Travel Disco

 **S0-ABA-971**

This coupon entitles you to special discounts when you book your trip through the

Hotels ♦ Airlines ♦ Car Rentals ♦ Cruises
All Your Travel Needs

Here's what you get: *

♦ A discount of $50 USD on a booking of $1,000** or more for two or more people!

♦ A discount of $25 USD on a booking of $500** or more for one person!

♦ Free membership for three years, and 1,000 free miles on enrollment in the unique Miles-to-Go™ frequent-traveler program. Earn one mile for every dollar spent through the program. Earn free hotel stays starting at 5,000 miles. Earn free roundtrip airline tickets starting at 25,000 miles.

♦ Personal help in planning your own, customized trip.

♦ Fast, confirmed reservations at any property recommended in this guide, subject to availability.***

♦ Special discounts on bookings in the U.S. and around the world.

♦ Low-cost visa and passport service.

♦ Reduced-rate cruise packages.

> Visit our website at http://www.travnet.com/Frommer or call us globally at 201-567-8500, ext. 55. In the U.S., call toll-free at 1-888-940-5000, or fax 201-567-1838. In Canada, call toll-free at 1-800-883-9959, or fax 416-922-6053. In Asia, call 60-3-7191044, or fax 60-3-7185415.

* To qualify for these travel discounts, at least a portion of your trip must include destinations covered in this guide. No more than one coupon discount may be used in any 12-month period, for destinations covered in this guide. Cannot be combined with any other discount or program.

**These are U.S. dollars spent on commissionable bookings.

***A $10 USD fee, plus fax and/or phone charges, will be added to the cost of bookings at each hotel not linked to the reservation service. Customers must approve these fees in advance.

Valid until December 31, 1998. Terms and conditions of the Miles-to-Go™ program are available on request by calling 201-567-8500, ext. 55.

  VIE123

Frommer's®

1st Edition

Vienna & the Danube Valley

by Darwin Porter and Danforth Prince

Macmillan • USA

ABOUT THE AUTHORS

Co-authors **Darwin Porter,** a native of North Carolina, and Ohio-born **Danforth Prince** wrote and researched the first ever Frommer's guide to Austria. These veteran travel writers are authors of several best-selling Frommer's guides, notably Germany, the Caribbean, Spain, England, and France. As frequent travelers to this alpine country's illustrious capital, Vienna, they know their destination well. In this guide, they share their secrets and discoveries with you.

MACMILLAN TRAVEL

A Simon & Schuster Macmillan Company
1633 Broadway
New York, NY 10019

Find us online at **http://www.mgr.com/travel** or
on America Online at Keyword: **Frommer's.**

ISBN 0-02861222-1
ISSN 1090-3178

Editor: Alicia Scott
Production Editor: John Carroll
Design by Michele Laseau
Digital Cartography by Peter Bogaty and Ortelius Design
Maps copyright ©1997 by Simon & Schuster, Inc.

SPECIAL SALES

Contents

List of Maps

An Invitation to the Reader

In researching this book, we discovered many wonderful places—hotels, inns, restaurants, shops, and more. We're sure you'll find others. Please tell us about them, so we can share the information with your fellow travelers in upcoming editions. If you were disappointed with a recommendation, we'd love to know that, too. Please write to:

Darwin Porter & Danforth Prince
Frommer's Vienna & the Danube Valley, 1st Edition
Macmillan Travel
1633 Broadway
New York, NY 10019

An Additional Note

Please be advised that travel information is subject to change at any time—and this is especially true of prices. We therefore suggest that you write or call ahead for confirmation when making your travel plans. The authors, editors, and publisher cannot be held responsible for the experiences of readers while traveling. Your safety is important to us, however, so we encourage you to stay alert and be aware of your surroundings. Keep a close eye on cameras, purses, and wallets, all favorite targets of thieves and pickpockets.

What the Symbols Mean

✪ Frommer's Favorites

Hotels, restaurants, attractions, and entertainment you should not miss.

ⓢ Super-Special Values

Hotels and restaurants that offer great value for your money.

The following abbreviations are used for credit cards:

AE	American Express	EU	Eurocard
CB	Carte Blanche	JCB	Japan Credit Bank
DC	Diners Club	MC	MasterCard
DISC	Discover	V	Visa
ER	enRoute		

The Road to Vienna

City of music, cafes, waltzes, parks, pastries, and *Gemütlichkeit*—that's Vienna. The capital of Austria became a showplace city during the tumultuous reign of the Habsburg dynasty and unlike many other European capitals managed to retain its most beautiful landmarks through two world wars.

Vienna is a true cosmopolitan city, where different tribes, races, and nationalities have for centuries fused their cultural identities to become the intriguing and often cynical Viennese.

From the time the Romans selected a Celtic settlement on the Danube for one of its most important central European forts, "Vindobona," the city we now know as Vienna has played a vital role in European history. Austria grew up around the city and developed into a mighty empire. At the splendid and brilliant Habsburg court, uniforms, decorations, gems, and precious metals made a dazzling, if sometimes tiring, show. Before the fall of the empire, Vienna was described as a "royal palace amidst surrounding suburbs." The face of the city has been altered time and again by war, siege, victory, defeat, death of an empire, birth of a republic, bombing, foreign oc-cupation, and the passage of time. But, fortunately, the Viennese character—a strict devotion to the good life—has remained solid.

Music, art, literature, theater, architecture, education, food, and drink (perhaps wine from the hills where the Romans had vineyards in the 1st century A.D.) are all part of Vienna's allure.

The Viennese have always been hospitable to foreigners, but there was a time at the end of the 18th century when the emperor felt that tourists might spread pernicious ideas, and all non-Austrians were limited to a one-week stay in the capital. This, of course, is no longer so, nor has it been for two centuries. In the pages that follow, we'll show you all the brilliance this city has to offer.

1 Frommer's Favorite Vienna Experiences

- **Listening to Mozart:** It is said that at any time of the day or night in Vienna someone somewhere is playing the music of Wolfgang Amadeus Mozart. You might hear it at an opera house, a church, a festival, an open-air concert, or more romantically in a *belle époque* cafe performed by a Hungarian orchestra. Regardless, "the sound of music" drifting through Vienna is likely the creation of this child prodigy. Try to arrange to hear Mozart on his home turf, in Vienna, where he knew such acclaim.

- **Cruising the Danube (*Donau*):** Johann Strauss took a bit of poetic license in calling the Donau "The Blue Danube," as it's actually a muddy-green color. But cruising the river by boat is nevertheless a highlight of any Viennese vacation. The legendary **DDSG,** Blue Danube Shipping Company (☎ 01/727-50-0), offers mostly one-day trips with cruises priced for every budget. On board, you'll pass some of the most famous sights in Eastern Austria, including quintessential towns like Krems and Melk.

- **Watching the Lippizaner Stallions:** Nothing evokes that heyday of imperial Vienna more than the **Spanish Riding School** (☎ 0222/533-90-32). Here, the sleek, white stallions and their expert riders demonstrate the classic art of "dressage" in choreographed leaps and bounds. The stallions, a crossbreed of Spanish thoroughbreds and Karst horses, are the finest equestrian performers on earth. Riders wear black bicorn hats with doeskin breeches and brass buttons. The public is admitted to watch but reservations should be made six to eight weeks in advance.

- **Heurigen Hopping in the Vienna Woods:** *Heurigen* are rustic wine taverns that celebrate the arrival of each year's new wine (*heuriger*) by placing a pine branch over the door. The Viennese rush to these taverns to drink the new local wines and feast on a country buffet. Some heurigen have garden tables with panoramic views of the Danube Valley, while others provide shaded, centuries-old courtyards where revelers can enjoy live folk music. Try the red wines from Vöslau, the Sylvaner of Grinzing, or the Riesling of Nussberg.

- **Feasting on *Tafelspitz,*"The Emperor's Dish":** No Austrian dish is more typical than the fabled Tafelspitz (boiled beef dinner) favored by Emperor Franz Joseph. Boiled beef sounds dull, but tafelspitz is far from bland. Boiled to a tender delicacy, the "table end" cut is flavored with a variety of spices including juniper berries, celery root, and onions. An apple and horseradish sauce further enlivens the dish, which is usually served with fried grated potatoes. For Vienna's best Tafelspitz, try the **Hotel Sacher** (☎ 0222/514-560).

- **Revisiting the Habsburgs:** One of the great dynastic ruling families of Europe, the Habsburgs ruled the Austro-Hungarian Empire from their imperial court in Vienna. You can still witness the grandeur of their lost lifestyle as you stroll through the Inner City. The Hofburg is the family's winter palace, and appears like a living architectural textbook, dating from 1279. Also, be sure to visit Schönbrunn, the Habsburgs' sprawling summer palace, which lies on the outskirts of the city and boasts magnificent gardens.

- **Cycling Along the Danube:** The Lower Danube Cycle Track is a cyclist's paradise. The most exciting villages and stopoffs along the Danube, including Melk and Dürnstein, are linked by a riverside bike trail between Vienna and Naarn. As you pedal along, you'll pass castles of yesteryear, medieval towns, and latticed vineyards. Route maps are available at the Vienna Tourist Office, and you can rent bikes from the ferry or train stations.

- **Attending an Auction at Dorotheum:** Vienna is a treasure trove of art and antiques, and as many estates break up, much of it goes on sale. The main venue for buying art and antiques is **Dorotheum,** Dorotheergasse 17 (☎ 0222/515-60), the state-owned auction house in Vienna. Founded in 1707, it remains one of the great European depositories of *objets d'art*. Most items here are likely to be expensive; however, if you're looking for something more affordable, try the summer

Saturday and Sunday outdoor art and antiques market along the Danube Canal in Vienna (between Schwedenbrücke and Salztorbrücke).

- **Savoring the Legendary Sachertorte: Café Demel** (☎ 0222/533-55-16), the most famous cafe of Vienna, has long feuded with the **Hotel Sacher** (☎ 0222/514-460) over who has the right to sell the legendary and original Sachertorte, a rich chocolate cake with a layer of apricot jam. Actually, the court settled that matter in 1965, ruling in favor of Hotel Sacher. But Demel still claims that the chef who invented the torte brought "the original recipe" with him when he left the Sacher to work for Demel. Settle the dispute yourself by sampling the Sachertorte at both of these venerated establishments.

- **Unwinding in a Viennese Coffeehouse:** Although no longer unique to Vienna, the coffeehouse still flourishes here in its most perfect form. You can spend hours reading newspapers (supplied free), writing memoirs, or planning the rest of your stay in Vienna. And, of course there's the coffee, prepared 20 to 30 different ways, from *Weissen Ohne* (with milk) to *Mocca Gespritzt* (black with a shot of rum or brandy). A glass of ice-cold water always accompanies a cup of coffee in Vienna, as should a delectable pastry or slice of cake.

- **Strolling the Kärntnerstrasse:** Lying at the heart of Viennese life is the bustling, pedestrian-only Kärntnerstrasse. From morning to night, shoppers parade along this merchandise-laden boulevard, and street performers, including musicians and magicians, are always out to amuse. For a break, retreat to one of the cafe terraces for some of the best people-watching in Vienna.

- **Playing at the Prater:** Ever since Emperor Joseph II opened the Prater to the public in 1766, the Viennese have been flocking to this park for summer fun—and understandably so. The Prater has abundant tree-lined paths in which to jog or stroll (the Viennese, in general, are much fonder of strolling). The amusement park boasts a looming Ferris wheel that was immortalized in Orson Welles's film, *The Third Man.* Open-air cafes line the park, which also provides an array of sports facilities such as tennis courts and a golf course.

- **A Night at the Opera:** There is nothing more Viennese than dressing up and heading to the Staatsoper, one of the world's greatest opera houses, where ascending the grand marble staircase is almost as exhilarating as the show. Built in the 1860s, the Staatsoper suffered severe damage during World War II, but reopened in 1955 with a production of Beethoven's *Fidelio,* marking Austria's independence from occupation. Both Richard Strauss and Gustav Mahler directed here and the world's most renowned opera stars continue to perform, accompanied, of course, by the Vienna Philharmonic Orchestra.

- **Hearing the Vienna Boy's Choir:** In this city steeped in musical traditions and institutions, one group has distinguished itself among all others: the Vienna Boy's Choir or *Wiener Sängerknaben.* Created by that great patron of the arts, Maximilian I, in 1498, the choir still performs masses by Mozart and Haydn at the Hofburgkapelle on Sundays and holidays, except in July and August. The children's voices are among the purest in all of Europe, and the chance to hear them is reason enough to come to Vienna.

- **Discovering the Majesty of St. Stephan's Cathedral:** Crowned by a 450-foot steeple, *Dompfarre St. Stephan,* the Cathedral of Vienna, is one of Europe's great Gothic structures. Albert Stifter, the great Austrian writer, claimed that its "sheer beauty lifts the spirit." The cathedral's vast tiled roof is exactly twice the height of its walls. Intricate altarpieces, stone canopies and masterful Gothic sculptures are just some of the treasures that lie within. Climb the spiral steps to the South Tower for a panoramic view of the city.

2 Vienna Today

In 1996, a year after Austria joined the European Union, this alpine nation continues to solidify its integration into Western Europe. Vienna now stands at the crossroads of Europe, between the east and west, just as it did in the heyday of the
Austro-Hungarian Empire. During the long, dark post-war era, the government, centered at Vienna, pretended to a neutrality it did not possess, as Austrian leaders feared
the return of the Russians, who left peacefully in 1955. But, with the collapse of the
Iron Curtain, Austria is moving toward greater cooperation and unity with the western powers.

Despite the optimism surrounding Austria's political strides abroad, neo-Nazism
is gaining ground at home. The Freedom Movement, led by Jörg Haider, has gained
increasing popularity among voters. The party seems to be capitalizing on the anti-
immigration backlash that followed in the wake of the collapse of the Soviet Union,
when the down-and-out from the former Communist nations flooded into Austria,
particularly into Vienna.

Environmental awareness is also on the rise in Vienna, especially among its younger
generation who feel that they live in one of the most beautiful countries on earth—
and rightfully so. Recycling is more evident in Vienna than any other European capital; in fact, recycling bins are commonplace on the city's streets, and the Viennese
are often seen sorting their paper, plastic, and tin cans.

Another concern among the Viennese is the rapid growth of tourism. In fact, one
man we met feared that his city "was becoming a giant Disneyland." To some
extent, that is true. Tourism is becoming more and more important to Vienna, as
thousands arrive every year to view the great art and architecture, feast on the lavish
pastries, cruise the Danube, and listen to the "music that never stops."

Vienna hasn't presided over an empire since the last Habsburg was sent packing
in 1918, but much of the glory and grandeur of those heady days remain. The treasures now stocking the museums were mostly from imperial days, and so many
baroque palaces are still standing, in spite of two world wars, that Vienna has been
called an "architectural waltz." Marble statues, lovely old squares, the grand palaces,
the voluptuous music of Richard Strauss, Gustav Klimt's paintings, the concert
halls—it's all still here, as if the empire were still flourishing.

Visitors today face a newer and brighter Vienna, a city with more *joie de vivre* than
it's had since before World War II. But, there's also a downside to all this optimism:
Prices are on the rise. They haven't reached the height of the Ferris wheel at the
Prater, but they are climbing.

3 A Look at the Past

Dateline

- 23,000 B.C. Venus of
  Willendorf, a representative
  of a Danubian fertility
  goddess, crafted near Vienna.
- 1000 B.C. Illyrian tribes
  establish a society near
  Vienna.

continues

Vienna's history was heavily influenced by its
position astride the Danube, midway between the
trade routes linking the prosperous ports of
northern Germany with Italy. Its position at the
crossroads of three great European cultures (the
Slavic, the Tetonic, and the Roman/Italian) transformed the settlement into a melting pot, and more
often than not, a battlefield, even in prehistoric
times.

FROM PREHISTORIC TO EARLY MEDIEVAL TIMES The 1906 discovery of the Venus of Willendorf, a fecund-looking Stone Age figurine, in the Danube Valley shows that the region around Vienna was inhabited long before the advent of recorded history.

Around 1,000 B.C., the mysterious Indo-European Illyrians established a high level of barbarian civilization around Vienna. Then came the Celts, who migrated eastward from Gaul around 400 B.C. They arrived in time to greet and resist the Romans, who began carving inroads into what is now known as Austria. Around 10 A.D., the Romans chose the site of modern-day Vienna for its fortified military camp, Vindobona. This strategic outpost occupied a well-documented site that's bordered today by Vienna's Rotenturm-strasse, St. Rupert's Church, Graben, and Tiefer Graben. Its position marked the northeastern border of the Roman Empire, and functioned as a blood-soaked buffer zone between warring Roman, Germanic, and Slavic camps.

BABENBURGS & BOHEMIANS Murky tribal politics dominated the landscapes around Vienna until 803 when the Frankish emperor Charlemagne swept through the Danube Valley establishing his new territory called *Ostmark* (The Eastern March). When Charlemagne died in 814, his squabbling heirs divided the once-mighty empire into feeble subdivisions. Vindobona struggled to survive within the oscillating Danube Valley, and was rebuilt atop the ancient Roman foundations. The earliest known reference to the site (*Wenia*) appeared in a proclamation of the archbishop of Salzburg in 881.

In 976, Leopold von Babenburg, representing his powerful Bavarian family, established control over Austria through inheritance, marriage, treaty, and politics. Commerce thrived under Babenburg rule and Vienna sprouted to one of the largest towns north of the Alps. By the end of the 10th century, the region had already been mentioned as *Ostarrichi*, which later became *Osterreich* (Austria).

In 1192, as part of a messy series of betrayals, the king of England, Richard *Coeur de Lion*, was arrested on Austrian soil, and the ransom paid to retrieve him was used for the construction of Vienna's ring of city walls, which were completed in 1200. A city charter was granted to Vienna in 1221, complete with trading privileges that encouraged the town's further economic development.

- **400 B.C.** Vendi tribes migrate from Gaul eastward to region around Vienna.
- **100 B.C.** Romans make military inroads into southern Austria.
- **A.D. 10** Vindobona (Vienna) established as a frontier outpost of the Roman Empire. Within 300 years, it's a thriving trading post.
- **400** Vindobona burnt and rebuilt, but the event marks the gradual withdrawal of the Romans from Austria.
- **500** Vienna overrun by Lombards.
- **630** Vienna taken by the Avars.
- **803** Charlemagne conquers the Danube Valley and site of Vienna, labeling what's now Austria as "Ostmark."
- **814** Death of Charlemagne signals dissolution of his empire.
- **881** First documented reference to Vienna (*"Wenia"*).
- **955** Charlemagne's heir, Otto I, reconquers Ostmark.
- **962** Otto I elected Holy Roman Emperor after papal stringpulling in his favor.
- **976** Leopold von Babenburg, first of his dynasty, rises to power in the Danube Valley.
- **996** Austria is referred to for the first time with a derivation (*Ostarrichi*) of its modern name.
- **1030** Vienna, after Cologne, is the largest town north of the Alps.
- **1147** A Romanesque predecessor of St. Stephan's Cathedral is consecrated as the religious centerpiece of Vienna.
- **1192** English king Richard The Lion-Hearted is arrested and held hostage by the

continues

Viennese. His ransom pays
for construction of the city's
walls, completed in 1200.

- **1221** City charter granted
  to Vienna, with trading
  privileges.
- **1246** Last of the Babenburgs,
  Friedrich the Warlike, dies in
  battle. He's succeeded with
  the brief reign of Bohemian
  king Ottokar II.
- **1278** Ottokar II killed at
  Battle of Marchfeld. Rudolf
  II of Habsburg begins one of
  the longest dynastic rules in
  European history.
- **1335 and 1363** Habsburgs
  add Carinthia and the Tyrol
  to Austrian territory.
- **1433** Central spire of
  St. Stephan's completed.
- **1453** Friedrich II elected as
  Holy Roman Emperor and
  rules from a base in Vienna.
- **1469** Vienna elevated to a
  bishopric.
- **1477** A Habsburg son
  marries the heiress to
  Burgundy, adding east-
  central France and the
  Netherlands to Austrian
  territory.
- **1485–90** Hungarian king
  Matthias Corvinus occupies
  Vienna's Hofburg for a five-
  year domination.
- **1496** A Habsburg son
  marries the *Infanta* of Spain,
  an act that eventually places a
  Habsburg in control of vast
  territories in the New World.
- **1519** Charles I, Habsburg
  ruler of Spain is elected Holy
  Roman Emperor.
- **1521** Charles I cedes Vienna
  and the central European
  portion of his holdings to his
  brother for more effective
  rule.
- **1526** Rebellion in Vienna
  leads to brutal repression
  by the Habsburgs.
- **1529** Half of Vienna
  destroyed in a fire. The same

continues

In 1246, the last of the Babenburgs, Friedrich II,
died without an heir, leaving the door wide open for
a fanatical struggle between the Roman popes
and the German princes as to who would control
Austria.

Into the power vacuum rose the powerful but
brief reign of the Bohemian king Ottokar II, whose
impressive empire eventually extended from the edge
of the Adriatic Sea to the western edge of what's
known today as the Czech Republic. When Ottokar
refused to swear an oath of fealty to the new emperor, Rudolf of Habsburg, the opposing armies
joined in one of Vienna's most pivotal battles, the
Battle of Marchfeld, in 1278. Ottokar perished, but
despite a short-lived administration, he is credited
for the earliest version of Vienna's Hofburg.

THE HABSBURG DYNASTY   Shortly after his
victory, Rudolf of Habsburg divided the territory
into the fiefdoms of Austria and Styria, placing
two of his sons in control of a powerful and long-
lived dynasty whose grip on Vienna and much of
central Europe would continue until the end of
World War I. Rudolf II (1552–1612), the son who
inherited Vienna, got off to a rocky start. When he
tried to eradicate the city's privileges, its citizens
broke into armed revolt, eventually forcing him to
grant them a municipal charter and administration
by mayor.

The next 200 years unveiled a series of annex-
ations and consolidations of power that incorporated
both Carinthia and the Tyrol into the Austrian fold.
In Vienna, Rudolf IV (1358–65) laid the corner-
stone of what was later consecrated as Vienna's
St. Stephan's Cathedral, and also founded the University of Vienna as a competitive response to the
academic facilities in neighboring Prague. In 1433
the spire of St. Stephan's was completed in the form
visitors see it today.

Stalwart Catholics in an age of Protestant rebel-
lions, the Habsburgs wrangled an advantageous
series of politically expedient marriages with many
of Europe's Catholic courts, including Spain,
Burgundy, and the Netherlands. In 1496, four years
after the colonization of the New World by
Spain, the Habsburgs married Phillip the Fair to the
Spanish *infanta* (heiress), a union that produced
Charles I (also known as Carlos I), who became ruler
of Spain and its New World holdings in 1516.
Three years later he was crowned Holy Roman
Emperor as Charles V.

Faced with mounting civil unrest in Vienna, Charles ceded control of Austria and the family's central European holdings to his Vienna-based younger brother, Ferdinand, in 1521. Ferdinand later married Anna Jagiello, heiress to Hungary and Bohemia, adding those countries into the growing empire.

In 1526, discontent in Vienna broke into civil war, which catalyzed brutal repression from Ferdinand, including a new city charter that placed control directly under Habsburg jurisdiction.

FIRES, REVOLUTIONS, PLAGUES & TURKISH INVASIONS Unfortunately, Vienna's "sea of troubles" had really just begun. In 1529, half of it was destroyed by fire. Also during that year, Turkish armies laid siege to the city for 18 intensely neurotic days. When the Turks withdrew, they left Vienna's outer suburbs in smoldering ruins, but luckily never breached the inner walls. Partly as a gesture of solidarity, Ferdinand I declared Vienna the site of his official capital in 1533.

Ironically, Vienna's building programs during most of the Renaissance were stifled by the obsessive need to reinforce the city's fortifications, which were completed in 1556 and drained most of the city's funds. In 1572 Maximilian II established the Spanish Riding School, a monument that is still closely identified with Vienna's sense of tradition and style.

Meanwhile, in Austria, no one could really decide whether Christians, Muslims, or the plague made the fiercest enemies, since incursions into the Balkans by Ottoman Turks continued to upset the power structures of Central Europe. Simultaneously, outbreaks of the Black Death reached their peak in 1679, when between 75,000 and 150,000 Viennese died. Leopold I commemorated the city's deliverance from the plague with the famous Pestaule column, which stands today on one of Vienna's main venues, the Graben.

The end of the Turkish menace, along with a decline in plague-related deaths spurred the sometimes frantic construction of baroque churches and memorial columns across Vienna. Architects like Johann Bernhard Fischer von Erlach and Johann Lukas von Hildebrandt designed some of the most lavish buildings in the Christian world, and composers and musicians flooded into the revitalized city.

HEREDITARY SUCCESSION & POLITICAL REFORM Years of inbreeding among Europe's royal families often resulted in infertility, not to

year sees the first of several Turkish sieges.

- **1533** Vienna declared as the official Habsburg capital.
- **1556** The Spanish king (a Habsburg) cedes his position as Holy Roman Emperor to his brother, the Austrian king, Ferdinand.
- **1560** Strengthening of Vienna's city walls.
- **1571** Ferdinand grants religious freedom to all Austrians. Before long, 80% of Austrians have converted to Protestantism.
- **1572** Establishment of the Spanish Riding School.
- **1576** The new king, Rudolf II, orders a reconversion to Catholicism of all Austrians. Beginning of the Counter-Reformation.
- **1600–1650** Hundreds of Catholic monks, priests, and nuns establish bases in Vienna as a means of encouraging the Habsburg role in the Counter-Reformation.
- **1618–48** Thirty Years' War almost paralyzes Vienna.
- **1679** The worst year of the plague, killing 75,000 to 150,000 Viennese.
- **1683** Turks besiege Vienna again before being routed by the armies of Lorraine and Poland.
- **1699** Turks evacuate strongholds in Hungary, no longer a threat to Austrian sovereignty.
- **1700** Death of the last of the Spanish Habsburgs, followed a year later by the War of the Spanish Succession.
- **1740** Maria Theresa ascends the Austrian throne after initial tremors from the War of the Austrian Succession (1740–48).
- **1769** Schönbrunn Palace completed.

continues

- **1770** Relations are cemented between Austria and France with the marriage of a Habsburg princess (Marie Antoinette) and Louis XVI of France.
- **1780** Death of Maria Theresa, and accession to power of her liberal son, Joseph II.
- **1789** Revolution in France leads eventually to the beheading of Marie Antoinette.
- **1805 and 1809** Vienna is occupied twice by armies of Napoléon.
- **1810** Marriage of Napoléon with Habsburg archduchess Marie-Louise.
- **1811** Viennese treasury is bankrupted by military spending.
- **1814–15** Congress of Vienna rearranges the map of Europe following the defeat of Napoleon.
- **1832** First steamship company organized to navigate along the Danube.
- **1837** Austria's first railway line.
- **1815–48** Vienna's *Biedermeier* period, supervised by Metternich, marks the triumph of the well-heeled *bourgeoisie*.
- **1848** Violent revolution in Vienna ousts Metternich, threatens the collapse of Austrian society, and ushers 18-year-old Franz Joseph I into power.
- **1850** Vienna's population reaches 431,000.
- **1859** Austria loses control of its Italian provinces, including Venice and Milan.
- **1862** Flooding on the Danube leads to a reconfiguration of its banks to a channel within Vienna's suburbs.

continues

mention ugliness, among the scions of the Habsburg line. In 1700, Charles II, last of the Spanish Habsburgs, died without an heir, signaling the final gasps of Habsburg control in Spain.

Provoked by what was happening in Spain, and confronted with the possibility that the Austrian Habsburgs might die without a clearly defined male heir, Austrian emperor Charles VI penned the Pragmatic Sanction, resembling a last will and testament, which ensured that his daughter, Maria Theresa, would succeed him. Accordingly, Maria Theresa ascended to power in 1740 at the age of 23, and retained her post for 40 years. She produced 16 potential heirs, more than Austria could ever reasonably need, and ushered Austria into a golden age.

During Maria Theresa's reign, the population of Vienna almost doubled, from 88,000 to 175,000. Her most visible architectural legacies include sections of Vienna's Hofburg and Schönbrunn Palace, her preferred residence that was completed in 1769. Simultaneously, modern reforms were implemented in the National Army, the economy, the civil service, and in education.

This buoyant ambiance was marred, however, by two traumatic events: the War of the Austrian Succession (1740–48), which contested the Empress's accession to the throne, and the Seven Years' War (1756–63), in which threats to Habsburg dominance of Central Europe were squelched, but with great fiscal and emotional sacrifices.

THE NAPOLEONIC WARS   The spectacular empire-building of the French general Napoleon added more havoc to the vast political landscapes controlled by Vienna. Napoléon's incursions onto Habsburg territories began in 1803, and culminated in the French occupation of Vienna in 1805 and 1809. The new Austrian Emperor, Franz II, was ordered to abdicate his position as Holy Roman Emperor. The Viennese treasury soon fell bankrupt, in 1811, causing a collapse of Austria's monetary system, events that instilled a deep mistrust of Austria's fiscal policies for generations to come.

In one of the 19th century's more bizarre marriages, and a new twist on the Habsburg gift for advantageous political weddings, Napoléon married the Habsburg archduchess Marie-Louise in 1810 as a means whereby each could maintain influence within the vast dominions controlled at the time from Vienna and Paris.

Napoleon's defeat in 1814 triggered the pivotal Congress of Vienna (1814–15), attended by representatives of Europe's major powers. Organized as a means of picking up the pieces of the Napoleonic debacle and redefining the borders, the forum developed into a showcase for the brilliant diplomacy and intrigue of Austria's foreign minister, Klemens von Metternich, whose skill left Austria with a regained pride and continued influence within a redefined confederation of German-speaking states.

Political developments and advancing technology changed the sociology and skyline of Vienna as the 19th century progressed. The first of many steamship companies to navigate up and down the Danube was established in 1832, and Austria's first railway line (linking the provinces to Vienna) opened in 1837.

FROM METTERNICH TO THE OUTBREAK OF THE WORLD WARS   Despite his brilliance as an international diplomat, Metternich managed to reconfigure the Austrian bureaucracies in ways that almost guaranteed civil unrest. His dominance of the Austrian government between 1815 and 1848 catalyzed another golden age in Vienna, the *Biedermeier* period, distinguished by the rise of the bourgeoisie and increased prosperity for the middle class. Metternich's policies, however, led to a deliberate eradication of civil rights, the postwar imposition of a police state, and the creation of an economic climate that favored industrialization at the expense of worker's wages and rights.

In March of 1848, events exploded in Vienna and Hungary and across most of Europe. Threatened by revolutionary chaos, Metternich was ousted from power and fled the city in terror, while some of the government's most prominent representatives were executed. The Austrian army imposed a new version of absolute autocracy and Emperor Franz Joseph I, the last scion of the Habsburg dynasty, became the new beneficiary of the restored order at age 18. During his autocratic 68-year reign (1848–1916), few other monarchies of Europe would be marked with as many tragedies, deceptions, and disillusionments.

Franz Joseph's austere comportment created the perfect foil for an explosion of artistic development in the newly revitalized Austria. Architecturally, his accomplishments included the development of the vast Ringstrasse, the boulevard that encircles Vienna's First District, from a position atop the

- **1867** Hungary and Austria are merged as the Austro-Hungarian Empire, headed by the Emperor, Franz Joseph I.
- **1869** Completion of Vienna's State Opera House.
- **1873** Vienna World's Fair.
- **1889** Controversial death of Crown Prince Rudolf at Mayerling.
- **1890–1900** Vienna's outer suburbs are incorporated into the city as Districts 11 to 20.
- **1914** Assassination of the heir to the Habsburg Empire, Archduke Ferdinand, sparks the beginning of World War I.
- **1916** Death of Franz Joseph, who is succeeded by Charles I, last of the Habsburg monarchs.
- **1918** End of World War I, defeat of Austria, abdication of Charles I, and the radical dismantling of the Austro-Hungarian Empire.
- **1919** Liberalization of Austrian voting laws enacts monumental changes in the social structure of Vienna. Beginnings of "Red Vienna" period where the city swings radically to the left.
- **1927** Violent discords rock through Vienna.
- **1929** Economic depression that begins with the collapse of stock prices on Wall Street, in New York, spread throughout the rest of the world.
- **1933** Austria's authoritarian chancellor, Dollfuss, outlaws the Austrian Nazi party.
- **1934** Dollfuss is assassinated by Nazis within his office.
- **1938** German Nazi troops complete an amicable invasion of Austria that leads to the union of the two nations (*Anschluss*) and the deep immersion of Austria

continues

into World War II as a Nazi ally.

- **1943–45** Massive bombings by Allied forces leave most public monuments in ruins.
- **1945** Defeat of Germany and Austria by Allied forces. Vienna is "liberated" by Soviet troops on April 11. On April 27, Austria redefined as a country distinctly separate from Germany, and divided, like Germany, into four zones of occupation. Vienna itself is subdivided into four separate zones as well.
- **1955** Evacuation of Austria by Allied forces and redefinition of Vienna as capital of a neutral nation.
- **1961** Summit meeting, in Vienna, between Kennedy and Khruschev.
- **1979** Summit meeting, in Vienna, between Brezhnev and Carter.
- **1986** Investigations into the wartime activities of Austrian chancellor, Kurt Waldheim, profoundly embarrasses many Austrians.
- **1989** The last heiress to the Habsburg dynasty, Empress Zita of Bourbon-Parma, in exile since 1919 dies and is buried in one of the most elaborate funerals in Viennese history.
- **1995** Austria, along with Sweden and Finland, admitted into the European Union.

remnants of city walls. Vienna's State Opera was completed in 1869 and was so instantly vilified that its architect soon after committed suicide.

Meanwhile, advanced technology helped launch Vienna into the Industrial Age, transforming the city into a glittering showcase. The empire's vast resources were funneled here in an effort to keep its theaters, coffeehouses, concert halls, palaces, and bourgeois homes well lit, cleaned, and maintained.

The foundations of Vienna were shaken again in 1889 by the mysterious deaths of 30-year-old Crown Prince Rudolf, an outspoken and not particularly stable liberal, and his 18-year-old mistress at the royal hunting lodge of Mayerling. The possibility that they were murdered, and the insistence of his family that every shred of evidence associated with the case be destroyed, led to some of the most lurid speculation of the 19th century. Tragedy, and the realization that all was not well within the Austro-Hungarian Empire, struck again in 1898 when Franz Joseph's estranged wife, Sisi, was stabbed to death by an Italian-born anarchist as she was about to step aboard a cruiser on Lake Geneva.

In 1890, many of the city's outer suburbs (Districts 11–19) were incorporated into the City of Vienna, and in 1900 a final, 20th district, Brigittenau, was also added.

Women received the right to vote throughout the Austro-Hungarian Empire beginning in 1906. By 1910, Vienna, with a population of two million comprised from at least a dozen of the Empires widely divergent nationalities, was the fourth-largest city in Europe after London, Paris, and Berlin.

THE WAR TO END ALL WARS & THE VERSAILLES TREATY During the *belle époque* of the early 20th century, Europe sat on a powderkeg of frustrated socialist platforms and conflicting colonial ambitions. The Austro-Hungarian Empire was linked to both Germany and Italy through the Triple Alliance. The flashpoint that sucked most of Europe into armed conflict occurred when Franz Joseph's nephew and designated heir, the Archduke Ferdinand, was shot to death by a Serbian terrorist as Ferdinand rode with his wife, Sophie, in an open car through Sarajevo on June 28, 1914. Within 30 days, the Austro-Hungarian Empire declared war on Serbia, signaling the outbreak of what eventually exploded into World War I. An embittered Franz Joseph died in 1916, midway through the conflict, and he was succeeded by the last of the Habsburg monarchs, Charles I, who was forced to abdicate in 1918 as part of the peace treaty at the end of the war.

The punitive peace treaty concluded at Versailles, and, tainted by the poisonous policies of France's Clemenceau, was harsher than most Viennese could bear. The victors, acknowledging the growing appeal for government reform, reconfigured

Vienna as the seat of an Austrian Republic, and replaced its royal precedents with an elected body of governors. The victors ordered the reconfiguration of vast Austro-Hungarian territories, which became the independent republics of Hungary, Poland, and even Yugoslavia and Czechoslovakia. The new Austria would adhere to the boundaries established by Charlemagne in his designation of the early *Ostmark.*

This overnight collapse caused profound dislocations of populations and trade patterns. Some of the new nations refused to deliver raw materials to Vienna's factories, or in some cases, food to Vienna's markets. That, coupled with the punitive effects of the Versailles treaty and the massive losses of manpower and resources during the war years, quickly led Vienna to the brink of starvation. Despite staggering odds, the new government—assisted by a massive loan in 1922 from the League of Nations—managed to stabilize the currency while Austrian industrialists hammered out new sources of raw materials.

In 1919, voting laws in Vienna were liberalized to the point whereby the secret ballot became the norm for all bona fide city residents. Vienna immediately took an abrupt turn toward socialism, embarking on a period known as "Red Vienna."

THE RISE OF FASCISM & THE ANSCHLUSS   In 1933, social tensions about the imminent collapse of Austrian society spurred Austria's authoritarian chancellor, Engelbert Dollfuss, to inaugurate a political regime dedicated to the punishment of left-wingers, National Socialists, and liberals. After riots in 1934, Vienna's liberal city council was eradicated, along with many social programs, and the Austrian National Socialist (Nazi) party was declared illegal.

Later that year, emboldened by their rise to power in Germany, Austrian Nazis assassinated Dollfuss in his offices, and pressured his successor to the point where, under massive pressure from many of his compatriots, he included the Austrian Nazis within the new coalition government.

On March 11, 1938, German troops marched into Austria, proclaiming the virtues and benefits of a pan-Germanic union. They met with virtually no resistance and, according to many observers, with some degree of enthusiasm. Austria was incorporated into Germany's Third Reich two days later, following Hitler's triumphant return to the city he had occupied several decades previously as an impoverished and embittered artist. In a national referendum held within a month of the Nazi rallies on Vienna's Heldenplatz, 99.75% of Austrians voted to support the *Anschluss* (Annexation) as a worthy and viable act. Austria, in effect, became an overnight province of the German Reich.

WORLD WAR II & ITS AFTERMATH   The rise of Austria's Nazis devastated Vienna's academic and artistic communities, as many of its members, including Sigmund Freud, fled to safer climes. Their fears were more than justified: The death camps that decimated Germany's Jewish, homosexual, and gypsy populations were duplicated in Austria. About 60,000 Austrian Jews were sent to concentration camps and only an estimated 2,000 managed to survive.

Beginning in 1943, Allied bombing raids demolished vast neighborhoods of the city, damaging virtually every public building of any stature, and as many as 86,000 private homes. The city's most prominent landmark, St. Stephan's cathedral, suffered a roof collapse and fires in both towers—damage that wasn't repaired until 1948. For the Viennese, at least, the war ended abruptly on April 11, 1945, when Russian troops moved into the city from bases in Hungary. The city's death rate was estimated as one of the highest in Europe.

During a confused interim that lasted a decade, Austria was divided into four zones of occupation, each controlled by one of the four Allies (the United States, the Soviet Union, Britain, and France). Vienna, deep within the Soviet zone, was also subdivided into four zones, each occupied by one of the victors. Control of what is today known as the city's 1st District (then known as the Central Zone) alternated every month between each of the four powers. It was a dark and depressing time in Vienna, one where rubble was cleared only slowly away from bomb sites, and the most glorious public monuments in Europe lay in ashes. Espionage, black market profiteering, and personal betrayals were rampant, leaving a poison that's still palpable within the memories of many older Viennese today.

On May 15, 1955, Austria was redefined as an independent, perpetually neutral, and unoccupied nation. It emerged as a hotbed of Cold War conflicts and espionage, and the preferred venue for meetings between such personalities as Kennedy and Khruschev (in 1961) and Brezhnev and Carter (1979). Because of Vienna's role as the capital of a neutral nation, many international organizations (including OPEC and the Atomic Energy Authority) established branches or headquarters there.

Following their reunification, the Viennese aggressively pursued the activities for which they are the most famous: promoting their self-image as cultural barons; an allegiance to the grandeur, pomp, and ceremony of their imperial past; and engaging in such everyday activities as opera-going, Sachertorte tasting, and gossiping.

However, Vienna's image as a lighthearted centerpiece for Strauss, strudel, and song suffered greatly during the scandals that centered around Austria's president, Kurt Waldheim, who was elected in 1986. Waldheim had been an officer in the Nazi army and had countenanced the deportation of Jews to extermination camps. The United States declared him *persona non grata.* Many Austrians defiantly stood by Waldheim, declaring that they would not let world opinion dictate their choice for president. Other Austrians were deeply embarrassed. Waldheim did not seek reelection, and in May 1992, Thomas Klestil, a career diplomat, was elected president. His candidacy was supported by the Austrian People's Party, representing the center of the political spectrum.

In 1989, the last heiress to the Habsburg dynasty, Empress Zita of Bourbon-Parma, in exile since 1919, was buried in one of the most lavish and emotional funerals ever conducted in Vienna. Aged 96, and the last Empress of Austria and Queen of Hungary, she had always been held with some degree of reverence by the Viennese, in the hopes that she might reinitiate the glorious days of the Austrian monarchy.

4 Architecture 101

Although Vienna is best known for the splendor of its baroque and rococo palaces and churches, it also contains a wealth internationally renowned of gothic and modern architecture.

ANCIENT ROME & THE EARLY MIDDLE AGES

Austria's most comprehensive Roman ruins lie in the Carinthian hamlet of St. Veit an der Glan about 200 miles south of Vienna, which has no known ruins that compare.

The Christianization of Austria began around 700 A.D. with the arrival of Anglo-Saxon and Scottish-Irish monks and missionaries, and triggered a mini-building boom in ecclesiastic architecture. Their duties involved the construction of their own monasteries as well as isolated outposts for the conversion of the surrounding tribes. Their churches were squat, small, and solid, usually with a single aisle and a square or rectangular sacristy (room for the storage of sacred objects and ceremonial robes) lying adjacent. Regrettably, excavations in Vienna have unearthed little more than the ruined foundations of a few early churches, which architects speculate were basilica-type structures. In Vienna, remnants, in the form of dusty excavations, can be seen in the neighborhoods of the Michaelerplatz, Hoher Markt, and Am Hof 9. Much altered from their original constructions, later churches, like St. Stephan's Cathedral and the Church of St. Michael, incorporated older foundations.

GOTHIC ARCHITECTURE

In Austria, Gothic architecture permeated the country's aesthetic consciousness beginning around 1200, and was officially encouraged in Vienna after the accession of the Habsburgs in 1278. The engineering techniques that made the construction of these cathedrals possible originated in France and quickly spread throughout the rest of Europe. Despite their French-inspired structural "skeletons," much of their ornamentation was inspired by models that originated in Germany and Italy. A good example of early Gothic architecture in Austria is the Dominikanerkirche (Church of the Dominicans) built around 1260 in Friesach, near Vienna.

Competing for prevalence during this era was a different architectural plan, the *Hallenkirche* (hall church), whose more unified interior spaces made large windows technically feasible. Widespread in Austria during the 1300s, and based on models that had originated earlier in Germany, these buildings featured interiors that resembled enormous hallways, with nave and aisles of the same height. The earliest example of this style was the choir added in 1295 to an older Romanesque building, the abbey church of Heiligenkreuz, 15 miles west of Vienna.

The most famous building erected in the Gothic Hallenkirche style is St. Stephan's Cathedral, in Vienna. For the first time decorative techniques from France permeated the interior of an Austrian church, although later modifications greatly altered the details of its original construction. Today only the foundations, the main portal, and the modestly proportioned western towers remain as part of the original plan. Much more dramatic is the cathedral's needle-shaped central spire, completed in 1433, which still soars high above Vienna's skyline.

During the late 1400s, Gothic architecture retreated from the soaring proportions of the Hallenkirche style and focused instead on more modestly proportioned buildings whose interiors were more richly decorated. Stonemasons chiseled out geometric patterns (tracery) onto ceilings, walls, and full-rounded or low-relief sculpture became a trend. One feature distinctive to Austrian Gothic—triple naves, each of the same uniform height—is shared in Vienna by St. Stephan's Cathedral as well as by the Minorite Church and the Church of St. Augustine. Gothic churches continued to be built in Austria until the mid-1500s, but the country's creative drive abandoned Gothic motifs when ecclesiastics turned their energies to the religious upheavals sweeping Central Europe.

FROM GOTHIC TO BAROQUE

One of the unusual aspects of the Viennese skyline is its relative lack of Renaissance architecture. That's because when Vienna was periodically besieged by the Turks from 1529 until the 1680s, the city endured debilitating plagues, and constant attacks from both Muslim and Christian armies. The resulting insecurities forced Viennese city planners to focus most of their attention on fortifications, many of which were demolished during the city's 19th-century building boom.

This lack of Renaissance (late 16th century and early 17th century) architecture was sorely missed by 19th-century city planners who did their best to fill up the Ringstrasse (see below) with neoclassical monuments reflecting some Renaissance motifs you might expect to find in Italy or southern Germany.

This was not the case, however, in other regions of Austria that were more politically stable during the Renaissance. Late in the 1500s many Italian builders settled in the regions of Tyrol, Carinthia, and Styria. Modest country churches, private homes, and civic buildings assimilated Italian motifs in subtle but distinctive ways. These included a widespread use of open porticoes, balconies, and loggias. The most famous building in Austria constructed during this transition was the Landhaus (the old city hall) at Graz, a reasonable train ride from Vienna. These Italian influences permeated the consciousness of Austria for more than a century before eventually blossoming into the full-blown and dramatic aesthetic known as the baroque.

BAROQUE & ROCOCO ARCHITECTURE

In 1620 Protestantism was outlawed in Austria, and around this time began the revival of architecture as an art form. This wholehearted rejection of Protestant theology and art, combined with the official endorsement of Catholicism encouraged theatrical buildings filled with curved lines arranged into spheres of dynamic tension. The result demonstrated the confidence and verve of a newly triumphant church.

The first baroque buildings were erected in Salzburg, far from the Turkish menace then plaguing Vienna. Importing such Italian architects as Santino Solari (1596–1646), the city added a baroque cathedral whose floor plan was inspired by Michelangelo's plan for St. Peter's Basilica in Rome. Flooded with sunlight and richly adorned with stucco, plaster, and gilt, it became a novelty throughout Austria, much-envied (and later used for inspiration) by the Habsburgs in Vienna.

After 1648, when the Peace of Westphalia signaled the end of the Thirty Years' War, the baroque mode became the preferred style of civic buildings and royal mansions in Vienna. The 47-year rule of Leopold I (1658–1705) witnessed the beginning of the golden age of Austrian baroque architecture. Italian-born Dominico Martinelli (1650–1718) designed the Liechtenstein Palace—built between 1694 and 1706 in Vienna, inspired by the Renaissance-era Palazzo Farnese in Rome.

Austria soon began to produce its own native-born architects, nearly all of whom gravitated to the center of the empire's money, power, and building commissions, Vienna. One of the most influential was **Johann Bernhard Fischer von Erlach** (1656–1723), who had trained with both Bernini and Borromini in Rome. His style was restrained but monumental, drawing richly from the great buildings of antiquity. His greatest achievements in Austria's capital are the Karlskirche and the original plan for Schönbrunn Palace and the National Library.

Von Erlach was succeeded by two other great names in the history of architecture: **Johann Lucas von Hildebrandt** (1668–1745) and **Jacob Prandtauer** (1660–1727). Both developed the opulent transition from baroque to the more heavily ornamented rococo style. Von Hildebrant's design for Prince Eugene's Belvedere Palace—a series of interlocking cubes with sloping mansard-style roofs—is the culmination of the architectural theories initiated by Fischer von Erlach. Other von Hildebrandt designs in Vienna include the Schwarzenberg Palace (converted after World War II into a well-managed hotel, Hotel Im Palais Schwarzenberg) and St. Peter's Church. The facades of grand homes, either of the emerging bourgeoisie or titled aristocracy, swarmed with stylized renderings of gods and caryatids. Many 18th-century buildings around Vienna feature heroic-looking giants squelching sea monsters or Turks while supporting a particularly heavy pediment or cornice.

The rococo style developed as a more ornate, somewhat fussier progression of the baroque, in which decoration was deliberately carried to extremes. Gilt stucco, brightly colored frescoes, and interiors that drip with embellishments are the hallmark of this distinctly Austrian style. Excellent examples include the Abbey of Durnstein (1731–35) and Melk Abbey, both of which are in Lower Austria (See Chapter 10, "Excursions from Vienna"). Prandtauer and Joseph Munggenast were two of the movement's chief designers. One of its most powerful proponents was Maria Theresa herself, who used its motifs so extensively within Schönbrunn Palace during its 1744 renovation that the school of Austrian rococo is sometimes referred to as late-Baroque Theresian style.

Rococo architecture eventually burned out as builders and patrons reacted against the ornate excesses of the baroque and returned to the restrained dignity inspired by ancient Greece and Rome. The result was a restrained neoclassicism whose tenets transformed the skyline of Vienna well into the 19th century. A good example of this style is Vienna's Technical University, whose dignified austerity was imposed in an emulation of the academic rigors legendarily associated with ancient Greece and Rome.

THE 19TH CENTURY

As Austria's wealthy bourgeoisie began to impose their tastes on public architecture, buildings during the 19th century grew more visually solid and monumental. The neoclassical style became the preferred style of government authorities, as evidenced by Vienna's Mint and its Palace of the Provincial Government. By the latter half of the century, after Austria's revolution in 1848, renewed emphasis was placed on an eclectic allegiance to a variety of architectural styles.

Between 1850 and the 1880s, monuments in Vienna reflected everything from French Gothic (*Votivkirche*); Flemish Gothic (*Rathaus*), Greek Revival (Parliament); the French Renaissance (*Staatsoper*), and the Tuscan Renaissance (Museum of Applied Arts). As for private homes, styles ranged from palatial and clearly defined historical styles to less defined styles that emulate a gamut of inspirations. Within the city's verdant outer districts, half-timbered facades inspired by the Teutonic legends of the Black Forest might appear in a garden adjacent to a turreted mansion capped with neo-feudal crenellations, oriel windows, and watchtowers. Although many of Vienna's showcase buildings within the Ring were rebuilt after the bombings of World War II, many of the outlying and idiosyncratic private homes weren't so fortunate.

The 19th century's most impressive architectural achievement involved the construction of the Vienna Ring (1857–91), a monumental beltway that today whizzes traffic in a circle around Old Vienna. The medieval walls that had previously fortified the inner city were demolished, along with hundreds of older buildings, to make room for the new avenues. The ring was lined with showcase buildings, including those mentioned just above. Regrettably, some of the charm of the Ring's original layout is diminished today by endless traffic. Nevertheless, a circumnavigation of the Ring, preferably by taxi or tram, provides aficionados of 19th-century architecture with a panorama of eclectic building styles.

MODERN ARCHITECTURE

By the late 19th century, young-minded artists and architects rebelled against the pomp and formality of the architectural styles endorsed by their elders. In 1896 young **Otto Wagner** (1841–1918) published a tract called *Moderne Architektur,* which argued for a return to more natural architectural forms. The result was the establishment of art nouveau (*Jugendstil* or as it applies specifically to Vienna, *Sezessionstil*). Jugenstil architects reaped the benefits from technological advances in building materials that became available after the Industrial Revolution. Wagner, designer of Vienna's Kirche am Steinhof and the city's *Postsparkasse* (Post Office Savings Bank), became a founding member of the "Vienna Secession" that drenched turn-of-the-century Austria with more functional building styles.

Joseph Hoffman (1870–1955) and **Adolf Loos** (1870–1933) also promoted a use of natural materials, including newly developed steel alloys and aluminum. In the process they discarded nearly all ornamentation, a rejection which contemporary Vienna found distasteful and profoundly shocking. Loos was particularly critical, even hostile, towards the mishmash of eclectic and sometimes pompous styles adorning the edges of the Ringstrasse. Fond of using glass and steel, he appeared most controversial in the design of the Michaeler Platz Building. Sometimes referred to as the Loos House, erected at Michaeler Platz 3 in 1908, it's a streamlined structure that received bitter criticism because of its total lack of ornamentation, its similarities to the "gridwork of a sewer," and its position adjacent to one of the entrances used by Emperor Franz Joseph in his travels in and out of the Hofburg. According to legend, the emperor found it so offensive that he ordered his drivers to avoid the Michaeler Platz entrance altogether.

Some of these architectural philosophies behind these buildings were affected by the "Red Vienna" socialist movements. Recognizing the need for public housing to alleviate the grinding social problems exacerbated by World War I, the Austrian Social Democratic Party—yielding to intense pressure from the city's blue-collar (or unemployed) work force—began erecting "palaces for the people." Based on cost-effective construction techniques and industrial materials, they're reminiscent of some of the Depression-era WPA projects of North America, yet on a more staggering scale. The most obvious of these is the Karl-Marx-Hof, Heiligenstadterstrasse 82-92, A-1190, which includes 1,600 apartments and stretches out for more that half a mile. Despite its banal exterior, it manages to incorporate public areas and landscaped courtyards that detract somehow from an otherwise overpowering sense of socialist anonymity.

Since the end of World War II, architecture has primarily been streamlined and functional, which says a lot about the severity of Viennese winters and the ongoing allure of cost-saving construction. Other than a profound allegiance to restoring older buildings to their pre-war grandeur, much of modern Vienna has adopted the same kind of neutral modernism you're likely to find in postwar Berlin or Frankfurt.

Post-modern masters who have broken the mold of the 1950s and 1960s include the iconoclastic mogul Hans Hollein, designer of a silvery, curved-sided Haas Haus (1990) adjacent to St. Stephan's Cathedral. Also noteworthy is the self-consciously avant-garde **Friedenreich Hundertwasser,** whose multicolored, ecologically inspired apartment building at the corner of Löwengasse and Kegelgasse appears randomly stacked, almost as a child might have heaped brightly-colored building blocks.

5 Art Through the Ages

Vienna's location at the crossroads of the Germanic, Mediterranean, and eastern European worlds contributed to the most rich and varied artistic heritage in central Europe.

EARLY CHRISTIAN ART

Beginning around A.D. 700, Benedictine monks from Ireland, Scotland, and England poured their energies into the conversion of the Austrians, founding monasteries and introducing Christian motifs into painting and sculpture.

Sculpture of the early medieval period was mainly decorative and/or abstract. Celtic-inspired animal motifs with braided borders of intertwined plant forms were introduced by the Benedictines. No large paintings or murals of any kind from the Carolingian period survive in Austria today, although a handful of illuminated manuscripts are preserved in carefully monitored settings, including some within Vienna's National Library. Most famous of these is the *Cutbercht Evangeliar,* crafted around 800. A richly illuminated copy of the four gospels, it was laboriously copied by a monk or team of monks residing in an Anglo-Saxon monastery in Upper Austria.

ROMANESQUE ART

Austria's Romanesque period reached its peak between A.D. 1000 and 1190 and was marked by a period of ecclesiastical wealth, power, and prestige. Most of the enduring monuments of the age were conceived as cathedrals, chapels, and monasteries, whose construction motifs are more fully described in "Architecture 101" above. Sculpture, however, was distinctly related to the architecture of the buildings it adorned. Most of the era's sculptures were carved in high relief, placed against niches, atop columns, or on walls. Many represented grotesque or imaginary animals, plant motifs, and demons. Around 1100, wood sculpture, mainly in the form of crucifixes and mortuary sculpture (coffins or sarcophagi carved with a portrait of the person whose body it contained), became fashionable.

Romanesque painting was mostly confined to religious frescoes, and was strongly affected by Byzantine concepts of spacing and ornamentation. The few remaining examples in Austria include the church choir of Nonnberg Convent in Salzburg, and the west gallery of the Cathedral at Gurk, near Klagenfurt. The monasteries of Salzburg soon developed as the country's centerpiece for the illumination of manuscripts. One of the best examples is the *Admont Great Bible,* crafted around 1140, which is today one of the prized treasures of Vienna's National Library.

The spatial techniques developed through the illumination of manuscripts was eventually applied to enamelwork and goldsmithing. In 1181 the famous goldsmith, Nicolas de Verdun, produced the finest enamel works in Europe for the pulpit at Klosterneuberg Abbey. Verdun's 51 small panels, crafted from enamel and gold, depict scenes from the religious tracts of the Augustinians. After a fire in the 1300s the panels were repositioned onto an altarpiece at Klosterneuberg, which is known today as the Verdun Altar.

THE GOTHIC AGE

The Gothic Age in Austria is better remembered for its architecture than its painting and sculpture. Even so, painting and the plastic arts evolved accordingly as Austria continued to assimilate new artistic concepts from Italy, France, and Germany.

Early Gothic sculpture was influenced by the *Zachbruchiger Stil* (zigzag style), identified by angular and vivid outlines of forms against contrasting backgrounds. The era's greatest surviving sculptures date from around 1320, and include *The Enthroned Madonna of Klosterneuburg* and *The Servant's Madonna,* showcased in Vienna's St. Stephan's Cathedral.

By the late 1300s, Austrian sculpture was strongly influenced by Bohemia. The human form became elongated, exaggerated, and idealized, often set in graceful but unnatural S curves. Wood became increasingly widespread as an artistic medium, and was often painted in vivid colors. A superb example of gothic sculpture is *The Servant's Madonna* within Vienna's St. Stephan's Cathedral. Carved around 1320, it depicts Mary enthroned and holding a fully standing Christ child.

By the end of the Gothic Age, the artistic vision of western and central Europe had merged into a short-lived union known today as "International Gothic." Especially evident in the illumination of manuscripts, the movement was encouraged by what was at the time Europe's only truly international organization, the Catholic Church, and partially funded by a coterie of feudal aristocrats. The finest assemblage of Gothic paintings in Austria lies in Vienna, at the Orangery of the Belvedere Palace.

THE RENAISSANCE

The introduction of the Italian Renaissance into Austria was largely encouraged by the Habsburg emperor Maximilian I (ruled 1493–1519), whose grip on political and, to some degree artistic developments, in Vienna was almost unshakable. His greatest incentive for sculpture was the commission for his own tomb, and for the construction of the Hofkirche in Innsbruck to contain it. Ironically, during most of the Renaissance, the Austrian Empire's capital, Vienna, painting during the Renaissance came from Germany was so preoccupied with fending off invasions, sieges, and an ongoing series of plagues that artistic expression was not a priority.

THE 17TH & 18TH CENTURIES

Viennese sculpture and painting during the 17th and 18th centuries were mainly appreciated for their decorative enhancement of larger aesthetic wholes. One of the baroque style's major features was its emphasis on symmetry and unity, and to this degree, architects used illusion (through the form of *trompe l'oeil*) to give extra dimension to a building's sculptural and architectural motifs. During this period, Vienna surged forward artistically, racing to surpass the artistic wealth already accumulated in such cities as Salzburg, Munich, Warsaw, Innsbruck, and most of the Italian cities. Grandiose churches and spectacular palaces sprang up across Vienna, and artists, suspended high above the floor on scaffolding, labored to adorn them with religious or allegorical frescoes.

The first noteworthy Austrian-born painter during the baroque age was **Johann Rottmayr** (1654–1730), the preferred painter of the two most influential architects of the baroque age, Hildebrandt and Fischer von Erlach. Rottmayr's works adorn some of the ceilings of Vienna's Schönbrunn Palace and Vienna's Peterskirche. The core of Vienna's baroque frenzy derived from the aesthetic presuppositions of Italy: Many of the baroque age's most enduring large-scale frescoes were the result of such imported artists as Andrea Pozzo (1642–1709), whose masterpiece, *The Apotheosis of Hercules,* appears on the ceilings of Vienna's Liechtenstein Palace.

Landscapes of Vienna as it emerged from a base of muddy fields into a majestic fantasy of baroque architecture were captured on the canvasses of **Bernardo Bellotto** (1720–80), nephew and pupil of the famous Venetian painter, Canaletto. Brought to Vienna at the request of Maria Theresa, Bellotto managed to bathe the city in a flat but clear light of arresting detail and pinpointed accuracy. Today, his canvasses are interpreted both as skillful artistic renderings as well as social and historical documents.

Not every painting of this era was devoted to depictions of religious ecstasy or heroic metaphors. Dutch-born, Sweden-trained **Martin van Meytens** (1695–1770), court painter to Maria Theresa, devoted his career to scenes of the lavish balls and assemblies that depicted Vienna's aristocracy to their most intensely-coifed and bejeweled. His canvases, though awkwardly composed and overburdened with more than the eye can reasonably absorb, are considered the best visual record of the Austrian Empress' parties and receptions. In 1730 Van Meytens was appointed director of Vienna's Fine Arts Academy.

Despite the fact that baroque architecture dominated the age's visual arts, a handful of famous names emerged as masters of the sculptural form. These included **Georg Raphael Donner** (1693–1741), best known for the remarkable life-size bronzes of the Fountain of Providence, which pervades the Neuer Markt in Vienna. Meanwhile **Balthasar Permoser** crafted equestrian likenesses of Prince Eugene for the courtyard of the Belvedere Palace, and **Balthasar Moll** designed baroque funeral caskets for Maria Theresa and Franz I.

Equally influential was **Franz Xaver Messerschmidt** (1737–83), the German-trained resident of Vienna who became justifiably famous as master of the portrait bust. His legacy contains some of the most physically and emotionally-accurate representations ever made of such luminaries as Maria Theresa and Emperor Joseph I.

THE 19TH CENTURY

During the early part of the 19th century most Viennese painting was not overly imaginative. Preoccupied with heroic themes from the past, paintings tended to be overscale, grandiose, sentimental, and pompous. This "official art," however, contrasts with the hundreds of folk-art sculptures and paintings produced in and around Vienna during the same era.

In rebellion against "official art," a school of Romantic painters drew upon biblical themes, Austrian folklore, and central European musical history. Scenes from popular operas were painted lovingly and evocatively on the walls of the Vienna Opera House. Landscape paintings which were influenced by the 17th-century Dutch masters came into vogue as well. One notable artist, **Georg Waldmüller** (1793–1865), a self-proclaimed enemy of "academic art" and an advocate of realism, created one of the best pictoral descriptions of Viennese society during the Biedermeier era in his *Wiener Zimmer* (1837). Over 120 of his paintings are on display at the Upper Belvedere museum.

Another vivid realist whose subject matter involved sensitive portrayal of the workaday concerns of middle-class Viennese was **Carl Moll** (1861-1945) whose graceful and evocative portrayals of everyday, workaday scenes are prized in Viennese collections today. Equally important was **Joseph Engelhart** (1864-1941), known for his voluptuous renderings of *belle époque* coquettes flirting with Viennese gentlemen.

More important than paintings, however, were the landmark achievements of the art nouveau (*Jugendstil* or *Sezessionstil*) school of sculpture and the decorative arts. Reflecting avant-garde themes equivalent to those in contemporary Munich and Paris, the Secessionist movement was founded in 1897 by young painters, decorators, and architects from Vienna's Academy of Fine Arts. The name derived from their retreat (Secession) from the *Künstlerhaus* (Vienna Artists' Association), which they considered pompous, sanctimonious, artificial, mediocre, and mired in the historicism favored by Emperor Franz Joseph. As an architectural and sculptural statement, they elevated the curved line to levels of sinuous grace that have yet to be equaled. The Jugendstil interpretation of organic forms added distinctive ornamentation to the Gilded Age buildings and monuments of Vienna.

The Secessionist headquarters, on the Friedrichstrasse (at the corner of the Opernring) was inaugurated in 1898 as an iconoclastic exhibition space for avant-garde artists. Foremost among them was **Gustav Klimt** (1862–1918) whose work developed rapidly into a highly personal and radically innovative form of painting. Later viewers defined his work as a psychedelic adaptation of the central tenets of bourgeois central European turn-of-the-century art. His masterpieces include a mammoth frieze, 110 feet long, encrusted with gemstones, dedicated to the genius of Beethoven. Executed in 1902, it's one of the artistic focal points of the above-mentioned Secessionist Pavilion. Other pivotal works include *Portrait of Adèle Bloch-Bauer* (1907), an abstract depiction of a prominent Jewish Viennese socialite whose gilded geometric forms evoke memories of ancient Byzantine art.

THE MODERN AGE

Klimt's talented disciple was **Egon Schiele** (1890–1918). Tormented, overly sensitive, and virtually unknown during his brief lifetime, he is now considered a modernist master whose work is the equivalent of Vincent Van Gogh and Modigliani. Vilified by critics, his works seem to dissolve the boundaries between humankind and the landscapes of nature, granting a kind of anthropomorphic (and traumatized) humanity to landscape painting. One of the most revered (and disturbing) of his paintings, *The Family* (1917) originally conceived as decoration for a mausoleum, shows tremendous compassion for the torment of his subjects.

Modern sculpture in Vienna is inseparable from the international trends that have dominated the 20th century art. One of the city's most noteworthy sculptors is **Fritz Wotruba** (1907–75), who introduced a neocubist style of sculpture into the Austrian consciousness. Many of his sculptural theories were manifested in his "Wotruba Church" (The Church of the Most Holy Trinity), erected toward the end of his life in Vienna's outlying 23rd District. Adorned with his sculptures, and representative of his architectural theories in general, the building is an important touristic and spiritual attraction.

Oscar Kokoschka (1886–1980) always makes the list of Vienna's most important contemporary painters. Well-versed in the visual techniques of both the Austrian baroque and the German expressionist schools, Kokoschka expressed the frenzied psychological confusion of the years before and after World War II. His portraits of such personalities as the artist Carl Moll are bathed in either psychological realism or violent emotions.

6 The Music of Vienna

RENAISSANCE POLYPHONY

As political, ecclesiastical, and academic power gravitated toward Vienna, the city on the Danube became the musical center for most of central Europe. The music of the Austrian monasteries became more complex, with an evolution toward vocal harmonies (polyphony). St. Stephan's Cathedral, spiritual center of the Austrian Empire, employed full-time choir directors who did much to develop their art form.

By the early 1500s, Vienna enjoyed the presence of one of the largest international congregations of musicians in Europe. Nurturing all this creativity was the Habsburg court, which paid stipends to its preferred musicians.

Less privileged was the music created by merchants, farmers, and artisans. A tradition of *Lieder* (songs), sometimes used as accompaniments for dancing, and performed either with or without instrumentation, were familiar to all classes of society. During this era the preferred instrument was the lute, an Asian instrument with a pear-shaped body, a fretted fingerboard, and between 6 and 13 pairs of strings.

THE BAROQUE AGE

The main contribution of the baroque age was the development of **opera.** Originally from Italy, opera was almost immediately received in Vienna with passion. A flood of brilliant and not-so-brilliant librettists, composers, singers, and musicians moved from Italy to the Habsburg capital to fill the insatiable musical needs of the imperial court. Rejecting their native German, Austrian composers hurried to learn Italian, the musically superior language of the period. One of the first truly important operas, performed endlessly in Vienna for almost a full year, was *Il Pomo d'Oro (The Golden Apple)*, composed in 1667 by Marcantonio Cesti.

THE CLASSICAL PERIOD

Audiences in Vienna began to appreciate more natural and graceful musical forms devoid of the sometimes excessive baroque ornamentation. Classicism's first great manifestation occurred with the development of *Singspiele,* a reform brought into opera by **Christoph Willibald von Gluck** whose most famous operas included *Orpheus and Eurydice* (1762) and *Alceste* (1767).

Franz Joseph Haydn (1732–1809), a contemporary of Gluck, created the classical sonata, which is the basis of classical chamber music. Haydn's most famous works included the Austrian national anthem (1797), which he later elaborated in his quartet Opus 76 no. 3. He also wrote oratorios, which included *The Creation* and *The Four Seasons;* and an array of masses, symphonies, and operas.

The most famous composer to emerge from Austria's classical period was **Wolfgang Amadeus Mozart** (1756–91). Viewed as a prodigious talent from the age of 5 in Salzburg, his native city, he was tutored by Haydn in Vienna. Later he toured Italy with his difficult and demanding father, Leopold, all the while absorbing that country's fertile musical traditions. Partially patronized by the aristocrats of Vienna, he composed more than 600 works in practically every musical form known to Europe at the time, many unmatched in beauty and profundity. Despite his position as royal chamber composer to Emperor Joseph II, he died in obscure poverty, buried in a pauper's grave in Vienna, the whereabouts of which are uncertain.

THE ROMANTIC AGE

Franz Schubert (1797–1828), the most Viennese of musicians, adapted central European dances and folk songs to create the hundreds of songs, concertos, and symphonies which have labeled him a master of the melodic line. Successfully setting the poetry of German poet Goethe to music when he was only 18 (in *Margaret at the Spinning Wheel* and *The Elf King*), he worked out a distinct and original style that culminated in his *Unfinished Symphony* and Quintet Opus 163.

THE RISE OF THE BOURGEOISIE

After 1850 Vienna became the world's capital of light music, exporting it to every corner of the globe. The **waltz,** originally developed as a rustic Austrian country dance, was adopted as the preferred pursuit of Viennese society.

Johann Strauss (1804–49), composer of more than 150 waltzes, and his talented and entrepreneurial son, **Johann Strauss Jr.** (1825–99), who further developed the art form, helped to spread the stately and graceful rhythms of the waltz around Europe. The younger Strauss's most famous waltzes included "The Blue Danube," "Tales from the Vienna Woods," and the opera *Die Fledermaus* (*The Bat,* 1874).

The tradition of Viennese light opera continued to thrive thanks to the efforts of **Franz von Suppé** (1819–95) and Hungarian-born **Franz Lehár** (1870–1948). Lehár's witty and mildly scandalous *The Merry Widow* (1905) is the most popular and amusing light opera ever written.

Other 19th-century composers wrote in more serious tones like **Anton Bruckner** (1824–96), composer of nine symphonies and a handful of deeply evocative masses.

Equally important was **Hugo Wolf** (1860–1903), who reinvented key elements of the German lieder with his five great song cycles. Most innovative of all was **Gustav Mahler** (1860–1911). A pupil of Bruckner, he expanded the size of the orchestra, added a chorus and/or vocal soloists, and composed weirdly evocative music, much of it set to poetry.

THE NEW VIENNA SCHOOL

Mahler's musical heirs forever altered the world's concepts of harmony and tonality, and introduced then-shocking concepts of rhythm. **Arnold Schoenberg** (1874–1951) expanded Mahler's style in such atonal works as *Das Buch der Hangenden Garten* (1908), and later developed a 12-tone musical technique referred to as dodecaphony (*Suite for Piano,* 1924). By the end of his career, he pioneered what was referred to as "serial music," whereby patterns or series of notes would have no key center, shifting confusingly from one tonal group to another. **Anton von Webern** (1883–1945) and **Alban Berg** (1885–1935), composer of the brilliant but esoteric opera *Wozzeck,* were pupils of Schoenberg who adapted his system to their own musical personalities.

Last, this discussion of Viennese music would not be complete without mention of the vast repertoire of folk songs, Christmas carols, and country dances which have inspired both professional musicians and common folk for generations. The most famous Christmas carol in the world, "Stille Nacht, Heilige Nacht" (Silent Night, Holy Night) was composed and performed for the first time in Salzburg in 1818 and heard in Vienna for the first time that same year.

7 Viennese Cuisine: From Wiener Schnitzel to Apfelstrudel

It's pointless to argue whether a Viennese dish is of Hungarian, Czech, Austrian, Slovenian, or even Serbian origin. Personally, we've always been more interested in taste than in tracing the province in which a dish was born. Our palates respond well to *Wienerküche* (Viennese cooking), a centuries-old blend of foreign recipes and homespun concoctions.

THE CUISINE

Soups are a savory and inexpensive choice among Viennese diners. Most popular are *gulyassuppe* (a Hungarian gulasch soup) and *leberknödlsuppe* (meat broth with round dumplings containing chicken liver). *Gulasches* (stews of beef or pork with paprika) are prepared many different ways throughout the city. The local version, *Wiener gulasch,* is usually lighter on the paprika than most Hungarian versions.

Viennese **bread** is among the best in the world. It comes in all shapes, sizes, and colors, and is made with many different grains and flours. **Strudels,** too, come in all shapes, sizes, and flavors, the most popular being *Apfelstrudel* (apple strudel).

Impressions

Oh, my friends, if you know how wonderful Vienna is! . . . Enormous churches, yet they do not oppress you by their bulk, but caress the eyes because they seem to be woven of lace. The Cathedral of St. Stephan and the Votivekirche are especially admirable. They are not edifices, but tea biscuits.

—Anton Chekhov

It's no secret that the Viennese are meat-eaters or that their city's most famous dish is *Wiener schnitzel* (breaded veal cutlet). The most authentic local recipes insist that the schnitzel be fried in lard, while the others prefer butter or at least a combination of the two. But everyone agrees on one point: The schnitzel should have the golden-brown color of a Stradivari violin.

Another renowned meat specialty is boiled beef, or *tafelspitz,* said to reflect "the soul of the empire." It's the *specialité de la nation.* You won't find a single discriminating Viennese who hasn't, at least once in his or her life, eaten this celebrated dish. For the best try it at Hotel Sacher, but if the price is too high, then order tafelspitz at a much cheaper *beisel,* cousin of the French bistro.

Roast goose is served on festive occasions such as Christmas, but at any time of the year you can order *eine gute fettgans,* a good fat goose. After such a rich dinner, you may want to relax over some strong coffee, followed by schnapps.

The Viennese are exceedingly fond of **desserts,** which are rich and varied. The city's pastries and cakes are world-famous, including *Rehruken,* a chocolate "saddle of venison" cake that's studded with almonds.

Even if you're not addicted to sweets, there's a gustatory experience you mustn't miss in Vienna: the Sachertorte. Many gourmets claim to have the original recipe for the "king of tortes," a rich chocolate cake with a layer of apricot jam. Master pastry baker Franz Sacher created the Sachertorte for Prince von Metternich in 1832, and it is still available in the Hotel Sacher in many sizes. Outstanding imitations, however, can be found throughout Vienna (see page 106 for the recipe).

COFFEE

Although it may sound heretical, Turkey is credited with establishing the tradition of the famous Viennese coffeehouse. The first *kaffeehaus* was established in Vienna in 1683, almost 40 years after coffee drinking became popular among the Austrian Empire's neighbors, the Ottoman Turks. Legend holds that Turks retreating from the siege of Vienna abandoned several sacks of coffee, which, when tasted by the victorious Viennese, established the Austrian passion for coffee drinking.

In Vienna, *jause* is a 4pm coffee-and-pastry ritual that is practiced daily throughout the city's classic coffeehouses. You can order your coffee several different ways—everything from *verkehrt* (almost milk-pale), to *mocca* (ebony-black). *Kaffee mit schalagobers* (with whipped cream) is the easiest, simplest, and most traditional method of preparing coffee in Vienna. You might even order *doppelschlag* (double whipped cream).

BEER, WINE & LIQUEURS

Vienna imposes few restrictions on the sale of alcohol, so except in alcohol-free places you should be able to order beer or wine with your meal—even if it's 9am. Many Viennese have their first strong drink in the morning, preferring beer to coffee to get them going.

In general, **Austrian wines** are served when new and most are consumed where they're produced. We prefer the white wine to the red, and perhaps you will, too. More than 99% of all Austrian wine is produced in vineyards in eastern Austria, principally Vienna, Lower Austria, Styria, and Burgenland. The most famous Austrian wine, *Gumpoldskirchen,* which is sold all over Vienna, comes from Lower Austria, the country's largest wine producer. At the heart of the Baden wine district, known as the *Sudbahnstrecke,* is the village of Gumpoldskirchen, which gives the wine its name. This white wine is heady, rich, and slightly sweet.

Located in an outer district of Vienna, Klosterneuburg, an ancient abbey on the right bank of the Danube, produces what is—arguably—the finest white wine in

Austria. Monks have been making wine at this Augustinian monastery for centuries. The Wachau district, lying to the west of Vienna, also produces some fine wines known for their delicate bouquet, including *Loibner Kaiserwein* and *Duernsteiner Katzensprung,* which are fragrant and fruity.

By far the best red wine, and on this there is little disagreement, is *Vöslauer* from Vöslau. It's strong but, even though red, not quite as powerful as Gumpoldskirchen and Klosterneuburger. From Styria comes Austria's best-known rosé, *Schilcher,* which is slightly dry, fruity, and sparkling.

Because many Viennese visiting the *heurigen* (wine taverns) outside their capital didn't want to get too drunk, they started diluting the new wine with club soda or mineral water. Thus the **spritzer** was born, a drink that swept Europe and North America as well. The mix is best with a very dry wine. If you use a sweetish wine, you're likely to get what Marlene Dietrich once called "weak lemonade."

In all except the most deluxe places it's possible to order a carafe of wine, *offener wein,* which will be much less expensive.

Austrian beers are relatively inexpensive and quite good, and they're sold throughout Vienna. *Gösser,* produced in Styria, is one of the most favored brews and comes in both light and dark. *Augustiner Bräu* and *Adambräu,* two other native beers, are also sold in Vienna's bars and taverns, along with some lighter, Bavarian-type beers like *Weizengold* and *Kaiser.* Austria brews most of its own beer. Vienna is one of its major production centers and home to what we believe is the finest beer in the city, *Schwechater.* For those who prefer the taste without the alcohol, *Null Komma Josef* is a local alcohol-free beer.

Two of the most famous and favored **liqueurs** among Austrians are *slivovitz* (a plum brandy which originated in Croatia) and *barack* (made from apricots).

Imported whisky and bourbon are likely to be lethal in price. When you're in Vienna, it's a good rule of thumb to drink the "spirit of the land." In this case, that means wine and beer.

The most festive drink is **bowle** (pronounced *bole*) which the Viennese often serve at parties. First made for us by the great chanteuse Greta Keller, we've been devotees of it ever since. She preferred the lethal method of soaking berries and sliced peaches overnight in brandy, pouring three bottles of dry white wine over the fruit and letting it stand for another two to three hours. Before serving, she'd pour a bottle of champagne over it. In her words, "You can drink it as a cocktail, during and after dinner, and on . . . and on . . . and on!"

THE HEURIGEN

In 1784, Joseph II decreed that each vintner in the suburbs of Vienna could sell his own wine right on his doorstep to paying guests. And thus a tradition was born that still continues today.

Heurig means "new wines" or, more literally, "of this year." These wine taverns lie on the outskirts of Vienna, mainly in Grinzing but also in Nussdorf and Sievering, and are often designated by a branch above the doorway. Most are rustic with wooden benches and tables, but much of the drinking takes place in vine-covered gardens in fair weather. In some of the more old-fashioned places, on a nippy night you'll find a crackling fire in an often flower-bordered ceramic stove. Many heurigen today are in fact quite elaborate restaurants, serving a buffet of meats, cheeses, breads, and vegetables. Others are still simple, and it's perfectly acceptable to bring your own snacks.

Schmaltzy Viennese songs are often featured in the courtyards here. There's likely to be a gypsy violin, an accordion, or perhaps a zither. Remember Orson Welles's movie *The Third Man*?

Beware: The wine is surprisingly potent, in spite of its innocent taste.

2 Planning a Trip to Vienna

So, you've decided on a trip to Vienna. Now you need to figure out how much it will cost, how to get there, and when to go. This chapter will answer these questions and more, with useful tips on pretrip planning to help you get the most from your stay.

1 Visitor Information, Entry Requirements & Customs

VISITOR INFORMATION

Before you go, your travel agent can supply basic information about Vienna, but we recommend you contact the **Austrian National Tourist Office,** P.O. Box 1142, New York, NY 10108-1142 (☎ **212/944-6880**); on the West Coast, write or call P.O. Box 491938, Los Angeles, CA 90049 (☎ **310/478-8376**). If you have Internet access, the Vienna Tourist Board has a useful web site, Vienna Scene (**http://wtv.magwien.gv.at/**), which provides current tourist information on special events and festivals, restaurants, hotels, and more.

As you travel throughout Vienna and Austria, you'll see signs indicating a fat **"i."** Most often that will stand for "information," and you'll be directed to a local tourist office where, chances are, you can obtain maps of the area and might even be assisted in finding a hotel should you arrive without a reservation.

ENTRY REQUIREMENTS & CUSTOMS

Citizens of the United States, Canada, the United Kingdom, Australia, Ireland, and New Zealand need only a valid passport to enter Austria. No visa is required.

Austria's duty-free allowances are as follows, and as a matter of necessity, are divided into two categories: nonresidents arriving from European countries, and nonresidents arriving from non-European countries (i.e., the U.S. or Canada).

Visitors arriving from other European Union countries may import the following items: 800 cigarettes, 200 cigars, or 1,000 grams of pipe tobacco, 20 liters of liqueur (up to 44 proof), and 10 liters of distilled liquor (more than 44 proof).

Visitors arriving from non-European Union countries may import 200 cigarettes, 50 cigars, or 250 grams of pipe tobacco. They may also include ¹/₄ liter of eau de toilette, and 50 grams of perfume. As far as spirits go, visitors may bring one liter of liqueur (up to 44 proof), or one liter of distilled liquor (over 44 proof), as well as two liters of wine.

U.S. CUSTOMS   Returning to the United States from Vienna, American citizens may bring in $400 worth of merchandise duty free, provided that you have not made a similar claim within the past 30 days. Remember to keep your receipts for purchases made in Austria. For more specific guidance, write to the U.S. Customs Service, P.O. Box 7407, Washington, DC 20044, and request the free pamphlet "Know Before You Go."

BRITISH CUSTOMS   Members of EU countries do not necessarily have to go through Customs when returning home providing that all their travel was within EU countries. There are certain EU guidelines for returning passengers, who can bring in 400 cigarillos, 200 cigars, 800 cigarettes, and one kilogram of smoking tobacco. They can also bring in 20 liters of fortified wine, 90 liters of wine, and 110 liters of beer. For further details on U.K. Customs, contact HM Customs and Excise, Excise and Inland Customs Advice Centre, Dorset House, Stamford Street, London SE1 9NG (☎ **0171/202-4227**).

CANADIAN CUSTOMS   For total clarification, Canadians can write for the booklet "I Declare," issued by Revenue Canada Customs Department, Communications Branch, Mackenzie Avenue, Ottawa, ON K1A 0L5. Canada allows its citizens a $300 exemption, and they can bring back duty free 200 cigarettes, 2 pounds of tobacco, 40 ounces of liquor, and 50 cigars. In addition, they are allowed to mail unsolicited gifts into Canada from abroad at the rate of $40 (Canadian) a day (but *not* alcohol or tobacco). On the package, mark UNSOLICITED GIFT, UNDER $40 VALUE. All valuables you own and take with you should be declared before departure from Canada on the Y-38 form, including serial numbers.

AUSTRALIAN CUSTOMS   The duty-free allowance in Australia is A$400 or, for those under 18, A$200. Personal property mailed back from Austria should be marked AUSTRALIAN GOODS RETURNED to avoid payment of duty. Upon returning to Australia, citizens can bring in 200 cigarettes or 250 grams of loose tobacco and one liter of alcohol. If you're returning with valuable goods you already own, such as foreign-made cameras, you should file form B263. A helpful brochure, available from Australian consulates or Customs offices, is "Customs Information for All Travellers." For more information, contact the Australian Customs Service, 5 Constitution Ave., Canberra, ACT 2601 (☎ 6/275-62-55).

NEW ZEALAND CUSTOMS   The duty-free allowance is NZ$500. Citizens more than 16 years of age can bring in 200 cigarettes or 250 grams of loose tobacco or 50 cigars, and 4.5 liters of wine or beer or 1.125 liters of liquor. New Zealand currency does not carry restrictions regarding import or export. A Certificate of Export listing valuables taken out of the country allows you to bring them back without paying duty. Most questions are answered in a free pamphlet, "New Zealand Customs Guide for Travellers," available at New Zealand consulates and Customs offices. For more information, contact New Zealand Customs, 50 Anzac Ave., P.O. Box 29, Auckland (☎ 9/377-35-20).

2 Money

Foreign and Austrian money can be brought into Vienna without any restrictions, and there is no restriction on taking foreign money out of the country either.

The Austrian Schilling

For American Readers   At this writing $1 = approximately 10.5 schillings (or 1 schilling = approximately 9½ cents), and this was the rate of exchange used to calculate the dollar values given in this book (rounded to the nearest nickel).

For British Readers   At this writing £1 = approximately 16.8 schillings (or 1 schilling = approximately 6 pence), and this was the rate of exchange used to calculate the pound values in the table below.

Note: Since international exchange rates fluctuate, this table should be used only as a guide.

AS	U.S.$	U.K.	AS	U.S.$	U.K.
1	.10	0.06	75	7.13	4.43
2	.19	0.12	100	9.50	5.90
3	.29	0.18	125	11.88	7.38
4	.38	0.24	150	14.25	8.85
5	.48	0.30	175	16.63	10.33
6	.57	0.35	200	19.00	11.80
7	.67	0.41	225	21.38	13.28
8	.76	0.47	250	23.75	14.75
9	.86	0.53	275	26.13	16.23
10	0.95	0.59	300	28.50	17.70
15	1.43	0.89	350	33.25	20.65
20	1.90	1.18	400	38.00	23.60
25	2.38	1.48	500	47.50	29.50
50	4.75	2.95	1,000	95.00	59.00

The basic unit of currency is the Austrian **schilling (AS),** which is made up of 100 **groschen.** There are coins with denominations of 2, 5, 10, and 50 groschen, and 1, 5, 10, and 20 schillings, and banknotes with denominations of 20, 50, 100, 500, 1,000, and 5,000 schillings.

EXCHANGING YOUR MONEY   It's always wise to exchange enough money before departure to get you from the airport to your hotel. This way, you avoid delays and the lousy rates at the airport exchange booths.

Austrian banks generally offer the best rates of exchange; they're open Monday through Wednesday, and Fridays from 8am to 3pm, and Thursdays from 8am to 5:30pm (most banks also close daily from 12:30 to 1:30pm). The most tourist-friendly bank in Vienna is the one run by American Express at Kärntnerstrasse 21-23 (☎ 0222/515-40-0), open Monday through Friday, 9am to 5:30pm, and Saturday, 9am to noon. During off-hours you can exchange money at bureaux de change throughout the Inner City (there's one at the intersection of Kohlmarkt and the Graben), as well as at travel agencies, train stations, and at the airport. There's also a 24-hour exchange service at the Post Office (*Haubtpostamt*) at Fleischmarkt 19. Examine the prices and rates carefully before handing over your dollars, and try not to exchange money at your hotel; the rates they offer tend to be horrendous.

If you need to prepay a deposit on hotel reservations by check, it's cheaper and easier to pay with a check drawn on an Austrian bank. This can be arranged by a large commercial bank or **Ruesch International,** 700 11th St. NW, Washington, DC 20005 (☎ **800/424-2923** or 202/408-1200), which performs many conversion-related tasks, usually for only $2 per transaction.

CREDIT CARDS   The way to get the best rate of exchange is to not change your money, but to buy whatever you can with credit cards. They virtually always offer a rate of exchange better than any you can get by changing your money, and there's no accompanying service charge. Credit cards are widely accepted in Austria; American Express, Visa, and Diners Club are the most commonly recognized. A Eurocard or Access sign displayed at an establishment means that it accepts MasterCard.

ATM NETWORKS   Plus, Cirrus, and other networks connecting automated-teller machines (ATMs) operate in Vienna and throughout Austria. By using your bank card to withdraw money you'll debit the amount from your account. When using an ATM abroad, the money will be in local currency; the rate of exchange tends to be as good, if not better, than what you would receive at an airport money counter or a hotel. Note that international withdrawal fees will be higher than domestic—ask your bank for specifics. Always determine the frequency limits for withdrawals and cash advances of your credit card. Also, check to see if your PIN code must be re-programmed forusage in Austria. Most ATMs outside the U.S. require a four-digit PIN number.

To receive a directory of **Cirrus** ATMs, call 800/424-7787; for **Plus** locations, call 800/843-7587. You can also access the Visa/PLUS International ATM Locator Guide through Internet: http://www.visa.com/visa.

What Things Cost in Vienna	U.S. $
Taxi from the airport to the city center	38.00
U-Bahn (subway) from St. Stephan's to Schönbrunn Palace	1.90
Local phone call	.10
Double room at the Park Hotel Schönbrunn (expensive)	242.50
Double room at the Pension Barich (moderate)	152.00
Double room at the Graf Stadion (inexpensive)	80.75
Lunch for one, without wine, at Drei Husareu (expensive)	37.05
Lunch for one, without wine, at Do & Co (moderate)	28.50
Dinner for one, without wine, at Stet (expensive)	57.00
Dinner for one, without wine, at Nicky's Kuchmastorei (moderate)	40.00
Dinner for one, without wine, at Zwölf-Apostelkeller (inexpensive)	19.95
Glass of wine (one-eighth liter)	2.50
Half-liter of beer	3.80
Coca-Cola (in a cafe)	2.30
Cup of coffee (in a cafe)	2.50
Roll of ASA 100 color film, 36 exposures	8.50
Admission to Schönbrunn Palace	7.25
Movie ticket	6.75
Theater ticket (at the Staatsoper)	36.50

TRAVELER'S CHECKS   Traveler's checks are the safest way to carry cash while traveling. Most banks will give you a better exchange rate for traveler's checks than cash.

Major issuers of traveler's checks include **American Express** (☎ 800/221-7282); **Citicorp** (☎ 800/645-6556 in the U.S. and Canada, or 813/623-1709 collect from anywhere else in the world); **Thomas Cook** (☎ 800/223-7373 in the U.S. and Canada, or 609/987-7300 collect from other parts of the world); and **Interpayment Services** (☎ 800/221-2426 in the U.S. and Canada, or 212/858-8500 collect from other parts of the world).

MONEYGRAM   If you find yourself out of money, a new wire service provided by American Express can help you tap willing friends and family for emergency funds. Through **MoneyGram,** 6200 S. Québec St., P.O. Box 5118, Englewood, CO 80155 (☎ 800/926-9400), money can be sent around the world in less than 10 minutes. Call AMEX to learn the address of the closest outlet that handles MoneyGrams. Cash, credit card, or the occasional personal check (with ID) are acceptable forms of payment. AMEX's fee for the service is $10 for the first $300 with a sliding scale for larger sums. The service includes a short telex message and a three-minute phone call from sender to recipient. The beneficiary must present a photo ID at the outlet where money is received.

3 When to Go

Vienna experiences its high season from April through October, with July and August and the main festivals being the most crowded times. Bookings around Christmastime are also heavy because many Austrians themselves visit the capital city during this festive time. Always arrive with reservations during these peak seasons. During the off seasons, hotel rooms are generally plentiful and less expensive, and there is less demand for tables in the important restaurants.

CLIMATE

The temperature in Austria varies greatly depending on your location. However, in Vienna—less subject to drastic temperature fluctuations than Innsbruck or other alpine locales—the January average is 32°F, whereas for July it's 66°F. In a subalpine climate it's neither very, very hot nor, on the other hand, is it Siberian cold. A New Yorker who lived in Vienna for eight years told us that the four seasons were "about the same." Summers in Vienna, which generally last from Easter until mid-October, are not usually as humid as those in sea-fronting New York City, but, ironically, the past three or four years have been uncomfortably sticky. The ideal times for visiting Vienna are spring and fall, when mild weather prevails, but the winter air is usually crisp and clear, with plenty of sunshine.

Average Daytime Temperature (°F) & Monthly Rainfall (inches) in Vienna

	Jan	Feb	Mar	Apr	May	June	July	Aug	Sept	Oct	Nov	Dec
Temp.	30	32	38	50	58	64	68	70	60	50	41	33
Rainfall	1.2	1.9	3.9	1.3	2.9	1.9	.8	1.8	2.8	2.8	2.5	1.6

HOLIDAYS

Bank holidays in Vienna are as follows: January 1, January 6 (Epiphany), Easter Monday, May 1, Ascension Day, Whitmonday, Corpus Christi Day, August 15, October 26 (*Nationalfeiertag*), November 1 and 26, and December 25–26.

VIENNA CALENDAR OF EVENTS

January
- **New Year's Eve/New Year's Day.** Vienna's biggest night is launched by the famed concert of the Vienna Philharmonic Orchestra. New Year also marks the beginning of **Fasching,** the famous Vienna Carnival season, which lasts until Ash Wednesday. For tickets and information, contact the Wiener Philharmoniker Bösendorserstrasse 12, A-1010 Vienna (☎ **0222/505-65-25**). It's followed by the Kaiserball in the Hofburg. For information and tickets, contact the WKV, Hofburg, Heldenplatz, A-1014 Vienna (☎ **0222/587-36-66**).

February
- **Opera Ball.** On the last Thursday of the Fasching, Vienna's high society gathers at the Staatsoper for the grandest ball of the Carnival season. The evening opens with a performance by the Opera House Ballet. You don't need an invitation, but you do need to buy a ticket, which, as you might guess, isn't cheap. For information call the Opera House (☎ **0222/514-4429-55**) directly.

May
- ✪ **Vienna International Festival** (*Wiener Festwochen*). This is the premier cultural event of the Austrian capital featuring theater, music, films, and other exhibitions, which are celebrated throughout the city. Musical performances emphasize both traditional and avant-garde compositions. To a lesser degree, the festival also offers unusual, often cutting-edge theater presentations, usually in both German and English. The festival takes place in various theaters, churches, and auditoriums throughout Vienna from early May to mid-June. For tickets and information, contact the Wiener Festwochen, Léhargasse 11, A-1060 Vienna (☎ **0222/ 586-16-76**).

July
- **Vienna Summer of Music.** From July 1 to August 31 this premier event fills the cultural calendar with concerts at City Hall, Schönbrunn Palace, and at many landmark homes of great 19th-century Viennese musicians. Densely packed with musical options, the festival often features a series of different musical events on any given night. For tickets, schedules, and information, contact the Wiener Musiksommer Laudongasse 19, A-1080 Vienna (☎ **0222/4000-84-722**).

October
- **Vienna Cinema Festival.** Showing everything from the most daringly avant-garde to golden oldies of the (mostly European) silver screen. For tickets and information, contact the Wiener Festwochen Viennale, Stiftgasse 6, A-1070 Vienna (☎ **0222/526-59-47**). The festival runs throughout October.

November
- **Vienna Schubert Festival.** A relative newcomer to the Viennese music scene, this all-Schubert celebration marks its 15th annual observance in 1997. For information, contact Wiener Musikverein, Bösendorferstrasse 12, A-1010 Vienna (☎ **0222/505-81-90**). Late November.

December
- **Chriskindl.** Between late November and New Year's, look for pockets of folkloric charm (and in some cases kitsch) associated with the Christmas holidays. Small outdoor booths known as *Chriskindlmarkts*—usually adorned with evergreen boughs, red ribbons, and in some cases religious symbols— sprout up in clusters around the city. They're selling old-fashioned toys, *tannenbaum* decorations, and

gift items. Food vendors will also be nearby offering sausages, cookies and pastries, roasted chestnuts, and *kartoffel*, charcoal-roasted potato slices. The greatest concentration of these open-air markets can be found in front of the Rathaus, in the Spittleberg Quarter (7th District), at Freyung, the historic square in the northwest corner if the Inner City.

4 Health & Insurance

STAYING HEALTHY

You'll encounter few health problems traveling in Vienna. The tap water is generally safe to drink, the milk pasteurized, and health services good. Occasionally the change in diet may cause some minor diarrhea so you may want to take some antidiarrhea medicine along.

Carry all your vital medicines in your carry-on luggage and bring enough prescribed medicines to last you during your stay. Bring along copies of your prescriptions that are written in the generic—not brand-name—form. If you need a doctor, your hotel can recommend one or you can contact your embassy or consulate. You can also obtain a list of English-speaking doctors before you leave from the **International Association for Medical Assistance to Travelers (IAMAT)** in the United States at 417 Center St., Lewiston, NY 14092 (☎ **716/754-4883**); in Canada, at 40 Regal Rd., Guelph, ON N1K 1B5 (☎ **519/836-0102**).

INSURANCE

Before going out and spending money on various sorts of travel insurance, check your existing policies to see if they'll cover you while you're traveling. For example, your homeowner's or renter's insurance might cover off-premises theft and loss wherever it occurs. And check that your health insurance will cover you when you're away from home.

Some credit and charge cards offer automatic flight insurance when you purchase an airline ticket with that card. These policies insure against death or dismemberment in case of an airplane crash. If you are traveling on a tour or have prepaid a large chunk of your travel expenses, you might want to ask your travel agent about trip-cancellation insurance.

If you are going to rent a car in Austria, check to see whether your automobile insurance, automobile club, or charge card covers personal accident insurance (PAI), collision damage waiver (CDW), or other insurance options. You may be able to avoid additional rental charges if you are already covered. See "Car Rentals" for more information.

The following companies sell a variety of travel insurance policies: **Healthcare Abroad (MEDEX),** c/o Wallach & Co., P.O. Box 480 (107 W. Federal St.), Middleburg, VA 22117-0480 (☎ 800/237-6615 or 540/687-3166); **Mutual of Omaha** (Tele-Trip), Mutual of Omaha Plaza, Omaha, NE 68175 (☎ 800/ 228-9792); **Travel Guard International,** 1145 Clark Street, Stevens Point, WI 54481 (☎ 800/826-1300 or 715/345-0505); and **Travel Insured International, Inc.,** P.O. Box 280568, East Hartford, CT 06128-0568 (☎ 800/243-3174 in the U.S., or 203/528-7663 outside the U.S., between 7:45am and 7pm EST).

5 Tips for Travelers with Special Needs

FOR TRAVELERS WITH DISABILITIES

BEFORE YOU GO   Before you go, there are many agencies that you can check with for advance-planning information.

For a $25 annual fee, **Mobility International USA,** P.O. Box 10767, Eugene, OR 97440 (☎ 541/343-1284 voice & TDD), will answer your questions on various destinations and also give discounts on videos, publications, and programs it sponsors.

You can also obtain a copy of **"Air Transportation of Handicapped Persons,"** published by the U.S. Department of Transportation. It's free if you write to Free Advisory Circular No. AC12032, Distribution Unit, U.S. Department of Transportation, Publications Division, M-4332, Washington, DC 20590.

If you're interested in tours run for travelers with disabilities, contact the **Society for the Advancement of Travel for the Handicapped,** 347 Fifth Ave., New York, NY 10016 (☎ 212/447-7248). Annual membership dues are $45, or $25 for senior citizens and students. Send a stamped, self-addressed envelope.

FEDCAP Rehabilitation Services (formerly known as the Federation of the Handicapped), 154 W. 14th St., New York, NY 10011 (☎ 212/727-4200), operates summer tours to Europe and elsewhere for its members. Membership costs $4 yearly.

For persons who are blind or have visual impairments, the best source is the **American Foundation for the Blind,** 15 W. 16th St., New York, NY 10011 (☎ 800/232-5463,** or 212/502-7600 in the U.S.). It offers information on travel and various requirements for the transport and border formalities for seeing-eye dogs. It also issues identification cards to those who are legally blind.

IN VIENNA   As with most European cities, services for disabled travelers in Vienna are limited, but luckily a lot of the sights in the city center are close together and are accessible by wheelchair. The **Vienna Tourist Board,** Obere Augartenstrasse 40, A-1025 (☎ 0222/211-14-0;** fax 0222/216-8492) publishes a helpful booklet for disabled visitors, including information on riding public transportation.

FOR GAY & LESBIAN TRAVELERS

Unlike Germany, Austria still has a prevailing anti-homosexual attitude, in spite of the large number of gay people who live within the country. There is still much discrimination; gay liberation has a long way to go. Vienna, however, has a large gay colony with many bars and restaurants. For information about gay-related activities in Vienna, call the **Gay/Lesbian Visitor Center** at Novargasse 40 (☎ 0222/216-6604).

To learn about gay and lesbian travel in Austria, you might want to consult the following publications before you go. Men can order *Spartacus,* the international gay guide ($32.95), or *Odysseus 1997, The International Gay Travel Planner,* a guide to international gay accommodations ($25). Both lesbians and gay men might want to pick up a copy of *Gay Travel A to Z* ($16), which provides general information and lists bars, hotels, restaurants, and places of interest for gay travelers throughout the world. These books and others are available from **Giovanni's Room,** 1145 Pine St., Philadelphia, PA 19107 (☎ 215/923-2960).

The magazine ***Our World,*** 1104 North Nova Rd., Suite 251, Daytona Beach, FL 32117 (☎ 904/441-5367), covers options and bargains for gay and lesbian travel worldwide. It costs $35 for 10 issues. ***Out and About,*** 8 W. 19th St., Suite 401, New York, NY 10011 (☎ 800/929-2268), has been hailed for its "straight" reporting about gay travel. It profiles the best gay or gay-friendly hotels, gyms, clubs, and other places at destinations throughout the world. It costs $49 for 10 information-packed issues. Both of these publications are also available at most gay and lesbian bookstores.

The **International Gay Travel Association** (IGTA), P.O. Box 4974, Key West, FL 33041 (☎ 800/448-8550 for voice mailbox, or 305/292-0217), encourages gay and lesbian travel worldwide. With around 1,200 member agencies, it specializes in networking travelers with the appropriate gay-friendly service organization or tour specialist. It offers quarterly newsletter, marketing mailings, and a membership directory updated four times a year.

In Austria, the minimum age for consensual homosexual activity is 18.

FOR SENIORS

Many senior discounts are available, but note that some may require membership in a particular association.

If you're a member of the **AARP (American Association of Retired Persons),** 601 E St. NW, Washington, DC 20049 (☎ **202/434-AARP**), you may get discounts on car rentals, hotels, and airfares.

SAGA International Holidays, 222 Berkeley St., Boston, MA 02116 (☎ **800/343-0273** in the U.S.), runs all-inclusive tours for those 50 years and older.

You can write for a helpful publication, **101 Tips for the Mature Traveler,** available free from Grand Circle Travel, 347 Congress St., Suite 3A, Boston, MA 02210 (☎ **800/221-2610** in the U.S., or 617/350-7500).

Information on travel for seniors is also available from the **National Council of Senior Citizens,** 1331 F St. NW, Washington, DC 20005-1171 (☎ **202/347-8800**). This nonprofit organization charges $12 per person or per couple for which you receive a monthly newsletter and membership benefits, including reduced discounts on hotel and car rentals.

Mature Outlook, P.O. Box 10448, Des Moines, IA 50306 (☎ **800/336-6330**), is a membership program for people more than 50 years of age. Members are offered discounts at ITC-member hotels and will receive a bimonthly magazine. The annual membership fee of $14.95 entitles you to discounts on selected car rentals and restaurants, plus free coupons for discounted merchandise from Sears, Roebuck & Co.

Uniworld, 16000 Ventura Blvd., Suite 200, Encino, CA 91436 (☎ **800/733-7820** in the U.S., or 818/382-7820), specializes in single tours for the mature person. They either arrange for you to share an accommodation with another single person, or they get you a low-priced single supplement.

For information before you go, write for a free booklet called "101 Tips for the Mature Traveler," available from **Grand Circle Travel,** 347 Congress St., Suite 3A, Boston, MA 02210 (☎ **800/221-2610** in the U.S., or 617/350-7500).

Elderhostel, 75 Federal St. Boston, MA 02110-1941 (☎ **617/426-7788**), offers an array of university-based summer educational programs for senior citizens worldwide, including Vienna. Most courses are three weeks long and are remarkable values, considering that airfare, accommodations (in student dormitories or modest inns), meals, and tuition are included. Courses include field trips but no homework, and participants must be at least 55 years old.

FOR FAMILIES

Vienna is a great place to take your kids. The pleasures available for children (which most adults enjoy just as much) range from watching the magnificent Lippizaner stallions fly through the air at the Spanish Riding School to exploring the city's many castles and dungeons.

Another outstanding and kid-friendly Viennese attraction is the Prater amusement park, with its giant Ferris wheel, roller coasters, merry-go-rounds, games arcades, and a tiny railroad that loops around the park. Even if your kids aren't very interested in touring the state rooms of palaces, take them to Schönbrunn, where the zoo and coach collection will surely be enjoyed. In summer, beaches along the Alte Donau (an arm of the Danube) are suitable for swimming. And, don't forget the lure of the *konditorei,* those little shops where scrumptious Viennese cakes and pastries are sold.

Baby-sitting services are available through most hotel desks or by applying at the Tourist Information Office in the town where you're staying. Many hotels have children's games rooms and playgrounds.

The *Family Travel Times* newsletter costs $40 for quarterly issues. Subscribers can also call in with travel questions, but only on Wednesday from 10am to 1pm eastern standard time. Contact **Travel With Your Children (TWYCH),** 40 5th Ave., New York, NY 10011 (☎ **212/471-5524**).

FOR STUDENTS

Council Travel (a subsidiary of the Council on International Educational Exchange) is America's largest student, youth, and budget travel group, with more than 60 offices worldwide. The main office is at 205 E. 42nd St., New York, NY 10017 (☎ **800/226-8624** or 212/661-1450); call to find the location nearest you. Council Travel sells publications for young people about how to work, study, and travel abroad.

International Student Identity Cards, issuable to all bona fide students for $16, entitle holders to generous travel and other discounts. Discounted international and domestic air tickets are available, and Eurotrain rail passes, YHA passes, weekend packages, overland safaris, and hostel/hotel accommodations are bookable. The card, which costs only $16, is available at Council Travel offices nationwide (☎ **800/ GET-AN-ID** in the U.S.), as well as on hundreds of college and university campuses. Proof of student status and a passport-size (two by two-inch) photograph are necessary.

For real budget travelers, it's worth joining **Hostelling/International/IYHF** (International Youth Hostel Federation). For information, write Hostelling Information/American Youth Hostels (HI-AYH), 733 15th St. NW, No. 840, Washington, DC 20005 (☎ 202/783-6161). Membership costs $25 annually; those under age 18 pay $10 and those over 54 pay $15.

6 Getting There

BY PLANE

Since the collapse of the Iron Curtain, Vienna has played an increasingly important role as a gateway between western and eastern Europe causing a subsequent increase in air traffic into the city. Although Vienna is serviced by a number of well-respected European airlines, most flights coming from the western hemisphere require a transfer in other European cities like London or Frankfurt.

THE MAJOR AIRLINES

From the United States, you can fly directly to Vienna on **Austrian Airlines** (☎ **800/843-0002** in the U.S. and Canada), the national carrier of Austria. There's nonstop service from New York to Vienna (approximately 9 hours) and more recently from Atlanta to Vienna. Austrian Airlines also flies from Chicago to Vienna via Zurich, and from Washington, D.C., via Geneva.

In 1994 Austrian Airlines inaugurated a block seat arrangement with **Delta Airlines** (☎ **800/241-4141** in the U.S.), whereby certain flights from New York's JFK would be operated by both carriers. Delta also maintains two independent routings into Vienna from New York and Atlanta. The first departs daily from New York's JFK, stopping in Munich with no change of aircraft. Flights from Atlanta to Vienna depart every day, although a change of equipment is required in Frankfurt.

British Airways (☎ 800/AIRWAYS in the U.S. and Canada) provides excellent service into Vienna. Passengers fly first to London—usually nonstop—from 18 gateways in the United States, three in Canada, two in Brazil, and from Bermuda, Mexico City, and Buenos Aires. From London, British Airways has two to five daily nonstop flights to Vienna from either Gatwick or Heathrow airports.

Also worthwhile is **Lufthansa** (☎ 800/645-3880 in the U.S. and Canada), the German national carrier. Flights depart from North America very frequently for Frankfurt, Düsseldorf, and Munich, any of which have connections to Vienna.

Affiliated with Lufthansa is **Lauda Air** (☎ 800/325-2832), which offers direct service three times a week between Miami and Vienna, with a brief touchdown in Munich. With some restrictions, round-trip fares from Miami range from $716 to $1,117. Lauda also operates flights to Vienna from European hubs like Barcelona, Madrid, London, Brussels, and Paris.

American Airlines (☎ 800/624-6262 in the U.S. and Canada), which funnels Vienna-bound passengers to their through gateways in Zurich, London, or Frankfurt.

If you're traveling from Canada, you can usually connect from your hometown to **British Airways'** (☎ 800/AIRWAYS in Canada) Canadian gateways in Toronto, Montréal, and Vancouver. Separate nonstop flights from both Toronto's Pearson Airport and Montréal's Mirabelle Airport depart every day for London, whereas flights from Vancouver depart for London three times a week. In London, you can stay for a few days (arranging discounted hotel accommodations through the British Airways tour desk) or head directly for any of the two to five daily nonstop flights from either Heathrow or Gatwick on to Vienna.

FINDING THE BEST AIRFARE

The lowest airfares at Austrian Airlines are called nonrefundable PEX (not to be confused with APEX), and these require a purchase of 21 days in advance and a European stopover of between 7 and 30 days. Once issued, no changes or refunds are permitted. A slightly different, slightly more expensive ticket is an Advance Purchase Excursion fare, or APEX, which requires a purchase of only 14 days in advance and a stopover of between seven days and two months. For changes in flight dates within 14 days prior to the initial departure, a $150 penalty is imposed.

With an excursion fare, no advance purchase is ever necessary. For this type of ticket, Austrian Airlines offers a $30 each-way discount on a round-trip midweek flight but makes no restrictions about early reservations or minimum time logged abroad. The return half of the ticket is valid for a year after departure.

A Note Regarding Senior-Citizen & Student Fares   Austrian Airlines offers a 10% discount off regularly published fares between New York and Vienna and Chicago and Vienna for passengers age 62 and over, and for a traveling companion regardless of that companion's age.

The airline also offers breaks to anyone between the ages of 12 and 25. Its round-trip Youth Fare requires only that tickets be reserved and purchased three days or less before departure. The return half of the ticket can be used any time within a year of departure.

OTHER GOOD-VALUE CHOICES

CHARTER FLIGHTS   Charter flights occur on an aircraft reserved months in advance for a one-time-only transit to some predetermined point. Before paying for a charter, check the restrictions on your ticket or contract. You'll pay a stiff penalty (or forfeit the ticket entirely) if you cancel. Charters are sometimes canceled when the plane doesn't fill up.

One reliable charter-flight operator is **Council Charter,** run by the Council on International Educational Exchange, 205 E. 42nd St., New York, NY 10017 (☎ 800/2-COUNCIL or 212/661-1450). You could also try **Travac,** 989 Sixth Ave., New York, NY 10018 (☎ 800/TRAV-800 or 212/563-3303).

BUCKET SHOPS & CONSOLIDATORS   You might be able to get a great deal on airfare by calling a bucket shop or a consolidator, outfits that act as clearinghouses for blocks of tickets that airlines discount and consign during normally slow periods of air travel. Tickets are usually priced 20% to 35% below the full fare. However, payment terms can vary and you might be assigned a poor seat on the plane at the last minute.

In the United States, bucket shops abound from coast to coast. You might try **Travac,** 989 Sixth Ave., New York, NY 10018 (☎ 800/TRAV-800 in the U.S., or 212/563-3303) or 2601 E. Jefferson St., Orlando, FL 32803 (☎ 407/896-0014); **TFI Tours International,** 34 W. 32nd St., 12th Floor, New York, NY 10001 (☎ 800/745-8000 outside of New York State, or 212/736-1140); **Travel Avenue,** 10 S. Riverside Plaza, Suite 1404, Chicago, IL 60606 (☎ 800/333-3335); or **TMI** (Travel Management International), 3617 Dupont Ave. South, Minneapolis, MN 55409 (☎ 800/245-3672). There's also **1-800-FLY-4-LESS,** RFA Building 5440 Morehouse Dr., San Diego, CA 92121, a nationwide airline reservation and ticketing service that specializes in finding only the lowest fares. For information on available consolidator airline tickets for last minute travel, call 800/359-4537.

REBATORS   Most rebators offer discounts ranging from 10% to 25% plus a $25 handling charge. They are not the same as travel agents but sometimes offer similar services, including discounted accommodations and car rentals.

Some rebators include **Travel Avenue,** 10 S. Riverside Plaza, Suite 1404, Chicago, IL 60606 (☎ 800/333-3335 or 312/876-1116); and **The Smart Traveller,** 3111 SW 27th Ave., (P.O. Box 330010) Miami, FL 33133 (☎ 800/448-3338 or 305/448-3338; fax 305/443-3544).

TRAVEL CLUBS   Travel clubs supply an unsold inventory of tickets at 20% to 60% discounts. After you pay an annual fee, you're given a "hotline" number to call to find out what's available. You have to be fairly flexible in your travel plans to take advantage of these offers. Some good travel clubs include **Moment's Notice,** 7301 New Utrecht Ave., New York, NY 11228 (☎ 212/486-0500), with a members' 24-hour hotline (☎ 718/234-6295) and a $25 annual fee; and the **Sears Discount Travel Club,** 3033 S. Parker Rd., Suite 1000, Aurora, CO 80014 (☎ 800/433-9383 in the U.S.), with a $50 annual fee and a catalog listing offers.

VIENNA'S AIRPORT

Vienna's international airport, **Wien Schwechat** (☎ 0222/711-10-2233 for flight information), is about 12 miles southeast of the inner city. One of Europe's most modern airport's, the Scwechat is quick and easy to navigate. There's even a supermarket here, in addition to several banks, restaurants, and duty-free shops. In the arrival hall, don't miss the official Vienna Tourist Information Office, which is open daily from 9am to 10pm, October through May; 9am to 11pm, June through September.

GETTING DOWNTOWN   When you come out of Customs, signs for taxis and buses are straight ahead. A one-way taxi ride from the airport into the inner city is likely to cost 410 AS ($38.95), and maybe more if traffic is bad. Therefore, it's better to take the bus.

There is regular bus service between the airport and the **City Air Terminal** which is adjacent to the Vienna Hilton and directly across from the **Wien Mitte/**

Landstrasse rail station, where you can easily connect with subway and tram lines. Buses run every 20 minutes from 6:30am to 11:30pm, and then every hour from midnight until 5:00am. The trip takes about 25 minutes and costs AS70 ($6.65) per person. Tickets are sold on the bus and must be purchased with Austrian money. There's also bus service between the airport and two railroad stations, the Westbahnhof and the Südbahnhof, leaving every 30 minutes to an hour. Fares are also 70 AS ($6.65).

There's also local train service, *Schnellbahn,* between the airport and the Wien Nord and Wien Mitte rail stations. Trains run hourly between 5:00am and 9:30pm and leave from the basement of the airport. Trip time varies from 40 to 45 minutes, and the fare is 34 AS ($3.25).

BY TRAIN

If you plan to travel heavily on the European and/or British railroads en route to Vienna, you'd do well to secure the latest copy of the *Thomas Cook European Timetable of Railroads.* It's available exclusively in North America from **Forsyth Travel Library,** P.O. Box 2975, Shawnee Mission, KS 66201 (☎ **800/FORSYTH**), at a cost of $27.95 plus $4.50 postage (priority airmail) in the United States and $2 (U.S.) for shipments to Canada.

Vienna has rail links to all the major cities of Europe. From Paris, the *Orient Express* leaves the Gare de l'Est at 7:43pm, arriving in Vienna at 9:25am. From Munich, a train leaves daily at 7:40am, arriving in Vienna at 4:08pm. and then again at 11:30pm (sleepers only), arriving in Vienna at 8:45am. From Zurich you can take a 9:33 p.m. train that arrives in Vienna at 6:30pm.

Rail travel within Austria itself is superb, with fast, clean trains taking you just about anywhere in the country and bypassing some incredibly scenic regions.

Train passengers using the **Chunnel** under the English Channel can go from London to Paris in just 3 hours and from London to Brussels in 3¼ hours. Inaugurated in 1994, the train, *Le Shuttle,* transports passengers along the 31-mile journey in just 35 minutes. The train accommodates passenger cars, charter buses, taxis, and motorcycles through a tunnel from Folkestone, England, to Calais, France. Service is year-round, 24 hours a day.

EURAIL

Austria is part of the Eurail system, and a **Eurailpass** is good for unlimited trips on all routes of the Austrian Federal Railways and on many Danube boats. The Eurailpass permits unlimited first-class rail travel in any country in western Europe (except the British Isles) and also includes Hungary in eastern Europe.

Here's how it works: The pass is sold only in North America. A 15-day pass costs approximately $522; a 21-day pass $678; a one-month pass $838; a two-month pass $1,148; and a three-month pass $1,468. Children under 4 travel free providing they don't occupy a seat (otherwise, they're charged half fare); children under 12 pay half fare. If you're under 26, you can obtain unlimited second-class travel wherever Eurailpass is honored, on a **Eurail Youthpass,** which costs $598 for one month or $798 for two months.

You can buy a Eurailpass at your travel agent or at a railway agent in major cities. You can also buy the pass at the North American offices of CIT Travel Service, the French National Railroads, the German Federal Railroads, and the Swiss Federal Railways.

The **Eurail Saverpass** offers discounted 15-day travel for a group of three people who travel constantly and continuously together between April and September, or if two people travel constantly and continuously together between October and March. The price of a Saverpass, valid all over Europe, good for first class only, is $452 for 15 days.

Eurail Flexipass allows passengers to visit Europe with more flexibility. It's valid in first class and offers the same privileges as the Eurailpass. However, it provides a number of individual travel days which can be used over a much longer period of consecutive days. That makes it possible to stay in one city and yet not lose a single day of travel. There are two passes: 10 days of travel within two months for $616, and 15 days of travel within two months for $812.

With many of the same qualifications and restrictions as the previously described Flexipass is a **Eurail Youth Flexipass.** Sold only to travelers under age 26, it allows 10 days of travel within two months for $438 and 15 days of travel within two months for $588.

VIENNA'S TRAIN STATIONS

Vienna has four principal rail stations, with frequent connections to all Austrian cities and towns and to all major European cities, from Munich to Milan. Train information for all stations can be obtained by calling **0222/17-17.**

The **Westbahnhof** (West Station), on Europaplatz, is for trains arriving from western Austria, France, Germany, Switzerland, and some eastern European countries. It has frequent links to all major Austrian cities such as Salzburg, which is a 3-hour train ride from Vienna. The Westbahnhof connects with local trains, the U3 and U6 underground lines, and several tram and bus routes.

The **Südbahnhof** (South Station), on Südtirolerplatz, has train service to southern and eastern Austria, Italy, Hungary and the new countries of Slovenia, Croatia (formerly part of Yugoslavia.) It is linked with local rail service and tram and bus routes.

Both of these stations house useful travel agencies (Österreichisches Verkehrsbüro) that provide tourist information and help with hotel reservations. In the Westbahnhof it's in the upper hall and at the Südbahnhof, in the lower hall.

Other stations in Vienna include **Franz-Josef Bahnhof,** on Franz-Josef-Platz, used mainly by local trains, although connections are made here to Prague and Berlin. You can take the D-tram line to the city's Ringstrasse from here. **Wien Mitte,** at Landstrasser Hauptstrasse 1, is also a terminus of local trains, plus a depot for trains to the Czech Republic and to Vienna's Schwechat Airport.

BY CAR

If you're already on the continent you might want to drive to Vienna. That is especially true if you're in a neighboring country such as Italy or Germany; however, arrangements should be made in advance with your car-rental company.

Inaugurated in 1994, the Chunnel running under the English Channel cuts driving time between England and France to 35 minutes. Passengers drive their cars aboard the train, *Le Shuttle,* at Folkestone in England, and vehicles are transported to Calais, France.

Vienna can be reached from all directions via major highways called *Autobahnen* or by secondary highways. The main artery from the west is Autoban A-1, coming in from Munich (291 miles), Salzburg (209 miles), and Linz (116 miles). Autobahn-2 arrives from the south from Graz and Klagenfurt (both in Austria). Autobahn-4 comes in from the east, connecting with route E-58 which runs to Bratslavia and Prague. Autobahn A-22 takes traffic from the northwest, and Route E-10 brings you to the cities and towns of southeastern Austria and Hungary.

Unless otherwise marked, the speed limit on autobahns is 130kmph (80 mph); however, when estimating driving times, figure on 50 to 60 mph due to traffic, weather, and road conditions.

As you drive into Vienna, you can get maps, information, and hotel bookings at **Information-Zimmernachweis** at the end of the A-1 (Westautobahn) at Wiental-strasse/Auhof (☎ **0222/979-1271**) or at the end of A-2 (Südautobahn) at Triester-strasse 149 (☎ **022/616-0071**).

BY BUS

Because of the excellence of rail service funneling from all parts of the Continent into Vienna, bus transit is not especially popular. But there is some limited service.

Eurolines, 52 Grosvenor Gardens, Victoria, London SW1 England (☎ **01582/ 404511** or 0171/730-8235), operates two express buses per week between London's Victoria Coach Station and Vienna. The trip takes about 29 hours and makes 45-minute rest stops en route about every four hours during the transit through France, Belgium, and Germany. Buses depart from London at 8:30am every Friday and Sunday, traverse the Channel between Dover and Calais, and are equipped with reclining seats, toilets, and reading lights. The one-way London–Vienna fare is £72 each way. If you opt for a round-trip fare, priced at £115, you won't need to declare your intended date of return until you actually use your ticket (although advance reservations are advisable), and the return half of your ticket will be valid for six months. The return to London departs from Vienna every Sunday and Friday at 7:45pm, arriving at Victoria Coach Station about 29 hours later. You can reserve tickets in advance through the Eurolines office listed above; through most British travel agencies; or through Eurolines' largest sales agent, National Express (☎ **0171/ 730-0202** or 0582/40-45-11).

Eurolines also maintains affiliates in every major city of Western Europe. In Munich, contact Deutsch Touring Office (☎ **069/790-3281**). In Vienna, contact O.B.B./Blaguss Reisen (☎ **0222/501-80-147**), and in Paris, contact Eurolines Gare Routière International de Paris-Gallieni, at its bus station in the Paris suburb of Bagnolet (☎ **01-49-72-51-51**).

VIENNA'S BUS STATION

The **City Bus Terminal** is at the Wien Mitte rail station, at Landstrasser Hauptstrasse 1. This is the arrival depot for Eurolines, all of Austria's postal and federal buses and for private buses from other European cities. The terminal has lockers, currency-exchange kiosks, and a ticket counter open daily from 6:15am to 6pm. For bus information, call **0222/711-01** daily from 6am to 9pm.

Very extensive bus service to surrounding towns and cities far afield in Austria is provided by **Zentrale Bundesbusauskunft,** whose headquarters are at Erdberger Lände 36-48 (☎ **0222/711-01**), and by the **Austrian Federal Railways** at Elizabethstrasse 9 (☎ **0222/33-44-19**).

BY BOAT

To arrive in Vienna with flair befitting the city's historical opulence, take advantage of the many cruise lines that navigate the Danube. One of the most accessible carri-ers is **DDSG, Blue Danube Shipping Company,** Donaureisen, Handelskai 265, in Vienna (☎ **0222/727-500**), which offers mostly one-day trips into Vienna from as far away as Passau, Germany. They also travel from Bratislava (in Slovakia), Budapest, and beyond, depending on the season and their current itinerary. Extended trips can be arranged and cruises are priced to meet every budget. See "Cruising the Danube" in Chapter 6.

PACKAGE TOURS

Although a sampling of some well-recommended tour operators follows, you should consult a good travel agent for the latest offerings and advice.

One tour operator with strong links to the touristic infrastructure of Vienna is the **Kemwel Corporation** (☎ **800/666-7269**), North American agents for Swisspak (formerly known as Austrian Holidays), and loosely affiliated with both Austrian Airlines and Swissair. The company's most popular tours include fully-escorted overviews (five days, four nights) of some of central Europe's most legendary cities. Among them are "Imperial Capitals," which incorporates visits to Vienna, Prague, and Budapest. Air transport on Austrian Airlines can be arranged simultaneously when you book the tour, usually at favorable rates.

Cental Holidays (☎ **800/935-5000**) is also endorsed by Austrian Airlines and offers packages and touring options in Vienna and other central European destinations. For passengers who want maximum travel independence, the company's "Vienna Interlude," includes air transport from North America and hotel lodgings for three nights in Vienna. With round-trip airfare and accommodations for three nights the price ranges from $960 to $1,361 per person. There's also a 10-day jaunt through Vienna, Prague, and Budapest, and an 8-day package to Vienna and Budapest or Vienna and Prague.

A far-flung and reliable touring experience is offered by **British Airways** (☎ **800/262-2422**). Trips usually combine the scenery and architecture of Vienna with similar attractions across the border in Germany and Switzerland. BA can arrange a stopover in London en route for $50, and allow extra time in Vienna before or after the beginning of any tour for no additional charge.

Other attractive options are provided by one of North America's tour-industry giants, **Delta Dream Vacations** (☎ **800/872-7786**), **American Express Travel** (☎ **800/937-2639**), and an unusual, upscale (and very expensive) tour operator, **Abercrombie and Kent** (☎ **800/323-7308**), long known for its carriage-trade rail excursions through eastern Europe and the Swiss and Austrian Alps.

7 For British Travelers

BEFORE YOU GO

PASSPORTS   See "Entry Requirements," above.

CUSTOMS   See "British Customs," under "Visitor Information & Entry Requirements," above.

INSURANCE   Most big travel agencies offer their own insurance, and will probably try to sell you their package when you book a holiday. Think before you sign. Britain's Consumers' Association recommends that you insist on seeing the policy and reading the fine print before buying travel insurance.

You should also shop around for better deals. You might contact **Columbus Travel Insurance Ltd.** (☎ **0171/375-0011** in London), or, for students, **Campus Travel** (☎ **0171/730-3402** in London). Columbus Travel will sell travel insurance only to people who have been official residents of Britain for at least a year.

GETTING THERE
BY PLANE

London and Vienna are linked together with frequent flights, the majority of which depart from London's Heathrow Airport. Flight time is 2 hours and 20 minutes.

Austrian Airlines (☎ **0171/439-0741** in London) has four daily nonstop flights into Vienna from Heathrow. **British Airways** (☎ **0171/897-4000** in London) surpasses that, offering three daily nonstops from Heathrow and two from Gatwick, with easy connections through London from virtually every other part of Britain.

The lowest fares are offered to travelers who stay a Saturday night abroad and return to London on a predetermined date within one month of their initial departure. To qualify for this type of ticket on either of the above-mentioned airlines, no advance purchase is necessary.

A regular fare from the U.K. to Vienna is extremely high, so call a travel agent about charter flight or special air-travel promotions. If this is not possible, then an APEX ticket might be the way to trim costs. These tickets must be reserved in advance; however, a PEX ticket offers a discount without the usual booking restrictions. You might also ask the airlines about a "Eurobudget ticket," which carries restrictions or length-of-stay requirements.

British newspapers are always full of classified advertisements touting "slashed" fares from London to other destinations. One good source is *Time Out,* a magazine filled with cultural information about London. The *Evening Standard* maintains a daily travel section, and the Sunday editions of virtually any newspaper in the British Isles will run ads.

Although competition among airline consolidators is fierce, one well-recommended company is **Trailfinders** (☎ **0171/937-5400** in London). Buying blocks of tickets from such carriers as British Airways, Austrian Airlines, and KLM, they offer cost-conscious fares from London's Heathrow or Gatwick to Vienna.

In London, many bucket shops around Victoria and Earl's Court that offer low fares. Make sure that the company you deal with is a member of the IATA, ABTA, or ATOL. These umbrella organizations will help you if anything goes wrong.

CEEFAX, a British television information service airs on many home and hotel TVs, and runs details of package holidays and flights to Vienna and beyond. Just switch to your CEEFAX channel and you'll find a menu of listings that includes travel information.

Make sure that you understand the bottom line on any special deal. Ask if all surcharges, including airport taxes and other hidden costs, are included before committing. Upon investigation, some of these "deals" are not as attractive as advertised. Also, find out about any penalties incurred if you're forced to cancel at the last minute.

By Train

Many different rail passes are available in the U.K. for travel to and from Vienna. **Wasteels,** Victoria Station, London SW1V 1JZ (☎ **0171/834-7066**) can help you find the best option for the trip you're planning. Some of the most popular passes, including Inter-Rail and EuroYouth, are offered only to travelers under 26 years of age, entitling them to unlimited second-class travel in 26 European countries.

Eurotrain "Explorer" tickets are another worthwhile option for travelers under 26. They allow passengers to move leisurely from London to Vienna, with unlimited stopovers. All travel must be completed within two months of departure. Such a ticket sells for £195 round-trip.

Persons under 26 (with proof of age) who want to travel from London to Vienna quickly and directly pay £153 round trip for a ticket that allows no stopovers, and retraces an identical route (exclusively through France) both ways. The cost includes ferryboat transport across the Channel. **Campus Travel,** 52 Grosvenor Gardens, London SW1W OAG (☎ **0171/730-3402**), can give you prices and help you book tickets.

TIPS FOR TRAVELERS WITH SPECIAL NEEDS
FOR TRAVELERS WITH DISABILITIES

RADAR (the Royal Association for Disability and Rehabilitation), Unit 12, City Forum, 250 City Rd., London ECIV 8AF (☎ 0171/250-3222), publishes holiday "fact packs"—three in all—which sell for £2 each or £5 for all three. The first provides general information, including planning and booking a holiday, insurance, finances, and useful organizations. The second outlines transport and equipment options for traveling abroad, and the third deals with specialized accommodations.

Another good resource is the **Holiday Care Service,** 2nd Floor Imperial Building, Victoria Road, Horley, Surrey RH6 7PZ (☎ **01293/774-535;** fax 01293/784-647), a national charity that advises on accessible accommodations for the elderly and travelers with disabilities. It also provides a free reservations service offering discount rates. Annual membership costs £25.

The **Airport Transport Users Council,** 5/F Kingsway House, 103 Kingsway, London WC2B 6QX (☎ **0171/242-3882**), publishes a free pamphlet: "Flight Plan—A Passenger's Guide to Planning and Using Air Travel," which is packed with information for travelers with disabilities.

FOR SENIORS

Wasteels, Victoria Station (opposite Platform 2), London SW1V 1JY (☎ **0171/834-7066**), currently provides an over-60s Rail Europe Senior Card. Its price is £5 to any Britisher, with government-issued proof of his or her age. With this card, discounts are sometimes available on certain trains in Britain and western Europe.

FOR STUDENTS

Campus Travel, 52 Grosvenor Gardens, London SW1W 0AG (☎ **0171/730-3402**) opposite Victoria Station, open seven days a week, is Britain's leading specialist in student and youth travel worldwide. It provides comprehensive travel service specializing in low-cost rail, sea, and air travel; holiday breaks; and travel insurance; plus student discount cards.

The **International Student Identity Card (ISIC)** is an internationally recognized proof of student status that will entitle you to savings on flights, sightseeing, food, and accommodations. You can purchase the card at Campus Travel for £5 and it is well worth the cost. Always show your ISIC when booking a trip—you may not get a discount without it.

Youth hostels are the place to stay if you're a student. You'll need an **International Youth Hostels Association** card, which you can purchase from the youth hostel store at 14 Southampton St., London WC23 7HY (☎ **0171/836-1036**), or Campus Travel 52 Grosvenor Gardens, London SW1W 0AG (☎ **0171/823-4739**). Take both your passport and some passport-size photos of yourself, plus £9.30 for your membership.

The Youth Hostel Association puts together *The Hostelling International Budget Guide,* listing every youth hostel in 31 European countries. It costs £6.99 when purchased at the Southampton Street store in London. Add 61p postage if it's being delivered within the United Kingdom.

If you're traveling in summer, many youth hostels will be full. To avoid disappointment, it's best to book ahead. In London, you can make advance reservations at the membership department at 14 Southampton St. (see above).

3 Getting to Know Vienna

This chapter will help you get your bearings in Vienna. It will introduce you to Vienna's neighborhoods, explain how the city is laid out, and tell you how to get around. There's also a convenient list of "Fast Facts," covering everything from embassies to electrical outlets.

1 Orientation

VISITOR INFORMATION

Once you've arrived safely in Vienna, go to the official **Vienna Tourist Office** at Kärntnerstrasse 38 (☎ **0222/513-88-92,** fax 0222/216-84-92). Located in the heart of the inner city (directly behind the Opera, on the corner of Philharmoniker Strasse) it's open daily from 9am to 7pm and room reservations can be made. Be sure to pick up a free copy of the **Wien Monatsprogramm,** which lists what's going on in Vienna's concert halls, theaters, and opera houses. Also worthwhile here is "Vienna A to Z," a general, pocket-size guide with descriptions and locations for a slew of attractions. This booklet is also free, but don't rely on its cluttered map.

For information on Vienna and Austria, including easy excursions from the city, visit the **Austrian National Tourist Office** (☎ **0222/58-86-60**) at Margaretenstrasse 1, A-1040.

CITY LAYOUT

From its origins as a Roman village on the Danubian plain, Vienna has evolved over the years into one of the largest metropolises of central Europe, with a surface area covering 160 square miles. To facilitate its administration, it has been divided into 23 districts (*bezirke*), which are identified with Roman numerals. Each district carries its own character or reputation; for example, the 9th District is known as Vienna's academic quarter, while the 10th, 11th, and 12th Districts are home to blue-collar workers and are the most densely populated.

The 1st District, known as the **Innere Stadt (Inner City),** is where most foreign visitors first flock. This compact area is considered historic Vienna and boasts the city's most astonishing array of monuments, churches, palaces, and museums, in addition to its finest hotels and restaurants. Its size and shape roughly correspond to the original borders (then walls) of the medieval city; however, other than **St. Stephan's Cathedral,** very few buildings from that era remain.

The Inner City is surrounded by **Ringstrasse,** a circular boulevard about $2^1/_2$ miles long. Constructed between 1859 and 1888, it's one of the most ambitious examples of urban planning and restoration in central European history. Built over the foundations of Vienna's medieval fortifications, the Ringstrasse opened new urban vistas for the dozens of monumental 19th-century buildings that line its edges today. The name of this boulevard changes as it moves around the Inner City, which can get confusing. Names that correspond with the boulevard carry the suffix *Ring:* Opernring, Schottenring, Burgring, Dr.-Karl-Lueger-Ring, Stubenring, Parkring, Schubertring, and Kärntner Ring.

Ironically, the river for which Vienna is so famous, the Danube, doesn't really pass through city center, which is often disappointing for visitors. Between 1868 and 1877 the river was channeled into its present muddy banks east of town, and was replaced with a small-scale substitute, the **Donaukanal (Danube Canal),** which was dug for shipping foodstuffs and other supplies to the Viennese. The canal sits against the eastern edge of the Ring, and is traversed by five bridges in the 1st district alone.

Surrounding Ringstrasse and the Inner City, in a more or less clockwise direction, are the inner suburban districts (2nd–9th), which contain many hotel and restaurants as well as the villas and palaces of Vienna's 18th-century aristocrats, modern apartment complexes, and the homes of 19th century middle-class entrepreneurs. There are plenty of quality hotels and restaurants in these districts due to their proximity to the center of town. We'll profile them later in this chapter under "Neighborhoods in Brief."

The outer districts (10th–23rd) form another concentric ring of suburbs, hosting a variety of neighborhoods from industrial parks to rural villages. **Schönbrunn,** the Habsburg's vast summer palace, is located in these outlying areas in the 13th District, **Hietzing.** Also noteworthy is the 19th District, **Döbling,** with its famous Heuriger villages like Grinzing and Sievering, and the 22nd District, **Donaustadt,** which is home to the verdant Donau Park and the adjoining UNO-City, an impressive, modern complex of United Nations agencies.

FINDING AN ADDRESS

Street addresses are followed by a four-digit zip code, or sometimes a Roman numeral, that identifies the district in which the address is located. Often, the code is preceded by the letter "A." The district number is coded in the two middle digits, so if an address is in the 1st district ("01"), the zip code would read A-1010; in the 7th District, A-1070, and in the 13th District, A-1130. The layouts of many neighborhoods—especially those around St. Stephan's—are labyrinths of narrow side streets and are often hard to navigate. Fortunately, the most confusing of the Inner City's streets tend to be the shortest, a fact that limits the extent of numbers within its boundaries. If you're doubtful about finding a street address, ask a well-meaning passerby to point you in the right direction or make a quick call before heading out to get the name of the nearest *ecke* (cross street or corner).

A rule of thumb used by hotel concierges and taxi drivers involves the following broad-based guidelines: Odd street numbers are on one side of the street, and even numbers on the other. The lowest numbers are usually closest to the city's geographic and spiritual center, Stephansplatz, and get higher as the street extends outward. Naturally, this system won't work on streets running parallel to the cathedral, so you'll have to simply test your luck.

What about the broad expanses of Vienna's Ring? Traffic always moves clockwise on the Ring, and any backtracking against the direction of the traffic must be done via side streets that radiate from the general traffic flow. Numeration on the ring

Vienna at a Glance

Obere Augarten Str.

Tabor Str.

Lassalle Str.

Leopoldstadt

Untere Augarten Str.

Leopolds G.

Heine Str.

Obere Donau Str.

Blumauer Gasse

Wien Nord

Austellungs Str.

Holland Str.

Lilienbrum G.

Zirkus Gasse

Tabor Str.

Prater Str.

Prater

...er Str.

Franzensbrucken

Haupt Allee

Salzgries

Franz Josefs Kai

Untere Donau Strasse

Donau Kanal

Innere Stadt

Rotenturm Str.

Dominikaner Bastei

Stuber Ring

Lowen G.

Rustenschacher Allee

...bon G.

Wollzeile

Marxer G.

Stephans Dom

...ner G.

Marxer G.

Park Ring

Schubert Ring

Seidl G.

Schüttelstr.

Kärntner Str.

Stadtpark

Beatrix G.

Kundmann G.

Erdberger Lände

Staatsoper

Johannes G.

Am Heumarkt

Linke Bahn G.

Rochus G.

Erdberg Str.

Kärntner Ring

Lothringer Str.

Rechte Bahn G.

Ungar Gasse

Karlsplatz

Salesianer Gasse

Neuling Gasse

Landstrasse

Gusshaus Str.

Rennweg

Prinz Eugen Strasse

Upper Belvedere

Landstrasser Hauptstr.

Favoriten Str.

Belvedere G.

Fasan Gasse

Argentinier Str.

Lower Belvedere

Wiedner Gürtel

Landstrasser Gürtel

Rennweg

...er Gasse

Südbahnhof

Laxenburger Strasse

Favoriten Strasse

Sonnwendg.

Arsenalstr.

N

always goes from high numbers to lower numbers, as determined by the direction of the prevailing traffic: Odd street numbers appear on a driver's left, and even numbers on the right.

STREET MAPS   You'll need a very good and detailed map to explore Vienna, as it has some 1,500 miles of streets (many of them narrow). Since so many places, including restaurants and hotels, lie on these alleyways, routine overview maps that are given away at hotels or the tourist office won't do. You'll need the best city map in Vienna, which is published by **Falk** and sold at all major newsstands, bookstores, and often at upscale hotel newsstands. The vital index at the back clearly labels those heretofore impossible-to-find streets.

NEIGHBORHOODS IN BRIEF

Since visitors spend most of their time in the city center, many of Vienna's hotels and restaurants are conveniently located within or just outside the 1st District. In this section we'll profile the Inner City, or *Innere Stadt*, and the districts that immediately surround it.

Innere Stadt (1st District)   As we mentioned earlier, this compact area, bounded on all sides by the legendary Ring, is at the center of Viennese life. The Inner City has dozens of streets devoted exclusively to pedestrian traffic including **Kärntnerstrasse,** which bypasses the Vienna State Opera House, and the nearby **Graben,** which backs up to Stephansplatz, home to the famous cathedral. Competing with both the cathedral and the Opera House as the district's most famous building is the **Hofburg,** the famous Habsburg palace that's now a showcase of tourist attractions including the National Library, the Spanish Riding School, and six museums. Other significant landmarks include the *Rathaus* (City Hall), *Parlament* (Parliament), the *Universität* (University of Vienna), the *Naturhistorisches* (Natural History) and the *Kunsthistorisches* (Art History) museums, and Stadtpark.

Leopoldstadt (2nd District)   Once inhabited by Balkan traders, this area doesn't physically border the Ringstasse, but lies on the eastern side of the Danube Canal, just a short subway ride (U1) from the Inner City. Here you'll find the massive **Prater** park, which boasts an amusement park, miles of tree-lined walking paths, and numerous sports facilities, including a large sports stadium. Vienna's renowned trade fair exhibition site is also in this district, which has seen a spree of development along the canal in recent years.

Landstrasse (3rd District)   The bucolic **Stadtpark** spreads into this district, where you'll also discover more of Vienna's imperial charm. Streets are dotted with churches, monuments, and palaces, such as the grand **Schwarzenburg Palace** and the looming **Konzerthaus** (concert house). However, the top attraction remains Prince Eugene Savoy's **Belvedere Palace,** an exquisite example of baroque architecture. Several embassies make their home in a small section of Landstrasse that's known as Vienna's diplomatic quarter, and the **Wien Mitte rail station** and the **City Air Terminal** are also located here.

Wieden (4th District)   This small neighborhood extends south from Opernring and Kärtnering, and it's considered just as fashionable as the First District. Most activity centers around **Karlsplatz,** a historical city square that features its domed namesake, Karlskirche. Also seated around this hub are Vienna's **Technical University** and the **Historical Museum of the City of Vienna.** Kärnerstrasse, the main boulevard of the city center turns into **Wiedner-Hauptstrasse** as it enters this district, and the **Südbahnof,** one of the two main train stations, lies at its southern tip.

Impressions

The streets of Vienna are surfaced with culture as the streets of other cities with asphalt.

—Karl Kraus (1874-1936)

Margareten (5th District)   Squeezed between the 4th and 5th districts, this area does not border the Ring, and thus lies a bit farther from the Inner City. You'll start to see more residential neighborhoods, representing the continual growth of Vienna's middle class. The historic homes of composers Franz Schubert and Christoph Gluck still stand here amongst modern apartment complexes and industrial centers.

Mariahilf (6th District)   One of Vienna's busiest shopping streets, **Maria-hilferstrasse,** runs through this bustling neighborhood. The sprawling and lively **Naschmarkt** (Produce Market), selling fresh fruits, vegetables, breads, cheeses, and more, is an ideal scene for people watching. On Saturdays the adjacent *Flohmarkt* (Flea Market) adds to the lively, but sometimes seedy atmosphere as vendors sell antiques and other junk. The surrounding streets are packed with *beisls* (small eateries), theaters, cafes, and pubs. As you go farther from the city center, however, you'll find that the landscape becomes more residential.

Neubau (7th District)   Bordering the expansive Museum Quarter of the Inner City, this is an ideal place to stay, as it's easily accessible by public transportation. The picturesque, and once neglected **Spittleburg quarter** lies atop a hill just beyond Vienna's most famous museums. It's a vibrant, cultural community that's popular with both young and old visitors. The old Spittleburg houses have been renovated into boutiques, restaurants, theaters, and art galleries—a perfect backdrop for an afternoon stroll.

Josefstadt (8th District)   This is the smallest of Vienna's 23 districts and is named after Habsburg Emperor Joseph II and was once home to Vienna's civil servants. Like Neubau, this quiet, friendly neighborhood sits behind the city hall and the adjacent grand museums of the Ringstrasse. You'll find everything from shady and secluded parks to charming cafes to elaborate monuments and churches. Vienna's oldest and most intimate theater, **Josefstadt Theater,** was built here in 1788 and is still in operation. The clientele among Josefstadt's shops and restaurants is varied, featuring lawmakers from City Hall as well as students from the University.

Alsergrund (9th District)   This area is often referred to as the academic quarter, not just because of its position near the University of Vienna but also because of its many hospitals and clinics. This is Freud territory, and you can visit his home, now the Freud Museum, on Berggasse. Here, you'll also stumble upon the **Lichenstein Palace,** one of Vienna's biggest and brightest, which today houses the federal **Museum of Modern Art.** At the northern end of Alsergrund is the **Franz-Josef Bahnhof,** an excellent depot for excursions to Lower Austria.

2 Getting Around

BY PUBLIC TRANSPORTATION

Whether you want to visit the Inner City's historic buildings or the outlying Vienna Woods, Vienna Transport (*Wiener Verkehrs-betriebe*) can take you there. This vast transit network is safe, clean and easy to use. If you plan on taking full advantage of it, pay the 15 AS ($1.40) for a map that outlines the **U-Bahn** (subway), buses,

Vienna's Underground

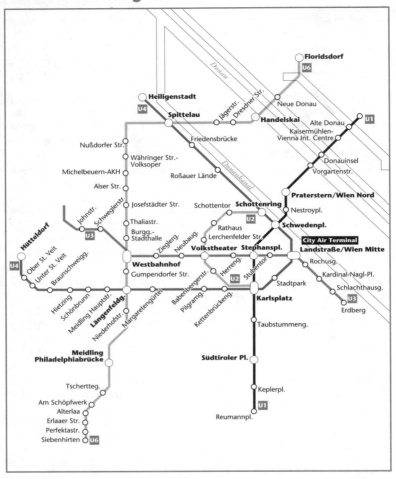

streetcars, and local trains Schnellbahn or S-train. It's sold at the **Vienna Public Transport Information Center** (*Informationdienst der Wiener Verkehrsbetriebe*), which has three locations at Opernpassage, the underground passageway at Karlsplatz (☎ **0222/587-31-86**); on Stephansplatz (☎ **0222/512-42-27**); and on Praterstern (☎ **0222/24-93-02**).

Vienna has a uniform fare, allowing the same tickets on all modes of public transport. It's smart to buy your tickets in advance at a *Tabak-Trafiks* (tobacco/newsstand) or at the public transport centers (see above).

Most buses and streetcars do not have conductors, so you must have the correct change, 21 AS ($2), when you buy your ticket on board at a machine. A ticket from the machine will be stamped with the date and time of purchase. No matter what vehicle you decide to ride in Vienna, remember that once a ticket is stamped (validated) by either a machine or rail attendant, it's good for one trip in one direction, including transfers.

DISCOUNT TICKETS

The **Vienna Card** is the best ticket to use when traveling within the city limits. At 180 AS ($17.10), it's extremely flexible and functional for tourists because it allows three days of unlimited travel, plus various discounts at city museums, restaurants and shops. You can purchase a Vienna Card at tourist information offices, public transport centers, and some hotels or order one over the phone with a credit card (☎ **0222/798-44-00-28**).

You can also buy money-saving tickets for one day, 50 AS ($4.75), and three days, 13 AS ($12.40). The green eight-day ticket, 265 AS ($25.20) is a great deal for visitors. It has eight strips, each of which, when stamped, is good for one day of unlimited travel. More than one person can use this ticket at the same time, which is convenient if you're with a group. A single ticket (one ride) costs 17 AS ($1.60) and can be bought in blocks of five for 85 AS ($8.10). Children under 6 ride for free.

These tickets are also available at *Tabak-Trafiks,* vending machines in underground stations, the airport's arrival hall (next to baggage claim), the DDSG landing pier (*Reichsbrücke*), and at the travel agencies (*Österreichisches Verkehrsbüro*) of the two main train stations.

BY U-BAHN (SUBWAY)

While most of the top attractions in the Inner City can be seen by foot, tram or bus, the U-Bahn is a fast way to get across town or reach the suburbs. It consists of five lines labeled as **U1, U2, U3, U4,** and **U6** (there is no U5). Karlsplatz, in the heart of the Inner City, is the most important underground station for visitors as the U4, U2 and U1 all converge here. The U2 traces part of the Ring, the U4 goes to Schönnbrun, and the U1 stops in Stephansplatz. The U3 also stops in Stephansplatz and connects with the Westbanhof. The underground runs daily from 6am to midnight.

BY TRAM (STREETCAR)

Riding the red and white trams (*Strassenbahn*) is not only a practical way to get around, it's a great way to see the city too. Tram stops are well-marked and lines are labeled as both numbers and letters. Lines 1 and 2 will bring you to all the major sights on the Ringstrasse. Line D skirts the outer Ring and goes to the Südbahnhof, while line 18 goes between the Westbanhof and the Südbahnhof.

BY BUS

Buses traverse Vienna in all directions and they operate Monday through Saturday from 6am to 10pm and on Sunday from 6am to 8pm. Buses 1A, 2A, and 3A will get you around the Inner City. Convenient night buses are available on weekends and holidays starting at 12:15 am. They go from Schwedensplatz, to the outer suburbs (including Grinzing). Normal tickets are not valid on these late "N" buses. Instead you pay a special fare of 25 AS ($2.38) on board.

BY FOOT

The best way to see Vienna is on foot. You can walk from one end of the Altstadt (Old Town) to the other in 10 to 15 minutes, depending on your pace. We suggest you take more time to stroll through the city's delightful squares and intricate cobblestone streets.

BY TAXI

Taxis are easy to find within the city center, but be warned that fares can quickly add up. Taxi stands are marked by signs, or you can call 31-300, 60-160, 81-400,

91-091, or 40-100. The basic fare is 26 AS ($2.45), plus 12 AS ($1.15) per kilometer. There are extra charges of 16 AS ($1.50) for luggage in the trunk. For night rides after 11pm, and for trips on Sundays and holidays, the basic fee is 27 AS ($2.55), plus 14 AS ($1.35) per kilometer. There are additional charges for more than one passenger and ordering by phone. The fare for trips outside the Vienna area (for instance, to the airport) should be agreed upon with the driver in advance, and a 10% tip is the norm.

BY HORSE-DRAWN CARRIAGE

Vienna's *fiakers,* or horse-drawn carriages, have transported people around the Inner City for some 300 years. You can clip-clop along for about 20 minutes at a cost of 680 AS ($64.60), but prices and the length of the ride must be negotiated in advance. In the 1st District you'll find a *fiaker* for hire at the following sites: On the north side of St. Stephan's, on Heldenplatz near the Hofburg, and in front of the Albertina on Augustinerstrasse.

BY BICYCLE

Some European cities, such as Madrid, are not bicycle-friendly due to pollution, but Vienna has more than 155 miles of marked bicycle paths within the city limits. In the summer months of July and August, many Viennese leave their cars in the garage and ride bikes. You can take bicycles on specially marked U-Bahn cars for free, but only Monday through Friday from 9am to 3pm and from 6:30pm to midnight. On weekends during July and August bicycles are also carried free from 9am until midnight.

Rental shops abound at the Prater (see Chapter 7) and along the banks of the Danube Canal, which is the favorite bicycling venue for most Viennese. One of the best-known and advertised shops is **Radverleih Salztorbrücke,** 1 Donaukanal-promenade near the Salztorbrüke, north of Stephansplatz (☎ **0222/535-34-22** for information). It's open from April through October from 10am to 7pm. The Vienna Tourist Board can also supply a list of rental shops and more information about bike paths. Bike rentals begin at about 200 AS ($19) per day.

BY CAR

Use a car only for excursions outside Vienna's city limits. Parking is a problem; the city is a maze of congested one-way streets, and the public transportation is too good to endure the hassle of driving around Vienna. If you do venture out by car, information on road conditions is available in English seven days a week from 6am to 8pm from the **Österreichischer Automobil-, Motorrad- und Touringclub (ÖAMTC),** Schubertring 3, A-1010 Vienna (☎ **0222/71-19-97**). This auto club also has a 24-hour emergency road service. Call **120** anywhere in Austria.

RENTALS   It's always best to reserve rental cars in advance, but it is possible to rent a car once you've arrived in Vienna. You'll need a passport and a driver's license that's at least one year old. Avoid renting a car at the airport as there is an extra 6% tax, in addition to the 21% value-added tax (VAT) on all rentals. For a one-to-two day rental of a small car (Ford Fiesta or Opal) expect to pay around 121 AS ($114.95) per day, which includes unlimited mileage, the whopping government tax, and the price of insurance. You'll save on the per-day cost if you rent your car for a minimum of one week.

Major car rental companies include: **Avis,** Opernring 1 (☎ **800/654-3001** in Vienna, **0222/587-62-41** in the U.S.); **Budget-Rent-a-Car,** City/Hilton Air

Terminal (☎ **800/472-3325** in the U.S., **0222/714-72-38** in Vienna) and **Hertz,** Kärntner Ring 17 (☎ **800/654-3001** in the U.S., **0222/512-86-77** in Vienna).

PARKING As we mentioned earlier, parking in Vienna, especially in the first district, is basically nonexistent. Restricted 90-minute parking zones, also known as "blue zones," can be used weekdays between 8am and 6pm, but require a parking voucher, which are sold at Vienna Public Transport offices, banks, tobacco/news shops and gas stations. Vouchers must be displayed in the windshield and must include the date and time of arrival. Be warned that towing is not an uncommon sight here.

 Parking garages are scattered throughout the city and most charge 30 to 40 AS ($2.85–$3.80) per hour. Ask at your hotel desk for nearby locations. Some convenient 24-hour garages in the first district are: Parkgarage Am Hof (☎ 0222/533-5571), Parkgarage Freyung/Herrengasse (☎ 0222/535-04-50), and Tiefgarage Kärtner Strasse (☎ 0222/587-17-97).

DRIVING Traffic regulations are similar to those in other European cities where you *drive on the right.* The speed limit is 50 kilometers per hour (31 mph) in built-up areas within the city limits unless otherwise specified. Out of town, in areas like the Wienerwald, the limit is 130 kmph (80 mph) on motorways, 100 kmph (62 mph) on all other roads.

FAST FACTS: Vienna

American Express The most convenient office in Vienna is at Kärntnerstrasse 21-23 (☎ **0222/515-40-0**), open Monday through Friday from 9am to 5:30pm and on Saturday from 9am to noon.

Area Code The telephone area code for Vienna is 01 when calling from outside the country and 0222 for calls within the Austrian border.

Baby-sitters Most hotels will be able to provide you with the name and number of potential English-speaking baby-sitters if they do not provide a service of their own. Sitters charge roughly 90 AS ($8.55) per hour. If you plan on utilizing their services beyond 11pm, expect to provide transportation home, most likely via a cab.

Bookstores **Gerold & Co.,** Graben 31 (☎ **0222/533-50-14**), is a good bookstore in Vienna for English-language publications. The sales personnel are helpful, and you can often pick up many titles not available elsewhere. Another good bookstore is **Morawa,** Wollzeile 11 (☎ **0222/515-62**), which is huge and rambling, occupying a labyrinth of vaulted rooms a short walk from St. Stephan's Cathedral. This outlet sells both English- and German-language books. Both stores are open Monday through Friday from 9am to 6pm and on Saturday from 9am to 1pm.

Business Hours Most shops are open Monday through Friday from 9am to 6pm and on Saturday from 9am to noon, 12:30pm, or 1pm, depending on the store. On the first Saturday of every month, shops remain open until 4:30 or 5pm, a tradition known as *langer Samstag.*

Car Rentals See "Getting Around," earlier in this chapter.

Climate See "When to Go," in Chapter 2.

Crime See "Safety," below.

Currency Exchange See "Money," in Chapter 2.

Customs See "Information and Entry Requirements," in Chapter 2.

Dentist For dental problems during the night or on Saturday and Sunday, call **0222/512-20-78.**

Doctor A list of physicians can be found in the telephone directory under *Arzte*. If you have a medical emergency during the night, call **141** daily from 7pm to 7am.

Documents Required See "Information and Entry Requirements" in Chapter 2.

Driving Rules See "Getting Around," earlier in this chapter.

Drug Laws Penalties are severe and could lead to either imprisonment or deportation. Selling drugs to minors is dealt with particularly harshly.

Drugstores Drugstores (chemist's shops) are open Monday through Friday from 8am to noon and 2 to 6pm, and on Saturday from 8am to noon. At night and on Sunday you'll find the names of shops whose turn it is to be open at those times listed on a sign outside every shop.

Electricity Vienna operates on 220 volts AC, with the European 50-cycle circuit. That means that U.S.-made appliances will need a transformer (sometimes called a converter). Many Viennese hotels stock adapter plugs but not power transformers. Electric clocks, record players, and tape recorders, however, will not work well even with transformers.

Embassies and Consulates The main building of the Embassy of the **United States** is at Boltzmanngasse 16, A-1090 Vienna (☎ **0222/313-39**). However, the consular section is at Gartenbaupromenade 2-4, A-1010 Vienna (☎ **0222/313-39**). Lost passports, tourist emergencies, and other matters are handled by the consular section. Both the embassy and consulate are open Monday through Friday from 8:30am to noon and 1 to 3:30pm.

The Embassy of **Canada,** Laurenzerberg 2 (☎ **0222/531-38-30-00**), is open Monday through Friday from 8:30am to 12:30pm and 1:30 to 3:30pm; the **United Kingdom,** Jauresgasse 12 (☎ **0222/713-15-75**), open Monday through Friday 9:15am to noon and 2 to 5pm; **Australia,** Mattiellistrasse 2-4 (☎ **0222/5128-580**), open Monday through Friday from 8:45am to 1pm and 2 to 5pm; and **New Zealand,** Springsiedelgasse 28 (☎ **0222/318-85-05**), open Monday through Friday from 8:30am to 5pm.

Emergencies Call **122** to report a fire, **133** for the police, or **144** for an ambulance.

Eyeglasses The most convenient place to handle any optical problems is **Trude Kleeman Optik,** Kärntnerstrasse 37 (☎ **0222/512-8425**), on the main shopping street of the city. It's open Monday through Friday from 9am to 6pm and on Saturday from 9:30am to 12:30pm.

Holidays See "When to Go," in Chapter 2.

Hospitals The major hospital is Allgemeines Krankenhaus, Währinger Gürtel 18-20 (☎ **0222/404-00**).

Hotlines The Rape Crisis Hotline is **0222/93-22-22,** in service on Monday from 10am to 1pm and on Tuesday and Thursday from 6 to 9pm. Threatened or battered women can call an emergency hotline at **0222/545-48-00** around the clock.

Information See "Visitor Information" in Chapter 2.

Language German is the official language of Austria, but since English is taught in the high schools, it's commonly spoken throughout the country, especially in tourist regions. Certain Austrian minorities speak Slavic languages, and Hungarian is commonly spoken in Burgenland.

Another way of communicating if you don't speak German is through **KWIKpoint,** a visual translator, allowing you to point at pictures to communicate. This four-panel brochure contains some 500 color illustrations of everyday items such as a pay phone or gasoline. You just point to the corresponding picture. Single copies cost $6 and can be ordered from Gaia Communications Inc., Dept. 102, P.O. Box 239, Alexandria, VA 22313-0239 (☎ **703/548-8794**).

Legal Aid   The consulate of your country is the place to turn, although officers cannot interfere in the Viennese legal process. They can, however, inform you of your rights and provide a list of attorneys. You'll have to pay for the attorney out of your pocket, however, as there is no free legal assistance. If you're arrested for a drug offense, about all the consulate will do is notify a lawyer about your case and perhaps inform your family.

Liquor Laws   Wine with meals has been a normal part of family life for hundreds of years in Vienna. Children are exposed to wine at an early age, and alcohol consumption is not anything out of the ordinary. Eighteen is the legal drinking age for buying or ordering alcohol. Alcohol is sold day and night throughout the year, as there are few restrictions on its sale.

Lost Property   A lost-property office, **Zentrales Fundamt** is maintained at Wasagasse 22 (☎ **0222/313-44-0**), open Monday through Friday from 8am to noon. Items found on trains are taken to the central lost-property office at the Westbahnhof. Items left on buses and streetcars are passed on to the Wasagasse office after three days. If you miss something as soon as you get off the bus, you can pick it up (providing it is returned) at Wiener Stadtwerke (Verkehrsbetriebe; ☎ **0222/501-30-0**) without waiting three days.

Luggage Storage/Lockers   All four main train stations of Vienna have lockers available on a 24-hour basis, costing 30-40 AS ($2.85-$3.80) for 24 hours depending on locker size. It's also possible to store luggage at these terminals daily from 4am to midnight (1:15am at the Westbahnhof) at a cost of 30 AS ($2.85).

Mail   Post offices (*Das Postamt*) in Vienna located in the heart of every district. If you're unsure of your address in Vienna, correspondence can be addressed in care of a local post office by labeling it either POST RESTANTE or POSTLAGERND. If you choose to do this, it's important to clearly designate the addressee, the name of the town, and its postal code. To claim any correspondence, the addressee must present his or her passport.

As an alternative to having your mail sent *post restante* to post offices, you might opt for the mail services offered in Vienna by American Express (see above). There's no charge for this service to anyone holding an American Express card or American Express traveler's checks.

The postal system in Vienna is, for the most part, efficient and speedy. You can buy stamps at any of the country's post offices, or in any of the country's hundreds of news and tobacco kiosks, designated locally as *Tabac/Trafiks*. Mailboxes are painted yellow, and in the case of the older ones, are emblazoned with the double-headed eagle of the Austrian Republic. Newer ones usually have the golden trumpet of the Austrian Postal Service. A blue stripe on a mailbox indicates that mail will be picked up there on a Saturday.

Letters weighing up to 20 grams (usually two sheets of paper inside an envelope) mailed to destinations in Europe cost 7 AS (65¢). Letters sent airmail to destinations in North America cost 11.50 AS ($1.10) for up to 10 ounces, and 16 AS ($1.40) for 10 to 20 ounces. Postcards sent airmail to North America cost 8.50 AS (80¢). Postcards and letters sent airmail to North America will usually take five to seven days to arrive.

Maps   See "Getting Around," earlier in this chapter.

Newspapers/Magazines   Most newsstands at major hotels or news kiosks along the streets sell copies of the *International Herald Tribune* and *USA Today*, and also carry copies of the European editions of *Time* and *Newsweek*.

Passports   See "Information and Entry Requirements," in Chapter 2.

Photographic Needs   The most central place for film and camera supplies is Foto Niedermayer, Graben 11, near Stephansplatz (☎ **0222/512-33-61**). Selling a wide range of equipment and film-processing services, it's open Monday through Friday from 9am to 6pm and on Saturday from 9am to 12:30pm.

Police   The emergency number is **133.**

Post Office   Addresses for these can be found in the telephone directory under "Post." Post offices are generally open for mail services Monday through Friday from 8am to noon and 2 to 6pm. The central post office, the Hauptpostamt, at Barbaragasse 2 (☎ **0222/515-09-0**), and most general post offices are open at night and 24 hours a day, seven days a week. Postage stamps are available at all post offices and at tobacco shops, and there are stamp-vending machines outside most post offices.

Radio/TV   The Austrian Radio Network (ÖRF) has English-language news broadcasts at 8:05am daily. "Blue Danube Radio" broadcasts daily in English from 7 to 9am, noon to 2pm, and 6 to 7:30pm on 103.8 FM in the Vienna area, and the Voice of America broadcasts have news, music, and feature programs at 1197 AM (middle wave, here) from 7am to 1pm and in the midafternoon and early evening. At noon every Sunday the TV network, FSI, broadcasts the English-language "Hello, Austria," covering sightseeing suggestions and giving tips about the country. Many first-class and deluxe hotels subscribe to CNN and also certain British channels. Films and programs from the United States and England are often shown in their original language with German subtitles.

Restrooms   Vienna has a number of public toilets, labeled WC, scattered at convenient locations throughout the city. All major sightseeing attractions also have public facilities.

Safety   In recent years, Vienna has been plagued by purse-snatchers. In the area around St. Stephan's Cathedral, signs (in German only) warn about pickpockets and purse-snatchers. Small foreign children often approach sympathetic adults and ask for money. As the adult goes for his wallet or her purse, full-grown thieves rush in and grab the money, fleeing with it. Unaccompanied women are the most common victims. If you're carrying a purse, do not open it in public.

Shoe Repairs   Call on Mister Minit, a branch of which is generally located in all the major department stores of Vienna, including Gerngross at Mariahilfer-strasse 48 (☎ **0222/52-45-654**).

Taxes   A 20% to 34% value-added tax (VAT) is included in the price of items sold in Vienna. Tourists must pay this VAT at the time of purchase, but can obtain a tax refund on purchases totaling 1,000 AS ($95) or more per store if the merchandise is taken out of the country unused. To get the refund, you must fill out Form U-34, which is available at most stores (a sign will say tax-free shopping). Get one for ÖAMTC quick refund if you plan to get your money at the border. Check whether the store gives refunds itself or uses a service. Sales personnel will help you fill out the form and will affix the store identification stamp. You will show the VAT *(MWSt)* as a separate item or will say that the tax is part of the total price. Keep your U-34 forms handy when you leave the country and have them validated by the Viennese Customs officer at your point of departure.

After returning home, mail the validated U-34 form or forms to the store where you bought the merchandise, keeping a copy of each form. The store will send you a check, bank draft, or international money order covering the amount of your VAT refund. Information and help is available at the Austrian Automobile and Touring Club (ÖAMTC), which has instituted methods of speeding up the refund process. Before you go call the Austrian National Tourist Office for the ÖAMTC brochure "Tax-free Shopping in Austria."

Taxis   See "Getting Around," earlier in this chapter.

Telegrams/Telex/Fax   The central telegraph office is at Börseplatz 1.

Telephone   Remember, never dial abroad from your hotel room unless you're forced to in an emergency. Place phone calls at the post office or some other location. Viennese hotels routinely add 40% surcharges, and some will add as much as 200% to your call! For help dialing, contact your hotel's operator; or dial **09** for placement of long-distance calls within Austria or for information about using a telephone company credit card; dial **16** for directory assistance; and dial **08** for help in dialing international long distance. Coin-operated phones appear all over Vienna. To make a local call if you don't have a phone card (see below), insert 2 AS (20¢) which gives you about three minutes, plus 1 AS (10¢) for each additional 90 seconds. Insert your coins, pick up the receiver, and dial the number you want; when your party answers, push the button that's indicated and your connection will be made.

Many Viennese avoid carrying lots of 1-schilling coins by buying a *Wertkarte* at tobacco/news kiosks or at post offices. Each card is electronically coded to provide 50 AS ($4.75), 100 AS ($9.50), or 200 AS ($19) worth of phone calls from pay phones. Buyers receive a slight discount, since cards worth 50 AS are priced at only 48 AS ($4.55), whereas cards worth 100 AS are priced at 98 AS ($9.30); the 200-AS card costs 190 AS ($18.05).

AT&T's USA Direct plan enables you to charge calls to your credit card or to call collect. The access number, **0222/90-30-11,** is a local call all over Austria.

The international access code for both the United States and Canada, incidentally, is **001,** followed by the area code and the seven-digit local number.

As for taxes and telex, virtually every hotel in Austria will have one or both of these machines, and will usually send a message for a nominal charge whose cost might be a lot less than that of a long-distance phone call. Your hotel will send faxes for you.

Time   Vienna operates on central European time, which makes it six hours earlier than U.S. eastern standard time. It advances its clocks one hour in summer, however.

Tipping   A service charge of 10% to 15% is included on hotel and restaurant bills, but it's a good policy to leave something extra for waiters and 25 AS ($2.40) per day for your hotel maid.

Railroad station, airport, and hotel porters get 20 AS ($1.90) per piece of luggage, plus a 10 AS (95¢) tip. Your hairdresser should be tipped 10% of the bill, and the shampoo person will be thankful for a 20-AS ($1.90) gratuity. Toilet attendants are usually given 5 AS (50¢), and hatcheck attendants expect 7 to 15 AS (65¢ to $1.45), depending on the place.

Tourist Offices   See "Information and Entry Requirements," in Chapter 2.

Transit Information   Information, all types of tickets, and maps of the transportation system are available at Vienna Transport's main offices on Karlsplatz (☎ **0222/587-31-86**) or at the St. Stephan's Square underground station (☎ **0222/ 582-42-27**) Monday through Friday from 8am to 6pm and on Saturday, Sunday, and holidays from 8:30am to 4pm.

Useful Telephone Numbers   Dial **0222/17-17** for rail information, **0222/ 711-01** for bus schedules, and **0222/211-14-0** for tourist information Monday through Friday from 8am to 4pm.

Visas   See "Information and Entry Requirements," in Chapter 2.

Accommodations 4

Vienna has some of the greatest hotels in Europe, and more than 300 recommendable ones. But finding a room can be a problem, especially in August and September, if you arrive without a reservation. During these peak visiting months you may have to stay on the outskirts of Vienna, in Grinzing or Hietzing, for example, and commute to the Inner City by streetcar, bus, or subway. But, if you're looking to cut costs, staying outside the Inner City is not a bad option. You can expect to pay a fifth to a quarter less for a hotel in the areas outside the Ringstrasse.

High season in Vienna encompasses most of the year: from May until October or early November, and during some weeks in midwinter when the city hosts major trade fairs, conventions, and other cultural events. If you're planning a trip around Christmas and the New Year holidays, room reservations should be made at least one month in advance. Some rate reductions (usually between 15% and 20%) are available during slower midwinter weeks—it always pays to ask.

Breakfast, usually continental style, is almost always included in the price of a room in Vienna, and if you've arrived via car, parking will cost around 350 AS ($33.25) per night in upscale hotels or as little as 100 AS ($9.50) in hotels that price their parking "promotionally." Most hotel staffs, renowned for their stellar service, are multilingual, which means that they speak English.

ACCOMMODATIONS AGENCIES

Any branch of the **Austrian National Tourist Office** (☎ 0222/58-86-60), including the Vienna Tourist Board, will help you book a room. They have branch offices in the arrival halls of the airport, train stations, and major highways that access Vienna (see Chapter 3, "Visitor Information"). They will not, however, reserve a room for you; call or write in advance.

If you prefer to deal directly with an Austrian travel agency, three of the city's largest include **Austropa,** Friedrichsgasse 7, A-1010 (☎ 0222/588-000); **Austrobus,** Dr. Karl Lueger-Ring 8, A-1010 (☎ 0222/534-110); and **Blaguss Reisen,** Wiedner Hauptstrasse 15 A-1040 (☎ 0222/501-8-0). They will not, however, reserve a room for you; call or write in advance.

Visitors wishing to stay outside the city limits should contact **Niederosterreich Information,** Heidenschluss 2, A-1010 (☎ 0222/533-31-14-28).

Vienna Accommodations

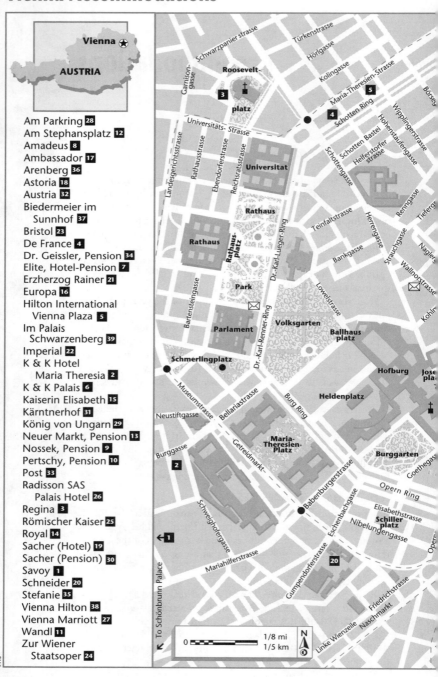

Am Parkring **28**
Am Stephansplatz **12**
Amadeus **8**
Ambassador **17**
Arenberg **36**
Astoria **18**
Austria **32**
Biedermeier im
  Sunnhof **37**
Bristol **23**
De France **4**
Dr. Geissler, Pension **34**
Elite, Hotel-Pension **7**
Erzherzog Rainer **21**
Europa **16**
Hilton International
  Vienna Plaza **5**
Im Palais
  Schwarzenberg **39**
Imperial **22**
K & K Hotel
  Maria Theresia **2**
K & K Palais **6**
Kaiserin Elisabeth **15**
Kärntnerhof **31**
König von Ungarn **29**
Neuer Markt, Pension **13**
Nossek, Pension **9**
Pertschy, Pension **10**
Post **33**
Radisson SAS
  Palais Hotel **26**
Regina **3**
Römischer Kaiser **25**
Royal **14**
Sacher (Hotel) **19**
Sacher (Pension) **30**
Savoy **1**
Schneider **20**
Stefanie **35**
Vienna Hilton **38**
Vienna Marriott **27**
Wandl **11**
Zur Wiener
  Staatsoper **24**

9110

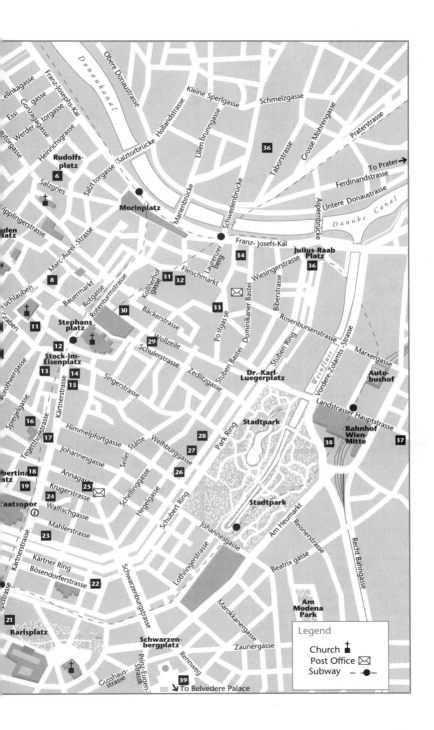

Donaukanal

Obere Donaustrasse

Franz-Josephs-Kai

Kleine Sperlgasse

Schmelzgasse

elinkagasse

Essi gasse

Gonzagagasse

Werder torgasse

torgasse

Heinrichsgasse

Lilien brunngasse

Hollandstrasse

Grosse Mohrengasse

Praterstrasse

36

Taborstrasse

Rudolfs-platz

6

Salzgries

To Prater →

Ferdinandstrasse

Salztorbrücke

Salztorgasse

Untere Donaustrasse

Marc-Aurel Strasse

vipplingerstrasse

den atz

Morinplatz

Marienbrücke

Schwedenbrücke

Aspernbrücke

Danube Canal

Franz- Josefs-Kai

Laurenzer berg

34

Wiesingerstrasse

Jullus-Raab Platz

36

8

Bauermarkt

Rotgasse

Rotenturmstrasse

Köllnerhof gasse

Fleischmarkt

31 32

Biberstrasse

uchlauben

raben

11

30

Bäckerstrasse

33

Postgasse

Rosenbursenstrasse

Stephans platz

12

Stock-Im-Eisenplatz

13

14

15

Wollzeile

29

Schulerstrasse

Zedlitzgasse

Stuben Bastei

Dominikaner Bastei

Stuben Ring

Dr.-Karl-Luegerplatz

Weinfluss

Vordere Zolamts-Strasse

Marxergasse

Auto-bushof

Singerstrasse

orotheetgasse

Kärntnerstrasse

16

Himmelpfortgasse

Tegetthofstrasse

17

Seiler Stätte

Weihburggasse

28

Park Ring

Stadtpark

Landstrasser Hauptstrasse

Bahnhof Wien-Mitte

38

37

Johannesgasse

27

26

ertina atz

18

19

Annagase

24

Krugerstrasse

25

Schellinggasse

Hegelgasse

Schubert Ring

Stadtpark

aatsopor

Walfischgasse

Mahlerstrasse

23

Johannesgasse

Am Heumarkt

Resnerstrasse

Kärtner Ring

Bösendorferstrasse

22

Schwarzenbergstrasse

Lothringerstrasse

Beatrix gasse

Recht Bahngasse

21

Karlsplatz

Schwarzen-bergplatz

Marokkanergasse

Zaunergasse

Am Modena Park

Prinz-Eugen-Strasse

Remweg

39

↓ To Belvedere Palace

Gusshaus-strasse

Legend

Church ⛪

Post Office ✉

Subway – ● –

61

SEASONAL HOTELS

In Vienna, between July and September, student dormitories are transformed into fully-licensed hotels. One popular chain is **Academia Hotels,** Pfeilgasse 3A, A-1080 (☎ **0222/406-16-61;** fax 0222/405-63-97). They offer comfortable rooms at reasonable rates and are among the best bargains in town. Plus, they're all within a 20-minute walk southwest of St. Stephan's Cathedral. Many of these accommodations are booked by groups, but individual travelers are welcomed. Depending on the hotel, doubles are usually 800 to 1,000 AS ($76 to $95) and triples run 930 to 1,290 AS ($88.35 to $122.55).

PRIVATE HOMES & FURNISHED APARTMENTS

For travelers who like to have a home base that is more spacious than an average hotel room, a limited number of private homes and furnished apartments are available to rent in Vienna. These accommodations can be a money-saving option depending on the season and the size of the place. Two agencies that deal in house rentals are **B&B Vienna,** Rielgasse 47b, A-1238 (☎ **0222/885-219**) and **Mitzwohnzentrale,** Laudongasse 7, A-1080 (☎ **0222/402-6061**). For apartments, contact **Vienna City Apartments,** Marc-Aurel Strasse 7, A-1010 (☎ **0222/535-03650**).

HOW WE'VE ORGANIZED THIS CHAPTER

Hotels are listed below, first by location, then by price, according to the following guide: **Very Expensive**—more than 3,200 AS ($304); **Expensive**—1,950 to 3,200 AS ($185.25 to $304); **Moderate**—1,500 to 1,950 AS ($142.50 to $185.25); and **Inexpensive**—1,000 to 1,500 AS ($95 to $142.50). Rates reflect the price of a double room in Vienna.

Note: Unless otherwise indicated, all accommodations listed here have a private bath.

1 Best Bets

- **Best Historic Hotel:** Built in 1869, the **Hotel Imperial** (☎ 0222/50-110-0) is actually the "official guest house of Austria." It has presided over much of the city's history, from the heyday of the Austro-Hugarian empire to defeat in two world wars. All the famous and infamous of the world have checked in here. Wagner, for example, worked on key sections of both *Tannhäuser* and *Lohengrin* here in 1875, and some of the great cultural icons of this century—from Fonteyn to von Karajan—have been guests.
- **Best for Business Travelers:** With state-of-the-art business equipment and an incredibly helpful staff, the **Hotel Bristol** (☎ 0222/515-160) is the preferred choice of the international business travelers who often flock here. Some suites are large enough for business meetings, and room service will quickly deliver hors d'oeuvres and champagne (for a price, of course) when the deal is closed. Many guests like to treat their clients to dinner at the Bristol's elegant restaurant, Korso, which is one of the most refined in town.
- **Best for a Romantic Getaway:** Set in 15 acres of manicured gardens, **Hotel in Palais Schwarzenberg** (☎ 0222/798-45-15) has an elegant, even noble atmosphere. Although perched in the center of a city, you feel like you've escaped to an old country estate. The palace was built three centuries ago by the baroque masters, Lukas Von Hildebrandt and Fisher Von Erlach, and remains a luxurious world of crystal, marble, and gilt.

- **Best Trendy Hotel:** The **Hilton International Vienna Plaza** (☎ 0222/ 31-39-0) is Vienna's "other Hilton," which has attracted the movers and shakers of the world—many from high finance, fashion, or other fields. They're attracted to the hotel's flair as well as its convenient location to the major sights, like the *Staatsoper*.
- **Best Lobby For Pretending You're Rich:** The romance and glamour of the Austro-Hungarian empire still live on at the **Hotel Sacher** (☎ 0222/514-56), which was built in 1876. The lobby and public rooms of this sumptuous hotel are done in red velvet, crystal chandeliers, and antiques, evoking Old Vienna.
- **Best for Families:** Only a four-minute walk from St. Stephan's Cathedral, **Hotel Kärntnerhof** (☎ 0222/512-19-23) is a small, kid-friendly hotel in the center of Vienna. The hotel attracts families because of its superb location, attentive staff, and good prices. Also, bedrooms are roomy enough to accommodate families and come equipped with all the modern amenities.
- **Best Moderately Priced Hotel:** Also in the heart of Old Vienna, less than a block from the cathedral, **Hotel Royal** (☎ 0222/51-568) was completely rebuilt in 1982. Within this price bracket, not many hotels can compete with the Royal in terms of class. In the lobby, you'll find the piano where Wagner composed *Die Meistersinger Von Nürnberg*.
- **Best Budget Hotel:** Between the State Opera and the famous Nasch Market, **Hotel Schneider** (☎ 0222/588-380) is a modern five-story building, traditionally furnished with 19th century antiques. It is comfortable and cozy, which attracts singers, musicians, artists, and actors (not the big stars). This hotel is also popular among families, since many of the rooms have kitchenettes.
- **Best B&B:** Next to Vienna's stock exchange, **Pension Elite** (☎ 0222/533 -25-18-0) is a homey and rather winning little boarding house where most rooms come with private bath. The service at this family-run pension is excellent and the ambience, as the name suggests, is quite refined.
- **Best Service:** The **Hotel de France** (☎ 0222/31-36-80) near the Votivkirche is hardly the best hotel in Vienna, but what makes a stay here particularly delightful is the attentive and highly professional staff. Room service is efficient, messages are received and delivered promptly, and the housekeepers turn down your bed at night.
- **Best Location:** Although it's no Bristol or Imperial, the **Hotel Ambassador** (☎ 0222/514-66) is definitely where you want to be. The hotel lies between the State Opera and St. Stephan's, with the Kärntnerstrasse on the other side. The Ambassador has enjoyed its position here since 1866—playing host to both Mark Twain and Theodore Roosevelt.
- **Best Health Club:** The **Vienna Hilton** (☎ 0222/71-700-0), under different management, sponsors the Pyrron Health Club on its premises. This is, by far, the most professional health club in town, with state-of-the-art equipment and facilities for both men and women. The price for hotel guests is 180 AS ($17.10) and 200 AS ($19) for non-guests.
- **Best Hotel Pool:** Hotels are not known for the breadth of their pools, but of the three hotels in town that have them, the biggest and best lies within the Body and Soul health spa in the windowless cellar of the **Vienna Marriott** (☎ 0222/ 515-18-6699). It's about 36 feet by 24 feet, and ringed with potted plants and tables. There's a pair of saunas, an exercise room, and massage facilities. Residents of the Marriott use the pool for free; nonresidents pay between 150 AS ($14.25) and 300 AS ($28.50), depending on the time of day. It's open daily from 7am to 10pm.

- **Best Views:** Overlooking the Danube Canal, the 18-story **Vienna Hilton** (☎ 0222/71-700-0) offers the most panoramic views from its top floors. Plush accommodations and elegant public rooms also lure guests. The cityscape views are quite dramatic at both dawn and sunset.

2 Innere Stadt (Inner City)

VERY EXPENSIVE

Hotel Ambassador

Kärntnerstrasse 22, A-1010 Vienna. ☎ **0222/514-66.** Fax 513-29-99. 106 rms, 1 suite. A/C MINIBAR TV TEL. 3,150–4,500 AS ($299.25–$427.50) double; 7,500 AS ($712.50) suite. AE, DC, MC, V. Parking 350 AS ($33.25). U-Bahn: Stephansplatz.

Until it became a hotel in 1866, the six-story Ambassador was a warehouse for wheat and flour, a far cry from its status as one of the four or five most glamorous hotels in Vienna today. It's no Bristol or Imperial, but it's quite posh, nonetheless. The Ambassador couldn't be better located: it's between the State Opera and St. Stephen's Cathedral, on the square facing the Donner Fountain. Shop-lined Kärntnerstrasse is on the other side. Mark Twain stayed here, as have a host of diplomats and celebrities, including Theodore Roosevelt.

Red, the hotel's trademark color, crops up all over: in the silk wall coverings, the bedspreads, the upholstery, or the long carpet that's often unrolled to the limousine of some famous personage. This hotel, with its sumptuous accommodations, is an ideal choice for devotees of rococo *fin-de-siècle* decor. Bedrooms are furnished with period pieces such as Biedermeier and art nouveau. The quieter rooms open onto Neuer Markt, although you'll miss the view of the lively Kärntnerstrasse.

Dining/Entertainment: The restaurant, Léhar, serves high-quality Austrian and international cuisine. The hotel also has an elegant bar.

Services: Room service, laundry, baby-sitting.

Facilities: Foreign-currency exchange.

✿ Hotel Bristol

Kärntner Ring 1, A-1015 Vienna. ☎ **0222/515-160.** Fax 0222/515-16-550. 137 rms, 9 suites. A/C MINIBAR TV TEL. 4,400–5,600 AS ($418–$532) double; 11,000–12,900 AS ($1,045–$1,225.50) suite. AE, DC, MC, V. Parking 400 AS ($38). U-Bahn: Karlsplatz. Tram: 1 or 2.

From the outside, this six-story landmark looks no different than Vienna's other grand buildings. But connoisseurs of Austrian hotels maintain that this is a superb choice, its decor evoking the full power of the Habsburg Empire. Only the Imperial is grander. The hotel was constructed in 1894 next to the State Opera, but has been updated to provide guests with black-tile baths and other modern conveniences. The memory of its former role as U.S. headquarters during the occupation have been erased.

Many of the architectural embellishments rank as *objets d'art* in their own right, including the black carved marble fireplaces and the oil paintings in the salons. On your way to the sumptuously appointed bedrooms, you'll see grandfather clocks in the corridors. The Bristol Club Rooms in the tower, for club-floor guests only, have comfortable chairs, an open fireplace, self-service bar, library, TV, video recorder, stereo, deck, and sauna. Each club accommodation consists of a bedroom with a living-room area, and many have a small balcony providing a rooftop view of the Vienna State Opera and Ringstrasse.

Dining/Entertainment: Corkscrew columns of rare marble grace the Korso, Bristol's restaurant, which is one of the best in Vienna. The modern Rôtisserie

Sirk and the elegant Café Sirk are also meeting places for gourmets and carry an *après-théâtre* ambience; the music room has a resident pianist who fills the ground floor with waltzlike melodies on the Böesendorfer grand.

Services: Room service, baby-sitting, laundry.

Facilities: Business center.

○ Hotel Imperial

Kärntner Ring 16, A-1015 Vienna. ☎ **800/325-3589** in the U.S., or 0222/50-110-0. Fax 501-10-440. 128 rms, 32 suites. A/C MINIBAR TV TEL. 5,100–7,500 AS ($484.50–$712.50) double; 11,000–39,000 AS ($1,045–$3,705) suite. AE, DC, MC, V. Parking 450 AS ($42.75). U-Bahn: Karlsplatz.

This hotel is definitely the grandest in Vienna. Luminaries from around the world use it as their headquarters, especially musical stars who prefer the location two blocks from the State Opera and one block from the Musikverein. Wagner stayed here with his family for a few months in 1875 (some scholars claim that he worked out key sections of both *Tannhäuser* and *Lohengrin* during that period). Other artists who have soothed opening-night jitters here include Domingo, Caballé, Carreras, Fonteyn, Ormandy, Fürtwangler, and Karajan, along with thousands of music-lovers who have come to see and hear them.

The hotel was built in 1869 as the private residence of the Duke of Württemberg. The Italian architect Zanotti designed the facade, which resembles a massive governmental building with a heroic frieze carved into the pediment below the roofline. It was converted into a private hotel in 1873. The Nazis commandeered it as their headquarters during World War II, and the Russians requisitioned it in 1945, turning it into a ghost of its former self. Since Austria regained its independence, massive expenditures have returned it to its former glory.

On the staircase leading up from the glittering salons you'll see archways supported by statues of gods and goddesses, along with two Winterhalter portraits of Emperor Franz Joseph and his wife, Elizabeth. Everything is outlined against a background of polished red, yellow, and black marble, crystal chandeliers, Gobelin tapestries, and fine rugs. The salons have arched ceilings, intricately painted with garlands of fruit, ornate urns, griffins, and the smiling faces of sphinxes. Some of the royal suites are downright palatial, but even the regular rooms today are sound-proof and generally spacious. Courtyard rooms are more tranquil but lack the view of the city.

Dining/Entertainment: The elegant restaurant, Zur Majestät, has a turn-of-the-century atmosphere, accented by antique silver, portraits of Franz Joseph, and superb service; the cuisine offers traditional Austrian dishes done with lightly and with excellent flavor. The Imperial Café downstairs plays Viennese music, whereas the hotel's bar, Maria Theresia, is an intimate rendezvous spot.

Services: 24-hour room service, baby-sitting, laundry.

Facilities: Hair salon, business center, foreign-currency exchange.

Hotel Sacher

Philharmonikerstrasse 4, A-1010 Vienna. ☎ **0222/514-56.** Fax 51-45-78-10. 116 rms, 3 suites. A/C MINIBAR TV TEL. 3,800–4,300 AS ($361–$408.50) double; from 10,800 AS ($1,026) suite. Rates include breakfast. AE, DC, MC, V. Parking 380 AS ($36.10). U-Bahn: Karlsplatz. Tram: 1, 2, 62, 65, D, or J. Bus: 4A.

The Sacher was built in 1876 and much of the glory of the Habsburg era is still evoked as you walk through the public rooms. Red velvet, crystal chandeliers, and brocaded curtains create a nostalgic feeling of Old Vienna. If you want truly grand, we think the Imperial and Bristol are superior, but the Sacher has its diehard admirers. The facade is appropriately elaborate, with neoclassical detailing, a striped awning over the sidewalk cafe, and flags from seven nations displayed near the caryatids on the second floor. Despite its popularity among spy novelists, both the crowned heads of Europe and the deposed heads (especially those of eastern European countries) have safely dined and lived here.

In addition to intrigue, the Sacher has produced culinary creations that still bear its name. Franz Sacher, the celebrated chef, left the world a fabulously caloric chocolate cake called the Sacher torte.

Demi-suites and chambers with drawing rooms are more expensive. The reception desk is fairly flexible about making arrangements for salons, apartments, or joining two rooms together, if possible.

Dining/Entertainment: Anna Sacher, the elegant coffeehouse, is the logical music-lover's choice in Vienna. You'll hear some kind of lilting classical music there in the afternoon, just as you had probably fantasized. The interior is a splendor of rococo.

Services: Concierge (who can probably produce "unobtainable" theater and opera tickets), room service, laundry, baby-sitting.

Facilities: Car-rental desk.

Hilton International Vienna Plaza

Am Schottenring 11, A-1010 Vienna. ☎ **800/445-8667** in the U.S., or 0222/31-39-0. Fax 0222/31-39-01-60. 218 rms, 37 suites. A/C MINIBAR TV TEL. 2,990–3,930 AS ($284.05–$373.35) double; from 6,400 AS ($608) suite. AE, DC, MC, V. Free parking. U-Bahn: U2, Schottentor. Tram: 1 or D. Bus: 40A.

This is Vienna's "other Hilton," and a much newer version, having opened in 1988. It rises imposingly for 10 stories in the city center, opening onto Ringstrasse just opposite the stock exchange. Its financial district location draws many business clients from around the world, but is also suitable for other visitors, as it's near many attractions such as the Burgtheater, City Hall, and the Kunsthistorisches and Naturhistorisches museums. Designed with flair and with the discriminating modern visitor in mind, the luxury hotel offers spacious guest rooms and suites. Each has a private safe, floor-to-ceiling windows, and a large marble bathroom fitted with hair dryers, phone, and radio. The hotel also offers a penthouse floor with balconies and a no-smoking floor.

Dining/Entertainment: You shouldn't have trouble finding a place to eat or drink at this hotel as it has three restaurants, a piano bar, a cocktail lounge, and a sidewalk terrace. You might begin with a champagne breakfast in Le Jardin, and in the afternoon enjoy apfelstrudel in the Plaza Café. La Scala restaurant features the northern Italian cuisine. To top the evening, order a nightcap in the Plaza Bar.

Services: 24-hour room service, free airport limousine.

Facilities: Business center, health and fitness club (with sauna, massage, gym, whirlpool, solarium, and health bar).

Radisson/SAS Palais Hotel

Weihburggasse 32, Parkring, A-1010 Vienna. ☎ **800/333-3333** or 0222/51-51-70. Fax 0222/512-22-16. 205 rms, 41 suites. A/C MINIBAR TV TEL. 3,800–4,500 AS ($361–$427.50) double; 5,800–9,800 AS ($551–$931) suite. AE, DC, MC, V. Parking 350 AS ($33.25). U-Bahn: Stadtpark. Tram: 2.

This hotel is one of Vienna's grandest renovations. An unused neoclassical palace was converted into a hotel in 1985 by SAS, the Scandinavian airline. In 1994, another palace next door was purchased, allowing the hotel to double its original size. Set near Vienna's most elaborate park (the Stadtpark), the hotel boasts facades accented with cast-iron railings, reclining nymphs, and elaborate cornices. The interior is plushly outfitted with 19th-century architectural motifs, all impeccably restored and dramatically illuminated. The lobby contains arching palms, a soaring ceiling, and a bar with evening piano music. The result is an uncluttered, conservative, and clean hotel that is managed in a breezy, highly efficient manner. Bedrooms are outfitted in either pink or blue and, in the new wing, in summery shades of green and white. The hotel also offers several duplex suites, or *maisonettes*, conventional suites, and rooms in the Royal Club, which has upgraded amenities and services.

Dining/Entertainment: An elegant basement-level restaurant, Le Siècle im Ersten, is decked out with peach-colored upholstery and a white ceramic stove. Here you can enjoy beautifully presented Austrian and Scandinavian dishes, while listening to live piano concertos.

Services: 24-hour room service, laundry, baby-sitting.

Facilities: Business center (upgraded and enlarged in 1994). Exercise buffs sometimes jog in the Stadtpark before relaxing in the hotel's sauna and whirlpool.

Vienna Marriott

Parkring 12A, A-1010 Vienna. ☎ **800/228-9290** in the U.S., or 0222/51-51-80. Fax 0222/ 51518-6736. 310 rms, 38 suites. A/C MINIBAR TV TEL. 1,980–3,500 AS ($188.10–$332.50) double; 3,500–4,900 AS ($332.50–$465.50) suite. AE, DC, MC, V. Parking 350 AS ($33.25). Tram: 1 or 2.

The Marriott has a striking exterior, and holds its own against SAS, the Palais Hotel, and the Hilton, although the latter two hotels do it somewhat better and manage to evoke a more Viennese atmosphere. Its Mississippi-riverboat facade displays expanses of tinted glass set in finely wrought enameled steel. When the hotel was built on the site of a covered garage, its designers allocated a third of the building for American Consulate offices and a few private apartments. The remainder contains comfortably modern bedrooms, some of which are larger than those in the city's other contemporary hotels.

Opposite Stadtpark, the hotel is ideally located for visitors, as it's within walking distance of such landmarks as St. Stephan's Cathedral, the State Opera, and the Hofburg. The hotel's lobby culminates in a stairway whose curved sides frame a splashing waterfall that's surrounded in plants.

Dining/Entertainment: Both in-house bars offer live entertainment at the cocktail hour, and a pair of restaurants feature appetizing and well-prepared Viennese and international specialties. In the gourmet restaurant, Symphonika, an array of plush pastel-colored banquettes encircle an art nouveau chandelier.

Services: 24-hour room service, laundry, baby-sitting.

Facilities: Swimming pool, sauna, Jacuzzi.

EXPENSIVE

Hotel Amadeus

Wildpretmarkt 5, A-1010 Vienna. ☎ **0222/533-87-38.** Fax 538-87-38-38. 30 rms. MINIBAR TV TEL. 1,950 AS ($185.25) double. Rates include breakfast. AE, DC, MC, V. U-Bahn: Stephansplatz.

Cozy and convenient, this hotel is only two minutes away from the cathedral and within walking distance of practically everything else of musical or historical note in Vienna. Behind a dull 1960s facade, the hotel maintains its bedrooms and carpeted public rooms in tip-top shape. Bedrooms are furnished in a comfortable, modern style, except for the uncomfortably low ceilings, and many open onto views of the cathedral. Double-glazing on the windows helps, but does not obliterate street noise. Some of the carpeting and fabrics look a little worse for wear. Only breakfast is served.

Hotel Astoria

Kärntnerstrasse 32–34, A-1015 Vienna. ☎ **0222/515-77-0.** Fax 515-77-82. 107 rms, 1 suite. MINIBAR TV TEL. 2,400 AS ($228) double; 3,800 AS ($361) suite. Rates include breakfast. AE, DC, MC, V. U-Bahn: Stephansplatz.

The Hotel Astoria is for nostalgists who want to experience life as it was in the closing days of the Austro-Hungarian Empire. A first-class hotel, the Astoria has an eminently desirable location, lying on the shopping mall near St. Stephan's Cathedral and the State Opera. Decorated in a slightly frayed turn-of-the-century style, the hotel offers well-appointed and traditionally decorated bedrooms. The interior rooms tend to be too dark, and singles are just too cramped. Of course, it has been renovated over the years, but the old style has been preserved, and management seems genuinely concerned about offering high-quality service and accommodation for what is considered a reasonable price in Vienna. The Astoria has long been a favorite with visiting performers such as the late Leonard Bernstein.

Dining/Entertainment: The restaurant, Astoria, is so special that it deserves (and gets) a special recommendation (see Chapter 5 on "Dining").

Services: Room service, laundry, baby-sitting.

Facilities: Car-rental desk.

Hotel de France

Schottenring 3, A-1010 Vienna. ☎ **800/223-5652** or 0222/31-36-80. Fax 0222/31-59-69. 206 rms, 10 suites. A/C MINIBAR TV TEL. 2,500–3,000 AS ($237.50–$285) double; 3,000–5,000 AS ($285–$475) suite. AE, DC, MC, V. U-Bahn: U2, Schottentor. Tram: 1, 2, 37, or D. Bus: 1A.

The Hotel de France is right on the Ring and has long been a favorite. It neighbors the university and the Votivkirche, which makes it a centrally located choice. Its chiseled gray facade looks basically as it did when it was first erected beside Ringstrasse in 1872. After World War II, the building was transformed into a hotel. Much renovation has made it a modern, savory establishment where you get comfortable, tasteful, and unobtrusively conservative decor. In such a subdued and appealing ambience, you often encounter businesspeople from all over the world. They appreciate the high-ceilinged public rooms and Oriental carpets, the generously padded armchairs, and, of course, the full-dress portrait of Franz Joseph. The bedrooms are among the finest for their price range in Vienna and all contain radios and a safe.

Dining/Entertainment At Bel Etage, you can enjoy such dishes as filet in Roquefort-and-whisky sauce, tafelspitz (the favorite dish of the emperor), and fogas, the highly prized fish from Lake Balaton in Hungary. There's also a French bistro as well as a beautiful atrium bar.

Services: Room service, laundry, baby-sitting.

Facilities: Sauna, solarium.

Hotel Europa

Neuer Markt 3, A-1010 Vienna. ☎ **0222/51-59-40.** Fax 0222/513-81-38. 102 rms. A/C MINIBAR TV TEL. 2,250–2,650 AS ($213.75–$251.75) double. Rates include buffet breakfast. AE, DC, MC, V. U-Bahn: Stephansplatz.

The welcoming parapet of this glass-and-steel hotel extends over the sidewalk almost to the edge of the street. You'll find the 10-story hotel midway between the State Opera and St. Stephan's Cathedral. It offers comfortable bedrooms done in Scandanavian modern. Some bedrooms are spacious, with lots of light coming in from the large windows, but nearly all the bathrooms are microscopic. Europa has a Viennese cafe, and a first-class restaurant, Zum Donnerbrunnen, which features zither music at night. The Europa Bar is also elegant.

Hotel König Von Ungarn

Schulerstrasse 10, A-1010 Vienna. ☎ **0222/515-84-0.** Fax 0222/515-848. 33 rms, 1 suite. A/C MINIBAR TV TEL. 2,200 AS ($209) double; 2,600 AS ($247) suite. Rates include breakfast. AE, DC, MC, V. Parking 200 AS ($19). U-Bahn: Stephansplatz.

On a narrow street near St. Stephan's, this hotel occupies a choice site in a nearby dormered building that dates back to the early 17th century. It has been receiving paying guests for more than four centuries and is Vienna's oldest continuously operated accommodation—in all, an evocative, intimate, and cozy retreat. It was once a *pied-à-terre* for Hungarian noble families during their stays in the Austrian capital. Mozart reportedly lived here in 1791. He wrote some of his immortal music when he resided in an apartment upstairs, where you'll find a Mozart museum.

The interior abounds with interesting architectural details, such as marble columns supporting the arched ceiling of the King of Hungary restaurant, which is one of Vienna's finest. There's also a mirrored solarium/bar area with a glass roof over the atrium, and a live tree growing out of the pavement. Tall hinged windows overlook the Old Town, and Venetian mirrors adorn some walls, evoking the atmosphere of Old Vienna. Everywhere you look you'll find low-key luxury, old tradition, and modern convenience. Room service (24 hours), laundry, and baby-sitting are available, and the professional staff is highly efficient, keeping the hotel spotless. Try for the two rooms with balconies.

Hotel Römischer Kaiser

Annagasse 16, A-1010 Vienna. ☎ **800/528-1234** in the U.S., or 0222/512-77-51. Fax 0222/512-77-51-13. 23 rms. A/C MINIBAR TV TEL. 1,990–3,050 AS ($189.05–$289.75) double. Rates include breakfast. AE, DC, MC, V. Parking 300 AS ($28.50). U-Bahn: Karlsplatz.

A Best Western affiliate, this hotel is housed in a national trust building that has seen its share of transformations. It's located in a traffic-free zone, between the cathedral of St. Stephan's and the Opera House, on a side street off the Kärntnerstrasse. It was constructed in 1684 as the private palace of the imperial chamberlain and later housed the Imperial School of Engineering before becoming a *fin-de-siècle* hostelry. The hotel rents romantically decorated rooms (our favorite has red satin upholstery over a chaise longue). All rooms have hair dryers, radio clock, cable TV (CNN), and a room safe. Double glazing keeps down the noise and baroque paneling adds to the nostalgic allure of the hotel. Some rooms—notably 12, 22, 30, and 38, can accommodate three or four beds, making this a family-friendly place.

Dining/Entertainment: The red-carpeted sidewalk cafe has bar service and features tables shaded with flowers and umbrellas. It evokes memories of Vienna as an imperial capital.

Services: 24-hour room service, laundry, baby-sitting.

Ⓢ K & K Palais Hotel

Rudolfsplatz 11, A-1010 Vienna. ☎ **800/528-1234** in the U.S., or 0222/533-13-53. Fax 0222/533-13-5370. 66 rms. A/C MINIBAR TV TEL. 1,980–2,290 AS ($188.10–$217.55) double. Rates include breakfast. AE, DC, MC, V. Parking 125 AS ($11.90). U-Bahn: Schottenring.

When its severely dignified facade was built in 1890, this hotel sheltered the affair of Emperor Francis Joseph and his celebrated mistress, Katherina Schratt. Occupying a desirable position near the river and a five-minute walk from the Ring, it remained unused for two decades until members of the Best Western chain renovated it in 1981.

Vestiges of its imperial past remain, in spite of the contemporary, but airy, lobby and the lattice-covered bar and coffeeshop, which serves Austrian fare. The public rooms are painted a shade of imperial Austrian yellow, and one of Ms. Schratt's antique secretaries occupies a niche near a white-sided tile stove. The bedrooms are comfortably outfitted and stylish. Room service operates 16 hours a day.

MODERATE

Hotel Am Parkring
Parkring 12, A-1015 Vienna. ☎ **0222/51-48-00.** Fax 0222/514-80-40. 56 rms, 7 suites. A/C MINIBAR TV TEL. 2,230–2,440 AS ($211.85–$231.80) double; 2,600–3,200 AS ($247–$304) suite. Rates include breakfast. AE, DC, MC, V. Parking 220 AS ($20.90). U-Bahn: Stadtpark or Steubentor. Tram: 1 or 2.

This well-maintained hotel occupies the 11th, 12th, and 13th floors of a 13-story office building that lies near the edge of Vienna's Stadtpark. A semiprivate elevator services only the streetside entrance and those floors affiliated with the hotel. Originally built in the early 1960s, this hotel offers sweeping views of the city from all of its bedrooms, some of which overlook nearby St. Stephan's Cathedral. Bedrooms are furnished in a conservative, but comfortable style, and are favored by business travelers and tourists alike, although the atmosphere is a bit sterile if you're seeking nostalgic Vienna. You can dine at the Himmelstube restaurant here and relax at the coffee bar, where Vienna's skyline spreads out before you. Room service, baby-sitting, and laundry are available.

Hotel Am Stephansplatz
Stephansplatz 9, A-1010 Vienna. ☎ **0222/534-05-0.** Fax 0222/534-05-711. 60 rms. MINIBAR TV TEL. 2,260 AS ($214.70) double. Rates include breakfast. AE, DC, MC, V. Parking 350 AS ($33.25). U-Bahn: Stephansplatz.

You'll walk out your door and face the front entrance to Vienna's cathedral if you stay in this hotel. The location, admittedly, is virtually unbeatable, although a lot of other Viennese hotels have more charm than this one, as well as a more helpful staff. Nevertheless, the place has many winning qualities; for example, it receives individual bookings, and is not overrun with group package tours. Marble, granite, crystal, and burled woods set the tone for the renovated lobby. Some of the bedrooms contain painted reproductions of rococo furniture and red-flocked wallpaper. Most rooms, however, are rather sterile and functional, and 10 come with showers only instead of club baths. Lack of air-conditioning could be a problem here in the evening, especially if guests must open their windows onto Stephansplatz, which is a noisy venue after dark. The singles are so plain and cramped that they're hardly recommendable. A typical Viennese coffee shop, the first-floor Dom Café, is a well-known rendezvous spot.

✪ Hotel Kaiserin Elisabeth
Weihburggasse 3, A-1010 Vienna. ☎ **0222/515-260.** Fax 0222/515-267. 620 rms, 3 suites. MINIBAR TV TEL. 1,900–2,300 AS ($180.50–$218.50) double; 2,600 AS ($247) suite. Rates include buffet breakfast. AE, DC, MC, V. Parking 350 AS ($33.25). U-Bahn: Stephansplatz.

A few blocks from the cathedral, this yellow-stoned hotel is conveniently located, lying only one block from the cathedral. The first thing you might notice about the interior is the number of Oriental rugs lying on well-maintained marble or wood floors. The main salon has a pale-blue skylight suspended above it, with mirrors and half-columns in natural wood. The soundproof rooms have been considerably updated since Richard Wagner, Franz Liszt, and Edvard Grieg stayed here, but modern composers are still attracted to the place. You're likely to see an up-to-date decor of polished wood, clean linen, and perhaps another Oriental rug in your room. In the breakfast area a portrait of Empress Maria Theresa hangs above the fireplace. Room service, laundry, and baby-sitting are provided.

Hotel-Pension Arenberg

Stubenring 2, A-1010 Vienna. ☎ **800/528-1234** in the U.S., or 0222/512-52-91. 22 rms, 1 suite. A/C TV TEL. 1,480–1,850 AS ($140.60–$175.75) double; 2,150 AS ($204.25) suite. Rates include breakfast. AE, DC, MC, V. Parking 350 AS ($33.25). U-Bahn: Schwedenplatz.

This genteel but unpretentious pension occupies the second and third floors of a six-story apartment house which was built around the turn of the century. Set in a prestigious neighborhood on Ringstrasse it offers soundproof bedrooms outfitted in old-world style with Oriental carpets, conservative furniture, and intriguing artwork. Breakfast is the only meal served.

⑤ Hotel Royal

Singerstrasse 3, A-1010 Vienna. ☎ **0222/51-568.** Fax 0222/513-96-98. 80 rms, 2 suites. MINIBAR TV TEL. 1,600–2,200 AS ($152–$209) double; 2,050–2,700 AS ($194.75–$256.50) triple; 2,800 AS ($266) suite. Rates include breakfast. AE, DC, MC, V. U-Bahn: Stephansplatz.

The outside of this nine-story hotel presents a restrained dignity to the older buildings around it. It's on one of the more prestigious streets of the old city, less than a block from St. Stephan's Cathedral. The lobby contains the piano where Wagner composed *Die Meistersinger von Nürnberg.* Each of the rooms is furnished differently, with some good reproductions of antiques and even an occasional original. The entire facility was built in 1960 and rebuilt in 1982. Try for a room with a balcony and a view of the cathedral. Corner rooms with spacious foyers are also desirable, although those facing the street tend to be noisy. Ristaurante Firenze, under separate management, serves a savory Italian cuisine on the premises, and has the largest selection of Italian wines in Austria. Room service is also available to guests.

INEXPENSIVE

Hotel Austria

Am Fleischmarkt 20, A-1011 Vienna. ☎ **0222/515-23.** Fax 0222/515-23-506. 46 rms (42 with bath). MINIBAR TV TEL. 910–1,160 AS ($86.45–$110.20) double without bath, 1,345–1,695 AS ($127.80–$161.05) double with bath; 1,710–2,125 AS ($162.45–$201.90) triple with bath. Rates include breakfast. AE, DC, MC, V. Parking 180 AS ($17.10). U-Bahn: Schwedenplatz. Tram: 1 or 2.

The staff here always seems willing to tell you where to go in the neighborhood for a good meal or a glass of wine, and often distributes typed sheets explaining the medieval origins of this section of Vienna. This unpretentious family-owned establishment sits on a small street whose name will probably be unfamiliar to many taxi drivers, although a corner building on the adjoining street, Fleischmarkt 20, is the point where you'll turn onto the narrow lane. The comfortable furnishings in the lobby and in the chandeliered breakfast room are maintained in tip-top shape.

Hotel Kärntnerhof

Grashofgasse 4, A-1010 Vienna. ☎ **0222/512-19-23.** Fax 0222/513-22-28-33. 43 rms (41 with bath), 1 suite. 900 AS ($85.50) double without bath, 1,680 AS ($159.60) double with bath; 2,250 AS ($213.75) suite. Rates include breakfast. AE, DC, MC, V. Parking 180 AS ($17.10). U-Bahn: Stephansplatz.

Only a four-minute walk from the cathedral, the Kärntnerhof advertises itself as a *Gutbürgerlich* family-oriented hotel. The decor of the public rooms is tastefully arranged around Oriental rugs, well-upholstered chairs and couches with cabriole legs, and an occasional 19th-century portrait. The bedrooms are more up-to-date, usually with the original parquet floors and striped or patterned wallpaper set off by curtains. The private baths glisten with tile walls and floors. The owner does what he can to be helpful, directing guests to the post office and other nearby Vienna landmarks.

◎ Hotel Post

Fleischmarkt 24, A-1010 Vienna. ☎ **0222/51-58-30.** Fax 0222/515-83-808. 107 rms (77 with bath). TV TEL. 820 AS ($77.90) double without bath, 1,350 AS ($128.25) double with bath; 1,060 AS ($100.70) triple without bath, 1,660 AS ($157.70) triple with bath. Rates include buffet breakfast. AE, DC, MC, V. Tram: 1 or 2.

The Hotel Post lies in the medieval slaughterhouse district, today an interesting section full of hotels and restaurants. The dignified front of this hotel is constructed of gray stone, with a facade of black marble covering the street level. The manager is quick to tell you that both Mozart and Haydn frequently stayed in a former inn at this address. Those composers would probably be amused to hear recordings of their music played in the coffeehouse/restaurant, Le Café/Alte Weinstube, attached to the hotel. Bedrooms are streamlined and functionally albeit simply furnished, each well maintained.

◎ Hotel Wandl

Petersplatz 9, A-1010 Vienna. ☎ **0222/53-45-50.** Fax 0222/53-455-77. 138 rms (134 with bath). TV TEL. 1,450 AS ($137.75) double without bath, 1,650–1,750 AS ($156.75–$166.25) double with bath. Rates include breakfast. No credit cards. Parking 300–400 AS ($28.50–$38). U-Bahn: Stephansplatz.

Stepping into this hotel is like stepping into a piece of a family's history—it has been under the same ownership for generations. The establishment lies in the Inner City and offers views of the steeple of St. Stephan's Cathedral from many of its windows, which often open onto small balconies with railings. The breakfast room is a high-ceilinged, two-toned room with hanging chandeliers and lots of ornamented plaster, whereas the bedrooms usually offer the kind of spacious dimensions that went out of style 60 years ago. Some units contain minibar and TV. The hotel faces St. Peter's Church. Laundry and baby-sitting are provided.

Pension Dr. Geissler

Postgasse 14, A-1010 Vienna. ☎ **0222/533-28-03.** Fax 0222/533-26-35. 26 rms (21 with bath). 780 AS ($74.10) double without bath, 980–1,180 AS ($93.10–$112.10) double with bath. Rates include buffet breakfast. Half board 150 AS ($14.25) per person extra. AE, DC, MC, V. Parking 150 AS ($14.25). U-Bahn: Schwedenplatz.

Unpretentious lodgings at reasonable prices are offered here to visitors who find themselves near well-known Schwedenplatz at the edge of the Danube Canal. The bedrooms in this attractively informal guesthouse are furnished with simple blond headboards and a few utilitarian pieces. You can order hot meals à la carte any time of the day.

◎ Pension Elite

Wipplingerstrasse 32, A-1010 Vienna. ☎ **0222/533-25-18-0.** Fax 0222/535-57-53. 27 rms (22 with bath). MINIBAR TEL. 940 AS ($89.30) double without bath, 1,360 AS ($129.20) double with bath. Rates include breakfast. No credit cards. Tram: 1, 2, or D. U-Bahn: Schottenor.

In a corner building, this pension is next to the Vienna stock exchange. The neighborhood is appropriately grand for this edifice, which looks like a former private palace. You'll be near the university, the Burgtheater, and the cathedral. The public rooms are tastefully furnished with a mixture of antiques and modern pieces, crystal chandeliers, lots of well-oiled paneling, green-tile fireplaces, and Oriental rugs. The family-run establishment lives up to its name and deserves a high recommendation for good service in a refined setting. Rates depend on the plumbing; TV is available upon request. Breakfast is served in the elegantly upholstered and carpeted dining room.

Pension Neuer Markt

Seilergasse 9, A-1010 Vienna. ☎ **0222/512-23-16.** Fax 0222/513-91-05. 36 rms. TV TEL. 880–1,380 AS ($83.60–$131.10) double. Rates include breakfast. Half board 150 AS ($14.25) per person extra. AE, DC, MC, V. Parking 360 AS ($34.20). U-Bahn: Stephansplatz.

Near the cathedral, this pension is housed in a white baroque building that faces a square with an ornate fountain. The carpeted rooms are clean and well maintained in an updated motif of white walls and strong colors. Some of the beds are set into niches, and many of the windows are large. Each of the units has central heating. We recommend you reserve 30 days in advance.

Pension Nossek

Graben 17, A-1010 Vienna. ☎ **0222/533-70-410.** Fax 0222/535-36-46. 26 rms (4 with shower only, 22 with bath). TEL. 1,100 AS ($104.50) double with shower; 1,500 AS ($142.50) double with bath. Rates include breakfast. No credit cards. U-Bahn: Stephansplatz.

Mozart lived in this building in 1781 and 1782, writing the *Haffner* symphony and *The Abduction from the Seraglio.* The establishment lies on one of Vienna's best shopping streets, just blocks away from the major sights. In 1909 the building was converted into a guesthouse, and has always been a good bet for clean, comfortable accommodations. Most of the bedrooms have been renovated and all but a few singles contain private baths; 16 rooms offer a minibar.

✪ Pension Pertschy

Habsburgergasse 5, 1010 Vienna ☎ **0222/534-49-0.** Fax 0222/534-49-49. 43 rms (all with bath, two with kitchen) MINIBAR TV TEL. 1,080–1,260 AS ($102.60–$119.70) double without kitchenette. DC, MC, V. U-Bahn: Stephansplatz.

Well-scrubbed and reputable, this simple but historic pension was originally built in the 1700s as the Palais Carviani in a restrained baroque style whose facade is scheduled for a renovation sometime during the life of this edition. Other than some scaffolding that might impair your view from the front rooms, it's business as usual among the hotel's four floors. Several rooms overlook a central courtyard and are scattered amongst six or seven private apartments, whose residents are used to foreign visitors roaming through the building. Bedrooms are high-ceilinged and outfitted in old-fashioned, almost dowdy tones of cream and pink. Most appealing is its prime location in the heart of Old Vienna (between Habsburgasse and Bräunergasse, just off the Graben).

✪ Pension Sacher

Rotenturmstrasse 1, A-1010 Vienna. ☎ **0222/533-32-38.** Fax 0222/533-32-38. 8 apartments. TV TEL. 900–1,230 AS ($85.50–$116.85) apartment for two. No credit cards. U-Bahn: Stephansplatz. Bus: 1-A.

The Pension Sacher is a well-run hostelry whose regular clients return year after year, partially because its located on Stephansplatz. Although it's not connected to the famous hotel with the same name, the Pension Sacher is owned by Claudia Racek-Sacher, the great-great-granddaughter of the man who invented the Sachertorte in 1832.

The pension, on the seventh floor of the building, consists of apartments with kitchenettes and bathrooms. There is no staff other than a maid who comes in Monday through Saturday to tidy the rooms. Higher-priced units have sitting rooms with an extra bed. Write well ahead of time for a reservation.

Zur Wiener Staatsoper

Krugerstrasse 11, A-1010 Vienna. ☎ **0222/513-12-74.** Fax 0222/513-12-74-15. 22 rms. TV. 1,400 AS ($133) double. Rates include breakfast. AE, V. Parking 200 AS ($19). U-Bahn: Karlsplatz. Tram: 1, 2, D, or J; Opernring.

You'll probably stop to admire the elaborately baroque facade of this family-run hotel even if you don't plan to stay here. Rooms are clean and comfortable, but furnishings are rather simple and functional. The elevator is convenient as is the hotel's location, near most Inner City monuments.

3 Leopoldstadt (2nd District)

MODERATE

Hotel Stefanie

Taborstrasse 12, A-1020 Vienna. ☎ **800/528-1234** in the U.S., or 0222/21-15-00. Fax 0222/211-50-160. 130 rms. MINIBAR TV TEL. 1,680–2,280 AS ($159.60–$216.60) double. Rates include buffet breakfast. AE, DC, MC, V. Parking 180 AS ($17.10). U-Bahn: Schwedenplatz. Tram: 21.

This updated four-star hotel is across the Danube Canal from St. Stephan's Cathedral, but still easily accessible to the rest of the city. The interior is partially decorated in beautifully finished wall paneling and gilded wall sconces. Upon closer examination much of the decor is reproduced, yet the hotel still emits a hint of 19th-century rococo splendor. The bar area is filled with black leather armchairs on chrome swivel bases, and the concealed lighting throws an azure glow over the artfully displayed bottles. All rooms have radios, and some are air-conditioned.

4 Landstrasse (3rd District)

VERY EXPENSIVE

✪ Hotel im Palais Schwarzenberg

Schwarzenbergplatz 9, A-1030 Vienna. ☎ **0222/798-45-15.** Fax 0222/798-47-14. 38 rms, 4 suites. MINIBAR TV TEL. 3,300–5,500 AS ($313.50–$522.50) double; 5,500–7,100 AS ($522.50–$674.50) suite. AE, DC, JCB, MC, V. Free parking. Tram: D. U-Bahn: Karlsplatz.

Just outside the Ring, this hotel—more a museum really—is hidden in 15 acres of manicured gardens. It's an excellent choice if you want a noble and elegant ambience. Unlike the Bristol and the Imperial, this hotel has the aura of a country estate in a formally landscaped and statue-dotted park. The palace was built 300 years ago by Lukas von Hildebrandt and Fischer von Erlach, masters of baroque architecture, and has held on to its splendid original touches. It was gutted during the Nazi era, but was completely reconstructed after the Soviet occupation of Vienna. Today the same striated marble, crystal chandeliers, mythical beasts, oval mirrors, and gilt—lots of it—fill the public rooms between painted murals of festive deities. The posh bedrooms and suites contain exquisite *objets d'art* and antique pieces, although they vary greatly in size. Only a few rooms are air-conditioned.

Dining/Entertainment: Guests enjoy the terrace restaurant, Wintergarten, which serves classical French and Viennese cuisine and overlooks the park. The Palais Bar, one of the most elegant in Vienna, is open daily from 10:30am to 2am.

Services: 24-hour room service, laundry, baby-sitting.

Facilities: Five tennis courts, croquet lawn, guest lounges, extensive private jogging tracks.

Vienna Hilton

Am Stadtpark, A-1030 Vienna. ☎ **800/445-8667** in the U.S., or 0222/71-700-0. Fax 0222/71-700-339. 600 rms, 29 suites. A/C MINIBAR TV TEL. 2,900–4,300 AS ($275.50–$408.50) double. From 4,900 AS ($465.50) suite. AE, DC, MC, V. Parking 256 AS ($24.30). The Hilton is attached to the City Air Terminal, the drop-off point for buses coming in at frequent intervals from the airport. U-Bahn: Landstrasse.

This 18-story box overlooks the Danube canal and offers plush accommodations and elegant public areas. Despite the hotel's modernity, it still manages to evoke plenty of Viennese flavor. Its soaring atrium lobby and bustling nightlife make it a vibrant home for business travelers.

The hotel offers well-appointed bedrooms in a range of styles, including Biedermeier, contemporary, baroque, and art nouveau. Since the Hilton towers over the city skyline, it affords great views from the top floors. Its suites and executive floors provide extra comfort for frequent travelers, but standard amenities in all bedrooms include a hair dryer and a basket of toiletries. The adjacent Stadtpark is connected to the hotel and the City Air Terminal by a bridge, which strollers and joggers use during excursions into the landscaped and bird-filled park.

Dining/Entertainment: The hotel's main restaurant, Arcadia, is recommended separately (see Chapter 5 on "Dining"). Other drinking and dining facilities include the Terminal Pub, offering an express breakfast, plus regional specialties throughout the day. The Mangostin Asia Restaurant features Thai, Chinese, and Japanese cooking, and the Klimt Bar, open daily from 9am to 2am, is one of the few bars left in Vienna that has live music.

Services: 24-hour room service, laundry, baby-sitting.

Facilities: Health club with sauna, business center.

MODERATE

Biedermeier im Sunnhof

Landstrasser Hauptstrasse 28, A-1030. ☎ **800/448/8355** or 0222/716710. Fax 0222/71671-503. 194 rms, 10 suites. MINIBAR TV TEL. 2,400 AS ($228) double, 4,900 AS ($465.50) suite. Rates include breakfast. AE, DC, MC, V. Parking 170 AS ($16.15) extra. U-Bahn: Rochusgasse.

This hotel was established in 1983 within the radically renovated premises of a late 19th century apartment house. It boasts a clearly defined theme that permeates both the public areas and the bedrooms—an allegiance to the blond and ebony tenants of Biedermeier furniture. Despite the hotel's position adjacent to the Wien Mitte bus station and roaring traffic on all sides, most bedrooms overlook a quiet pedestrian-only walkway lined with shops and cafes. On the premises are a formal restaurant, Zu den Deutschmeistern, plus a simpler, less formal Beisl, the Weissgerberstube. Both are open daily for lunch and dinner. There's also a bar and a cafe terrace overlooking a small garden, but other than that, the hotel has few other facilities.

Hotel-Pension Barich

Barichgasse 3, A-1030 Vienna. ☎ **0222/712-12-73.** Fax 0222/712-22-75-88. 16 rms, 1 apartment. MINIBAR TV TEL. 1,380–1,660 AS ($131.10–$157.70) double; 2,990 AS ($284.05) apt. for five. Rates include buffet breakfast. MC, V. Parking 150 AS ($14.25). Bus: 74A.

This spot might be the choice for guests who prefer serene residential surroundings. Northeast of the Südbahnhof, behind an unpretentious facade, this small hotel is quiet and well furnished. The proprietors, Ulrich and Hermine Platz, who manage the establishment, speak fluent English. All bedrooms are soundproofed and have radios, cable TV with CNN, hair dryers, electric trouser presses, and safes.

5 Wieden & Margareten (4th & 5th Districts)

EXPENSIVE

Hotel Erzherzog Rainer

Wiedner Hauptstrasse 27-29, A-1040 Vienna. ☎ **0222/50-111-316.** Fax 0222/50-111-350. 84 rms. MINIBAR TV TEL. 1,980 AS ($188.10) double. Rates include breakfast. AE, MC, V. Parking 200 AS ($19). U-Bahn: Taubstummengasse.

Family-Friendly Hotels

Hotel Kärntnerhof *(see page 71)*   A family-oriented *Gutbürgerlich* hotel, this establishment lies right in the Center of Vienna and its helpful management welcomes kids.

Hotel Graf Stadion *(see page 79)*   Many of the rooms at this hotel—a longtime favorite of families on a tight budget—contain two double beds, suitable for parties of three or four.

Hotel Römischer Kaiser *(see page 69)*   The former palace of the imperial chamberlain, this edifice, a Best Western affiliate, offers a glimpse of Imperial Vienna circa 1684 when it was constructed. Its staff is extremely hospitable and gracious to visiting families.

Hotel Schneider *(see page 77)*   Set between the State Opera and the flower market, this is one of Vienna's better small hotels. Families can rent rooms with kitchenettes to cut down on the high cost of dining in Vienna.

Popular with groups and business travelers, this family-run hotel was built just before World War I (around 1912), and was gradually renovated, room by room, between 1992 and 1994. It's only five minutes by foot to the State Opera and Kärntnerstrasse, with a U-Bahn stop just steps away. The bedrooms are well decorated, and you'll find radios, but not soundproofing, in all. The singles are impossibly small, and on certain days air-conditioning is sorely missed. A booking service for opera and theater tickets operates out of the lobby. An informal brasserie serves Austrian specialties, and the cozy bar is modishly decorated with accents of black and brass. Other convenient services include 10-hour dry cleaning, Monday through Friday.

Hotel Prinz Eugen

Wiedner Gürtel 14, A-1040 Vienna. ☎ **0222/505-17-41.** Fax 0222/505-17-41-19. 112 rms, 2 suites. MINIBAR TV TEL. 2,200 AS ($209) double or suite. Rates include breakfast. AE, DC, MC, V. U-Bahn: Südtiroler Platz or Südbahnhof.

Built in the 1960s, and renovated in stages between 1992 and 1994, this hotel has soundproof windows and balconies. In a section of Vienna favored by diplomats, the hotel is immediately opposite the Belvedere Palace and the Südbahnhof rail station. Subways will carry you quickly to the center of Vienna, and there are good highway connections as well. Inside, you'll find a cozy, paneled bar and a series of conference rooms and salons that are often in demand by local business. The decor is a mixture of antiques, Oriental rugs, and some glitzy touches like glass walls with brass trim and adaptations of crystal chandeliers. Suites are nothing more than slightly larger double rooms with an additional bathroom. Room service, baby-sitting, and laundry are available.

6 Mariahilf (6th District)

MODERATE

Hotel Kummer

Mariahilferstrasse 71A, A-1060 Vienna. ☎ **0222/588-95.** Fax 0222/587-81-33. 100 rms. MINIBAR TV TEL. 1,810 AS ($171.95) double. Rates include buffet breakfast. AE, DC, MC, V. Parking 208 AS ($19.75). U-Bahn: Neubaugasse. Bus: 13A or 14A.

Established by the Kummer family during the 19th century, this hotel was built in response to the growing power of the railways as they forged new paths of commerce and tourism through central Europe. A short walk from Vienna's Westbahnhof, the hotel sits in a busy, noisy location, but looks as ornamental as any public monument constructed during the imperial days. Restored and renovated in 1994, the facade is richly embellished with Corinthian capitals on acanthus-leaf bases, urn-shaped balustrades, and representations of four heroic demigods staring down from under the building's eaves.

The modern public rooms inside are not as delightful as the building's exterior, but they are comfortable and satisfactory, and often a favorite among large groups. The bedrooms have soundproof windows, but some of the singles are so small and dimly lit they aren't recommendable. The hotel contains a restaurant and bar, and provides room service, laundry, and baby-sitting.

Fürst Metternich Hotel

Esterházygasse 33, A-1060 Vienna. ☎ **0222/588-70.** Fax 0222/58-75-268. 53 rms, 1 suite. MINIBAR TV TEL. 1,620 AS ($153.90) double; 1,740 AS ($165.30) suite. Rates include breakfast. AE, DC, MC, V. Parking 300 AS ($28.50). U-Bahn: Kirchengasse. Tram: 5.

Pink and gray paint and ornate stone window trim identify this solidly built 19th-century hotel, which began as an opulent private home. It's located between the Ring and the Westbahnhof near Mariahilferstrasse, about a 20-minute walk from the cathedral. Many of the grander architectural elements were retained, including a pair of red stone columns in the entranceway and an old-fashioned staircase guarded with griffins, while the high-ceilinged bedrooms retain a neutral decor, with laminated furnishings, feather pillows, and duvets. Windows in the front rooms are soundproof in theory, but not in practice. If you want a more tranquil night's sleep, opt for a room in the rear. The Barfly's Club, a popular hang-out in Vienna, is open daily from 6pm to 2am, offering 120 different exotic drinks.

Hotel President

Wallgasse 23, A-1060 Vienna. ☎ **800/387-8842** or 0222/599-90. Fax 0222/596-76-46. 72 rms, 5 suites. A/C MINIBAR TV TEL. 1,950 AS ($185.25) double; 2,350 AS ($223.25) suite. Rates include buffet breakfast. AE, DC, MC, V. Parking 150 AS ($14.25). U-Bahn: Gumpendorfer. Bus: 57A.

This seven-story concrete-and-glass hotel was designed in 1975 with enough angles in its facade to allow each bedroom to have an irregular shape. Usually the units have two windows that face different skylines. Aside from the views, each of the decent-size bedrooms has comfortable furnishings, a radio, and a minisafe. Opt for a room—really a studio with a terrace—on the seventh floor, if one is available. The hotel also has a public rooftop terrace where many guests sit sipping drinks in summer. The Restaurant Casserole serves above average Viennese and international cuisine in an informal setting every night until 11pm. food. Room service, baby-sitting, and laundry are provided.

INEXPENSIVE

⑤ Hotel Schneider

Getreidemarkt 5, A-1060 Vienna. ☎ **0222/588-380.** Fax 0222/588-38-212. 71 rms. MINIBAR TV TEL. 1,600–2,160 AS ($152–$205.20) double. Rates include buffet breakfast. AE, DC, MC, V. Parking 250 AS ($23.75). U-Bahn: Karlsplatz.

Sitting at the corner of a well-known street, Lehargasse, this hotel is in the center of Vienna between the State Opera and the famous Nasch Market. It's a modern five-story building with panoramic windows on the ground floor and a red-tile roof. The interior is warmly decorated in part with 19th-century antiques and with comfortably upholstered chairs. Musicians, singers, actors, and other artists form part of the loyal clientele. This is one of Vienna's better small hotels, and families are especially fond of the place because 35 of the accommodations contain kitchenettes. All units also offer cable TV and some of them are air-conditioned.

7 Neubau (7th District)

EXPENSIVE

K & K Hotel Maria Theresia

Kirchberggasse 6-8 (Breitegasse 5), A-1070 Vienna. ☎ **800/528-1234** in the U.S., or 0222/ 52-123. Fax 0222/521-23-70. 117 rms, 6 suites. MINIBAR TV TEL. 1,980–2,290 AS ($188.10–$217.55) double; 3,700–4,600 AS ($351.50–$437) suite. Rates include breakfast. AE, DC, MC, V. Parking 100 AS ($9.50). U-Bahn: Volkstheater. Bus: 48.

The initials of this hotel are a reminder of the dual monarchy (Kaiserlich und Königlich—"by appointment to the Emperor of Austria and King of Hungary"). Even the surrounding neighborhood, marked by some major museums that lie just outside the Ring, is reminiscent of the days of Empress Maria Theresa. The hotel is in the artists' colony of Spittelberg, within walking distance of the Winter Palace gardens, the Volkstheater, and the famous shopping street, Mariahilferstrasse. The hotel, built in the late 1980s, offers comfortable and contemporary rooms that are amply sized. Its restaurant, Maria Theresia, serves standard continental cuisine, with some regional specialties added for variety.

MODERATE

Hotel Savoy

Lindengasse 12, A-1070 Vienna. ☎ **0222/523-46-40.** Fax 0222/93-46-40. 42 rms. MINIBAR TV TEL. 1,340-1,780 AS ($127.30-$169.10) double. Rates include breakfast. AE, DC, MC, V. U-Bahn: Neubaugasse.

Built in the 1960s, this well-managed hotel rises six stories above one of Vienna's busiest wholesale and retail shopping districts. Within walking distance of Ringstrasse, opposite a recently built station for the city's newest U-Bahn line (the U3), the hotel prides itself on tastefully decorated bedrooms designed to make you feel at home. Most offer picture-window views of the neighborhood. Although the only meal served in the hotel is breakfast, there's an Austrian restaurant under independent management in the same building, and dozens of neighborhood eateries serving everything from pasta and pizza to American-style burgers.

INEXPENSIVE

ⓢ Hotel-Pension Museum

Museumstrasse 3, A-1070 Vienna. ☎ **0222/523-44-26-0.** Fax 0222/523-44-26-30. 15 rms. TV TEL. 1,100–1,600 AS ($104.50–$152) double. Rates include breakfast. AE, MC, V. Parking 150 AS ($14.25). U-Bahn: Volkstheater.

This hotel was originally built in the 17th century as the home of an aristocratic family. But its facade was transformed around 1890 into the elegant art nouveau look it has today. Located across from the Imperial Museums, there are plenty of palaces, museums, and monuments nearby to keep you busy for days. You'll appreciate the spacious bedrooms.

8 Josefstadt (8th District)

EXPENSIVE

Theater-Hotel In der Josefstadt

Josefstadter Strasse 22, A-1080 Vienna. ☎ **0222/405-36-48.** Fax 0222/405-14-06. 54 rms, 11 suites. A/C MINIBAR TV TEL. 1,760–2,510 AS ($167.20–$238.45) double; 3,400 AS ($323) suite. Rates include breakfast. AE, DC, MC, V. Parking 140 AS ($13.30). U-Bahn: Rathaus.

Named because of its location next to one of Vienna's most visible theaters (Theater in der Josefstadt), this hotel was built from a 19th-century core that was radically modernized in the late 1980s. Today it's a favorite of Austrian business travelers, who profit from the hotel's proximity to the city's wholesale buying outlets. Each comfortable but simply furnished unit contains its own small but efficient kitchenette, which allows guests to save on restaurant. In addition to a cafe, the hotel also maintains a popular bar and restaurant, the Theater-Restaurant, which is especially busy before and after performances next door.

INEXPENSIVE

⑤ Hotel Graf Stadion

Burchfeldgasse 5, A-1080 Vienna. ☎ **0222/405-52-84.** Fax 0222/405-01-11-84. 40 rms. TV TEL. 1,100–1,450 AS ($104.50–$137.75) double; 1,400 AS ($133) triple; 1,800 AS ($171) quad. Rates include buffet breakfast. AE, MC, V. U-Bahn: Rathaus.

This is one of the few genuine Biedermeier-style hotels left in Vienna. It's located right behind the Rathaus, within a 10-minute walk from most of the central monuments. The facade evokes the building's early 19th-century elegance, with triangular or half-rounded ornamentation above many of the windows. The bedrooms (36 doubles and 4 singles) have been refurnished.

Hotel Rathaus

Lange Gasse 13, A-1080 Vienna. ☎ **0222/406-43-02.** Fax 0222/408-42-72. 40 rms. (36 with bath). TV TEL. 1,080 AS ($102.60) double with bath. Rates include breakfast. No credit cards. Parking 150 AS ($14.25). U-Bahn: Rathaus. Bus: 13.

You enter the Hotel Rathaus through a wrought-iron gate. The bedrooms are simple and functional, but some of the singles are without baths. This is a no-frills place, but because it's so well situated near the university and Parliament, and because its prices are so reasonable, we consider it a worthy choice.

Pension Zipser

Lange Gasse 49, A-1080 Vienna. ☎ **0222/404-54-0.** Fax 0222/408-52-666-13. 47 rms. TV TEL. 900–1,420 AS ($85.50–$134.90) double. Rates include breakfast. AE, DC, MC, V. Parking 180 AS ($17.10). U-Bahn: Rathaus. Bus: 13A.

A five-minute walk from the Rathaus, this pension offers rooms with wall-to-wall carpeting and central heating, many overlooking a private garden. Much of the renovated interior is tastefully adorned with wood detailing. Bedrooms are furnished in a functional and modern style, with some opening onto balconies above the garden.

Impressions

Östlich von Wien, fängt der Orient an. [East of Vienna, the Orient begins.]
—Prince Metternich (attrib.)

9   Alsergrund (9th District)

MODERATE

Hotel Regina

Rooseveltplatz 15, A-1090 Vienna. ☎ **0222/42-76-81.** Fax 0222/40-88-392. 125 rms, 10 suites. MINIBAR TV TEL. 1,900 AS ($180.50) double; 2,600–3,200 AS ($247–$304) suite. Rates include breakfast. AE, DC, MC, V. Parking 250 AS ($23.75). U-Bahn: Schottenring. Tram: 38, 40, or 41.

Established in 1896 near the Votive Church, this hotel has a structure that every Viennese would instantly recognize—the "Ringstrasse" style. The facade is appropriately grand, and looks a lot like a French Renaissance palace. The tree-lined street is usually calm, especially at night. The Regina is an old-world hotel with red salons and interminable corridors. Bedrooms are well maintained and furnished in a traditional style. Fully renovated in 1993, the hotel rises five floors and contains two elevators, a restaurant, a cafe, and a bar.

Hotel Bellevue

Althanstrasse 5, A-1091 Vienna. ☎ **0222/31-348.** Fax 0222/31348-801. 161 rms, 12 suites. MINIBAR TV TEL. 1,810–2,200 AS ($171.95–$209) double; 3,100 AS ($294.50) suite. Rates include breakfast. AE, DC, MC, V. Parking 100 AS ($9.50). U-Bahn: Friedensbrücke. Tram: 5 or D.

The ornate sandstone facade of this hotel was built in 1873, at about the same time as the Franz-Josefs Bahnhof, which lies a short walk away and whose passengers it was designed to house. Its wedge-shaped position on the acute angle of a busy street corner evokes the Flatiron Building in Manhattan. The Italianate embellishments seem to converge at a point on the fifth floor, where statues of two demigods support the corner of the roofline.

Most of the antique details have been stripped from the public rooms, leaving a clean series of lines and a limited handful of antiques. At least 100 of the hotel's bedrooms are in a new wing that was added to the establishment's antique core in 1982. Regardless of their location within the hotel, all bedrooms are clean, functional, and comfortable. Rooms are decorated in monochromatic color schemes of brown or blue and contain low beds, and utilitarian desks and chairs. Facilities include a sauna and solarium, laundry, baby-sitting facilities, and room service. The hotel maintains its own restaurant and cafe, serving standard Viennese and international cuisine.

Hotel Albatros

Liechtensteinstrasse 89, A-1090 Vienna. ☎ **0222/34-35-08.** Fax 0222/34-35-08-85. 70 rms. A/C MINIBAR TV TEL. 1,880 AS ($178.60) double. Rates include breakfast. AE, DC, MC, V. Parking 150 AS ($14.25). U-Bahn: Friedensbrücke. Tram: D.

This eight-floor hotel was built in 1971 and lies near the U.S. Embassy and the Franz-Josefs Bahnhof, a 10-minute tram ride north of the Rathaus on Ringstrasse. If you associate an albatross with bad luck, you'll need to change your thinking about this one. The comfortable bedrooms are cheerfully decorated, clean, and well furnished. The hotel also offers an indoor steam room and sauna, plus room service and laundry. The hotel restaurant Albatros, serves Viennese and international fare.

10 Near Schönbrunn

EXPENSIVE

Hotel Kaiserpark-Schönbrunn
Grünbergstrasse 11, A-1120 Vienna. ☎ **0222/813-86-10.** Fax 0222/813-81-83. 54 rms.
A/C TV TEL. 1,700 AS ($161.50) double. Rates include breakfast. AE, DC, MC, V. U-Bahn:
Schönbrunn. Tram: 52 or 58. Bus: 15A.

Not everyone can walk out his or her front door and stare immediately at Schönbrunn Palace and its glorious gardens, but if you stay here that's precisely what you'll
do. This elegant hotel is outfitted with dark paneling and red velvet. The bedrooms
are as comfortable as you'd expect from such a quality establishment. A public swimming pool in Schönbrunn Park is just a short walk away, and a tram will take you
into the center of Vienna in seven minutes.

✪ Parkhotel Schönbrunn
Hietzinger Hauptstrasse 10-20, A-1131 Vienna. ☎ **800/223-5652** in the U.S., or 0222/87-804.
Fax 0222/87-804-3220. 435 rms, 4 suites. MINIBAR TV TEL. 2,550 AS ($242.25) double;
4,500 AS ($427.50) suite. Viktoria annex, 1,550 AS ($147.25) double. Rates include breakfast.
AE, DC, JCB, MC, V. Parking 140 AS ($13.30). U-Bahn: Hietzing. Tram: 58 or 60.

Called the "guesthouse of the kaisers," this four-star hotel, $1^1/_2$ miles from the
Westbahnhof, 3 miles from the City Air Terminal, is today part of the Steigenberger
reservations system. It has had a long history since Franz Joseph I ordered its construction in 1907. Here the first performances of *Loreleyklänge* by Johann Strauss Sr.,
and of *Die Schönbrunner,* the famous waltz by Josef Lanner, took place. During its
heyday, guests ranged from Thomas Edison to Walt Disney.

Today the hotel is modern and updated, although its original core is still used for
once-elegant public rooms. Contemporary wings and annexes house many visitors
today. The newer additions include the Stöckl, Residenz, and Maximilian (the most
boring and cramped rooms), together with a villa formerly inhabited by Van Swieten,
the personal doctor of Empress Maria Theresa.

Rooms in the main building are generally more spacious and better appointed than
the annex selections which are often lackluster in decor. The well-furnished guest
rooms are done in a variety of styles ranging from classical to modern. Each accommodation is equipped with a private bath, radio and TV/VCR. An annex, the three-
star Hotel Viktoria, offers 60 well-equipped rooms, and helps make this the largest
hotel complex in Vienna. Opposite the magical Schönbrunn Castle and its park, the
Parkhotel is only a 10-minute tram ride from the Inner City.

Dining/Entertainment: Inside is a Biedermier coffeehouse, along with a series of
lavishly outfitted public salons. The Jagerstubl is traditionally decorated in forest colors. There's also a French restaurant, plus a winter-garden restaurant, a gypsy tavern,
and two bars.

Services: Room service, laundry, baby-sitting.

Facilities: Pool, fitness center, sauna, solarium.

INEXPENSIVE

Altwienerhof
Herklotzgasse 6, A-1150 Vienna. ☎ **0222/892-60-00.** Fax 0222/892-60-00-8. 21 rms (19 with
bath), 4 suites. TV TEL. 720 AS ($68.40) double without bath, 1,080 AS ($102.60) double with

bath; 1,800 AS ($171) suite. Rates include breakfast. V. Parking 100 AS ($9.50). U-Bahn: Gumpendorfer. Tram: 6, 8, or 18.

This is a highly acclaimed restaurant, one of the finest and most expensive in the city. But it's also a reasonably priced hotel, with traditionally furnished bedrooms, many of which were renovated in 1993. The place oozes with old-world charm, an atmosphere carefully nurtured by the owners, Rudolf and Ursula Kellner, and their helpful and welcoming staff. Both the singles and doubles range from those with hot and cold running water to those with private showers or baths. (See Chapter 5 on "Dining" for a complete description of the Altwienerhof restaurant.)

11 Elsewhere in Vienna

MODERATE

Hotel Maté

Ottakringer Strasse 34-36, A-1170 Vienna. ☎ **0222/40-45-50.** Fax 0222/40-45-58-88. 122 rms, 4 suites. MINIBAR TV TEL. 1,280–2,080 AS ($121.60–$197.60) double; 2,400 AS ($228) suite. Rates include breakfast. AE, MC, V. Parking 80 AS ($7.60). Tram: 44.

Built in 1973 by members of the Matejovsky family, this hotel rises seven stories and has rows of decorative geometric designs along a streamlined facade. The public rooms make ample use of handcrafted hardwood planks which are fastened together for unusual visual effects. There's a bar area lined with marble, an indoor swimming pool which rests under a roof that's shaped into a continuous barrel vault. The bedrooms are comfortable and cozy, with soundproofed windows, and benefit from a renovation completed in 1994. The hotel is classified four stars by the Austrian government. If you choose to stay here, you'll get a comforting sense that this hotel is run by a group of cooperative family members.

A short walk from the hotel is a less expensive three-star hotel **Maté Dependence,** Bergsteiggasse 22 (☎ 0222/404-66) under the same management. It has 44 rooms, each with TV and telephone, and was built in the 1960s. Breakfast is the only meal served. A double costs 1,480 AS ($140.60) including breakfast.

Dining 5

In Vienna, where eating out is a local pastime, you'll find restaurants of all types, serving not only Austrian and French cuisine, but Serbian, Slovenian, Slovakian, Hungarian, and Czech as well, along with Chinese, Italian, and Russian. Before dining out, refer to the section on Austrian cuisine, "From Wiener Schnitzel to Apfel-Strudel," in Chapter 1.

MEALS & DINING CUSTOMS

Although Viennese meals are traditionally big and hearty, innovative chefs throughout the city are now turning out lighter versions of the old classics. Even so, the Viennese still love to eat, often as many as six times a day. Breakfast usually consists of bread with butter, jam, or cheese along with milk and coffee. Around 10 o'clock it's time for *gabelfrühstück* (fork breakfast) when diners usually savor some type of meat, perhaps little finger sausages. Lunch at midday is normally a filling repast, and the afternoon *jause* consists of coffee, open-face sandwiches, and, if desired, the luscious cakes that Viennese cooks make so well. Dinners may also be hearty, although many locals prefer a light meal then.

Because Vienna cherishes its theaters, concert halls, and opera houses, many locals choose to dine after a performance. *Après-théâtre* is all the rage in this city, and many restaurants and cafés deliberately stay open late to cater to this entourage of cultural buffs.

Unlike many western European capitals, Vienna's restaurants still heed to Sunday closings (marked by SONNTAG RUHETAG signs). Also beware of those summer holiday closings, when chefs would rather rush to nearby lake resorts rather than cook for Vienna's visiting hordes. Sometimes vacation closings are announced only a week or two before the restaurant actually shuts down.

HOW WE'VE ORGANIZED THIS CHAPTER

The restaurants below are listed first by location and then by price according to the following guide: **Very Expensive**—more than 550 AS ($52.25); **Expensive**—350 to 550 AS ($33.25 to $52.25); **Moderate**—200 to 350 AS ($19 to $33.25) and **Inexpensive**—less than 200 AS ($19). Prices are based on dinner for one, excluding drinks but including tax and tip.

1 Best Bets

- **Best Spot for a Romantic Dinner:** The **Sacher Hotel Restaurant** (☎ 0222/514-560) is a showcase for imperial Vienna. Franz Joseph's favorite dish was Tafelspitz, a delectable boiled beef dinner that's still served daily here, along with various Viennese and international dishes that are deftly crafted from the finest ingredients. Of course, you'll naturally want to finish your elegant repast with the fabled Sacher international acclaim.
- **Best Spot for a Business Lunch:** Most afternoons you'll find the movers and shakers of Vienna at **Korso bei Der Oper** (☎ 0222/51-516-546) in the Hotel Bristol. The refined menu features Viennese/International cuisine, and business can be conducted with the assurance of good food and impeccable service, which is never obtrusive if you're trying to firm up that deal.
- **Best Spot for a Celebration:** When you want to take your significant other or a close group of friends to a special place, **Altwienerhof** (☎ 0222/892-60-00), serving Austrian/French cuisine, is a discriminating choice. Once a private home in the 1870s, it's been transformed into one of the city's premier restaurants. Of course, if it's a real celebration, you'll order champagne, but if not, you'll find one of Vienna's largest wine cellars here.
- **Best Decor:** At **Steirereck** (☎ 0222/713-3168), which means "corner of Styria," the decor is pristine and pure, with original beams and archways transplanted from an old Styrian castle. Murals also add to the elegant, yet cozy ambience, but it's still the food that brings most guests here.
- **Best Wine List:** There are far more elegant restaurants in Vienna and far better places serving haute cuisine, but the wine list at **Wein-Comptoir** (☎ 0222/51-21-760) is tops. Wines are mostly Austrian and reflect the best vintages from every province. Some discriminating diners come just for the wine. If you're seeking really expensive vintages, then head for the Steirereck (see above) instead.
- **Best Value:** If you're seeking a reliable Austrian/International kitchen, and don't want to go broke sampling its wares, head for the **Hotel Astoria Restaurant** (☎ 0222/515-771-72). This time-honored favorite retains the authentic *Jugenstil* (art nouveau) look of its past, and is an elegant spot to sample moderately priced, Old Viennese cooking.
- **Best for Kids:** When your kids rebel against sauerkraut and sausage, take them to **Spaghetti Factory** (☎ **0222/519-79-55**) for a spaghetti "fix." It's one of the most reasonably priced restaurants in town, and the chefs offer 21 different varieties of pasta, even some exotic variations for parents. There's also a wide selection of desserts.
- **Best Viennese Cuisine:** If the empire were ever to be restored in Austria, you'd want to take the new Kaiser to **Drei Husaren** (☎ 0222/512-10-92). Expect an impeccably prepared meal containing the finest ingredients. Antiques and abundant flowers add to the elegant setting, but it is the delectable menu itself that wins favor, including a nightly repertoire of some 35 hors d'oeuvres.
- **Best Continental Cuisine:** The **Gottfried Restaurant** (☎ 0222/713-82-56) has taken Vienna to some new culinary heights. Dishes are delicately flavored and crafted from the finest produce on the market. Although many dishes are innovative, the chefs are strongly grounded in the traditions of the continental kitchen.
- **Best Italian Cuisine:** Homemade pastas in savory sauces are served at **Firenze Enoteca** (☎0222/513-43-74), which lies in the heart of Vienna, near St. Stephan's Cathedral. Most of the food is Tuscany-inspired, but other regions of Italy are represented. Be sure to complement dinner with a bottle of classic Chianti.

- **Best Hungarian Cuisine:** If you can't visit neighboring Budapest, you can get a good preview of Hungarian fare at **Kardos** (☎0222-512-69-49). Try all the Gypsy *schmaltz* favorites, including fish soup in the style of Lake Balaton.

- **Best Seafood:** The freshest seafood in Vienna—flown in either from the North Sea or the Bosphorus—is served in the center of town at **Kervansaray und Hummer Bar** (☎0222/51-28-843). You might begin with a salmon caviar cocktail, and later sample Vienna's finest lobster catch.

- **Best for Game:** In a land of hunters, wild game is still very popular among the Viennese who flock to **Sailer** (☎ 0222/479-21-210). The chefs here prepare such dishes as wild boar, pheasant, and partridge—all according to time-honored recipes.

- **Best Place for Wiener Schnitzel:** The most classic Viennese dish—perhaps even more famous than tafelspitz—is Wiener schnitzel, a local, legendary version of a breaded veal cutlet. At **Figmüller** (☎ 0222/512-61-77) the cutlet is so big it sprawls off your plate. Although it sounds like a simple dish, everyone has a favorite recipe. Old Viennese chefs, for instance, insist that true Wiener schnitzel be cooked in lard. Regardless, the Wiener schnitzel here is the one most often recommended by locals.

- **Best Desserts:** Reigning supreme among sweet tooths is **Café Demel** (☎ 0222/533-55-16), a Viennese legend. This is the place that took the Hotel Sacher to court over the right to advertise who has the recipe for the original Sachertorte, which you can still sample here. Demel also boasts Vienna's finest array of pastries and other delectable desserts like the *Gugelhupfs* or cream-filled horns.

- **Best for Late Night Dining:** Because of its location in the Hotel Bristol, which is just around the corner from the State Opera, **Rôtisserie Sirk** (☎0222/515-16-552) attracts many après-opera diners for late-night meals. Orders are taken until midnight and the menu features both Viennese and international dishes. Try the chef's specialty—three petit filets of beef, pork, and veal.

- **Best Outdoor Dining:** The **Palais Schwarzenberg Restaurant** (☎ 0222/798-45-15), in one of Vienna's most famous hotels, boasts the most beautiful dining terrace in the entire city. Classic Viennese cuisine and a stellar wine list only enhance this summer delight.

- **Best Afternoon Tea:** Located across from the Hofburg, **Café Central** (☎0222/533-37-63) is quite grand and an ideal venue for a spot of tea as the decor evokes the rich trappings of late imperial Vienna. You'll not only find a wide selection of tea (and coffee), but a rich variety of pastries and desserts.

- **Best Brunch:** In a style that would have impressed Maria Theresa herself, **Café Imperial** (☎0222/50-110-389), in the Hotel Imperial, prepares an outstanding breakfast buffet on Sundays, beginning at 7am. After brunch and a little champagne, the day is yours!

- **Best Restaurant with Music:** To a true Viennese, a meal is not a meal without music. At **Wiener Rathauskeller** (☎0222/405-12-190), in City Hall, you'll enjoy all the schnitzel and sauerkraut you've ever desired while listening to virtual musical *soirees* that begin at 8pm nightly. Live musicians ramble through the world of operetta, waltz, and *Schrammerl.*

- **Best Picnic Fare:** Head for the **Naschmarkt,** the open-air food market that's a five-minute stroll from the Karlsplatz. Here you can gather all the ingredients for a spectacular picnic and then head for the Stadtpark, the Volksgarten, or even an excursion into the Vienna Woods.

2 Restaurants by Cuisine

AUSTRIAN

Altwienerhof (Near Schönbrunn, *VE*)
Augustinerkeller (Inner City, *I*)
Glacisbeisel (Neubau, *I*)
Griechenbeisl (Inner City, *M*)
Hotel Astoria Restaurant
(Inner City, *M*)
Leupold's Kupferdachl
(Inner City, *E*)
Piaristenkeller (Josefstadt, *M*)
Restaurant Fischerhaus
(Vienna Woods, *E*)
Sacher Hotel Restaurant
(Inner City, *VE*)
Sailer (Gersthof, *M*)
Steirereck (Landstrasse, *VE*)
Wein-Comptoir (Inner City, *I*)

BALKAN

Bukarest (Inner City, *I*)
Dubrovnik (Inner City, *I*)
Kardos (Inner City, *M*)

CLASSICAL VIENNESE

Palais Schwarzenberg Restaurant
(Landstrasse, *E*)

COFFEEHOUSES, TEA ROOMS & CAFES

Café Central (Inner City)
Café Demel (Inner City)
Café Dommayer (Near Schönbrunn)
Café Imperial (Inner City)
Café Landtmann (Inner City)
Café Leopold Hawelka (Inner City)
Café Tirolerhof (Inner City)
Café/Restaurant Prückel (Inner City)
Demmer's Teehaus (Inner City)

CONTINENTAL

Gottfried Restaurant
(Landstrasse, *VE*)

CROATIAN

Dubrovnik (Inner City, *I*)

DELI

Dö & Co. (Inner City, *M*)

FRENCH

Altwienerhof (Near Schönbrunn, *VE*)

HUNGARIAN

Alte Backstube (Josefstadt, *I*)
Kardos (Inner City, *M*)

INTERNATIONAL

Arcadia Restaurant (Landstrasse, *VE*)
Bohème (Neubau, *M*)
Drei Husaren (Inner City, *VE*)
Franz Zimmer Schubertstuberln
(Inner City, *M*)
Hotel Astoria Restaurant
(Inner City, *M*)
König von Ungarn (Inner City, *VE*)
Korso bei Der Oper (Inner City, *VE*)
Motto (Margareten, *M*)
Niky's Kuchlmasterei
(Landstrasse, *M*)
Restaurant Fischerhaus
(Vienna Woods, *E*)
Rotisserie Sirk (Inner City, *M*)
Sacher Hotel Restaurant
(Inner City, *VE*)
Wiener Rathauskeller
(Inner City, *M*)
Wein-Comptoir (Inner City, *I*)
Zum Schwarzen Kameel
(Inner City, *I*)

ITALIAN

Firenze Enoteca (Inner City, *M*)

PASTA

Spaghetti Factory
(Inner City, *I*)

ROMANIAN

Bukarest (Inner City, *I*)

RUSSIAN

Abend-Restaurant Fuervogel
(Alsergrund, *M*)

SANDWICHES

Buffet Trzesniewski
(Inner City, *I*)

Key to Abbreviations: *E*=Expensive, *I*=Inexpensive, *M*=Moderate, *VE*=Very Expensive

SEAFOOD
Kernansaray und Hummer Bar
(Inner City, *VE*)

TUSCAN
Firenze Enoteca (Inner City, *M*)

VEGETARIAN
Siddhartha (Inner City, *I*)

VIENNESE
Alte Backstube (Josefstadt, *I*)
Altes Jägerhaus (Leopoldstadt, *I*)
Bohème (Neubau, *M*)
Drei Husaren (Inner City, *VE*)
Dubrovnik (Inner City, *I*)
Figlmüller (Inner City, *I*)
Franz Zimmer Schubertstüberln
(Inner City, *M*)
Glacisbeisel (Neubau, *I*)
Gösser Bierklinik (Inner City, *I*)
Gottfried Restaurant
(Landstrasse, *VE*)
Hauswirth (Neubau, *E*)

König von Ungarn (Inner City, *VE*)
Korso bei Der Oper (Inner City, *VE*)
Leupold's Kupferdachl
(Inner City, *E*)
Loft (Mariahilf, *I*)
Niky's Kuchlmasterei
(Landstrasse, *M*)
Ofenloch (Inner City, *I*)
Raimundstüberl (Mariahilf, *M*)
Rotisserie Sirk (Inner City, *M*)
Sacher Hotel Restaurant
(Inner City, *VE*)
Sailer (Gersthof, *M*)
Schlossgasse 21 (Margareten, *M*)
Silberwirt (Maragareten, *I*)
Steirereck (Landstrasse, *VE*)
Wiener Rathauskeller
(Inner City, *M*)
Wienerwald (Inner City, *I*)
Zum Weissen Rauchfangkehrer
(Inner City, *I*)
Zwölf-Apostelkeller
(Inner City, *I*)

3 Innere Stadt (Inner City)

VERY EXPENSIVE

Kervansaray und Hummer Bar

Mahlerstrasse 9. ☎ **0222/51-28-843.** Reservations recommended. Kervansaray, main courses 200–300 AS ($19–$28.50). Hummer Bar, main courses 295–450 AS ($28.05–$42.75). AE, DC, MC, V. Mon–Sat noon–1am. U-Bahn: Karlsplatz. Tram: 1 or 2. Bus: 3A. SEAFOOD.

Here you'll sense the historic link between the Habsburgs and their 19th-century neighbor, the Ottoman Empire. This is actually a three-in-one place. In addition to the two restaurants, there's also a deli. The Kervansaray and Hummer Bar (Lobster Bar) occupy two different floors, but each serves an array of delectable seafood flown in frequently from the North Sea or the Bosphorus.

On the ground floor, in the Kervansaray, polite waiters, many of whom are Turkish, announce a changing array of daily specials and serve tempting salads from an hors d'oeuvre table. Upstairs, guests enjoy the bounties of the sea at the Lobster Bar.

A meal often begins with a champagne cocktail, followed by one of many appetizers, including a lobster and salmon caviar cocktail. The menu has a short list of meat dishes like filet mignon with Roquefort sauce, but most entrees feature seafood, including grilled filet of sole with fresh asparagus, Norwegian salmon with a horseradish and champagne sauce, and, of course, lobster. If shellfish is your weakness, tabs can run very high indeed.

König von Ungarn (King Of Hungary)

Schulerstrasse 10. ☎ **0222/512-53-19.** Reservations required. Main courses 250–350 AS ($23.75–$33.25); fixed-price menu 450 AS ($42.75) at lunch, 700 AS ($66.50) at dinner. MC. Sun–Fri noon–2:30pm and 6–10:30 pm. U-Bahn: Stephansplatz. Bus: 1A. VIENNESE/INTERNATIONAL.

Vienna Dining

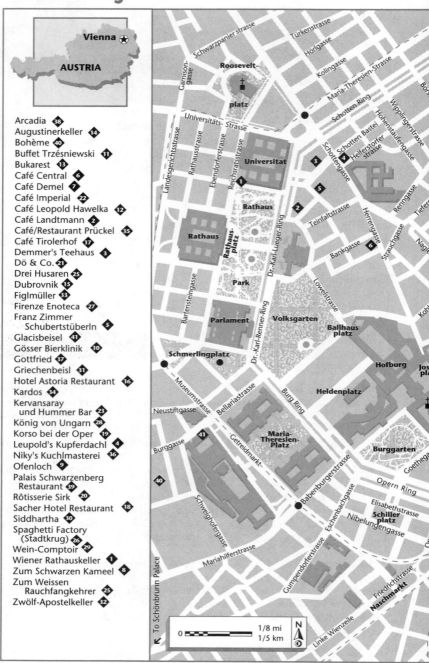

9111

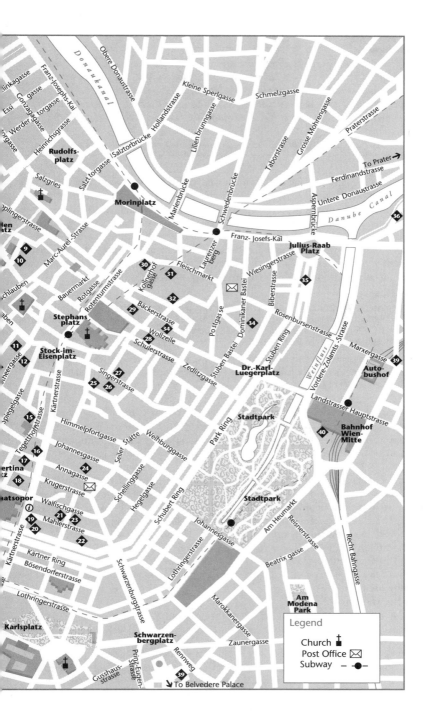

Housed by the famous hotel of the same name, this restaurant evokes a rich atmosphere with crystal chandeliers, antiques, marble columns, and vaulted ceilings. The service here is superb and the menu appealing. If you're unsure of what to order, try the tafelspitz, a savory boiled-beef specialty, elegantly dispensed from a trolley. Other choices, which change seasonally, include a ragoût of seafish with fresh mushrooms, tournedos of beef with a mustard-and-horseradish sauce, and an array of appetizers like scampi in caviar sauce. Chefs balance flavors, textures, and colors to create a cuisine long favored by locals, who often bring out-of-town guests here.

✪ Drei Husaren

Weihburggasse 4. ☎ **0222/512-10-92.** Reservations required. Main courses 255–395 AS ($24.25–$37.55); *menu dégustation* (six courses) 880 AS ($83.60); fixed-price four-course business lunch 390 AS ($37.05). AE, DC, MC, V. Daily noon–3pm and 6–11 pm. Closed mid-July to mid-Aug. U-Bahn: Stephansplatz. VIENNESE/INTERNATIONAL.

This establishment is an enduring favorite for inventive and classic Viennese cuisine. Some consider it as much an institution as St. Stephan's Cathedral, which looms nearby. Few social or business moguls would consider a trip to Vienna without dining here. Over the years it has entertained the famous (the Duke and Duchess of Windsor) and the not-so-famous. Just off Kärntnerstrasse, it has a large plate-glass window with plaster mannequins of the Hungarian officers who established the restaurant after World War I. A look inside reveals Gobelin tapestries, antiques, fine rugs, and lots of flowers. The owner, Uwe Kohl, is perhaps the most gracious restaurant host in Vienna.

Drei Huseran is expensive and select, with a delectable cuisine rated by most as the best traditional food in Vienna. Enjoy Gypsy melodies while you savor lobster-cream soup with tarragon, freshwater salmon with pike soufflé, or breast of guinea fowl. The chef specializes in veal, including his deliciously flavored *kalbsbrücken Metternich.* A renowned repertoire of more than 35 hors d'oeuvres is served from a roving trolley, but, if you choose to indulge, your bill is likely to double as the hors d'oeuvres aren't priced. Finish with the Husaren pfannkuchen (Hussar's pancake), or the cheese-filled crêpe topped with chocolate sauce, a secret recipe that's been a favorite since the 1960s.

Korso bei Der Oper

In the Bristol Hotel, Mahlerstrasse 2. ☎ **0222/51-516-546.** Reservations required. Main courses 250–390 AS ($23.75–$37.05); fixed-price menu 390 AS ($37.05) at lunch, 630–780 AS ($59.85–$74.10) at dinner. AE, DC, MC, V. Sun–Fri noon–2pm; daily 7–11pm. Closed Aug 8–28. U-Bahn: Karlsplatz. Tram: 1 or 2. VIENNESE/INTERNATIONAL.

This citadel of gastronomic chic contains expensive paneling, sparkling chandeliers, and—flanking either side of a baronial fireplace—two of the most breathtaking baroque columns in Vienna. Set in the elegant Bristol Hotel, the restaurant has its own entrance directly across from the State Opera, a position that has always attracted a legendary clientele of opera stars, including Leonard Bernstein, Plácido Domingo, and Agnes Baltza.

The kitchen concocts an alluring mixture of traditional and modern cuisine for discriminating palates. Your meal may feature filet of char with a sorrel sauce, saddle of veal with cèpe mushrooms and homemade noodles, or the inevitable tafelspitz. The rack of lamb is excellent as are the medaillons of beef with a shallot-flavored butter sauce and Roquefort-flavored noodles. The wine list here is extensive, and the service, as you'd expect, is impeccable.

✪ Sacher Hotel Restaurant

Philharmonikerstrasse 4. ☎ **0222/514-560.** Reservations required. Main courses 250–380 AS ($23.75–$36.10); fixed-price menu 580 AS ($55.10). AE, DC, MC, V. Daily noon–2:30pm and 6–11pm. U-Bahn: Karlsplatz. AUSTRIAN/VIENNESE/INTERNATIONAL.

Most celebrities who visit Vienna can eventually be seen in this scarlet dining room, where they're likely to order the restaurant's most famous dish, tafelspitz. The chef at Sacher prepares the boiled beef ensemble with a savory, herb-flavored sauce that is truly fit for the Emperor's table. Other delectable dishes include fish terrine and veal steak with morels. For dessert, the Sachertorte enjoys world renown. It's primarily a chocolate sponge cake that's sliced in half and filled with apricot jam. The most famous pastry in Vienna, the torte was supposedly created in 1832 by Franz Sacher while he served as Prince Metternich's apprentice.

Wear your finest dining attire, and make sure to show up before 11pm, even though the restaurant officially closes at 1am. Despite the adherence to form and protocol here, latecomers will never go hungry as the hotel maintains tables in the adjoining and less formal Red Bar, where the menu is available every day from noon to 11:30pm (last order). The Sacher has always been a favorite for dinner either before or after the opera.

EXPENSIVE

Leupold's Kupferdachl

Schottengasse 7. ☎ **0222/533-93-81.** Reservations recommended. Main course 200–280 AS ($19–$26.60). AE, DC, MC, V. Mon–Fri 10am–3pm; Mon–Sat 6pm–midnight. U-Bahn: Schottentor 7. Tram: 2, 43, or 44. VIENNESE/AUSTRIAN.

Run by the Leupold family since the 1950s, this eatery serves "new Austrian" cuisine, but the chef does prepare traditional dishes. Some reputable menu items are beef tenderloin (Old Viennese style) with dumplings boiled in a napkin, lamb loin breaded and served with potatoes, and chicken breast Kiev. The interior is both rustic and elegant, decorated with Oriental rugs and cozy banquettes with intricate straight-back chairs. Leupold also operates a beer pub, with good music and better prices. A large beer begins at 38 AS ($3.60), and you can order a big salad for 78 AS ($7.40). The pub is open daily from 10am to midnight.

MODERATE

Dö & Co.

Akademiestrasse 3. ☎ **0222/512-64-74.** Reservations recommended for one of the tables. Main courses 155–245 AS ($14.75–$23.30). AE, DC, MC, V. Mon–Fri 10:30 am–7:30 pm, Sat 9:30 am–3pm. U-Bahn: Karlsplatz. DELI.

Located next to the State Opera, this sophisticated delicatessen is connected by a corridor to the Kervansaray und Hummer Bar (see above). Sprawling glass display cases are filled with pâtés, seafood salads, quiches, Viennese pastries, and more. Try one of the three shrimp platters or a portion of Norwegian lobster Thermidor.

Customers can take their foodstuffs with them or sit at one of the tiny, somewhat-cramped tables near the entrance. The place is likely to be packed, especially at lunchtime, with demanding gastronomes willing to sacrifice space and ambience for a taste of the good life. The deli has extended its facilities to include two more restaurants: one is directly across from St. Stephan's Cathedral and the other has been named the official restaurant of Schönbrunn Palace.

Firenze Enoteca

Singerstrasse 3. ☎ **0222/513-43-74.** Reservations recommended. Main courses 100–350 AS ($9.50–$33.25). AE, DC, MC, V. Daily noon–2pm and 6–11pm. U-Bahn: Stephansplatz. TUSCAN/ITALIAN.

This is Vienna's premier Italian restaurant. In the heart of the monument quarter, near St. Stephan's Cathedral and next to the Royal Hotel, it's furnished in Tuscan Renaissance style, with copies of frescoes by Benozzo Gozzoli. The kitchen specializes in homemade pasta served with zesty sauces. According to the chef, the cuisine is "80% Tuscan, 20% from the rest of Italy." Start with selections from the antipasti table, then choose among dishes like spaghetti with "fruits of the sea," penne with salmon, veal cutlet with ham, cheese, and sardines, or perhaps filet mignon in a tomato-garlic sauce. Be sure to complement any meal here with a classic bottle of Chianti.

Franz Zimmer Schubertstüberln

Schreyvogelgasse 4. ☎ **0222/533-71-87.** Reservations recommended. Main courses 100–350 AS ($9.50–$33.25); fixed-price menu 450 AS ($42.75). DC, MC, V. Mon–Fri 11am–3pm and 6–11:30pm. U-Bahn: U2, Schottentor. Tram: 1, 2, or D. VIENNESE/INTERNATIONAL.

Established in the 1960s by its namesake, Franz Zimmer, this restaurant occupies a 600-year-old building on a quiet street near the Burgtheater. In summer, dining tables are set on a raised platform above the cobblestones and rows of begonias provide a garden-like atmosphere. Standing outside, you'd never believe that there's a sprawling interior with a modern bar and a labyrinth of small dining rooms. The least formal room is the Bistro, where prices, business hours, and menu items are the same, although the usual cover charge of 40 AS ($3.80) per person is not levied. Austrian politicians, many of whom *kibitz* over lunch or dinner here with constituents, have always loved it. Menu items include Hungarian fish soup; filet Stroganoff with Rösti; filet of veal "Old Vienna," served with a goose-liver and sour-cream sauce; and a cheese strudel for dessert.

⊗ Griechenbeisl

Fleischmarkt 11. ☎ **0222/533-19-77** or 0222/533-19-47. Reservations required. Main courses 165–225 AS ($15.70–$21.40); fixed-price menu 270–445 AS ($25.65–$42.30). AE, DC, MC, V. Daily 11am–1am (last orders at 11:30pm). Tram: N or Z. AUSTRIAN.

Griechenbeisl was established in 1450 and is still one of the city's leading restaurants. There's a maze of dining areas on three different floors, all with low vaulted ceilings, smoky paneling, and wrought-iron chandeliers. Watch out for the Styrian-vested waiters who scurry around the building with large trays of food. As you enter from the street, look down at the grate under your feet for an illuminated view of a pirate counting his money. As you go in, be sure to look for the so-called inner sanctum, with signatures of former patrons like Mozart, Beethoven, and Mark Twain.

The Pilsen beer is well chilled and the food is categorized as *Bürgerlich*—hearty, ample, and solidly bourgeois. Menu items include deer stew, Hungarian and Viennese gulasch, sauerkraut garni, and venison steak. As an added treat, the restaurant also features nighttime accordion and zither music.

Hotel Astoria Restaurant

Kärntnerstrasse 32 (entrance at Führichgasse 1). ☎ **0222/515-771-72.** Main courses 185–275 AS ($17.60–$26.15). AE, DC, MC, V. Mon–Fri noon–3pm and 6–9pm. Closed July 1–Aug 23. U-Bahn: Karlsplatz or Stephansplatz. AUSTRIAN/INTERNATIONAL.

The first-floor restaurant inside the Hotel Astoria (see Chapter 4, "Accommodations") dates from 1911 and remains the premier authentic *Jugendstil* dining room in Vienna. The foyer is lined with portraits of opera stars, and a handsome marble fireplace enhances the grandiose decor. They offer a varied opera menu which is served both before and after performances at the nearby Staatsoper. Typical dishes include tafelspitz, saddle of veal, and tournedos with morel sauce. The recipes are tried-and-true from the Old Vienna kitchen, so don't expect much in the way of innovation here.

Kardos

Dominikaner Bastei 8. ☎ **0222/512-69-49.** Reservations recommended. Main courses 100–220 AS ($9.50–$20.90). AE, MC, V. Tues–Sat 11am–2:30pm and 6–11pm. U-Bahn: U2, U4; Schwedenplatz. HUNGARIAN/BALKAN.

This restaurant specializes in the strong flavors and mixed grills of the Great Hungarian Plain, turning out traditional specialties like fish soup in the style of Lake Balaton, piquant little rolls known as grammel that are seasoned with minced pork and spices, and a choice of grilled meats. The atmospheric cellar is filled with pinewood accents and brightly-colored Hungarian accessories that create a sense of Gypsy *schmaltz.* During the winter months, you're likely to find a strolling violinist. Your meal might be preceded with a glass of *barack,* an apéritif made from fermented apricots.

Rotisserie Sirk

In the Hotel Bristol, Kärntnerstrasse 53. ☎ **022/515-16-552.** Reservations recommended. Main courses 200–300 AS ($19–$28.50). AE, DC, MC, V. Restaurant, daily noon–2:30pm and 6–11:30pm. Café, daily 10am–midnight. Closed July. U-Bahn: Karlsplatz. VIENNESE/INTERNATIONAL.

This modern restaurant prepares conservative but flavorful dishes with flair and gusto, and offers good value, especially when compared to other higher-priced citadels near the Opera House. On the lower street level you'll see an art nouveau cafe, complete with rich pastries, beveled glass, and picturesque windows.

However, most diners head straight to the second floor, where a traditional three-course opera supper is offered nightly. Specialties include "3 Kleine Filets" (beef, pork, and veal) served with mushrooms, spinach, and a pepper-cream sauce; crispy roast duck with red cabbage and bread dumplings; and medaillons of venison in a goose-liver sauce. The food, although hardly the best in Vienna, is consistently well-prepared.

Wiener Rathauskeller

Rathausplatz 1. ☎ **0222/405-12-190.** Reservations required. Main courses 90–240 AS ($8.55–$22.80); Vienna music evening with dinner (Tues–Sat at 8pm) 390 AS ($37.05). AE, DC, MC, V. Mon–Sat 11:30am–3pm and 6–11pm. U-Bahn: Rathaus. VIENNESE/INTERNATIONAL.

City halls throughout the Teutonic world have traditionally maintained restaurants in their basements, and Vienna is no exception. Although its famous Rathaus was built between 1871 and 1883, its cellar-level restaurant wasn't added until 1899. Today, in half a dozen richly atmospheric dining rooms, you'll enjoy the high vaulted ceilings and stained-glass windows of their neo-Gothic heyday, as well as good and reasonably priced food. The chef's specialty is a Rathauskellerplatte for two, consisting of various cuts of meat, including a veal schnitzel, lamb cutlets, and pork medaillons. One section of the cellar is devoted every evening to a Viennese

musical *soirée* beginning at 8pm. Live musicians ramble through the world of operetta, waltz, and *Schrammel* music—suitable entertainment as you dine. If you prefer to eat à la carte, or just have a drink and a salad, the price of the show without
food is 140 AS ($13.30).

INEXPENSIVE

Augustinerkeller

Augustinerstrasse 1. ☎ **0222/533-10-26.** Main courses 110–170 AS ($10.45–$16.15); glasses
of wine 28–32 AS ($2.65–$3.05). AE, DC, MC, V. Daily 11am–midnight. U-Bahn: Stephansplatz.
AUSTRIAN.

Since 1857 the Augustinerkeller has served wine, beer, and food from the basement
of one of the grand Hofburg palaces. It attracts a lively and diverse group of patrons
who get more and more boisterous as the *Schrammel* music is played late into the
night. Upon entering, you'll find yourself in a vaulted brick room with worn pine-
board floors and wooden banquettes. This long and narrow room is usually packed
with people and atmosphere, and often features roaming accordion players. An upstairs room looks much the same, although it's less crowded and usually doesn't have
music.

This place offers one of the best values for wine tasting in Vienna. The ground-
floor lobby lists prices of vintage local wines by the glass. Tasters can sample from
hundreds of bottles near the stand-up stainless-steel counter. Aside from the wine and
beer, the establishment serves simple food, including roast chicken on a spit, schnitzel,
and Viennese tafelspitz.

○ Buffet Trzesniewski

Dorotheergasse 1. ☎ **0222/512-32-91.** Reservations not accepted. Sandwiches 8 AS (75¢);
pastries 20 AS ($1.90). No credit cards. Mon–Fri 9am–7:30pm, Sat 9am–1pm. U-Bahn:
Stephansplatz. SANDWICHES.

Everyone in Vienna knows about this spot, from the most hurried office worker to
the most elite hostesses. Franz Kafka lived next door and used to come here for sandwiches and beer. It's unlike any buffet you've seen, with six or seven cramped tables
and a rapidly moving queue of clients who jostle for space next to the glass countertops. Indicate to the waitress the kind of sandwich you want, and if you can't read
German, just point.

Most people devour the delicious finger sandwiches, which come in 18 different
combinations of cream cheese, egg, onion, salami, mushroom, herring, green and red
peppers, tomatoes, lobster, and many other tasty ingredients. You can also order small
glasses of fruit juice, beer, or wine with your snack. If you do order a drink, the cash-
ier will give you a rubber token which you'll present to the person at the far end of
the counter.

⑤ Bukarest

Bräunerstrasse 7. ☎ **0222/512-37-63.** Reservations recommended. Main courses 80–275 AS
($7.60–$26.15). AE, DC, MC, V. Tues–Sun 11:30am–2:30pm and 6pm–11:30pm. Closed 2nd
week in Feb. U-Bahn: Stephansplatz. BALKAN/ROMANIAN.

This restaurant serves Balkan—mainly Romanian—specialties in a tunnel-like room
with old vaulting and an exposed charcoal grill. If you like this rather heavy Slavic
cuisine, this is the best in town. Specialties include Serbian bean soup, grilled sirloin
steak stuffed with chopped meat, Argentinean steak, and a Jamaican pepper-and-
garlic dish. The chef is rightly proud of his mixed grill, and his baklava is outstanding. For those who prefer to sit outside, there's a cafe in front with sidewalk tables.

Dubrovnik

Am Neumarkt 5. ☎ **0222/713-27-55.** Reservations recommended. Main courses 80–220 AS ($7.60–$20.90). AE, DC, MC, V. Daily 11am–3pm and 6pm–midnight. U-Bahn: Stadtpark. CROATIAN/BALKAN/VIENNESE.

Well-established as one of the best Yugoslav restaurants in Vienna, Dubrovnik redefined itself after the dissolution of Yugoslavia in the early 1990s and now stresses its culinary (and cultural) allegiance to Croatia. The restaurant is composed of three dining rooms on either side of a central vestibule that's filled with busy waiters in Croat costume. The menu lists a lengthy choice of Balkan dishes, including bean soup; homemade sausages; stuffed cabbage; filet of veal with boiled potatoes, sour cream, and sauerkraut; and grilled pork kidney. Among the fish dishes, the most exotic is *fogosch* (a whitefish), served with potatoes and garlic. For dessert, you should opt for baklava or, if you prefer, an assortment of Bulgarian cheeses.

⑤ Figlmüller

Wollzeile 5. ☎ **0222/512-61-77.** Reservations recommended for parties of four or more. Main courses 90–198 AS ($8.55–$18.80). No credit cards. Daily 11am–10pm. Closed Aug. U-Bahn: Stephansplatz. VIENNESE.

This restaurant is one of the most famous *beisels* (a typical Viennese tavern) in the city. A passageway leads to a room that's about 500 years old and inside you'll find the perfect setting for a good, simple Viennese meal. The Wiener schnitzel here is legendary—it's so big it spills over your plate. You'll also find an excellent selection of Viennese sausages, along with tafelspitz, fresh salads, and plenty of well-chosen wines. Expect big crowds during peak serving hours.

Gösser Bierklinik

Steindlgasse 4. ☎ **0222/535-68-97.** Reservations recommended for parties of three or more. Main courses 97–175 AS ($9.20–$16.65). AE, DC, MC, V. Mon–Sat 10am–11pm. Closed holidays. U-Bahn: Stephansplatz. Tram: 31 or 32. VIENNESE.

Also known as the *Güldene Drache* (Golden Dragon), this restaurant serves the Styrian-brewed Gösser, reportedly the finest beer in the city. It's an ancient rustic institution in a building that, according to tradition, dates from Roman times. An inn operated here in the early 16th century, when Maxmillian I ruled the empire, and so the decor is strictly Middle Ages. The waitresses are usually carrying ample mugs of Gösser beer, and are often rushed and harassed. When you finally get their attention, order up some hearty Austrian fare like veal chops with dumplings. A small mug of Gösser costs 30 AS ($2.85) and a large mug is 40 AS ($3.80).

Ofenloch

Kurrentgasse 8. ☎ **0222/533-88-44.** Reservations required. Main courses 128–255 AS ($12.15–$24.25). AE, DC, MC, V. Daily 11:30am–midnight. U-Bahn: U1, U3; Stephansplatz. Bus: 1A. VIENNESE.

The Viennese have known about this spot since the 1600s, when it functioned as a simple tavern. The present management dates from the mid-1970s, and maintains a well-deserved reputation as a nostalgic, old-fashioned eating house. Waitresses wear classic Austrian regalia, and will give you a menu that looks more like a magazine, with some amusing mock-medieval illustrations inside. The hearty soup dishes are popular, as is the schnitzel. For smaller appetites, the menu offers a variety of salads and cheese platters, plus an entire page devoted to one-dish meals, all of which go well with wine and beer. For dessert, choose from an array of old-style Viennese specialties.

Siddhartha

Fleischmarkt 16. ☎ **0222/513-11-97.** Reservations recommended for parties of three or more. Main courses 96–164 AS ($9.10–$15.60). No credit cards. Daily 11:30am–3pm and 6–11pm. U-Bahn: U2, U4; Schwedenplatz. VEGETARIAN.

Located at the end of a covered arcade in Old Vienna, this place is crowded, but clean with white stucco, candlelight, fresh flowers, and vaulted ceilings. The walls are adorned with Hindu and Buddhist art and artifacts. Only vegetarian food is served here, and it's so popular you'll be lucky to get a seat during peak hours. House specialties include ratatouille, quiche Lorraine, the "Siddhartha" combination plate for two, Roquefort crêpes, and mushrooms Romanoff. There are far better vegetarian restaurants around the world, but in Vienna, this one's the best.

Spaghetti Factory (Stadtkrug)

Weihburggasse 3-5. ☎ **0222/512-79-55.** Reservations recommended. Main courses 72–164 AS ($6.85–$15.60). AE, MC, V. Daily 11am–12:30am (last orders). U-Bahn:Stephansplatz. PASTA.

In 1994 this well-managed spaghetti house took over the site of a venerated restaurant (Stadtkrug) which had for generations been favored by visiting artists like Leonard Bernstein. After intensive renovations, a duet of dining rooms emerged in this 14th-century building. Today the place is informal, animated, and charming, offering about 21 different kinds of spaghetti. All the conventional spaghetti preparations are listed on the menu, as well as certain exotic variations such as smoked salmon in an herb cream sauce. This kid-friendly restaurant serves a wide variety of desserts, including chocolate mousse and tiramisù, and parents will find plenty of wines and beers from which to choose. During clement weather, tables are set up on the sidewalk in front.

Wein-Comptoir

Bäckerstrasse 6. ☎ **0222/51-21-760.** Reservations recommended. Main courses 125–290 AS ($11.90–$27.55). AE, DC, MC, V. Mon–Sat 5pm–2am (last orders at 1am). U-Bahn: Stephansplatz. AUSTRIAN/INTERNATIONAL.

This is one of the most charming wine-tavern restaurants in Old Vienna. You can stop by and sample a wide selection of wines, mostly Austrian, while relaxing at the street-level tables. You may also want to descend the steps into the brick-vaulted cellar, where tables are arranged for dining. Waiters hussle up and down the steep steps, serving wine and standard platters of Austrian and international food. Since most dishes are cooked to order, prepare yourself for a long wait. Full meals might include breast of venison in a goose-liver sauce, tafelspitz, or breast of pheasant with bacon. For an appetizer, try either the rich potato soup flavored with bacon bits or a terrine of pike and zander.

Wienerwald

Annagasse 3. ☎ **0222/512-37-66.** Main courses 74–175 AS ($7.05–$16.65). AE, DC, MC, V. Daily 11am–1am. U-Bahn: Stephansplatz. VIENNESE.

This is the most centrally-located branch of Vienna's largest restaurant chain, which has become so successful that they're now found all over Germany and Austria. Vienna has 20 branches alone, but most are in the suburbs. Wienerwald at Stephansplatz, like all the others, became famous for its delectable and reasonably-priced grilled chicken. The signature dish, preceded by soup, costs 136 AS ($12.90) and is the most popular menu item. However, you can also get Wiener schnitzel or chicken Cordon Bleu, and the inevitably fresh salad.

⑤ Zumm Schwarzen Kameel (Stiebitz)

Bognergasse 5. ☎ **0222/533-81-25.** Main courses 150–280 AS ($14.25–$26.60). No credit cards. Mon–Fri 9am–8pm, Sat 9am–3pm. U-Bahn: Schottentor. Bus: 2A or 3A. INTERNATIONAL.

This restaurant has remained in the same family since 1618. A delicatessen against one of the walls sells wine, liquor, and specialty meat items, although most of the action takes place among the chicly dressed clientele in the cafe. On a Saturday morning the cafe section is packed with weekend Viennese trying to recover from a late night. Uniformed waiters will bring you a beverage here and you can select open-face sandwiches from the trays on the black countertops.

Beyond the cafe is a perfectly preserved art deco dining room where jeweled copper chandeliers hang from beaded strings. The walls are a combination of polished paneling, yellowed ceramic tiles, and a dusky plaster ceiling frieze of grape leaves. The restaurant has just 11 tables, but it's a perfect place for a nostalgic lunch in Vienna. The cuisine features herring filet Oslo, potato soup, tournedos, Roman saltimbocca, and an array of daily fish specials.

Zum Weissen Rauchfangkehrer

Weihburggasse 4. ☎ **0222/512-34-71.** Reservations required. Main courses 110–205 AS ($10.45–$19.50). AE, DC, MC, V. Daily 11am–3pm and 6pm–midnight. U-Bahn: Stephansplatz. VIENNESE.

Established in the 1860s, this place is the former guildhall for Vienna's chimney sweeps. In fact the name, translated as the "white chimney sweep," comes from the story of a drunken and blackened wretch who fell into a kneading trough and woke up the next day covered in flour. The dining room here is rustic, with deer antlers, fancifully crafted chandeliers, and pine banquettes that vaguely resemble church pews. A piano in one of the inner rooms provides nighttime music and adds to the comfortable ambience. Big street-level windows let in lots of light and pieces of stained glass are also scattered among the woodwork. The menu offers Viennese fried chicken, both Tyrolean and Wiener schnitzel, wild game, veal gulasch, bratwurst, and several kinds of strudel. You'll certainly want to finish with the house specialty, a fabulously rich chocolate cream puff.

Zwölf-Apostelkeller

Sonnenfelsgasse 3. ☎ **0222/512-67-77.** Main courses 70–145 AS ($6.65–$13.80). No credit cards. Daily 4:30pm–midnight. Closed July. Tram: 1, 2, 21, D, or N. Bus: 1A. VIENNESE.

Sections of this old wine tavern's walls predate 1561. Rows of wooden tables stand under vaulted ceilings, with lighting partially provided by the streetlights that are set into the masonry floor. It's so deep that you feel you're entering a dungeon.

This place is popular with students because of its low prices and proximity to St. Stephan's. In addition to beer and wine, the establishment serves hearty Austrian fare. Specialties include Hungarian gulasch soup, meat dumplings, and a *schlachtplatte* (a selection of hot black pudding, liverwurst, pork, and pork sausage with a hot bacon-and-cabbage salad).

4 Leopoldstadt (2nd District)

INEXPENSIVE

Altes Jägerhaus

Freudenau 255. ☎ **0222/728-95-77-0.** Reservations recommended. Main courses 85–190 AS ($8.05–$18.05). No credit cards. Wed–Sun 9am to 11pm. U-Bahn: U3, Schlachthausgasse; then take Bus 77A. AUSTRIAN/GAME.

Little about the decor at this eatery has changed since it was established in 1899. Located one mile from the entrance to the Prater in a verdant park, it's a welcome escape to the more crowded restaurants of the Inner City. Select a seat in any of the four old-fashioned dining rooms, where the beverage of choice is equally divided between beer and wine. Seasonal game dishes like pheasant and venison are the house specialty, but you'll also find an array of seafood dishes that might include freshwater and saltwater trout, zander, or salmon. The menu also features a delicious repertoire of Austrian staples like tafelspitz (boiled beef) and schnitzel.

5 Landstrasse (3rd District)

VERY EXPENSIVE

Arcadia Restaurant

In the Vienna Hilton, Am Stadtpark. ☎ **0222/71-700.** Reservations recommended for dinner. Main courses 155–270 AS ($14.75–$25.65); breakfast buffet 260 AS ($24.70); lunch buffet 380 AS ($36.10); Sun brunch 460 AS ($43.70). AE, DC, MC, V. Daily 6:30am–11pm. U-Bahn: U4, Stadtpark. INTERNATIONAL.

Everything from an early business breakfast to an after-theater dinner is served here. The breakfast buffet is the most lavish in town, and at lunch a large selection of hot and cold specials, including delectable desserts and Viennese pastries, is spread out before you. In summer guests try for one of the tables on the outdoor terrace.

One section of the dinner menu is reserved for lamb, which this restaurant does exceptionally well. Start with a lamb appetizer such as smoked lamb with red-wine onions, followed by lamb from a carving trolley, perhaps a tender rack of lamb glazed with herbs. Other main courses include pan-fried filet of Norwegian salmon with chive sauce and grilled veal T-bone served with lime butter. The chef also dishes out two noteworthy classics, the famed tafelspitz (boiled beef) and a Wiener schnitzel prepared according to 19th-century traditions. Enjoy an "Austrian Steakweekend" meal for 490 AS ($46.55) Thursday through Saturday, or the famous summer barbecue for 460 AS ($43.70), prepared on the terrace with a charwood grill.

✪ Gottfried Restaurant

Untere Viaduktgasse 45 at Marxergasse 3. ☎ **0222/713-82-56.** Reservations required. Main courses 240–330 AS ($22.80–$31.35); fixed-price menu 690 AS ($65.55). AE, DC, MC, V. Tues–Sat noon–3pm and 6pm–midnight. Bus: 25A. VIENNESE/CONTINENTAL.

One of the top two or three restaurants in Vienna, the Gottfried was established in 1985 on a commercial street near the City Air Terminal. Many less successful restaurants envy its decor, which combines a perfectly controlled ambience with superb food. The pure-white walls and lace-covered windows are offset with ruby-colored Oriental carpets, pink napery, and unglazed terra-cotta floors. Add about a dozen polite and uniformed waiters, verdant plants, and comfortably contemporary armchairs covered in pastel-tinted upholstery, and you get an idea of what the Gottfried is all about.

This place seems to reach for new culinary heights, as it beautifully combines tradition with innovation. Dishes are delicately flavored and never overseasoned. Your meal might begin with potato soup with truffles carpaccio, a lobster salad with fresh asparagus, a wild duck, or a Provençal fish soup so rich it could almost be considered a relish.

✪ Steirereck

Rasumofskygasse 2. ☎ **0222/713-31-68.** Reservations required. Main courses 248–350 AS ($23.55–$33.25); three-course fixed-price lunch 395 AS ($37.55); five-course fixed-price dinner 880 AS ($83.60). AE, V. Mon–Fri 10:30am–3pm and 7pm–midnight. Closed holidays. Tram: N. Bus: 4. VIENNESE/AUSTRIAN.

Steirereck means "corner of Styria," which is exactly what Heinz and Margarethe Reitbauer have created in this intimate and rustic restaurant, which lies on the

Danube Canal between the Central Station and the Prater. The Reitbauers transplanted original beams and archways from an old castle in Styria to enhance the ambience here. Murals adorn the walls and also add to the cozy feel.

You'll find both traditional Viennese dishes and "new Austrian" selections on the menu. You might begin with a caviar-semolina dumpling, roasted turbot with fennel (served as an appetizer), or the most elegant and expensive item of all, goose-liver Steirereck. Some enticing main courses include asparagus with pigeon, saddle of lamb for two, prime Styrian roast beef, or red-pepper risotto with rabbit. The menu is wisely limited and well prepared, changing daily depending on what's fresh at the market. The restaurant is popular with after-theater diners, and patrons are invited to inspect the large wine cellar, which holds some 35,000 bottles.

EXPENSIVE

Palais Schwarzenberg Restaurant
Schwarzenbergplatz 9. ☎ **0222/798-45-15.** Reservations required. Main courses 270–420 AS ($25.65–$39.90); fixed-price business lunch 390 AS ($37.05); five-course fixed-price dinner 980 AS ($93.10). AE, DC, MC, V. Daily noon–3pm and 6:30–10pm. U-Bahn: U1, U2, U4; Karlsplatz. Tram: D. CLASSICAL VIENNESE.

Located in one of Vienna's premier hotels (see "Accommodations," in Chapter 4), The Palais Schwarzenberg, has one of the most elegant backgrounds of any restaurant in the city. It's owned by Prince Karl Johannes von Schwarzenberg, scion of one of the Austria's most aristocratic families.

Take your time over an apéritif in the deluxe cocktail lounge, where the waiter will most likely recite the daily specialties. In summer you can dine Habsburg-style on a magnificent terrace. The cuisine is refined, with many French entrees, and the chef adjusts his menu seasonally. His many specialties include filet of catfish on a ragoût of potatoes and morels with leek; medallions of venison roasted with fresh morels; and, for dessert, a chocolate-mint soufflé with passion fruit. Service is first class and very Old World, and the wine cellar is nothing less than superb.

MODERATE

Niky's Kuchlmasterei
Obere Weissgerberstrasse 6. ☎ **0222/712-90-00.** Reservations recommended. Main courses 198–300 AS ($18.80–$28.50); fixed-price menu 394 AS ($37.45) for three courses, 695 AS ($66.05) for seven courses. AE, DC, MC, V. Mon–Sat 11:30am–midnight. U-Bahn: Schwedenplatz. VIENNESE/INTERNATIONAL.

After a long and pleasant meal, your bill will arrive in an elaborate box suitable for jewels, along with an amusing message in German that offers a tongue-in-cheek apology for cashing your check. The decor features old stonework with some modern architectural innovations and the extensive menu boasts well-prepared food. The lively crowd of loyal habitués adds to the welcoming ambience, making Niky's a good choice for an evening meal, especially in summer when you can dine its unforgettable terrace.

6 Wieden & Margareten (4th & 5th Districts)

MODERATE

✪ Motto
Schönbrunnerstrasse 30 (entrance is at Rudigergasse 1). ☎ **0222/587-06-72.** Reservations recommended. Main courses 92–218 AS ($8.75–$20.70). No credit cards. Restaurant daily 6pm–3:30am; bar daily 6pm–4am. U-Bahn: Pilgramgasse. INTERNATIONAL.

Established in the 1970s, this restaurant slumbered in relative obscurity until the mid 1990s, when it was suddenly discovered by a sophisticated cross-cultural mishmash of Viennese trendsetters and artists. Today, any hint of the old-fashioned stodginess has been swept aside with the introduction of an oscillating roster of usually startling (often nude) paintings that change according to demand or when one is actually bought. Hang out at the bar, where many romances seem to get started, or in the courtyard in back, where there's an interesting hi-tech fountain that recirculates water into glass-covered channels below your feet. The international menu features most Austrian staples, including schnitzel that hangs over the plate, as well as an assortment of pastas like ravioli stuffed with salmon, cream, and herbs. If possible, try to eat here on Sunday, Monday, or Tuesday, when Hélene, a cult figure on the Viennese restaurant scene, flambées steaks at tableside while dispensing culinary advice.

Schlossgasse 21

Schlossgasse 21. ☎ **0222/544-0767.** Reservations recommended. Main courses 88–300 AS ($8.35–$28.50). No credit cards. Mon–Fri noon–12:30am; Sat–Sun 6pm–12:30am. U-Bahn: Pilgrimgasse. AUSTRIAN/INTERNATIONAL.

This cozy restaurant was the private, turn of the century home of its owner until the early 1990s when it was transformed. Decorated in a pleasant mishmash of old and new furnishings, much like you would find in someone's home, this place offers classic Austrian dishes, as well as some interesting and palate-pleasing Asiatic dishes such as Indonesian satay and Chinese stir-frys. An enduring favorite is the steak, prepared according to traditional French techniques.

INEXPENSIVE

Silberwirt

Schlossgasse 21. ☎ **0222/544-4907.** Reservations recommended. Main courses 75–195 AS ($7.15–$18.50). AE,DC,MC,V. Daily, noon–midnight. U-Bahn: Pilgrimgasse. VIENNESE.

Despite the fact that it opened just 20 years ago, this restaurant oozes with Old Viennese style and resembles the traditional *beisl* with its copious portions of conservative, time-honored Viennese food. You can dine within the pair of dining rooms inside or move into the beer garden, where foaming steins of beer and carafes of wine are staples. Menu items include stuffed mushrooms, tafelspitz, schnitzels, and filets of zanderfish, salmon, and trout. Be aware that this establishment shares the same building and address with Restaurant Schlossgasse listed above.

7 Mariahilf (6th District)

MODERATE

Raimundstüberl

Liniengasse 29. ☎ **0222/596-7784.** Reservations recommended. Main courses 80–230 AS ($7.60–$21.85). DC,V. Daily 10:30am–3:30pm and 5:30pm–midnight. U-Bahn: Gumpendorferstrasse or Westbahnhof. VIENNESE.

Appealing because of its emphasis on old-world decor and time-tested cuisine, this restaurant is also a good value, in a neighborhood loaded with simpler, and usually less worthy, choices. Established around the turn of the century, it features a pair of wood-sheathed dining rooms, a garden, and copious portions of schnitzels, goulasches and beefsteaks, which are smothered in mushrooms. The staff is polite and the ambience pure Viennese.

INEXPENSIVE

Loft

Mariahilferstrasse 19-21. ☎ **0222/586-6227.** Reservations not necessary. Main courses 60–100 AS ($5.70–$9.50); set menus 78 AS ($7.40). No credit cards. Daily 10am–3am. U-Bahn: Neubaugasse. VIENNESE/INTERNATIONAL.

Despite appearance as a simple, almost Spartan, cafe, this restaurant lures neighborhood residents for its reasonably-priced set menus, which change daily depending on the season and the chef. It's a great spot for lunch or for lingering over coffee or beer in the evening. The menu features homemade bagels, salads, sandwiches, roulades of beef and other Austrian specialties. This cozy eatery also attracts diners in their 20s and 30s, especially on the weekends, when they can head downstairs after dinner to the cellar disco, **Mekka,** which opens at 11pm.

8 Neubau (7th District)

EXPENSIVE

✪ Hauswirth

Otto-Bauer-Gasse 20. ☎ **0222/587-12-61.** Reservations recommended. Main courses 160–290 AS ($15.20–$27.55); fixed-price menu 450 AS ($42.75) for three courses, 850 AS ($80.75) for four courses for two diners. AE, DC, MC, V. Mon–Sat noon–3pm and 6pm–midnight. Closed Dec 23–Jan 8. U-Bahn: Zieglerstrasse. Tram: 52 or 58. VIENNESE.

The imposing entrance to this restaurant is under a rectangular corridor. Push open the leaded-glass door and discover the art nouveau enclave, which has become a stamping ground of well-dressed habitués. The summertime gardens are lovely, but in winter you'll eat in a paneled ambience accented by dark wood and crystal chandeliers. The chef adjusts his menu seasonally, obtaining whatever is fresh at local markets. Offerings might include quail, venison, asparagus, fresh berries, goose liver, sweetbreads, well-prepared steaks, seafood specialties, and a tempting array of homemade pastries.

The cellar holds not only a large variety of the finest Austrian wines, but also a well-chosen selection from some of the best European vineyards.

MODERATE

Bohème

Spittelberggasse 19. ☎ **0222/523-31-73.** Reservations recommended. Main courses 95–215 AS ($9.05–$20.45). AE, DC, MC, V. Mon–Sat 6–11:30pm. U-Bahn: Volkstheater. VIENNESE/INTERNATIONAL.

The carefully maintained house occupied by this restaurant won a municipal award in 1992 for the authenticity of its historic restoration. Originally built in 1750 in the baroque style, it once functioned as a bakery. Today, its historic street is an all-pedestrian walkway loaded with shops.

Since its opening in 1989, Bohème has attracted a clientele well versed in the nuances of wine, food, and the endless range of opera music that reverberates through the two dining rooms. Even the decor is theatrical; it looks like a cross between a severely dignified stage set and an artsy, turn-of-the-century cafe. Menu items are listed as movements in an opera, with overtures (apéritifs), prologues (appetizers), and first and second acts (soups and main courses, respectively). Some tempting items include thinly sliced cured ham with melons, Andalusian gazpacho, platters of mixed fish filets with tomato risotto, tafelspitz with horseradish, gourmet versions of bratwurst and sausages on a bed of ratatouille, and an array of vegetarian dishes like soya schnitzels in sesame sauce.

INEXPENSIVE

Glacisbeisel

Messepalast. ☎ **0222/526-67-95.** Reservations required. Main courses 110–265 AS ($10.45–$25.20). AE, DC, MC, V. Daily 11am–midnight. Closed Christmas–Feb 1. Bus: 48A. VIENNESE/AUSTRIAN.

Near the English Theater, inside a maze of palatial buildings whose entrances lie on Museumsstrasse, this restaurant is housed inside the walls of what was once the imperial stables. To reach it, you'll have to traverse a series of courtyards. Climb one flight above ground level to a wood-sheathed atmosphere filled with tin cake molds and regional pottery. The restaurant serves Wiener schnitzel, as tafelspitz (boiled beef with potato Rösti), plus a milk-and-cream strudel with vanilla sauce. In summer it seats more than 300 diners on an open-air terrace.

9 Josefstadt (8th District)

MODERATE

Piaristenkeller

Piaristengasse 45. ☎ **0222/405-91-52.** Reservations recommended. Main courses 110–320 AS ($10.45–$30.40). AE, DC, MC, V. Daily 6–midnight. U-Bahn: Rathaus. AUSTRIAN.

Erich Emberger has successfully renovated and reassembled this wine tavern with centuries-old vaulted ceilings in a vast cellar room. The place was founded in 1697 by Piarist monks as a tavern and wine cellar. The kitchen, which once served the cloisters, serves traditional Austrian specialties based on original recipes. The most expensive item on the menu is a mixed grill, with four different kinds of meat. Zither music is played from 7:30pm on, and in summer the garden at the church square is open from 11am to midnight. Wine and beer are available whenever the cellar is open. Advance booking is required for a guided tour of the cloister's old wine vaults. At least six guests pay 150 AS ($14.25) per person for the tour.

INEXPENSIVE

Ⓢ Alte Backstube

Lange Gasse 34. ☎ **0222/403-11-01.** Reservations required. Main courses 120–250 AS ($11.40–$23.75). AE, V. Tues–Sat 9am–midnight, Sun and holidays 2pm–midnight. Closed Aug. U-Bahn: Rathaus. VIENNESE/HUNGARIAN.

This spot is worth visiting just to admire the baroque sculptures that crown the top of the doorway. The building was originally built as a private home in 1697, and four years later it was transformed into a bakery, complete with wood-burning stoves. For more than 2¹/₂ centuries the establishment served the baking needs of its neighborhood, and then, in 1963, the Schwarzmann family added a dining room, a dainty front room for drinking beer and tea, and a collection of baking-related artifacts.

Once seated, you can order such wholesome, robust Teutonic specialties as braised pork with cabbage, Viennese-style gulasch, and roast venison with cranberry sauce and bread dumplings. There's an English-language menu if you need it. Try the house special dessert, cream-cheese strudel with hot vanilla sauce.

10 Alsergrund (9th District)

MODERATE

Abend-Restaurant Fuervogel

Alserbachstrasse 21. ☎ **0222/317-53-91.** Reservations recommended. Main courses 120–210 AS ($11.40–$19.95); fixed-price menu 595 AS ($56.55). AE, DC, V. Mon–Sat 6pm–1am. Closed July 15–Aug 15. U-Bahn: Friedensbrücke. Bus: 32. RUSSIAN.

Since World War I, this restaurant has been a Viennese landmark, bringing Russian cuisine to a location across the from the palace of the Prince of Liechtenstein. You'll eat in romantically Slavic surroundings with Gypsy violins playing Russian and Viennese music. Specialties include chicken Kiev, beef Stroganoff, veal Dolgoruki, borscht, and many other dishes that taste as if they came right off the steppes. For an hors d'oeuvre try *sakkuska*, a variety platter that's popular in Russia. You can also order a fixed-price *ourmet kreml dinner* with five courses. Be sure to sample the Russian ice cream known as *plombier*.

11 Near Schönbrunn

VERY EXPENSIVE

✪ Altwienerhof

Herklotzgasse 6. ☎ **0222/892-60-00.** Reservations recommended. Main courses 250–300 AS ($23.75–$28.50); fixed-price lunch 420 AS ($39.90); *menu dégustation* (dinner only) 715 AS ($67.95) for six courses, 1,000 AS ($95) for eight courses. MC, V. Mon–Sat 11:15am–2pm and 6–11pm. Closed first 3 weeks in Jan. Tram: 6, 8, or 18. AUSTRIAN/FRENCH.

A short walk from Schönbrunn Palace, this establishment is one of the premier dining spots in Vienna. The building is completely modernized, but it was originally designed as a private home in the 1870s. Rudolf and Ursula Kellner bring sophistication and charm to a wood-paneled series of dining rooms which retain many Biedermeier embellishments of the original construction. The chef prepares a nouvelle cuisine, using only the freshest and highest-quality ingredients. Since the menu changes frequently, we can't recommend specialties, but the maître d' is always willing to assist. Each night the chef prepares a *menu dégustation,* which is a sampling of the kitchen's best nightly dishes. The wine list consists of well over 700 items, while the cellar houses about 18,000 bottles; each of the wines is selected by Mr. Kellner himself. The Kellners also run a small (25-room) budget hotel on the premises (see Chapter 4, "Accommodations").

12 In the Outer Districts

EXPENSIVE

Restaurant Fischerhaus

An der Höhenstrasse. ☎ **0222/440-13-20.** Reservations required. Main courses 160–300 AS ($15.20–$28.50); fixed-price menu 400 AS ($38) at lunch, 500 AS ($47.50) at dinner. AE, MC, V. Mon–Fri 3–11pm, Sat–Sun noon–11pm. Closed Nov–Feb. AUSTRIAN/INTERNATIONAL.

Perched among the Vienna Woods—the remote 19th district of Vienna—this restaurant is popular with members of Vienna's diplomatic community and the city's business elite. Celebrities who have dined here include Arnold Schwarzenegger,

Robert Mitchum, and Elizabeth Taylor. The cellars read like an international directory of fine wines, especially those from the Napa Valley of California. The establishment is housed in a century-old farmhouse surrounded by plush greenery and an outdoor terrace. The interior features a wintertime fireplace and a collection of antique firearms and hunting memorabilia. Since its opening in 1954, Fischerhaus has lured the Viennese with its hearty Austrian and international fare.

MODERATE

Sailer

Gersthoferstrasse 14. ☎ **0222/479-21-210.** Reservations required. Main courses 130–260 AS ($12.35–$24.70); fixed-price menu 290–350 AS ($27.55–$33.25). MC. Daily noon–3pm; Mon–Sat 6–11pm. Closed Sat–Sun July–Aug. Tram: 45. Bus: 10A. VIENNESE/AUSTRIAN.

Located near the Türkenschanzpark, this restaurant is tastefully decorated in Old Vienna style, with wood paneling, Biedermeier portraits, and in one of the cellar rooms, antique chairs that are hand-carved in different designs. Both the restaurant and the house it's in were established in 1892 by the ancestors of the present owners. Their specialties include deer and elk, wild boar, pheasant, and partridge, each prepared according to time-honored Viennese recipes. The owners have given in to demands for an updated lighter cuisine with daily specials.

13 Coffeehouses, Tea Rooms & Cafes

Café Central

Herrengasse 14. ☎ **0222/533-37-63.**

The Café Central stands in the center of Vienna just across from the Hofburg (the imperial winter palace) and the Spanish Riding School. This grandly proportioned cafe offers a glimpse into 19th-century Viennese life. The cafe once served as the center of Austrian literature and the meeting place of the country's best-known writers. Even Lenin, under an assumed name, is said to have plotted the Russian Revolution here. The cafe offers a variety of Viennese coffees and a vast selection of pastries and desserts, costing 42 to 80 AS ($4 to $7.60). Coffee ranges from 41 to 85 AS ($3.90 to $8.05). The restaurant offers both Viennese and provincial dishes, and is a delightful spot for lunch. A three-course lunch will cost about 250 AS ($23.75). The cafe is open Monday through Saturday from 8am to 10pm; closed holidays. U-Bahn: Herrengasse.

✪ Café Demel

Kohlmarkt 14. ☎ **0222/533-55-16.**

The windows of this much-venerated establishment are filled with fanciful spun-sugar creations of characters from folk legends. Perhaps Lady Godiva's five-foot tresses will shelter a miniature village of Viennese dancers. Inside you'll find a splendidly baroque Viennese landmark of black marble tables, embellished plaster walls, elaborate half paneling, and crystal. Dozens of different pastries are available every day, including pralinentorte, Senegal torte, truffle torte, sandtorte, and Maximiliantorte, as well as cream-filled horns (*Gugelhupfs*). If you're not in the mood for sweets, Demel also serves a mammoth variety of tea sandwiches made with smoked salmon, egg salad, caviar, or shrimp. If you want to be traditional, ask for a Demel-Coffee, which is filtered coffee served with milk, cream, or whipped cream. Coffee costs 45 AS ($4.30), and those tempting desserts begin at 48 AS ($4.55). Open daily from 10am to 7pm. Bus: 1A or 2A. U-Bahn: Herrengasse.

Café Dommayer
Dommayergasse 1. ☎ **0222/877-54-65.**

Not far from Schönbrunn Palace you'll find one of the most atmospheric cafes in Vienna. This is the place where both Johann Strausses played waltzes for Vienna's *grande bourgeoisie.* Established in 1787 by a local writer, the cafe contains an old-world decor of Beidermeier accessories set amongst silver samovars. The formally dressed waiters dote on a stylish and very Viennese clientele. Longtime customers seem eminently comfortable here sipping *mélange,* adjusting the folds of their fur coats, cutting pastries into bite-size pieces, reading the German-language newspapers, and, of course, gossiping. Coffee prices can cost up to 38 AS ($3.60) for a Viennese mocha specialty, and meals cost around 175 AS ($16.65). Open Monday through Saturday from 7am to midnight. U-Bahn: Schönbrunn.

✪ Café Imperial
Karntner Ring 16. ☎ **0222/50-110-389.**

Housed in the deluxe Hotel Imperial (see Chapter 4, "Vienna Accommodations"), this cafe was a favorite of Gustav Mahler and a host of other celebrated cultural figures. The "Imperial Toast" is a mini-meal in itself: white bread with veal, chicken and leaf spinach that's gratinéed in the oven and served with hollandaise sauce. A Sunday breakfast/brunch buffet for 270 AS ($25.65), is served Habsburg-style on Sunday from 7am until closing at 11pm. It's said to be the only hotel buffet breakfast in Vienna that comes with champagne. Coffee costs 60 AS ($5.70), with pastries beginning at 45 AS ($4.30). Open daily from 7am to 11pm. U-Bahn: Karlsplatz.

✪ Café Landtmann
Dr.-Karl-Lueger-Ring 4. ☎ **0222/532-06-21.**

One of the Ring's great cafes, this spot has a history dating to the 1880s. Overlooking the Burgtheater, it has traditionally drawn a mixture of politicians, journalists, and actors. It was also Freud's favorite. The original chandeliers and the pre-war chairs have been refurbished. We highly suggest spending an hour or so here, whether it be perusing the newspapers, sipping on coffee, or planning the day's itinerary. A large coffee costs 40 AS ($3.80), and full meals are available. A fixed-price lunch costs 105 AS ($10). The cafe is open daily from 8am to midnight; lunch is served from 11:30am to 3pm and dinner from 5 to 11pm. Tram: 1, 2, or D.

Café Leopold Hawelka
Dorotheergasse 6. ☎ **0222/512-82-30.**

Just off the Graben, this cafe was once the most famous rendezvous point for poets, artists, and the literati. Nowadays it's Vienna's most frequented cafe among young people. Coffee costs range from 7 to 37 AS (65¢ to $3.50). Open on Monday and Wednesday through Saturday from 8am to 2am, and on Sunday from 4pm to 2am; closed July 12 to August 9. U-Bahn: Stephansplatz.

Café Tirolerhof
Tegetthoffstrasse 8. ☎ **0222/512-78-33.**

This cafe, which has been under the same management for decades, makes for a convenient sightseeing break, particularly from a tour of the nearby Hofburg complex. A slice of apple strudel costs 36 AS ($3.40). One coffee specialty is the Maria Theresia, a large cup of mocca flavored with apricot liqueur, and topped with whipped cream; it costs 125 AS ($11.90). If coffee sounds too hot, try the tasty milkshakes. You can also order a Viennese breakfast of coffee, tea, hot chocolate, two Viennese rolls, butter, jam, and honey for 60 AS ($5.70). Open Monday through Saturday from 7am to 9pm and on Sunday from 9:30 to 8pm. U-Bahn: Stephansplatz or Karlsplatz.

The Legendary Sachertorte

In a city fabled for its desserts, the Sachertorte has emerged as the most highly prized. At a party thrown for Prince Wenzel Clemens Metternich in 1832, Franz Sacher first concocted and served the confection. It was an instant success, and news of the torte spread throughout the Austro-Hungarian Empire. Back then, everyone wanted the recipe, but it was a closely guarded secret.

In 1876 Sacher's son, Eduard, launched the Hotel Sacher where the torte was served nightly to crowds of European aristocrats. Eduard's cigar-smoking wife, Frau Anna, transformed the place into a rendezvous for Austrian nobles who drank wine and devoured Sachertortes into the wee hours. Memory of this pastry faded during the tragedy of two world wars, but in 1951 the Sachertorte returned to the hotel's kitchen and reclaimed the renown it enjoyed in the 19th century. Today almost every pastry shop in Vienna sells the Sachertorte, and some confectioneries will ship it around the world.

Like all celebrities, the Sachertorte has even been the subject of a lawsuit. A 25-year-old legal battle over the exclusive right to the name "Original Sachertorte" was conducted between the Hotel Sacher and the patisserie Demel. An Austrian court in 1965 ruled in favor of the Hotel Sacher, granting the right to call its pastry the Original Sachertorte.

After endless samplings of the torte from both the Demel and the Hotel Sacher, only the most exacting connoisseur can tell the difference—if there is any. Here, with permission of the Hotel Sacher, is their recipe for Sachertorte:

Ingredients:

    5 oz dark chocolate
    1/2 cup butter
    1/2 cup granulated sugar
    1/2 cup confectioner's sugar
    6 eggs
    1 cup flour
    apricot jam (as desired)
    1 tsp. vanilla

Add the softened butter, the confectioner's sugar, and the vanilla and mix well. Add the egg yolks and beat. Mix in the chocolate. Whip the egg whites until stiff and add to the mixture, along with the granulated sugar. Knead with a wooden spoon. Add the flour; then place in a mold and bake at 340° for 15 minutes with the oven door ajar, then for a further 1 hour with the door shut. Turn out of the mold and allow to cool for 20 minutes. Coat with warm apricot jam.

Ingredients for Icing:

    4/5 cup confectioner's sugar
    1/2 cup water
    6 oz chocolate

Heat the sugar and water (5-6 minutes), add the melted chocolate and stir with a wooden spoon until the mixture is moderately thick. Layer the cake with the mixture ($^1/_4$ inch) and allow to cool.

Impressions

What if the Turks had taken Vienna, as they nearly did, and advanced westward? . . . Martial spoils apart, the great contest has left little trace. It was the beginning of coffee-drinking in the West, or so the Viennese maintain. The earliest coffee houses, they insist, were kept by some of the Sultan's Greek and Serbian subjects who had sought sanctuary in Vienna. But the rolls which the Viennese dipped in the new drink were modelled on the half-moons of the Sultan's flag. The shape caught on all over the world. They mark the end of the age-old struggle between the hot-cross-bun and the croissant.
                                        —Patrick Leigh Fermor, *A Time of Gifts,* 1977

Café/Restaurant Prückel
Stubenring 24. ☎ **0222/512-61-15.**

This place was built at the turn of the century, and renovated in 1955, just after Austria regained its independence. The spot plays host to an offbeat, artsy clientele who lounge in the Sputnik-era chairs amongst piles of dog-eared newspapers. The owner offers 20 different kinds of coffee, including the house favorite, Maria Theresia, a large black coffee with orange liqueur and whipped cream, costing 75 AS ($7.15). A fixed-price lunch costs 120 AS ($11.40). Open daily from 9am to 10pm. U-Bahn: Stubentor.

Demmer's Teehaus
Mölkerbastel 5. ☎ **0222/533-59-95.**

Thirty different kinds of tea are served here, along with dozens of pastries, cakes, toasts, and English sandwiches. Demmer's is managed by the previously recommended restaurant, Buffet Trzesniewski; however, the teahouse offers you a chance to sit down, relax and enjoy your drink or snack. Teas begin at 30 AS ($2.85). Open Monday through Friday from 10am to 6:30pm. U-Bahn: Schottenring.

PICNICKING

Picnic fanciers find Vienna among the best-stocked cities in Europe for food supplies. The best place—and the least expensive venue—is the **Naschmarkt,** an open-air market that's only a five-minute stroll from Karlsplatz (the nearest U-Bahn stop). Here you'll find hundreds of stalls selling fresh produce, breads, meats, cheeses, flowers, tea, and more. There are also fast-food counters and other stands peddling ready-made foods like grilled chicken, Austrian and German sausages, even sandwiches and beer, among literally hundreds of other items. The market is open Monday through Friday from 6am to 6:30pm and on Saturday from 6am to 1pm.

With your hand-selected picnic basket, head for such ideal settings as the **Stadtpark** or the **Volksgarten,** each lying on the famous Ring. Even better, if the weather is right, plan an excursion into the **Vienna Woods** for your picnic.

STREET FOOD

Street corners throughout Vienna are home to one of the city's most popular eating venues, the **Würstelstand.** These small stands sell frankfurters, bratwurst, curry wurst, and other Austrian sausages, which are usually served on a roll *mit senf* (with mustard). Try the *Käsekrainer,* a fat frankfurter infused with tasty bits of cheese. Conveniently located stands are on Seilergasse (just off Stephansplatz) and Kupfer-schmiedgasse (just off Kärntnerstrasse). Beers and soda are also sold at these frankfurter stands.

6

What to See & Do in Vienna

"**A**sia begins at Landstrasse." Prince von Metternich, the Austrian statesman, made that now-famous remark to suggest the power and influence of the far-flung Austrian Empire, whose destiny was controlled by the Habsburg dynasty from 1273 to 1918.

Viennese prosperity under the Habsburgs reached its peak under the long reign of Maria Theresa during the late 18th century. Many of the sights described below are traced directly to the great empress who escorted Vienna through the Age of Enlightenment. She welcomed Mozart, the child prodigy, to her court at Schönbrunn when he was just six years old.

With the collapse of the Napoleonic Empire, Vienna took over Paris's long-held position as "the center of Europe." The crowned heads of Europe met for the now-legendary Congress of Vienna in 1814–15 to restructure Europe's political boundaries. But so much time was devoted to galas that Prince de Ligne remarked, "The Congress doesn't make progress, it dances."

In this chapter we'll explore the many sights of this city of *Gemütlichkeit,* including its palaces, museums, churches, parks, attractions for kids and those with special sightseeing interests. Be warned that it's possible to spend a week here and only touch the surface of this multifaceted city. We'll take you through the highlights, but even this venture will take more than a week of fast-paced walking.

SUGGESTED ITINERARIES

Many readers will not have time to see Vienna as it deserves to be seen. Some visitors will have only a day or two, and with those people in mind, we've compiled a list of the major attractions a first-time traveler to Vienna will want to explore, as well as additional sights for those with more time. To help your touring strategies, we've outlined some suggested itineraries below on based on the length of your stay. Regardless of time, no one should miss the Inner City, Ringstrasse, Schönbrunn Palace, Hofburg Palace, Belvedere Palace, Kunsthistorisches Museum, and St. Stephan's Cathedral. You also might consider one of our three walking tours of the city which are mapped out in Chapter 7, "Vienna Strolls."

If You Have 1 Day

Sadly little time, but you'll have to make the best of it. Begin at St. Stephan's Cathedral and from there branch out for a tour of the enveloping Inner City, or Old Town. But, before you leave the cathedral, climb the south tower of the cathedral for a panoramic view of the city (you can also take an elevator to the top). Next, stroll down Kärntnerstrasse, the main shopping artery, and enjoy the 11am ritual of coffee in a grand cafe, such as the Café Imperial. In the afternoon, visit Schönbrunn Palace, the magnificent summer seat of the Habsburg dynasty. Have dinner in a Viennese wine tavern.

If You Have 2 Days

For Day 1, stick to the agenda listed above. On Day 2, explore other major attractions of Vienna, including the Hofburg, the Imperial Crypts, and the Kunsthistorisches Museum. In the evening, attend a performance of the opera or some other musical event, perhaps the famous Konzerthaus.

If You Have 3 Days

Spend Days 1 and 2 as planned above. On Day 3, try to work two important performances into your schedule: the Spanish Riding School (Tuesday through Saturday) and the Vienna Boys' Choir (singing at masses on Sunday). Also be sure to visit the Belvedere Palace and its fine art galleries. Take a stroll through the Naschmarkt, the city's major open-air market, and finish the day with our walking tour of Imperial Vienna (see Chapter 7, "Vienna Strolls").

If You Have 4 or 5 Days

Spend Days 1–3 as above. On Day 4, take a tour of the Vienna Woods and then visit Klosterneuburg Abbey, Austria's most impressive abbey (see Chapter 10, "Sidetrips from Vienna"). Return to Vienna for an evening of fun at the Prater amusement park.

On Day 5, "mop up" all the attractions you missed on your first four days. These might include a visit to the Albertina Graphische Sammlungen, the most important graphic-arts collection in the world; a visit to the Sigmund Freud Museum; or a walk through the Stadtpark, at Parkring.

Or if these less important attractions don't interest you, take a boat cruise on the Danube (available May through September only). End your Viennese experience by patronizing a *heurige,* a typically Viennese wine cellar in such districts as Grinzing or Heiligenstadt.

1 The Hofburg Palace Complex

Once the winter palace of the Habsburgs, the Hofburg sits in the heart of Vienna and is known for its vast, impressive courtyards. To reach it (you can hardly miss it), head up Kohlmarkt to Michaelerplatz 1, Burgring (☎ **0222/587-55-54**), where you'll stumble upon two enormous fountains embellished with statuary. You can also take the **U-Bahn** to Stephansplatz, Herrengasse, or Mariahilferstrasse, or else **Tram** 1, 2, D, or J to Burgring.

This complex of imperial edifices, the first of which was constructed in 1279, grew with the empire, so that today the palace is virtually a city within a city. The earliest parts were built around a courtyard, the **Swiss Court,** named for the Swiss mercenaries who performed guard duty here. This most ancient section of the palace is at least 700 years old.

The Hofburg's complexity of styles, which is not always harmonious, is the result of each emperor opting to add or take away some of the work done by his or her predecessors. The palace, which has withstood three major sieges and a great fire, is called simply *die Burg,* or "the palace," by Viennese. Of its more than 2,600 rooms, fewer than two dozen are open to the public.

✪ Schatzkammer (Imperial Treasury)

Hofburg, Schweizerhof. ☎ **0222/533-79-31.** Admission 60 AS ($5.70) adults; 30 AS ($2.85) children, senior citizens, and students. Wed–Mon 10am–6pm.

Reached by a staircase from the Swiss Court, the Schatzkammer is the greatest treasury in the world. It's divided into two sections: the Imperial Profane and the Sacerdotal Treasuries. The first displays the crown jewels and an assortment of imperial riches, and the other, of course, contains ecclesiastical treasures.

The most outstanding exhibit in the Schatzkammer is the imperial crown, which dates from 962. It's so big that, even though padded, it probably slipped down over the ears of a Habsburg at a coronation. Studded with emeralds, sapphires, diamonds, and rubies, this 1,000-year-old symbol of sovereignty is a priceless treasure, a fact recognized by Adolf Hitler, who had it taken to Nürnberg in 1938 (the American army returned it to Vienna after World War II ended). Also on display is the imperial crown worn by the Habsburg rulers from 1804 to the end of the empire. Be sure to have a look at the coronation robes of the imperial family, some of which date from the 12th century.

You can also view the saber of Charlemagne and the holy lance from the 9th century. The latter, a sacred emblem of imperial authority, was thought in medieval times to be the weapon that pierced the side of Christ on the cross. Among the great Schatzkammer prizes is the Burgundian Treasure. Seized in the 15th century, it is rich in vestments, oil paintings, gems, and robes. Highlighting this collection of loot are artifacts connected with the Order of the Golden Fleece, the romantic medieval order of chivalry.

✪ Kaiserappartements (Imperial Apartments)

Hofburg, Schweizerhof. ☎ **0222/533-7570.** German-language guided tour 70 AS ($6.65); English-language tours aren't available unless you hire one of the freelance tour guides loitering around the entryway, or prearrange one with the Vienna Tourist Information Office. Mon–Sat 8:30am–4:30pm, Sun 8:30am–1pm.

The Hofburg complex also includes the Kaiserappartements, on the first floor, where the emperors and their wives and children lived. To reach these apartments, enter through the rotunda of Michaelerplatz. The apartments are richly decorated with tapestries, many from Aubusson. The court tableware and silver are outrageously ornate, reflecting the pomp and splendor of a bygone era. The **Imperial Silver and Porcelain Collection** descends directly from the Hapsburg household during the 18th and 19th centuries and provides a look into their court etiquette. Admission to this collection costs 70 AS ($6.65) and a combined tour is 90 AS ($8.55). Leopoldinischer Trakt, or Leopold's apartments, date from the 17th century. You can't visit the quarters once occupied by Maria Theresa, as they are now used by the president of Austria.

These Imperial Apartments seem to be more closely associated with Franz Joseph than with any other emperor because of his long reign. His wife, Elizabeth of Bavaria, lived here too when she wasn't traveling. You'll see the "iron bed" of Franz Joseph, who claimed he slept like his own soldiers. Maybe that explains why his wife spent so much time elsewhere!

✪ Hofmusikkapelle Wien (Vienna Boys' Choir)

Die Burgkapelle (Palace Chapel), Hofburg (entrance on Schweizerhof). ☎ **0222/533-99-27.** Tickets, 60-280 AS ($5.70-$26.60). Masses (performances) held only Jan–June and mid-Sept until the end of Dec, Sun and holidays at 9:15am.

Construction of this Gothic chapel began in 1447 during the reign of Emperor Frederick III, but it was later massively renovated. From 1449 it was the private chapel of the royal family. Today the Burgkapelle hosts the Hofmusikkapelle, an ensemble of the Vienna Boys' Choir and members of the Vienna State Opera chorus and orchestra, that performs works by classical and modern composers. Written applications for reserved seats should be sent at least eight weeks in advance, but do not send cash or checks. For reservations, write to Verwaltung der Hofmusikkapelle, Hofburg, A-1010 Vienna. If you failed to reserve in advance, you may be lucky enough to secure tickets from a block sold at the Burgkapelle box office every Friday from 3 to 5pm on, but the queue starts lining up at least half an hour before that. If you're willing to settle for standing room, it's free.

The Vienna Boys' Choir boarding school is at Palais Augarten, Obere Augartenstrasse.

Neue Burg

Heldenplatz. ☎ **0222/521-770.** Admission to Hofjagd and Rüstkammer, Musikinstrumentensammlung, and Ephesos-Museum, 30 AS ($2.85) adults, 15 AS ($1.45) children. Hofjagd and Rüstkammer and Musikinstrumentensammlung and Ephesos-Museum, Wed–Mon 10am-6pm.

The most recent addition to the Hofburg complex is the Neue Burg, or New Château. Construction was started in 1881 and continued through 1913. The palace was the residence of Archduke Franz Ferdinand, the nephew and heir apparent of Franz Joseph, whose assassination at Sarajevo set off the chain of events that led to World War I.

The **arms and armor collection** is second only to that of the Metropolitan Museum of Art in New York. It's in the Hofjagd and Rüstkammer, on the second floor of the New Château. On display are crossbows, swords, helmets, pistols, and other armor, mostly the property of Habsburg emperors and princes. Some of the exhibits, such as scimitars, were captured from the Turks as they fled the their lost sieges of Vienna. Of bizarre interest is the armor worn by the young Habsburg princes.

Another section, the **Musikinstrumentensammlung** (☎ 0222/521-77-470), is devoted to old musical instruments, mainly from the 17th and 18th centuries, but with some from the 16th century. Some of the instruments, especially pianos and harpsichords, were played by Brahms, Liszt, Mahler, and Beethoven.

In the **Ephesos-Museum** (Museum of Ephesian Sculpture), Neue Burg 1, Heldenplatz, with an entrance behind the Prince Eugene monument (☎ 0222/521-77-0), you'll see high-quality finds from Ephesus in Turkey and the Greek island of Samothrace. It's in the Neue Hofburg, an annex of the Collection of Greek and Roman Antiquities of the Kunsthistoriches Museum. Here the prize exhibit is the Parthian monument, the most important relief frieze from Roman times ever found in Asia Minor. It was erected in celebration of the Romans' victorious conclusion of the Parthian wars (A.D. 161–65).

Visit the **Museum für Völkerkunde** (Museum of Ethnology), Neue Burg, Hofburg (☎ 0222/534-30) for no other reason than to see the only original Aztec feather headdress in the world. Also on display are Benin bronzes, Cook's collections of Polynesian art, and Indonesian, African, Eskimo, and pre-Columbian exhibits. Admission is 50 AS ($4.75) for adults, 25 AS ($2.40) for children. The museum is open Wednesday through Monday, 10am to 4pm.

Vienna Attractions

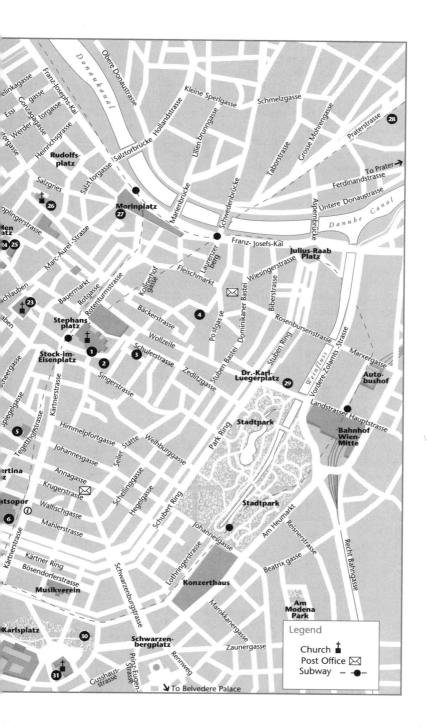

Österreichische Nationalbibliothek (Austrian National Library)

Josef-platz 1. ☎ **0222/534-10-397.** Admission 30 AS ($2.85) adults, 15 AS ($1.45) children; 50 AS ($4.75) during summer exhibition. Oct 30–Apr, Mon–Sat 11am–noon; June–Oct 29, Mon and Wed–Sat 10am–4pm, Tues 10am–6pm, Sun and public holidays 10am–1pm.

The royal library of the Habsburgs dates back to the 14th century, and the library building, developed on the premises of the court from 1723 on, is still expanding to the Neue Hofburg. The Great Hall of the present-day library was ordered by Karl VI and designed by those masters of the baroque, the von Erlachs. Its splendor is captured in the frescoes of Daniel Gran and the equestrian statue of Joseph II. The complete collection of Prince Eugene of Savoy is the core of the precious holdings shelved in front of the library building. With its heritage of manuscripts, rare autographs, globes, maps, and other memorabilia, it's among the finest libraries in the world.

Graphische Sammlung Albertina (Albertina Collection)

Augustinerstrasse 1. ☎ **0222/53-483.** Admission 45 AS ($4.30) adults; 20 AS ($1.90) students; free for children under 11. Mon–Thurs 10am–4pm, Fri 10am–2pm, Sat–Sun 10am–1pm.

The development of graphic arts since the 14th century is explored at this Hofburg museum. Housing one of the world's greatest graphics collections, the museum was named for a son-in-law of Maria Theresa. The most outstanding treasure in the Albertina is the Dürer collection, although what you'll usually see are copies—the originals are shown only on special occasions. Be sure to view Dürer's *Praying Hands*, which has been reproduced throughout the world. The 20,000-some drawings and more than 250,000 original etchings and prints include work by such artists as Poussin, Fragonard, Rubens, Rembrandt, Michelangelo, and Leonardo da Vinci. Exhibitions of both ancient and modern drawings and prints are always changing.

Augustinerkirche (Church of the Augustians)

Augustinerstrasse 3. ☎ **0222/533-70-99.** Guided tour, 10 AS (95¢) contribution. To arrange a visit, contact the church office, Pfarre St. Augustin, Augustinerstrasse 3, or the music office (☎ 0222/533-69-63).

This 14th-century church was built within the Hofburg complex to serve as the parish church of the imperial court. In the latter part of the 18th century it was stripped of its baroque embellishments and returned to the original Gothic features. The Chapel of St. George, dating from 1337, is entered from the right aisle. The tomb of Maria Christina, the favorite daughter of Maria Theresa, is housed in the main nave near the rear entrance, but there's no body in it. (The princess was actually buried in the Imperial Crypt, which is described later in this section.) The richly ornamented empty tomb here is one of Canova's masterpieces. A small room in the Loreto Chapel is filled with urns, containing the hearts of the imperial Habsburg family. They can be viewed through a window in an iron door. The Chapel of St. George and the Loreto Chapel are only open to the public by prearranged guided tour.

This church is as much a place of life as it is death. Maria Theresa married François of Lorraine here in 1736, and the Augustinerkirche was also the site of other royal weddings: Marie Antoinette to Louis XVI of France in 1770, Marie-Louise of Austria to Napoléon in 1810 (by proxy—he didn't show up), and Franz Joseph to Elizabeth of Bavaria in 1854.

The most convenient—and perhaps the most dramatic—time to visit the church is on Sunday at 11am, when a high mass is celebrated, with choir, soloists, and orchestra. On selected Sundays of the church year and in July and August, beautiful organ masses are presented during services. Admission for the masses is free, but donations are most welcome. On Friday at 7:30pm from the end of May until the end of September—and on certain selected Fridays throughout the year—organ recitals and concerts are also presented here. Tickets range from 80 to 200 AS ($7.30 to $18.20), depending on the event. Otherwise, you can only visit the church by appointment (see below), as it keeps no regular hours anymore.

✪ Spanische Hofreitschule (Spanish Riding School)

Michaelerplatz 1, Hofburg. ☎ **0222/533-90-32.** Regular performances, 240–800 AS ($22.80–$76.00) seats, 190 AS ($18.05) standing room. Training performances with music, 240 AS ($22.80). (Children under 3 not admitted, but children 3–6 attend free with adults.) Training session, 100 AS ($9.50) adults, 20 AS ($1.90) children. Regular performances, Mar–June and Sept to mid-Dec: Sun at 10:45am, most Weds at 7pm. Training performances with music, May and Sept: Sat at 10am. Training sessions, mid-Feb to June, end of Aug to mid-Dec: Tues–Fri 10am–noon except on public holidays.

This riding school is a reminder that horses were an important part of everyday life for many centuries, particularly during Vienna's imperial heyday. The school is housed in a white, crystal-chandeliered ballroom in an 18th-century building of the Hofburg complex. You'll marvel at the skill and beauty of the sleek Lippizaner stallions as their adept trainers put them through their paces in a show that hasn't changed for four centuries. These are the world's most famous, classically styled equine performers. Many North Americans have seen them in the States, but to watch the Lippizaners prance to the music of Johann Strauss or a Chopin polonaise in their home setting is a pleasure you shouldn't miss.

Reservations for performances must be made in advance, as early as possible. Order your tickets for the Sunday and Wednesday shows in writing to Spanische Reitschule, Hofburg, A-1010 Vienna (fax 43/1/535-01-86), or through a travel agency in Vienna. (Tickets for Saturday shows can be ordered only through a travel agency.) Tickets for training sessions with no advance reservations can be purchased at the entrance.

2 Other Top Attractions

THE INNER CITY

✪ Dompfarre St. Stephan (St. Stephan's Cathedral)

Stephansplatz 1. ☎ **0222/515-52.** Admission to Cathedral, free; tour of catacombs, 40 AS ($3.80), 15 AS ($1.45) children under 14. Guided tour of cathedral, 40 AS ($3.80) adults, 15 AS ($1.45) children under 14. North Tower, 40 AS ($3.80) adults, 15 AS ($1.45) children under 15; South Tower, 25 AS ($2.40) adults, 15 AS ($1.45) students, 5 AS (45¢) children under 15. Evening tours, including tour of the roof, 130 AS ($12.35) adults, 50 AS ($4.75) children under 15. Cathedral, daily 6am–10pm except times of service. Tour of catacombs, Mon–Sat at 10, 11, and 11:30am and 2, 2:30, 3:30, 4, and 4:30pm; Sun at 2, 2:30, 3:30, 4, and 4:30pm. North Tower, daily 9am–6pm; South Tower, daily 9am–5:30pm. Guided tour of cathedral, Mon–Sat at 10:30am and 3pm; Sun 3pm. Special evening tour Sat 7pm (May–Sept). U-Bahn: Stephansplatz.

A basilica built on the site of a Romanesque sanctuary, the cathedral was founded in the 12th century in what was, even in the Middle Ages, the town's center.

Stephansdom was virtually destroyed in a 1258 fire that swept through Vienna, and toward the dawn of the 14th century the ruins of the basilica gave way to a gothic building. The cathedral suffered terribly in the Turkish siege of 1683, but experienced peace until the Russian bombardments of 1945. Destruction continued as the Germans continued to fire on Vienna as they fled the city following World War II. Restored and reopened in 1948, the cathedral is today one of the greatest Gothic structures in Europe, rich in woodcarvings, altars, sculptures, and paintings. The steeple, rising some 450 feet, has come to symbolize the very spirit of Vienna.

The 352-foot-long cathedral is inextricably entwined in Viennese and Austrian history. It was here that mourners attended Mozart's "pauper's funeral" in 1791, and it was on the cathedral door that Napoléon posted his farewell edict in 1805.

The **pulpit** of St. Stephan's was carved from stone by Anton Pilgrim, his enduring masterpiece. But the chief treasure of the cathedral is the carved, wooden **Wiener Neustadt altarpiece** that dates from 1447. Richly painted and gilded, the altar was discovered in the Virgin's Choir. In the Apostles' Choir look for the curious tomb of Emperor Frederick III. Made of a pinkish Salzburg marble in the 17th century, the carved tomb depicts hideous little hobgoblins trying to enter and wake the emperor from his eternal sleep. The entrance to the catacombs or crypt is on the north side next to the Capistran pulpit. Here you'll see the funeral urns that contain the entrails of 56 members of the Habsburg family. (As we noted earlier, the hearts are inurned in St. George's Chapel of the Augustinerkirche and the bodies are entombed in the Imperial Crypt of the Kapuziner Church.)

You can climb the 343-step south tower of St. Stephan's, which dominates the Viennese skyline, for a view of the Vienna Woods. Called *Alter Steffl* (Old Steve), the tower, marked by its needlelike spire, was built between 1350 and 1433. The North Tower (Nordturm), reached by elevator, was never finished to match the South Tower, but was crowned in the Renaissance style in 1579. From here you get a panoramic sweep of the city and the Danube.

✪ Staatsoper (State Opera)

Opernring 2. ☎ **0222/51444-29-60.** Tours are given almost daily year-round, often two to five times a day, depending on demand. Tour times are posted on a board outside the entrance. The cost is 40 AS ($3.80) per person. Tickets 120–2,300 AS ($11.40–$218.50). U-Bahn: Karlsplatz.

This is one of the three most important opera houses in the world, and the upkeep is apparently a necessity to the Austrians as its operation costs taxpayers some million schillings a day. When it was originally built in the 1860s, criticism of the structure apparently so upset one of the architects, Eduard van der Null, that he killed himself. In 1945, at the end of World War II, despite other pressing needs such as that for public housing, Vienna started restoration work on the theater, finishing it in time to celebrate the country's independence from occupation forces in 1955.

With the Vienna Philharmonic Orchestra in the pit, some of the leading opera stars of the world perform here. In their day, Richard Strauss and Gustav Mahler worked as directors. Daily performances are given from the first of September until the end of June.

Gemäldegalerie Akademie der Bildenden Künste (Academy of Fine Arts)

Schillerplatz 3. ☎ **0222/58-816.** Admission 30 AS ($2.85) adults and children. Tues, Thurs, and Fri 10am–1pm, Wed 10am–1pm and 3–6pm, Sat–Sun 9am–1pm. U-Bahn: Karlsplatz.

When in Vienna, always make at least one visit to this painting gallery to see the *Last Judgment* triptych by the incomparable Hieronymus Bosch. In this masterpiece, the artist conjured up all the demons of the nether regions for a terrifying view of the suffering and sins that humankind must endure. You'll also be able to view many Dutch and Flemish paintings, some from as far back as the 15th century, although the academy is noted for its 17th-century art. The gallery boasts works by van Dyck, Rembrandt, Botticelli, and a host of other artists. There are several works by Lucas Cranach the Elder, the most outstanding being his *Lucretia,* completed in 1532. Some say it's as enigmatic as *Mona Lisa.* Rubens is represented here by more than a dozen oil sketches. You can see Rembrandt's *Portrait of a Woman* and scrutinize Guardi scenes from 18th-century Venice.

✪ Kunsthistorisches Museum (Museum of Fine Arts)

Maria-Theresien-Platz, Burgring 5. ☎ 0222/521-77-0. Admission 95 AS ($9.05) adults, 60 AS ($5.70) students and senior citizens, free for children under 11. Tues–Sun 10am–6pm. U-Bahn: Mariahilferstrasse. Tram: 52, 58, D, or J.

Across from the Hofburg Palace, this huge building houses many of the fabulous art collections gathered by the Habsburgs when they added new territories to their empire. One highlight is the fine collection of ancient Egyptian and Greek art. The museum also has works by many of the greatest European masters, such as Velásquez and Titian.

On display here are Roger van der Weyden's *Crucifixion* triptych, a Memling altarpiece, and Jan van Eyck's portrait of Cardinal Albergati. But it's the works of Pieter Brueghel the Elder for which the museum is renowned. This 16th-century Flemish master is known for his sensitive yet vigorous landscapes. He did many lively studies of peasant life, and his pictures today seem almost a storybook of life in his time. Don't leave without a glimpse of Brueghel's *Children's Games and Hunters in the Snow,* one of his most celebrated works.

Many visitors go to the gallery that displays the work of van Dyck, especially to see his *Venus in the Forge of Vulcan.* You'll see Peter Paul Rubens's *Self-Portrait* and *Woman with a Cape,* for which he is said to have used the face of his second wife, Helen Fourment. The Rembrandt collection includes two remarkable self-portraits as well as a moving portrait of his mother and one of his son, Titus.

Other than revisiting the works of Brueghel, the thrill of any trip to Vienna is seeing the Kunsthistorisches Museum's collection of works by Albrecht Dürer, the German painter and engraver (1471–1528), known for his imaginative art and his painstakingly detailed workmanship. His noted *Blue Madonna* is here as are some of his realistic landscapes like *Martyrdom of 10,000 Christians.*

The glory of the French, Spanish, and Italian schools is also visible in this Viennese museum, having often come into Habsburg hands as "gifts." Titian is represented by *A Girl with a Cloak;* Veronese by an *Adoration of the Magi;* Caravaggio by his *Virgin of the Rosary;* Raphael by *The Madonna in the Meadow,* and Tintoretto by his painting of Susanna caught off guard in her bath when the Peeping Tom elders came along. One of our all-time favorite painters is Giorgione, and here visitors can gaze long at his *Trio of Philosophers.*

Secession Building

Friedrichstrasse, 12 (on the western side of Karlsplatz). ☎ 0222/587-53-07-347. Admission 30 AS ($2.85) adults, 15 AS ($1.45) children. Special exhibitions 60 AS ($5.70) adults, 30 AS ($2.85) children. Tues–Fri 10am–6pm, Sat–Sun 10am–4pm. U-Bahn: Karlsplatz.

Come here if for no other reason than to see Gustav Klimt's *Beethoven Frieze,* a 30-meter-long visual interpretation of Beethoven's *Ninth Symphony.* Built in 1898, this building—a virtual art manifesto proclamation—stands south of the Opernring, beside the Academy of Fine Arts. The building is crowned by a dome once called "outrageous in its useless luxury." The empty dome—covered in triumphal laurel leaves—echoes that of the Karlskirche on the other side of Vienna.

The Secession building was the home of the Viennese avant-garde, which extolled the glories of *Jugendstil* or art nouveau. A young group of painters and architects launched the Secessionist movement in 1897 in rebellion against the strict confines of the Academy of Fine Arts. Klimt was a leader of the movement, and defied the historicism favored by the Emperor Franz Joseph. The works of Kokoschka were featured here, as was the "barbarian" Gauguin. Instead of having a memorial to the great Secessionist artists of yesterday, the pavilion here instead displays substantial contemporary exhibits. The Belvedere Palace is still the best repository for Secessionist art, not this building.

OUTSIDE THE INNER CITY

✪ Schönbrunn Palace

Schönbrunner Schlossstrasse. ☎ **0222/81-113.** Admission 95 AS ($9.05) adults, 40 AS ($3.80) children 6–15, free for children under 6. Apartments, Apr–Oct, daily 8:30am–5pm; Nov–Mar, daily 9am–4:30pm. U-Bahn: U-4 to Schönbrunn.

A Habsburg palace of 1,441 rooms, Schönbrunn was designed by those masters of the baroque, the von Erlachs. It was built between 1696 and 1712, at the request of Emperor Leopold I for his son, Joseph I. Leopold envisioned a palace whose grandeur would surpass that of Versailles. However, Austria's treasury, drained by the cost of wars, would not support the ambitious undertaking, and the original plans were never carried out.

When Maria Theresa became empress, she had the original plans changed greatly, and Schönbrunn looks today much as she conceived it, with delicate rococo touches designed for her by Austrian Nikolaus Pacassi. Schönbrunn was the imperial summer palace during Maria Theresa's 40-year reign, and it was the scene of the great ceremonial balls, lavish banquets, and fabulous receptions held during the Congress of Vienna. At the age of 6, Mozart performed in the Hall of Mirrors before Maria Theresa and her court, and the empress held secret meetings with her chancellor, Prince Kaunitz, in the round Chinese Room.

Franz Joseph was born within the palace walls, which became the setting for the lavish court life associated with his reign, and he also spent the final years of his life here. The last of the Habsburg rulers, Karl I, signed a document here on November 11, 1918, renouncing his participation in affairs of state—not quite an abdication, but tantamount to one.

Schönbrunn Palace was damaged in World War II by Allied bombs, but restoration has obliterated the scars. In complete contrast to the grim, forbidding Hofburg, Schönbrunn Palace, done in "Maria Theresa ochre," has **Imperial Gardens,** embellished by the Gloriette, a marble summerhouse topped by a stone canopy that showcases the imperial eagle. The so-called Roman Ruins here consist of a collection of marble statues and fountains, dating from the late 18th century, when it was fashionable to simulate the ravaged grandeur of Rome. The park, which can be visited until sunset daily, was laid out by Adria van Steckhoven and contains many fountains and heroic statues, often depicting Greek mythological characters.

The **State Apartments** are the most stunning display in the palace. Much of the interior ornamentation is decorated in the rococo style, done in red, white, and more often than not $23^1/_2$ karat gold. Of the 40 rooms that you can visit, particularly fascinating is the "Room of Millions," decorated with Indian and Persian miniatures and the grandest rococo salon in the world. Guided tours of many of the palace rooms, lasting 50 minutes, are narrated in English every half hour beginning at 9:30am. You should tip the guide.

The palace's grandest summer attraction is the **Mozart Festival** in July and August. The open-air festival, initiated at Schönbrunn in 1992, is set in the Imperial Gardens. It attracts top-notch international artists and is bound to include a performance of the opera *Don Giovanni*. The most recent festivities included an all-new staging of *Die Zauberflöte*, perhaps Mozart's most enigmatic—albeit, highly popular—opera. Under the starry summer sky, a night of enchantment awaits visitors in a city renown for its charmed musical progeny. For more information on the

In case you want to see the world.

At American Express, we're here to make your journey a smooth one. So we have over 1,700 travel service locations in over 120 countries ready to help. What else would you expect from the world's largest travel agency?

do more

Travel

http://www.americanexpress.com/travel

In case you want to be welcomed there.

We're here to see that you're always welcomed at establishments everywhere. That's why millions of people carry the American Express® Card — for peace of mind, confidence, and security, around the world or just around the corner.

do more

In case you're running low.

We're here to help with more than 118,000 Express Cash locations around the world. In order to enroll, just call American Express before you start your vacation.

do more

Express Cash

And just in case.

We're here with American Express® Travelers Cheques
and Cheques *for Two*.® They're the safest way to carry
money on your vacation and the surest way to get a
refund, practically anywhere, anytime.

Another way we help you...

do more

**Travelers
Cheques**

Festival Mozart in Schönbrunn, 24 Fleischmarkt, A-1010 Vienna, dial **0222/ 512-01-00.**

Also on the grounds at Schönbrunn is the **Schlosstheater** (Palace Theater), which is still has summer performances. Marie Antoinette appeared on its stage in pastorals during her happy youth, and Max Reinhardt, the theatrical impresario, launched an acting school here. The **Wagenburg** or Carriage Museum (☎ **0222/877-32-44**) is also worth a visit. It contains a fine display of imperial coaches from the 17th, 18th, 19th, and 20th centuries. The coronation coach of Karl VI (Charles, 1711–40), which was pulled by eight white stallions, is here. It was also used for several Habsburg coronations. This intriguing museum is open from April through October, Tuesday through Sunday from 9am to 6pm; and November through March, Tuesday through Sunday, 10am to 4pm.

✪ Belvedere Palace

Prinz-Eugen-Strasse 27. ☎ **0222/795-57.** Admission 60 AS ($5.70) adults, 30 AS ($2.85) children. Tues–Sun 10am–5pm. Tram: D to Schloss Belvedere.

Southeast of Karlsplatz, the Belvedere sits on a slope above Vienna. The approach to the palace through a long garden with a huge circular pond is memorable as the water reflects the sky and the looming palace buildings. Designed by Johann Lukas von Hildebrandt, who was the last major Austrian baroque architect, the Belvedere was built as a summer home for Prince Eugene of Savoy. It consists of two palatial buildings, made up of a series of interlocking cubes. The interior is dominated by two great, flowing staircases.

Unteres Belvedere (Lower Belvedere), with its entrance at Rennweg 6A, was constructed from 1714 to 1716. **Oberes Belvedere** (Upper Belvedere) was started in 1721 and completed in 1723.

The Gold Salon in Lower Belvedere is one of the most beautiful rooms in the palace. Anton Bruckner, the composer, lived in one of the buildings until his death in 1896, and the palace was the residence of Archduke Franz Ferdinand, who was slain in 1914. In May 1955 the peace treaty recognizing Austria as a sovereign state was signed in Upper Belvedere by foreign ministers of the four powers that occupied this country at the close of World War II—France, Great Britain, the United States, and the Soviet Union.

Today visitors can come to the splendid baroque palace to enjoy the panoramic view of the **Wienerwald** (Vienna Woods) from the terrace. A regal French-style garden lies between Upper and Oberes Belvedere, both of which feature impressive art collections that are open to the public.

Lower (Unteres) Belvedere has a wealth of sculptural decorations and houses the **Barockmuseum** (Museum of Baroque Art). The original sculptures from the Neuer Markt fountain, the work of Georg Raphael Donner, who died in 1741, are displayed here. During his life, Donner dominated the development of 18th century Austrian sculpture, well founded in Italian art. On the fountain, four figures represent the four major tributaries of the Danube. Works by Franz Anton Maulbertsch, an 18th-century painter, are also exhibited. Maulbertsch, strongly influenced by Tiepolo, was the most original and the greatest Austrian painter of his day. He was best known for his iridescent colors and flowing brushwork.

The **Museum Mittelalterlicher Kunst** (Museum of Medieval Austrian Art) is located in the Orangery at Lower Belvedere. Here you'll see works from the Gothic period as well as a Tyrolean Romanesque crucifix that dates from the 12th century. Outstanding works include seven panels by Rueland Frueauf, scenes from the life of the Madonna and the Passion of Christ.

Upper (Oberes) Belvedere houses the **Galerie des 19. and 20. Jahrhunderts** (Gallery of 19th- and 20th-Century Art). In a large salon decorated in red marble you can view the 1955 peace treaty mentioned above. A selection of Austrian and international paintings of the 19th and 20th centuries is on display, including works by Oskar Kokoschka, Vincent van Gogh, James Ensor, and C.D. Freidrich.

Most outstanding are the works of Gustav Klimt (1862–1918), who was one of the founders of the 1897 Secession movement. Klimt used a geometrical approach to painting, blending figures with their backgrounds in the same overall tones. Witness the extraordinary *Judith,* in which the artist reveals his fascination with patter. Other notable works by Klimt are displayed such as *The Kiss, Adam and Eve,* and five panoramic lakeside landscapes from Attersee. Sharing almost equal billing with Klimt is Egon Shiele (1890–1918), whose masterpieces displayed here include *The Wife of an Artist.* Schiele could be both morbid, as exemplified by *Death and Girl,* or cruelly observant, as in *The Artist's Family.* Art lovers from around the world come to Vienna just to see the various works of Schiele and Klimt.

Hundertwasserhaus

Löwengasse and Kegelgasse 3. ☎ **0222/713-6093.** U-Bahn: Landstrasse; Tram: N.

In a city filled with baroque palaces and other architectural adornments, this sprawling public-housing project in the rather bleak 3rd District of Vienna, is visited—or at least seen from the window of a tourist bus—by about a million visitors annually. Completed in 1985, it was the work of self-styled "eco-architect" Friedensreich Hundertwasser. The complex, which has a facade like a gigantic black-and-white game board, is relieved with scattered splotches of red, yellow, and blue. Trees stick out at 45° angles through apartments designed to accommodate human tenants as well as the foliage.

There are 50 apartments here and signs warn not to go inside. However, there's a tiny gift shop at the entrance, where you can buy Hundertwasser posters and postcards, plus a coffee shop on the first floor. With its irregular shape, its turrets and its "rolling meadows" of grass and trees, the Hundertwasserhaus is certainly the most controversial building in Vienna, which makes it a must for any Viennese itinerary.

Museum Moderner Kunst Stiftung Ludwig Wien
(Museum of Modern Art)

Schweizer Garten and Fürstengasse 1. ☎ **0222/317-69-00** or 0222/799-69-00. Admission 45 AS ($4.30)adults to each house, 60 AS ($5.70) for both houses; 25 AS ($2.40) for students and senior citizens to each house, 30 AS ($2.85) for both houses; free for children under 11. Both houses, Tues–Sun 10am–6pm. U-Bahn: Südtirolerplatz for Museum des 20. Jahrhunderts. Tram: D to Fürstengasse for Palais Liechtenstein.

This museum comprises two exhibition buildings, the Museum des 20. Jahrhunderts, which was first opened to the public in 1962, and the Palais Liechtenstein, a building rented in 1979 to add more exhibition space. The **Museum des 20. Jahrhunderts** at the Schweizer Garten is housed in a pavilion originally constructed for the world exposition in Brussels in 1958. On the first floor of the museum, large alternating exhibitions are presented, while the international collection is exhibited on the second floor, featuring the works of such artists as Donald Judd, Lawrence Weiner, Bertrand Lavier, and Jannis Kounellis. In the sculpture gardens, you'll discover works by Henry Moore, Fritz Wotruba, and Alberto Giacometti.

The baroque **Palais Liechtenstein,** built between 1698 and 1711, today displays a cross section of 20th-century international art. Special rooms are dedicated to various art movements from expressionism (Jawlensky, Pechstein) to cubism (Léger, Gleizes) to futurism (Balla), and on and on, ranging from surrealism (Magritte,

Ernst) to Vienna Actionism (Nitsch, Rainer), and ending with pop art (Warhol, Rauschenberg).

3 Churches

See also section 1 of this chapter for listings of the Hofburg Palace Chapel, where the Vienna Boy's Choir performs, and the Augustinerkirche. Section 2, "Other Top Attractions" contains the listing for St. Stephan's Cathedral.

THE INNER CITY

✪ Kapuzinerkirche, with the Kaisergruft (Imperial Crypt)

Neuer Markt. ☎ **0222/512-68-53.** Admission 40 AS ($3.80) adults, 30 AS ($2.85) children. Daily 9:30am–4pm. U-Bahn: Stephansplatz.

The Kapuziner Church (just inside the ring behind the Opera) has housed the Imperial Crypt, the burial vault of the Habsburgs for some three centuries. Capuchin friars guard the family's final resting place, where 12 emperors, 17 empresses, and dozens of archdukes are entombed. But, only their bodies are here. Their hearts are in urns in the Loreto Chapel of the Augustinerkirche in the Hofburg complex, and their entrails are similarly enshrined in a crypt below St. Stephan's Cathedral.

Most outstanding of the imperial tombs is the double sarcophagus of Maria Theresa and her consort, Emperor Francis I (François of Lorraine), the parents of Marie Antoinette. Before her own death, the empress used to descend into the tomb often to visit the gravesite of her beloved Francis. The "King of Rome," the ill-fated son of Napoléon and Marie-Louise of Austria, was also buried here in a bronze coffin after his death at 21. (Hitler managed to anger both the Austrians and the French by having the remains of Napoléon's son transferred to Paris in 1940.) Although she was not a Habsburg, Countess Fuchs, the governess who practically reared Maria Theresa, lies in the crypt.

Emperor Franz Joseph was interred here in 1916, a frail old man who outlived his time and died just before the final collapse of his empire. His wife, Empress Elizabeth, was buried in the crypt following her assassination in Geneva in 1898, as was their son, Archduke Rudolf, who allegedly committed suicide at Mayerling.

Die Deutschordenkirche (Church of the Teutonic Order)

Singerstrasse 7. ☎ **0222/512-10-65.** Admission to Church, free; treasury, 30 AS ($2.85), free for children under 11. Church, daily 9am–6pm; treasury, Sun–Thurs 10am–noon, Fri–Sat 3–5pm. U-Bahn: Stephansplatz.

Die Deutschordenkirche and its treasury, Schatzkammer des Deutschen Ordens, will stir thoughts of the Crusades in the minds of history buffs, but the relics of vanished glory may make some visitors wish they had been among the medieval nobility. The Order of the Teutonic Knights was a German society founded in 1190 in the Holy Land. The order came to Vienna in 1205, but the church they built dates from 1395. The building never fell prey to the baroque madness that swept the city after the Counter-Reformation. Subsequently, you see it pretty much in its original form, a Gothic church dedicated to St. Elizabeth. A choice feature is the 16th-century Flemish altarpiece standing at the main altar, which is richly decorated with woodcarving, much gilt, and painted panel inserts. Many knights of the Teutonic Order are buried here, their heraldic shields still mounted on some of the upper walls.

In the knights' treasury, on the second floor of the church, you'll see mementos such as seals and coins illustrating the history of the order, as well as a collection of arms, vases, gold, crystal, and precious stones. Also on display are the charter given to the Teutonic Order by Henry IV of England and a collection of medieval paintings. A curious exhibit is a Viper Tongue Credenza, said to have the power to detect poison in food and render it harmless.

Maria Am Gestade (St. Mary's on the Bank)

At Passauer Platz. ☎ **0222/533-22-82.** Free admission. Daily 6am–6pm. U-Bahn: Stephanplatz.

This church, also known as the Church of Our Lady of the Riverbank, was once just that. With an arm of the Danube flowing by, it was a favorite place of worship for fishers. But the river was redirected and now the church draws people with its own beauty. A Romanesque church on this site was rebuilt in the Gothic style between 1394 and 1427. The western facade is flamboyant, with a remarkable seven-sided Gothic tower; it's surmounted by a dome that culminates in a lacelike crown.

Michaelerkirche (Church of St. Michael)

Michaelerplatz. ☎ **0222/533-80-00.** Free admission. Mon–Sat 6:45am–8pm, Sun 8am–6:30pm. U-bahn: Herrengasse. Bus: 1A, 2A, or 3A.

This church can trace some of its Romanesque portions to the early 1200s. The exact date of the chancel is not known, but it's probably from the mid-14th century. Over its long history the church has felt the hand of many architects and designers, resulting in a medley of styles, not all harmonious. Perhaps only the catacombs would be recognized by time travelers from the Middle Ages.

Most of St. Michael's as it appears today dates from 1792, when the facade was done in the neoclassical style; however, the spire is from the 16th century. The main altar is richly decorated in baroque style, and the altarpiece, entitled *The Collapse of the Angels,* completed in 1781, is the last major baroque work completed in Vienna.

Minoritenkirche (Church of the Minorites)

Minoritenplatz 2A. ☎ **0222/533-41-62.** Free admission. Mon–Sat 9am–6pm. U-Bahn: Herrengasse.

If you're tired of baroque ornamentation, visit this church of the Friar Minor Conventual, a Franciscan order also called the Minorite friars (inferior brothers). Construction of this church began in 1250, but was not completed until early in the 14th century. Its tower was damaged by the Turks in their two sieges of Vienna, and it later fell prey to baroque architects and designers in the 18th century. But in 1784 Ferdinand von Hohenberg ordered that the baroque additions be removed and the simple lines of the original Gothic church be returned, complete with Gothic cloisters. Inside you'll see a mosaic copy of da Vinci's *The Last Supper.* Masses are said on Sunday at 8:30 and 11am.

Peterskirche (St. Peter's Church)

Peterplatz. ☎ **0222/533-64-33.** Free admission. Daily 7am–6:30pm. U-Bahn: Stephansplatz.

This is the second-oldest church in Vienna, but the spot on which it stands may well be the oldest Christian church site. Many places of worship have stood here, the first believed to date from the second half of the 4th century. Charlemagne is credited with having founded a church on the site during the late 8th or early 9th century.

The present St. Peter's, the most lavishly decorated baroque church in Vienna, was designed in 1702 by Gabriel Montani. Von Hildebrandt, the noted architect who designed the Belvedere Palace, is believed to have finished the building in 1732. The fresco in the dome is a masterpiece by J. M. Rottmayr, depicting the Coronation of the Virgin. The church contains many frescoes and much gilded carved wood, plus altarpieces done by many well-known artists of the period.

Impressions

This is one of the most perplexing cities that I was ever in. It is extensive, irregular, crowded, dusty, dissipated, magnificent, and to me disagreeable. It has immense palaces, superb galleries of paintings, several theatres, public walks, and drives crowded with equipages. In short, everything bears the stamp of luxury and ostentation; for here is assembled and concentrated all the wealth, fashion, and nobility of the Austrian empire.
          —Washington Irving, letter to his sister, from *The Travellers'*

Ruprechtskirche (St. Rupert's Church)

Ruprechtsplatz, Seittenstettengasse 4–5. ☎ **0222/553-60-03.** Free admission. Easter–Sept, Mon–Fri 10am–1pm. Closed Oct–Easter. U-Bahn: Schwedenplatz.

The oldest church in Vienna, Ruprechtskirche has stood here since 740, although much that you see now, such as the aisle, is newer—from the 11th century. Beautiful new stained-glass windows—the work of Lydia Roppolt—were installed in 1993. It's believed that much of the masonry from a Roman shrine on this spot was used in the present church. The tower and nave are Romanesque, the rest of the church is Gothic. St. Rupert is the patron saint of the Danube's salt merchants.

Universitätskirche (Church of the Jesuits)

Dr.-Ignaz-Seipel-Platz 1. ☎ **0222/512-52-32.** Admission to Church, free. Tickets to SPECTACVLVM (☎ 0222/512-52-32), 50–650 AS ($4.75–$61.75). Daily 7am–7pm. U-Bahn: Stephansplatz or Stubentor. Tram: 1 or 2. Bus: 1A.

Built at the time of the Counter-Reformation, this church is rich in baroque embellishments, a trend that swept the city during the 17th century. This was the university church, dedicated to the Jesuit saints Ignatius of Loyola and Franciscus Xaverius. The high-baroque decorations—galleries, columns, and the *trompe-l'oeil* painting on the ceiling, which gives the illusion of a dome—were added from 1703 to 1705. The embellishments were the work of a Jesuit lay brother, Andrea Pozzo, at the orders of Emperor Leopold I. Look for Pozzo's painting of Mary behind the main altar. Choir and orchestra services (mostly classical) are celebrated on Sunday and Holy Days at 10am.

In July the church is a central point of the SPECTACVLVM, a summer festival held by the Society for Music Theater in the old university district. Baroque operas and contemporary ballets are performed in the church, with other segments performed elsewhere. Information about this event is available from the **Society for Music Theater**, Türkenstrasse 19, A-1090 Vienna (☎ **0222/34-06-99**).

OUSIDE THE INNER CITY

✪ Karlskirche (Church of St. Charles)

Karlsplatz. ☎ **0222/504-61-87.** Free admission. Self-guided tours, 10 AS (95¢) adults, 5 AS (50¢) for children. Mon–Fri 7:30am–7pm, Sat 8am–7pm, Sun 9am–7pm. Bus: 4.

Construction on Karlskirche, dedicated to St. Charles Borromeo, was begun in 1716 by order of Emperor Charles VI. The Black Plague swept Vienna in 1713 and the emperor made a vow to build the church if the disease would abate. The master of the baroque, Johann Bernard Fischer von Erlach, did the original work on the church from 1716 to 1722, and his son, Joseph Emanuel, completed it between 1723 and 1737. The lavishly decorated interior stands as a testament to the father-and-son duo that led the baroque movement.

The well-known ecclesiastical artist J. M. Rottmayr painted many of the frescoes inside the church from 1725 to 1730. The green copper dome of Karlskirche is 236 feet high, a dramatic landmark on the Viennese skyline. Two columns, spin-offs from Trajan's Column in Rome, flank the front of the church, which opens onto Karlsplatz. There's also a sculpture by Henry Moore in a little pool.

Piaristenkirche (Church of the Piarist Order)
Piaristeng 54. ☎ **0222/405-95-53.** Free admission. Daily 8am–8pm. U-Bahn: Rathaus.

Work on the Piaristenkirche, more popularly known as Piaristenplatz, was launched in 1716 by a Roman Catholic teaching congregation known as Piarists (fathers of religious schools). The church, however, was not consecrated until 1771. Some of the designs submitted during that long period are believed to have been drawn by von Hildebrandt, the noted architect who designed the Belvedere Palace, but many builders had a hand in its construction. This church is noteworthy for its fine classic facade as well as the frescoes by F. A. Maulbertsch, which adorn the inside of the circular cupolas.

Votivkirche
Rooseveltplatz 8. ☎ **0222/431-192.** Free admission. Daily 9am–4pm. U-Bahn: Schottenor.

After a failed assassination attempt on Emperor Franz Joseph, a collection was taken for the construction of the Votive Church, which sits across from the site where the attempt was made. Heinrich von Ferstel began work on the neo-Gothic church in 1856, but it was not consecrated until 1879. The magnificent facade features awesome lacy spires and intricate sculpture. Most noteworthy is the Renaissance sarcophagus tomb of Niklas Salm, who commanded Austrian forces during the Turkish siege in 1529.

4 Museums & Galleries

See sections 1 and 2 of this chapter for additional museums and galleries.

THE INNER CITY

Niederösterreichisches Landesmuseum (Museum of Lower Austria)
Herrengasse 9. ☎ **0222/53-110.** Admission 25 AS ($2.40) adults, 10 AS (95¢) children. Tues–Fri 9am–5pm, Sat noon–5pm, Sun 9:30am–1pm. Closed Aug. U-Bahn: Herrengasse. Bus: 2A or 3A.

This museum has exhibits of the geology, flora, and fauna of the area surrounding Vienna. It also exhibits a collection of art, including baroque and Biedermeier. Temporary shows featuring 20th-century works are also presented. These exhibits are displayed in a palace dating from the 17th century. Best of all, it's only a 5-minute walk from Stephansplatz.

Österreichisches Museum für Angewandte Kunst
(Museum of Applied Art)
Stubenring 5. ☎ **0222/711-36.** Admission 90 AS ($8.55) adults, 45 AS ($4.30) children 12–18, free for children 11 and under. Tues–Wed and Fri–Sun 10am–6pm, Thurs 10am–9pm. U-bahn: Stubentor. Tram: 1, 2.

Of special interest here is a rich collection of applied tapestries, some from the 16th century, and the most outstanding assemblage of Viennese porcelain in the world. Look for a Persian carpet depicting *The Hunt* as well as the group of 13th-century Limoges enamels. Exhibits typically display Biedermeier furniture and other antiques, glassware and crystal, plus outstanding objects of *Wiener Werkstatte*, and large collections of lace and textiles. An entire hall is devoted to art nouveau.

Uhrenmuseum der Stadt Wien (Municipal Clock Museum)

Schulhof 2. ☎ **0222/533-22-65**. Admission 50 AS ($4.75) adults, 20 AS ($1.90) children. Tues–Sun 9am–4:30pm. U-Bahn: Stephansplatz.

A wide-ranging assemblage of timepieces—some ancient, some modern, and some in between—are on view here. Housed in what was once the Obizzi town house, the museum dates from 1917 and displays clocks of all shapes and sizes. Clock collectors from all over Europe and North America come here to gaze and perhaps to covet. See Rutschmann's astronomical clock made in the 18th century. There are several interesting cuckoo clocks and a gigantic timepiece that was once mounted in the tower of St. Stephan's.

OUTSIDE THE INNER CITY

Heeresgeschichtliches Museum (Museum of Military History)

Arsenal 3. ☎ **0222/79-561-0**. Admission 40 AS ($3.80) adults, 20 AS ($1.90) children. Sat–Thurs 10am–4pm. Tram: 18 or D.

The oldest state museum in Vienna, this building was constructed from 1850 to 1856, a precursor to the Ringstrasse style. The Moorish-Byzantine and the neo-Gothic designs draw attention to the museum, where the military history of the Habsburgs, including both triumphs and defeats, is delineated.

A special display case in front of the Franz-Josef Hall contains the six orders of the House of Habsburg that Franz Joseph sported on all public occasions. The colors are faded and the pins and other fasteners almost worn away. We find the Sarajevo room fascinating—it contains mementos of the assassination of Archduke Franz Ferdinand and his wife on June 28, 1914, the event that set off the deadly bonfire of World War I. The archduke's bloodstained uniform is displayed, along with the bullet-scarred car in which the royal couple rode. Many exhibits concentrate on the navy of the Austro-Hungarian Empire, and frescoes depict important battles, including those fought against the Turks in and around Vienna.

Historisches Museum der Stadt Wien (Historical Museum of Vienna)

Karlsplatz 4. ☎ **0222/505-87-47**. Admission 50 AS ($4.75) adults, 10 AS (95¢) children. Tues–Sun 9am–4:30pm. U-Bahn: Karlsplatz.

History buffs should seek out this fascinating but apparently little-visited collection. Here the full panorama of Old Vienna's history folds, beginning with the settlement of prehistoric tribes in the Danube basin. Roman relics, artifacts from the reign of the dukes of Babenberg, and a wealth of leftovers from the Habsburg sovereignty are on display, as well as arms and armor from various eras. A scale model shows Vienna as it looked in the Habsburg heyday. You'll see pottery and ceramics dating from the Roman era, 14th-century stained-glass windows, mementos of the Turkish sieges of the city in 1529 and 1683, and Biedermeier furniture. There's also a section on Vienna's art nouveau.

Sigmund Freud Haus

Berggasse 19. ☎ **0222/319-15-96**. Admission 60 AS ($5.70) adults, 40 AS ($3.80) senior citizens and students, 25 AS ($2.40) children 10–16, free for children 9 and under. Daily 9am–4pm. Tram: D to Schlickgasse.

With its dark furniture (only part of it original), lace curtains, and collection of antiquities, this museum gives you the feeling that the doctor might walk in at any moment and tell you to make yourself comfortable on the couch. His velour hat, dark walking stick with ivory handle, and other mementos are on view in the study and waiting room he used during his residence here from 1891 to 1938.

The museum also has a bookshop where souvenirs are available, including a variety of postcards of the apartment, books by Freud, posters, prints, and pens.

5 Parks & Gardens

When the weather is fine, the typical Viennese shuns city parks in favor of the *Wienerwald* (**Vienna Woods**), a wide arc of forested countryside that surrounds the northwestern and southwestern sides of Vienna (for more details, see Chapter 10, "Side Trips from Vienna"). But if you're an aficionado of parks, you'll find some magnificent ones in Vienna, where there are more than 4,000 acres of gardens and parks within the city limits and no fewer than 770 sports fields and playgrounds. You can, of course, visit **Schönbrunn Park** and **Belvedere Park** when you tour those once-royal palaces. Below, we highlight only the most popular parks of Vienna.

THE INNER CITY

Burggarten

Operrning-Burgring, next to the Hofburg. Tram: 1, 2, 52, 58, or D.

The former gardens of the Habsburg emperors, were built soon after the Volkgarten (see below) was completed. Look for the monument to Mozart as well as an equestrian statue of Franz I, beloved husband of Maria Theresa. The only open-air statue of Franz Joseph in all Vienna is also here and there's a statue of Goethe at the park entrance.

✪ Stadtpark

Parkring. Tram 1, 2, J, or T. U-Bahn: Stadtpark.

This lovely, "City Park" is open 24 hours daily and lies on the slope where the Danube used to overflow into the Inner City prior to the construction of the Danube Canal. Many memorial statues stand in the park, the best known depicts Johann Strauss Jr., composer of operettas and waltzes like "The Blue Danube Waltz." Here, too, are monuments to Franz Schubert and to Hans Makart, a well-known artist whose work you'll see in churches and museums throughout Vienna. These monuments are surrounded by verdant squares of grass, well-manicured flower gardens, and plenty of benches.

From Easter to October, the **Spa Pavilion,** built in 1867, hosts waltz concerts. The Kursalon, an elegant cafe-restaurant, stands at the south end of the Stadtpark. Here you can sit at a garden table and often enjoy Viennese as you sip the local wine.

Volksgarten

Dr.-Karl-Renner-Ring, between the Hofburg and the Burgtheater. Tram: 1, 2, or D.

Known as the "people's park", this oasis was laid out on the site of the old city wall fortifications and can be entered from Dr.-Karl-Lueger-Ring. The oldest public garden in Vienna, dating from 1820, it's dotted with monuments, including a 1907 memorial to assassinated Empress Elizabeth. Construction of the so-called Temple of Theseus, a copy of the Theseion in Athens, was begun in 1820.

OUTSIDE THE INNER CITY

✪ Praterverband (The Prater)

Prater 9. ☎ **0222/218-05-16.** Free admission, but you'll pay for various rides and amusements. Apr–Sept, daily 9am–11pm; Mar and Oct, daily 10am–10pm. U-Bahn: Praterstern.

This extensive tract of woods and meadowland in the 2nd district has been Vienna's favorite recreation area since 1766, when Emperor Joseph II opened it to the

Tales of the Vienna Woods

Yes, dear reader, there really are Vienna Woods (*Wienerwald* in German). They weren't simply dreamed up by Johann Strauss Jr. as the subject of musical tales in waltz time. The Wienerwald is a land of gentle paths and trees several thousand acres in size in a delightful hilly landscape that borders Vienna on its southwestern and northwestern sides. If you stroll through this area, a weekend playground for the Viennese, you'll be following in the footsteps of Strauss and Schubert. Beethoven, when his hearing was failing, claimed that the chirping birds, trees, and leafy vineyards of the Wienerwald made it easier for him to compose.

A round-trip through the woods takes about 3¹/₂ hours by car, a distance of some 50 miles. Even if you don't have a car, the woods can be visited relatively easily on your own. Board tram no. 1 near the State Opera, going to Schottentor; there, switch to tram no. 38 (the same ticket is valid) going out to **Grinzing,** the village that's home to the famous *heurigen* (wine taverns).Here you can board a bus that goes through the Wienerwald to Kahlenberg. The whole trip takes about one hour each way. You might rent a bicycle nearby to make your own exploration of the woods.

Many of the attractions of the Wienerwald are described in Chapter 10, "Side Trips from Vienna."

When you go to the Vienna Woods by public transportation, after you reach Grinzing (if you can resist the *heurigen*), you board bus no. 38A up the hill to **Kahlenberg** on the northeasternmost spur of the Alps (1,585 feet). If the weather is fair and clear, you can see all the way to Hungary and Slovakia from here. At the top of the hill is the small Church of St. Joseph, where King John Sobieski of Poland stopped to pray before leading his troops to the defense of Vienna against the Turks. For one of the best views overlooking Vienna, go to the right of the Kahlenberg restaurant. From the terrace there you'll have a panoramic sweep, including the spires of St. Stephan's.

Many Austrian visitors from the country, a hardy lot, walk along a footpath to the suburb of **Nussdorf** and **Heiligenstadt,** perhaps along the very path Beethoven trod when he lived here. At Nussdorf, it's possible to take tram D back to the center of Vienna.

public. Prior to its institution as a public park, it had been used as a hunting preserve and riding ground for the aristocracy.

The Prater is the birthplace of the waltz and it was first introduced here in 1820 by Johann Strauss Sr. and Josef Lanner. However, it was under Johann Strauss Jr., who became known as "the king of the waltz," that this music form reached its greatest popularity.

The best-known part of the huge park is at the end nearest the entrance from the Ring. Here you'll find the **Riesenrad,** the giant Ferris wheel, which was constructed in 1897 and reaches 220 feet at its highest point.

Just beside the Riesenrad is the terminus of the **Lilliputian railroad,** the 2.6-mile narrow-gauge line that operates in summer using vintage steam locomotives. The amusement park, right behind the Ferris wheel, has all the typical entertainment facilities—roller coasters, merry-go-rounds, tunnels of love, games arcades, whatever. There are also swimming pools, riding schools, and race courses here and there between woodland and meadows. International soccer matches are held in the Prater stadium.

The Prater is not a fenced-in park, but not all amusements are open throughout the year. The season lasts from March or April until October, but the Ferris wheel operates from the beginning of March until November 1. Some of the more than 150 booths and restaurants stay open in winter, including the pony merry-go-round and the gambling venues. If you drive here, don't forget to observe the no entry and no parking signs, which apply after 3pm daily. The place is usually jammed on Sunday afternoon in summer.

Botanischer Garten (Botanical Garden of the University of Vienna)

Rennweg 14. ☎ 0222/797-94. Free admission. Mid-April to October 1, daily from 9am– dusk. Tram: 71 to Unteres Belvedere.

These lush gardens contain exotic plants from all over the world, many of which are extremely rare. Located in Landstrasse (3rd District) right next to the Belvedere Park, the Botanical Garden grew out of a place where Maria Theresa once ordered medicinal herbs to be planted. Always call in advance if the weather is doubtful.

Donaupark

Wagramer Strasse. U-Bahn to Reichsbrücke.

This 247-acre park, located in the 22nd district between the Danube Canal and the *Alte Donau* (Old Danube), was converted in 1964 from a garbage dump to a recreation park with flowers, shrubs, and walks, as well as a bird sanctuary. Within the park you'll find a bee house, a birdhouse with native and exotic specimens, a small-animal paddock, a horse-riding course, playgrounds, and games.

An outstanding feature of the park is the **Donauturm** (Danube Tower), Donauturmstrasse 4 (☎ 0222/23-53-68), an 828-foot tower with two rotating cafe-restaurants from which you have a panoramic view of the city. One restaurant is at the 528-foot level, the other at 561 feet. International specialties and Viennese cuisine are served in both, with meals beginning at 250 AS ($23.75). There's also a sightseeing terrace at 495 feet. Two express elevators take people up in the tower, which in summer is open daily from 9am to midnight, and in winter, daily from 10am to 10pm. The charge for the elevator ride is 65 AS ($6.20) for adults and 45 AS ($4.30) for children.

6 Especially for Kids

The greatest attraction for kids is the **Prater Amusement Park,** but there's much more in Vienna that children find amusing, especially the performances of the horses at the **Spanish Riding School.** They also love the adventure of the climbing the tower of **St. Stephan's Cathedral.** And, nothing quite tops a day like a picnic in the **Vienna Woods.** Below, we list other fun-filled attractions that you and your children will enjoy. (See also **"Outdoor Activities"** at the end of this chapter.)

Schönbrunner Tiergarten, Schönbrunn Gardens (☎ 0222/877-92-94-0) is the world's oldest zoo, founded by Franz Stephan von Lothringen, husband of Empress Maria Theresa. Maria Theresa liked to have breakfast here with her brood, enjoying the antics of the animals. The baroque buildings in the historical park landscape present a unique setting for modern animal keeping; the tranquil setting makes for relaxing, yet interesting outing. Admission is 90 AS ($8.55) for adults, 40 AS ($3.80) for children. It's open from March to September, daily 9am to 7pm; October to February, daily 9am to 5pm. Take the U-Bahn to Hietzing.

The **Puppen & Spielzeug Museum** (Doll and Toy Museum), Schulhof 4, (☎0222/535-68-60), located near the Clock Museum (see Section 4, "More Museums & Galleries" above), is a museum for all ages. Its collection of dolls and dollhouses is one of the most remarkable in the world, ranging from the 1740s to the 1930s. Some of the most outstanding dolls featured in the exhibits are from Germany, which has a rich doll-making heritage. Admission 60 AS ($5.70) adults, 30 AS ($2.85) children. The museum is open from Tuesday to Sunday from 10am to 6pm. Take the U-Bahn to Stephansplatz or Herrengasse.

Other worthwhile museums for children include the **Zirkus und Clownmuseum** (Circus and Clown Museum), Karmelitergasse 9 (☎ **0222/346-8615**), and the **Wiener Straasenbahnmuseum** (Streetcar Museum), Erdbergstrasse 109 (☎ **0222/712-1201**).

7 For Music Lovers

If you're a fan of Mozart, Schubert, Beethoven, Strauss, or Haydn, you've landed in the right city. While in town, you'll not only be able to hear their music in the concert halls and palaces where they performed, but also visit the houses and apartments in which they lived and worked as well as the cemeteries where they were buried.

Haydns Wohnhaus (Haydn's House)
Haydngasse 19. ☎ **0222/596-13-07.** Admission 25 AS ($2.40) adults, 5 AS (50¢) students and children. Tues–Sun 9am–12:15pm and 1–4:30pm. Tram: 52 or 58.

This is where Franz Josef Haydn conceived and wrote his magnificent later oratorios *The Seasons* and *The Creation*. He lived in this house from 1797 until his death in 1809. Haydn gave lessons to Beethoven here. There's also a room in this house, which is a branch of the Historical Museum of Vienna, honoring Johannes Brahms.

Johann-Strauss-Memorial Rooms
Praterstrasse 54. ☎ **0222/214-01-21.** Admission 25 AS ($2.40) adults, 10 AS (95¢) children. Tues–Sun 9am–12:15pm and 1–4:30pm. U-Bahn: Nestroyplatz.

"The King of the Waltz," Johann Strauss Jr., lived at this address for a number of years, composing "The Blue Danube Waltz" here in 1867. The house is now part of the Historical Museum of Vienna.

Mozart-Wohnung / Figarohaus (Mozart Memorial)
Domgasse 5. ☎ **0222/513-62-94.** Admission 15 AS ($1.45) adults, 5 AS (50¢) students and children. Tues–Sun 9am–12:15pm and 1–4:30pm. U-Bahn: Stephansplatz.

This 17th-century house is called the House of Figaro because Mozart composed his opera *The Marriage of Figaro* here. The composer resided here from 1784 to 1787, a relatively happy period in what was otherwise a rather tragic life. It was here that he often played chamber-music concerts with Haydn. Over the years he lived in a dozen houses in all, which became more squalid as he aged. He died in poverty and was given a "pauper's" blessing at St. Stephan's Cathedral in 1791, then buried in St. Marx Cemetery. The Domgasse apartment has been turned into a museum.

Pasqualati House
Mölker Bastei 8. ☎ **0222/535-89-05.** Admission 25 AS ($2.40) adults, 10 AS (95¢) children. . Tues–Sun 11am–12:15pm and 1–4:30pm. U-Bahn: Schottentor.

Beethoven lived in this building on and off from 1804 to 1814. It's likely that either the landlord was tolerant or the neighbors deaf. Beethoven is known to have composed his Fourth, Fifth, and Seventh symphonies here, as well as *Fidelio* and other works.

There isn't much to see except some family portraits and the composer's scores, but you may feel it's worth the climb to the fourth floor (there's no elevator).

Schubert Museum

Nussdorferstrasse 54. ☎ **0222/317-36-01**. Admission 25 AS ($2.40) adults, 10 AS (95¢) students and children. Tues–Sun 9am–12:15pm and 1–4:30pm. U-bahn: U4. S-Bahn: Nussdorferstrasse.

Son of a poor schoolmaster, Schubert was born here in 1797 in a house built earlier in that century. Many Schubert mementos are on view. You can also visit the house at Kettenbrückengasse 6, where he died at age 31.

8 Organized Tours

Wiener Rundfahrten (Vienna Sightseeing Tours), Stelzhamergasse 4-11 (☎ **0222/ 712-468-30**), offers many tours, ranging from a 75-minute **"Vienna—Getting Acquainted"** trip to a one-day excursion by motorcoach to Budapest costing 1,250 AS ($118.75) per person. The get-acquainted tour costs 220 AS ($20.90) for adults and is free for children 12 and under. It's ideal for visitors who are pressed for time and yet want to be shown the major (and most frequently photographed) monuments of Vienna. It takes you past the historic buildings of Ringstrasse—the State Opera, Hofburg Palace, museums, Parliament, City Hall, Burgtheater, the University, and the Votive Church—into the heart of Vienna. Tours leave the State Opera daily at 10:30 and 11:45am and at 3 and 4:30pm.

"Vienna Woods—Mayerling," another popular excursion, lasting about four hours, leaves from the State Opera and takes you to the towns of Perchtoldsdorf and Modling, and also to the Abbey of Heiligenkreuz, a center of Christian culture since medieval times. The commemorative chapel in the village of Mayerling reminds visitors of the tragic suicide of Crown Prince Rudolph, only son of Emperor Franz Joseph. The tour also takes you for a short walk through Baden, the spa that was once a favorite summer resort of the aristocracy. Tours cost 480 AS ($45.60) for adults and 160 AS ($15.20) for children.

A **"Grand City Tour,"** which includes visits to Schönbrunn and Belvedere palaces, leaves the State Opera daily at 9:30am and again at 2:30pm, lasting about three hours and costing 390 AS ($37.05) for adults and 160 AS ($15.20) for children.

A variation on the city tour includes an optional visit to the Spanish Riding School, where the world-renowned Lippizaner horses are trained and showcased. This tour is offered Tuesday through Saturday, leaving from the State Opera building at 9:30am. In addition to driving in a bus past the monuments of Vienna, with guided commentary, the tour includes a half-hour performance by the Lippizaners on their home turf. Adults pay 480 AS ($45.60) and children are charged 160 AS ($15.20); children under 12 tour for free.

Information and booking for these tours is possible either through Vienna Sightseeing Tours (see above) or through their affiliate, **Elite Tours,** Operngasse 4 (☎ **0222/513-22-25**).

9 Active Pursuits

STAYING ACTIVE

BICYCLING

Vienna maintains almost 200 miles of cycling lanes and cycling paths, some of which meander through some of the most elegant parks in Europe. Depending on their location, they'll be identified either by a yellow image of a cyclist stenciled directly onto the pavement, or crafted from rows of red brick set amid the cobblestones or concrete of the busy boulevards in the city center. Some of the most popular paths run parallel to both the Danube and the Danube Canal.

Several entrepreneurs will rent you a bicycle at a cost of around 40 AS ($3.80) per hour. You'll usually be asked to leave either your passport or a form of ID as a deposit. Among the most convenient venues is **Radverleih Salztorbrücke,** at the corner of the Salztorbrücke in the city center (☎ **0222/535-34-22**). Another possibility, one that might enhance a visit to one of the most famous eco-friendly housing projects in Europe, is on the grounds of the architecturally famous Hundertwasserhaus; **Radverleih Hundertwasserhaus** (☎ **0222/713-93-95**), near the entrance to the Hundertwasserhaus.

A final note: One unusual bike itinerary known for almost no interruptions encompasses the long and skinny island that separates the Danube from the Neue Donau Canal, which parallels it. Low-lying and occasionally marshy, but with paved paths along most of its length, it provides clear views of central Europe's industrial landscape and the endless river traffic that flows by on either side.

BOATING

Wear a straw boating hat and hum a few bars of a Strauss waltz as you paddle your way around the quiet eddies of the Alte Donau. This gently curving stream bisects residential neighborhoods to the north of the Danube, and is preferable to the muddy and swift-moving currents of the river itself.

Newrkla, An der Obere Alte Donau (☎ **0222/38-61-05**) rents motorboats on the Danube. A short walk from the Donaupark, beside An der Obere Alte Donau no. 186, it anchors a row of recreational outposts, some renting canoes and kayaks.

GOLF

If you're even considering it, think again. The two golf courses in or near Vienna are chronically overbooked, forcing even long-term members to be highly flexible about their starting times. The busier of the two courses is in the Prater, at **Golfplatz Wien-Freudenau,** Freudenau 65a, (☎ **0222/728-95-64**). More distant, with space which might conceivably be available on a weekday (but almost never on a weekend) is **Föhrenwald,** Bodenstrasse 54, an 18-hole course about 30 miles south of Vienna, in the suburb of Wiener Neustadt (☎ **02622/21-900**).

HEALTH CLUBS

Even if you're not registered at the Vienna Hilton, you are welcome to use the popular health club, **Fitness Center Pyron,** in the Vienna Hilton, Am Stadtpark (☎ **0222/71-20-955**), on the third floor of the deluxe hotel. After registering at the desk, you'll be given a locker key, a towel, and access to the sauna, cold baths, and showers; women and men share the facilities equally. After a sauna, guests relax, draped in towels, beside the TV of the clubroom. Entrance fees for a sauna visit and gym are 200 AS ($19) for nonresidents, 180 AS ($17.10) for hotel guests. The club is open daily from 11am to 10pm September through May, and daily, 2pm to 10pm June through August. Women who prefer to have their sauna alone are directed to a private room.

HIKING

You're likely to expend plenty of shoe leather simply navigating from one of Vienna's museums and palaces to another, but if you yearn for more isolated settings, the city tourist offices will provide information about its eight **Stadt-Wander-Wege.** These are carefully marked hiking paths which usually originate at a point within the city's far-flung network of trams.

Cruising the Danube

Why not take a boat trip on the Danube? Until the advent of railroads and high-ways, the Danube played a vital role in the Vienna's history, helping to build the complex mercantile society that eventually became the Habsburg Empire. In the early 1990s, as boundaries between eastern and western Europe continued to erode, a handful of reputable companies launched a renaissance of travel on this fabled river.

Passenger boats on the Danube are operated by the **First Danube Steamship Co.** (Erste Donau-Dampfschiffahrts-Gesellschaft, or **DDSG**), with main offices at Handelskai 265, A-1024 Vienna (☎ **0222/727-50-0**). Daily trips are made the company's White Fleet from May through October, and special excursions are often available. There is also daily service between Passau and Linz, Linz and Vienna, and Melk and Krems from about mid-April through September.

Cruise programs range from local sightseeing cruises around Vienna to three-hour evening jaunts with dancing on board. Combined boat/rail day trips from Vienna to the Wachau, even to Bratislava or Budapest, or from Linz to Passau, are also operated. Speedboat trips to Bratislava and Budapest are available, as well as two-day cruises between Passau and Vienna in both directions. The "Imperial Austria" cruises cover Linz, Bratislava, and Budapest and then return to Vienna.

Children under 6 ride free, and those aged 6 to 15 go for half fare. International railroad tickets are valid on the Danube River boats, but with an extra supplement. You must present your rail ticket at the DDSG ticket counter before embarking.

A less structured option involves heading east of town into the vast precincts of the **Lainzer Tiergarten,** where hiking trails entwine themselves amid forested hills, colonies of deer, and abundant bird life. To reach it from Vienna's center, first take the U-bahn to the Kennedy Brücke/Heitzing station, which lies a few steps from the entrance to Schönbrunn Palace. A trek among the formal gardens of Schönbrunn might provide exercise enough, but if you're hungry for more, then take tram 60 and then bus 60B into the distant but verdant confines of the Lainzer Tiergarten.

HORSEBACK RIDING

The Prater amusement park, east of the center, contains a network of bridle paths and a stable, the **Reitclub Donauhof,** Hafenzufahrtstrasse 63 (☎ **0222/728-36-46**), willing to rent mounts to qualified riders.

ICE SKATING

There's a public rink, the **Wiener Eislaufverein,** Lothringer Strasse 22 (☎ **0222/713-6353**), within a 20-minute walk southeast of the cathedral. Located just outside the famous Am Stadtpark, near the Inter-Continental Hotel, and especially crowded on weekends, the rink rents skates and is open between late October and early March.

SKIING

Skiing isn't really a very good idea if you plan on staying within the city limits of Vienna. Most Viennese head for the easily accessible slopes of Land Salzburg, Tyrol, or Vorarlberg. If you insist, however, some limited skiing is available on the **Hohe Wand,** west of town. To reach it, take the U4 subway to the Hütteldorf station, then take bus 49B to the city's 14th District. The area around the Semmering (about an hour from the city) is a favorite Viennese location for a quick skiing getaway. For information on skiing in Austria, contact the Austrian National Tourist Office, Margaretenstrasse 1, A-1040 (☎ **0222/588-66**).

SWIMMING

Despite the popularity of certain beaches on islands in the Alte Donau Canal in summer, swimming in either the Danube or any of its satellite canals is not recommended, both because of pollution and because of a dangerous undertow in the main river.

To compensate, Vienna has dozens of swimming pools. Your hotel's receptionist will tell you about options in your neighborhood that are suitable. One of the most modern lies within the confines of the Prater. For pool locations and information, contact Rathaus (City Hall), Friedrich Schmidt-Platz (☎ **0222/4000-5**).

TENNIS

You'll find that many of the tennis courts in Vienna are almost constantly busy. Your hotel might have connections with one or another of them, but if not, contact the city's largest tennis agency: **Sportservice Wien-Sport,** Bacherplatz 14 (☎ **0222/ 545-31-31** or **0222/545-12-01**), which maintains ties to dozens of indoor and outdoor tennis courts throughout Vienna, and can guarantee playing time at some of them for a modest fee.

SPECTATOR SPORTS

HORSE RACING

It all takes place on the legendary pleasure grounds of the **Prater,** at Trabbrennplatz (☎ **0222/218-9535**). The season runs from April to November, and includes both sulky and flat racing. The Vienna Derby is one of the equestrian season's highlights, and takes place on the third Sunday in June.

SOCCER

The sport is known throughout Europe as football, although it tends to draw a less impassioned response in Austria than, for example, in Italy or France. Most of the city's matches are played in the Prater's **Weiner Stadion,** Meiereistrasse 7 (☎ **0222/ 728-0854**). Smaller matches or those played during midwinter or during unfavorable weather usually take place under the protective roof of the **Stadthalle,** Vogelweidplatz 14 (☎ **0222/98-100**).

Tickets to any of these events are usually available at the gate on the day of the match, although it's usually wiser to reserve tickets through one of Vienna's ticket agencies. These can be picked up at the **Kartenbüro Flamm,** Kärntner Ring 3 (☎ **0222/512-4225**), or ordered through the mail several weeks in advance from the **Vienna Ticket Service,** Borscgasse 1, A-1010 Vienna (☎ **0222/534-13-63,** fax 0222/534-13-79), or at a second location, Linke Wienzeile 4, A-1060 Vienna (☎ **0222/587-9843,** fax 0222/587-98-44).

7

Vienna Strolls

Few other cities in the world represent the cultural polyglot of Vienna, former seat of an empire that until 1918 encompassed dozens of linguistic, cultural, and national groups. The result is a rich and evocative treasure trove of architecture that includes buildings erected during virtually every period of the city's history. And even though much of the city's inner core lay in ashes after the bombings of World War II, few other cities in Europe have been as meticulous in their reconstruction.

Many of the streets in the revered First District are designated exclusively for pedestrians, either because they're too narrow for cars, or because local merchants and restaurateurs have demanded that cars be banished (except for deliveries, usually early in the morning) as an incentive for urban revitalization. Vienna has one of the most richly accessorized inner cities in Europe, and an immense potential for rewarding walking tours.

We propose three walking tours, each geared toward a different kind of Viennese aesthetic. No one will mind if you stare in amazement at the city's architectural wealth—just beware of cars, as they sometimes roar through narrow streets at relatively high speeds.

WALKING TOUR 1
Imperial Vienna

Start: State Opera House.
Finish: State Opera House.
Time: 3 hours.
Best Time: During daylight hours or at dusk.
Worst Time: Rainy days.

Although there are dozens of potential itineraries through the historic center of Vienna, this meandering tour through the urban haunts of the Habsburgs will give you at least an exterior view of many of them. The tour is mainly designed to reveal lesser-known sights best seen from the outside, on foot. Later, you can pick and choose the attractions you most want to revisit. (Details on many of these sights are given in Chapter 6.)

Our tour begins at the southernmost loop of **Ringstrasse,** the beltway that encircles most of the historic core of the city, within the shadow of the very symbol of Austrian culture itself, the:

Walking Tour: Imperial Vienna

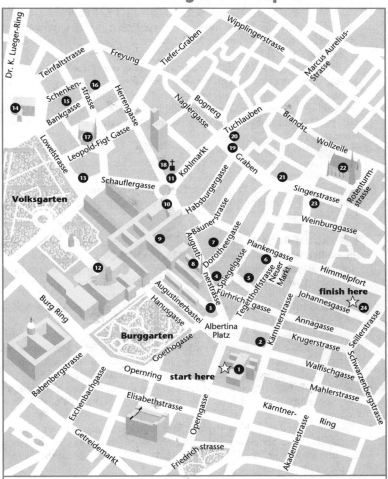

1. Staatsoper
2. Hotel Sacher
3. Albertina Collection
4. Lobkowitz Palace
5. Church of the Capuchin Friars
6. Donner Fountain
7. Dorotheum
8. Hofburg
9. Josefsplatz
10. Spanish Riding School
11. Loos House
12. Heldenplatz
13. Chancellery
14. Burgtheater
15. Palais Liechtenstein
16. Hungarian Embassy
17. Church of the Minorites
18. St. Michael's Church
19. Plague Column
20. Peterskirche
21. Stock-im-Eisen
22. St. Stephan's Cathedral
23. Kärntnerstrasse
24. Savoy Foundation for Noble Ladies

1. Staatsoper (State Opera House). Built between 1861 and 1865 in a style inspired by the French Renaissance, it was so severely criticized after its unveiling that one of its architects, Eduard van der Null, committed suicide. (The other died of a stroke several months later.)

   On Opernring, walk one block northward on the most famous pedestrian street of Austria, Kärntnerstrasse. This tour will eventually take you past this street's rows of glamorous shops and famous houses, but, for the moment, turn left behind the arcaded bulk of the State Opera onto Philharmonikerstrasse. On the right-hand side, you'll see the lushly carved caryatids and globe lights of Vienna's best-known hostelry, the:

2. Hotel Sacher. If you're interested, a confectionery store with a separate streetside entrance sells portions of the hotel's namesake, Sachertorte, which can be shipped anywhere in the world.

   A few steps later you'll find yourself amid the irregular angles of Albertinaplatz, where you'll be able to plunge into the purely Viennese experience of the *kaffeehaus*.

   ☕ **TAKE A BREAK** If you'd rather indulge in heartier fare, try the **Augustinerkeller,** Augustinerstrasse 1 (☎ **0222/533-10-26**), in the basement of the Hofburg palace sheltering the Albertina collection. This popular wine tavern, open daily from 10am to midnight, offers wine, beer, and Austrian food.

   In the same building as your rest stop is one of Vienna's best-known buildings, the headquarters of the:

3. Albertina Collection. A monumental staircase built into its side supports the equestrian statue that dominates the square. Its subject is Field Marshal Archduke Albrecht, in honor of a battle he won in 1866. Adjacent to Albertinaplatz, at Lobkowitzplatz 2, lies one of the many baroque jewels of Vienna, the:

4. Lobkowitz Palace. (Its position is confusing because of the rows of buildings partially concealing it. To get here, walk about 50 paces to the right of the Albertina Collection.)

   At the far end of Lobkowitzplatz, take Gluckgasse past a series of antiques shops filled with art deco jewelry and silverware. At the end of the block, at Tegetthoffstrasse, go left. About 50 paces later you'll be in front of the deceptively simple facade of the:

5. Church of the Capuchin Friars. Originally constructed in the 1620s, its facade was rebuilt in a severely simple design following old illustrations in 1935. Despite its humble appearance, the church contains the burial vaults of every Habsburg ruler since 1633. The heavily sculpted double casket of Maria Theresa and her husband, Franz I, is flanked with weeping nymphs and skulls, but capped with a triumphant cherub uniting the couple once again in love.

   The portal of this church marks the beginning of the Neuer Markt, whose perimeter is lined with rows of elegant baroque houses. The square's centerpiece is one of the most beautiful works of outdoor art in Austria, the:

6. Donner Fountain. Holding a snake, the gracefully undraped Goddess of Providence is attended by four laughing cherubs struggling with fish. The waters flowing into the basin of the fountain are provided by four allegorical figures representing nearby tributaries of the Danube. The fountain is a copy of the original, which was moved to the Baroque Museum in the Belvedere Palace. The original was commissioned by the City Council in 1737, executed by Georg Raphael Donner, but

judged obscene and immoral when viewed for the first time by Maria Theresa. Today it's one of Austria's masterpieces of baroque sculpture.

Now take the street stretching west from the side of the fountain, Plankengasse, where a yellow baroque church fills the space at the end of the street. As you approach it, you'll pass an array of shops filled with alluringly old-fashioned merchandise. Even the pharmacy at the corner of Spiegelgasse has a vaulted ceiling and rows of antique bottles. The store at Plankengasse 6, as well as its next-door neighbor at the corner of Dorotheergasse, is well stocked with museum-quality antique clocks, many of which ticked their way through the dying days of the early 19th century. Turn left when you reach Dorotheergasse, past the turn-of-the-century Italianate bulk of no. 17. Therein lies one of the most historic auction houses of Europe, the:

7. **Dorotheum,** established in 1707, and rebuilt in the neo-baroque style in 1901.

About half a block later, turn right onto Augustinerstrasse, whose edge borders the interconnected labyrinth of palaces, museums, and public buildings known as the:

8. **Hofburg.** The grime-encrusted grandeur of this narrow street is usually diminished by the traffic roaring past its darkened stone walls. Despite that modern intrusion, this group of buildings is the single most impressive symbol of the former majesty of the Viennese Habsburgs.

In about half a block you'll arrive at:

9. **Josefsplatz,** where a huge equestrian statue of Joseph II seems to be storming the gate of no. 5, the Palffy Palace, originally built around 1575 with a combination of classical and Renaissance motifs. Its entrance is guarded by two pairs of relaxed caryatids who seem to be discussing the horseman's approach. Next door, at no. 6, is another once-glittering private residence, the Palavicini Palace, which was completed in 1784 for members of the Fries family, and later purchased by the family whose name it bears today. A few steps later, a pedestrian tunnel leads past the:

10. **Spanish Riding School** (Spanische Reitschule). The district becomes increasingly imperial, filled with slightly decayed vestiges of a long-ago empire whose baroque monuments are flanked by outmoded, too-narrow streets and thundering traffic.

Michaelerplatz now opens to your view. Opposite the six groups of combative statues struggling with their own particular adversaries is a streamlined building with rows of unadorned windows. Known as the:

11. **Loos House,** Michaelerplatz 3, it was designed in 1910 and immediately became the most violently condemned building in town. That almost certainly stemmed from the unabashed (some would say provocative) contrast between the lavishly ornamented facade of the Michaelerplatz entrance to the Hofburg and what contemporary critics compared to "the gridwork of a sewer." Franz Joseph himself hated the building so much that he used the Michaelerplatz exit as infrequently as possible so that he wouldn't have to look at the building, which faced it.

A covered tunnel that empties both pedestrians and automobiles into the square takes you beneath the Hofburg complex. Notice the passageway's elaborate ceiling where spears, capes, and shields crown the supports of the elaborate dome. Cars seem to race beside you, making this one of the most heavily embellished traffic tunnels in the world. As you walk through the tunnel, an awesomely proportioned series of courtyards reveal the Imperial Age's addiction to conspicuous grandeur.

When you eventually emerge from the tunnel, you'll find yourself surrounded by the magnificent curves of:

12. Heldenplatz. Its carefully constructed symmetry seems to dictate that each of the stately buildings bordering it, as well as each of its equestrian statues and ornate lampposts, seems to have a well-balanced mate.

Gardens stretch out, flowering in summer, in well-maintained splendor. Enjoy the gardens if you want, but to continue the tour, put the rhythmically spaced columns of the Hofburg's curved facade behind you and walk catercorner to the far end of the palace's right-hand wing. At Ballhausplatz, notice the:

13. Chancellery, at no. 2. It's an elegant building, yet its facade is modest in comparison with the ornamentation of its royal neighbor. The events that transpired within have influenced the course of European history hundreds of times since the building was erected in 1720. Here, Count Kaunitz plotted with Maria Theresa again and again to expand the influence of her monarchy. Prince Metternich used these rooms as his headquarters during the Congress of Vienna in 1814–15. Many of the decisions made here were responsible for the chain of events leading to World War I. In 1934 Dollfuss was murdered here. Four years later Hermann Göring, threatening a military attack, forced the ouster of the Austrian cabinet with telephone calls made to an office in this building. Rebuilt after the bombings of World War II, this battle-scarred building has housed Austria's Foreign Ministry and its Federal Chancellor's office since 1945.

Walk along the side of the Chancellery's adjacent gardens, along Lowelstrasse, until you reach the:

14. Burgtheater, the national theater of Austria. Notice the window trim of some of the buildings along the way, each of which seems to have its own ox, satyr, cherub, or Neptune carved above it.

At the Burgtheater, make a sharp right-hand turn onto Bankgasse. The ornate beauty of the:

15. Palais Liechtenstein, completed in the early 18th century, is on your right, at no. 9. A few buildings farther on, stone garlands and glimpses of crystal chandeliers are visible at the:

16. Hungarian Embassy, at no. 4-6 on the same street.

Now retrace your steps for about half a block until you reach Abraham-a-Sancta-Clara-Gasse. At its end you'll see the severe Gothic facade of the:

17. Church of the Minorites, on Minoritenplatz. Its 14th-century severity contrasts sharply with the group of stone warriors struggling to support the gilt-edged portico of the baroque palace facing it.

Walk behind the blackened bulk of the church to the curve of the building's rear. At this point some maps of Vienna might lead you astray. Regardless of the markings on your particular map, look for Leopold-Figl-Gasse and walk down it. You'll pass between two sprawling buildings, each of which belongs to one or another of the Austrian bureaucracies, which are linked by an above-ground bridge. A block later, turn right onto Herrengasse. Within a few minutes, you'll be on the by-now-familiar Michaelerplatz. This time you'll have a better view of:

18. St. Michael's Church, where winged angels carved by Lorenzo Mattielli in 1792 fly above the entranceway and a single pointed tower rises. Turn left (north) along Kohlmarkt, noticing the elegant houses along the way: no. 14 houses Demel's, the most famous coffeehouse of Vienna; no. 9 and no. 11 bear plaques for Chopin and Haydn, respectively.

At the broad pedestrian walkway known as the Graben, turn right. The baroque:

19. Plague Column you see in the Graben's center has chiseled representations of clouds piled high like whipped cream, dotted profusely with statues of ecstatic saints fervently thanking God for relief from an outbreak of the Black Plague that erupted in Vienna in 1679 and may have killed as many as 150,000 people. Carved between 1682 and 1693 by a team of the most famous artists of the era, this column eventually inspired the erection of many similar monuments throughout Austria.

A few feet before the Plague Column, turn left onto Jungferngasse and enter what is our favorite church in Vienna:

20. Peterskirche. Believed to rise from the site of a crude wooden church built during the Christianization of Austria around A.D. 350, and later—according to legend—rebuilt by Charlemagne, it was lavishly upgraded during the 1700s by baroque artists who included the famous painter J. M. Rottmayr.

Return to the Graben, passing the papal tiaras at the base of the Plague Column. A few steps later, pass the bronze statue of a beneficent saint leading a small child in the right direction. You might, after all this, enjoy a sandwich. Leave the Graben at one of the first intersections on the right, Dorotheergasse, where you'll find a fine choice.

🍵 **TAKE A BREAK**   Despite its functional simplicity, **Buffet Trzesniewski,** Dorotheergasse 1 (☎ **0222/512-32-91**), has satisfied the hunger pangs of everyone who was ever important in Vienna during the last century. For more information on this place, see "Dining," in Chapter 5.

After your break, continue in a southeasterly direction down the Graben to its terminus. There you'll find a vaguely defined section of pavement which signs will identify as:

21. Stock-im-Eisen. Here two pedestrian thoroughfares, the Graben and Kärntnerstrasse, meet at the southernmost corner of Stephansplatz. To your right, notice the sheet of curved Plexiglas bolted to the corner of an unobtrusive building at the periphery of the square. Behind it are the preserved remains of a tree that used to grow nearby. In it, 16th-century blacksmiths drove a nail for luck each time they left Vienna for other parts of Austria. Today the gnarled and dusty log is covered with an almost uninterrupted carapace of angular, hand-forged nails.

By now, it will be difficult to avoid a full view of Vienna's most symbolic building:

22. St. Stephan's Cathedral. Many newcomers opt to circumnavigate the building's exterior, admiring its 12th- and 13th-century stonework before entering for a view inside. When you exit, turn left after passing through the main portal, passing once again the nail-studded stump in Stock-im-Eisen, and promenade down the pedestrian thoroughfare of what's the most evocative and famous street in Vienna's Inner City:

23. Kärntnerstrasse. Notice especially the exhibition of art objects—a kind of mini-museum of the glassmaking industry—that decorates the second floor of the world-famous glassmaker, Lobmyer, at no. 26.

If you still have the energy, make a detour off Kärntnerstrasse, turning left on Johannesgasse. You'll pass some old and very interesting facades before reaching the baroque carvings and stone lions that guard the 17th-century portals of the:

24. Savoy Foundation for Noble Ladies (Savoysches Damenstift, at no. 15), where countless generations of well-born Austrian damsels struggled to learn "the gentle arts of womanhood." Established by the Duchess of Savoy-Carignan, and originally built in 1688, its facade is adorned with a lead statue by the baroque sculptor F. X. Messerschmidt.

As you retrace your steps back to the shops and the pedestrian crush of Kärntnerstrasse, you might hear strains of music cascading into the street from the Vienna Conservatory of Music, which occupies several buildings on Johannesgasse. These buildings, except for their association with the conservatory, are not especially noteworthy. Turn left as you reenter Kärntnerstrasse, enjoying the views until you eventually return to your point of origin, the State Opera House.

WALKING TOUR 2
South of the Ring

Start: State Opera House.
Finish: Gumpendorferstrasse (on Saturdays, Flohmarkt).
Time: 3¹/₂ hours, not counting visits to museums.
Best Time: Saturday morning, when the Flohmarkt is functioning.
Worst Time: After dark, or in the rain.

The temptation is strong, especially for a first-time visitor to Vienna, to limit exposure to the city only to those monuments within the Ring—i.e., the Gothic, baroque, and Biedermeier architecture within the city's medieval core, the 1st District.

You'll break that tendency by following this tour, which incorporates visits to the sometime surreal manifestations of *fin-de-siècle* Habsburg majesty a short distance south of the Ring. The tour also includes views of less celebrated late 19th-century buildings that don't seem as striking today as when they were designed, but which, for their era, were almost revolutionary.

Regrettably, parts of the 6th District, site of most of this tour, were heavily damaged, then rebuilt, after the horrors of World War II, and will require navigating beside less-than-inspiring boulevards that contain heavy traffic. Fortunately, a network of underground walkways, designed by city planners as part of Vienna's subway system, will make transits through the densest traffic a lot easier.

Begin your tour near the southern facade of:

1. The Vienna State Opera. This was the first of the many monuments built during the massive Ringstrasse projects begun around 1850 by Franz Joseph, on land reclaimed from the razing of Vienna's medieval fortifications. Its French Renaissance theme was plagued with controversy and cost overruns from the moment its foundations were laid. Notice how, on the building's southern edge, bad overall planning caused the roaring traffic of the nearby Ringstrasse to be several feet higher than the foundation of the building. This discrepancy in the respective heights of the surrounding grade, coupled with an offhand—but widely reported—criticism of the situation by Franz Joseph, is believed to have triggered the eventual suicide (by hanging) of one of the building's architects, van der Null, and the death by stroke, a few weeks later, of its other architect, von Sicardsburg. The roof and much of the interior of the building you'll see today were largely rebuilt after the night bombing on March 12, 1945, that sent the original building up in flames. Ironically, the last performance before its near-destruction had been a rousing version of Wagner's *Götterdammerung*.

Since its reconstruction, it has nurtured such luminaries as Bruno Walter and Herbert von Karajan, who survived some of the most Byzantine and convoluted political intrigue of any concert house in the world.

Across the avenue, on your left as you face the Ring, at the intersection of the Kärntner Ring and the Kärntnerstrasse, notice one of the grandest hotels in Europe, the:

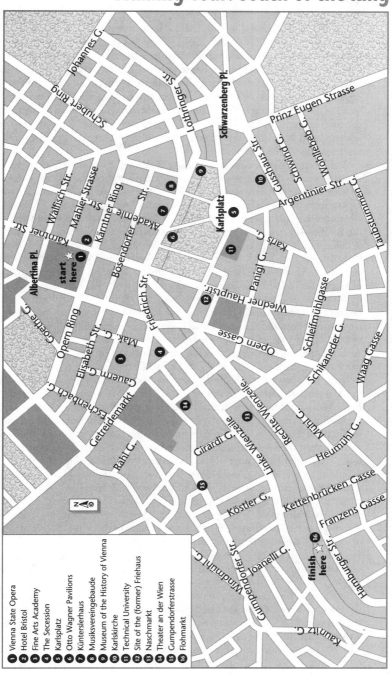

start here ①

finish here ⑯

- ① Vienna State Opera
- ② Hotel Bristol
- ③ Fine Arts Academy
- ④ The Secession
- ⑤ Karlsplatz
- ⑥ Otto Wagner Pavilions
- ⑦ Künstlerhaus
- ⑧ Musikvereingebaude
- ⑨ Museum of the History of Vienna
- ⑩ Karlskirche
- ⑪ Technical University
- ⑫ Site of the (former) Friehaus
- ⑬ Naschmarkt
- ⑭ Theater an der Wien
- ⑮ Gumpendorferstrasse
- ⑯ Flohmarkt

2. Hotel Bristol, Kärntner Ring 1. Ornate, socially impeccable, and tidy, it reigns along with the Sacher and the Imperial as the grande dame of Viennese hotels. A deceptively unpretentious lobby might disappoint you, as the most impressive reception areas are concealed inside within a labyrinth of upstairs corridors. Consider returning later for midafternoon tea or a drink in one of the bars.

Take a deep breath before descending into the depths of an underground passageway that begins at the corner of the Kärnerstrasse and the Kärntner Ring, just south of the Opera House. (You'll find it's a lot easier and safer than trying to cross the roaring traffic of the Ring as an unarmed pedestrian.) You'll bypass some underground boutiques, then climb up from the passage to a position on the southern edge of the Opernring.

Walk west along the Opernring, using another of those underground tunnels to cross beneath the Operngasse, till you reach the Robert Stolz Platz, named after an Austrian composer who died nearby in 1975. If you glance north, across the Opernring, you'll see a faraway statue of Goethe, brooding in a bronze chair, usually garnished with a roosting pigeon. The Robert Stolz Platz opens southward into the Schillerplatz, where, as you'd expect, an equivalent statue features an image of Schiller. The building on Schillerplatz's southern edge (Schillerplatz 3) is the:

3. Gemäldegalerie Akademie der Bildenden Kunst (Fine Arts Academy), erected between 1872 and 1876 by the Danish architect Theophil Hansen in a pastiche of Greek Revival and the Italian Renaissance style. It was here that the artistic dreams of an 18-year-old Adolf Hitler were dashed, in 1907 and 1908, when he failed twice to gain admission to what was at the time the ultimate arbiter of the city's artistic taste and vision. Ironically, a few years later, painter Egon Schiele, an artist of Hitler's age, eventually seceded from the same academy because of its academic restrictions and pomposity. For details about the exhibits contained within this building, refer to "What to See & Do" in Chapter 6.

Now, walk east for a half-block along the Niebelungengasse, then south along the Makartgasse, skirting the side of the Academy. Makartgasse was named after Hans Makart, the most admired and sought-after painter in 19th-century Vienna, the darling of the Academy you've just visited. The soaring and artfully cluttered studio he occupied was subsidized by Franz Joseph himself, and transformed into a salon every afternoon at 4pm for receptions of every prominent newcomer in town. Exhibitions of his huge historical canvases attracted viewings of up to 34,000 people at a time. Young Adolf Hitler is said to have idolized Makart's grandiloquent sense of flamboyance; Klimt and Schiele of the Secessionist school at first admired him, then abandoned his presuppositions and forged a bold new path of their own. Handsome, socially correct, charming, and promiscuous, Makart's *vernissages* were often filled with rumor and innuendo about the specific identities of the models who appeared as artfully undressed figures within his paintings. His fall from social grace began when he defied upper-class Viennese conventions to marry a ballet dancer, then contracted a fatal case of syphilis that killed him at age 44.

At the end of Makartgasse, turn left (east) for a half-block. Then turn right onto the Friedrichstrasse. Before the end of the block, at Friedrichstrasse 12, you'll reach the *Jugendstil* facade of a building that launched one of the most enviously admired artistic statements of the early 20th century.

4. The Secession. At the time of its construction in 1898, its design was much, much more controversial than it is today, and as such attracted hundreds of passersby who would, literally, gawk. Its severe cubic lines, Assyrian-looking corner towers, and gilded dome caused its detractors to refer to it as "the Gilded Cabbage," and

"Mahdi's Tomb," and was immediately interpreted as an insult to bourgeois sensibilities. Despite the controversy that surrounded it (or perhaps because of it), 57,000 people attended its inaugural exhibition of Secessionist works. The Secession's position within a short walk of the organization it defied (the previously visited Academy of Fine Arts) was an accident, prompted only by the availability of a suitable tract of real estate. Inside, a roster of innovative display techniques—revolutionary for their time—included movable panels, unadorned walls, and natural light pouring in from skylights. The inscription above the door, *Jeder Zein sein Kunst, Jeder Kunst sein Freiheit,* translates as "To every age its art, to every art its freedom." Damaged during World War II and looted in 1945, it lay derelict until 1973, when it was bought, and later restored, as a municipal treasure.

From here, retrace your steps in a northeasterly direction beside the dense traffic of the Friedrichstrasse for two blocks. At the corner of the Niebelungengasse and the Friedrichstrasse (which forks gently into the Operngasse at a point nearby) you'll find the entrance to an underground tunnel, part of Vienna's subway network, that will lead you safely beneath roaring traffic for several underground blocks to your next point of interest. Follow the underground signs to the subway and to the Wiedner Hauptstrasse. Turn right at the first major underground intersection, again following signs to the Wiedner Hauptstrasse. After what might seem a rather long underground walk, you'll see daylight from above, allowing you to ascend to a point near the sprawling and sunken perimeter of the:

5. **Karlsplatz.** For many generations, this sunken bowl contained Vienna's fruit and vegetable markets. Too large to be called a square, and too small to be defined as a park, it's an awkward space that's valued today mainly as a means of showcasing the important buildings that surround it. Climb from the Karlsplatz up a flight of stone steps to the platform that skirts the Karlsplatz' northern edge, and walk east for a minute or two. The small-scale pair of *Jugendstil* pavilions you'll notice are among the most famous of their type in Vienna, the:

6. **Otto Wagner Pavilions.** Originally designed by Otto Wagner as a station for his *Stadtbahn* (the subway system he designed around the turn of the century for Vienna), they are gems of functional Secessionist theory and preserved as monuments by the city. After their construction, many of their decorative adornments were copied throughout other districts of the Austro-Hungarian empire as part of their respective late 19th-century building booms. Regrettably, many were later demolished as part of the Soviet regime's control of the Iron Curtain countries during the Cold War. Art historians consider them Vienna's response to the art nouveau metro stations of Paris built around the same time, many of which have been elevated to museum status.

From there, continue walking eastward. The first building across the avenue on your left, at Friedrichstrasse 5, is the:

7. **Künstlerhaus.** Around 1900 its name was rigidly associated with conservative art, and as such, tended to enrage the iconoclastic rebels who later formed the Secessionist movement. Completed in 1868, and not particularly striking for its architecture, it functioned for years as the exhibition hall of works produced by students at the Fine Arts Academy. Today, it's used for temporary exhibitions, and devotes some of its space to a changing roster of film and theater experiments.

Immediately to the right (east) of the Künstlerhaus is the Renaissance-inspired:

8. **Musikvereinsgebaude** (Friends of Music Building), Karlsplatz 13, home of the Vienna Philharmonic, and site of concerts that are often sold out years in advance through fiercely protected private subscriptions. Constructed between 1867–69, and designed by the same Theophil Hansen who built the previously visited Fine

Arts Academy, it's another example of the way architects dabbled in the great historical styles of the past during the late 19th-century revitalization of the Ringstrasse.

Within the confines of the Karlsplatz, at Karlsplatz 4, a short walk to the southeast from the Musikverein, note the location of a monument that serves, better than any other, to bind together the complicated worlds, subcultures, and historic periods that interconnect to form the city of Vienna, the:

9. **Historisches Museum der Stadt Wien** (Museum of the History of Vienna). Because this is such a densely packed collection that might better be viewed as part of a separate visit, we advise that you continue your clockwise circumnavigation of the Karlsplatz to the majestic confines of the:

10. **Karlskirche** (Church of St. Charles). Built by Emperor Charles VI, father of Maria Theresa, who mourned the loss of Austria's vast domains in Spain, this church was conceived as a means of recapturing some of Vienna's imperial glory. It is almost always cited as the monument for which the baroque architect Fischer von Erlach the Elder is best remembered today and the most impressive baroque building in Austria. Built between 1716 and 1737, nominally in thanks for deliverance of Vienna from yet another disastrous bout with the plague, it manages to combine aspects of a votive church with images of imperial grandeur. Note that at the time of its construction, the Ringstrasse was not yet in place, and it lay within an easy and unrestricted stroll from the emperor's residence in the Hofburg. Rather coyly, Charles didn't name the church after himself, but after a Milanese prelate (St. Charles Borromeo), although the confusion that has ensued ever since was almost certainly deliberate. To construct the skeleton of the church's dome, 300 massive oak trees were felled. The twin towers in front, although not strictly synchronized with the theories of baroque architecture, were inspired by Trajan's column in Rome, the Pillars of Hercules (Gibraltar) in Spain, and Mannerist renderings of what contemporary historians imagined as the long-lost Temple of Jerusalem. The reflecting fountain in front of the church, site of a parking lot in recent times, contains a statue donated by Henry Moore to the city of Vienna in 1978.

Now, continue walking clockwise around the perimeter of the square to the Karlsplatz' southern edge. A short side street running into the Karlsplatz at this point is the Karlsgasse. Near the junction of the square with this small street, at Karlsgasse 4, you'll see a plaque announcing that a building that used to stand here, and commandeered later by the massive building program of the Technical University, was the site of an apartment house where Brahms died in 1897. The next major building you'll see is the showcase of Austria's justifiably famous reputation for scientific and engineering excellence, the:

11. **Technische Universität** (Technical University). Its ionic portico overlooks a public park with portrait busts of the great names associated with this treasure trove of Austrian inventiveness. Talent that's emerged from this institution includes Josef Ressel (whose name is perpetuated by nearby Ressel Park), inventor of the marine propeller; Josef Madersperger, original inventor of the sewing machine in 1815, who died impoverished while others, such as the Singer family, profited from his invention; and Siegfried Marcus, inventor of a crude version of the gasoline-powered automobile in 1864. Other Austrians associated with the school are Ernest Mach, whose experiments with sound led to the association of his name with the speed at which an aircraft breaks the sound barrier; and Josef Weineck, whose experiments with the solidification of fats laid the groundwork for the cosmetics industry.

Continue walking west along the southern perimeter of the Karlsplatz, past the Resselpark, and across the Wiedner Hauptstrasse, a modern manifestation of an ancient road that originally linked Vienna to Venice and Trieste. Although the neighborhood you're traversing, because of wartime damage that began as early as the Turkish sieges of 1683, doesn't look particularly antique, it's actually viewed by urban historians as Vienna's first suburb. The neighborhood to your left, stretching for about four blocks between the Wiedner Hauptstrasse and the Naschmarkt (which you'll soon visit), is now occupied by sprawling annexes of the Technical University and not-particularly-interesting modern buildings. But historians value it as the site that housed, during the 18th century, one of the largest communal housing projects in Europe, the since-demolished site of the former:

12. Freihaus, the sprawling home to more than 1,000 people who accessed their apartments by means of 31 different stairwells. In 1782, a theater was opened in a wing of that building, the *Theater auf der Wieden,* and soon after provided the venue for the premier performance of Mozart's *Zauberflote (Magic Flute).* During the 19th century, when the Friehaus degenerated into an industrial slum, and a civic embarrassment because of its proximity to the Karlskirche and the State Opera House, much of it was deliberately demolished to make room for the creation of the Operngasse. The bombings of World War II finished off the rest, and today, only memories of the subcultures that thrived within its massive premises remain.

Continue walking along the Treitlstrasse, which is the logical westward extension of Resselpark. Soon you'll reach the Rechte Wienzeile, a broad boulevard that once flanked the quays of a branch of the Danube before urban renewals in the 19th century diverted the course of the mighty river to a position outside town. Within the filled-in valley of what served as the bed for part of the Danube for thousands of years, you'll see the congested booths and labyrinthine stalls of Vienna's largest food and vegetable market, the:

13. Naschmarkt. Wander at will through the stalls, observing rules well-known to every Viennese who wants to avoid the wrath of the notoriously short-tempered women who sell produce, meats, cheese, and dairy products. Your visit will be more harmonious if you observe the following unwritten rules: Don't try to buy less than a half-kilo (about a pound) of potatoes, never touch merchandise without the intention of actually buying something, and don't even try to understand the nuances of a sometimes raunchy Viennese patois that even cultured Germans from such cities as Berlin can understand only after careful concentration. Know in advance that the more expensive and image-conscious shops lie near the Naschmarkt's eastern end. Its center tends to be devoted to housewares, and less glamorous food outlets, including lots of butcher shops.

After your exploration of the food market, walk along the market's northern fringe, the Linke Weinzeile. At the corner of the Millöckergasse, you'll see a historic theater that, during the decade-long renovation of the previously visited State Opera House, functioned as Vienna's primary outlet for the performing arts, the:

14. Theater an der Wien, Linke Weinzeile 6. Despite its modern facade (a result of an unfortunate demolition and rebuilding that occurred around 1900 and later damages during World War II), it's the oldest theater in Vienna, dating back to 1801. To get an idea of the age of this place, bypass the front entrance to the theater, and walk northwest along the Millöckergasse. Millöckergasse, incidentally, was named after an overwhelmingly popular composer of Viennese operettas, Karl Millöcker (1842–99). At no. 8, notice the theater's famous *Pappagenotor,* a stage door entrance capped with an homage to the Pan-like character in Mozart's

Magic Flute. The likeness of Pappageno was deliberately modeled after Emanuel Schikaneder, the first actor to play the role, the author who wrote most of the libretto to the score, and the first manager, in 1801, of what was at the time a new theater. Attached to the wall near the *Pappagenotor* is a plaque recognizing that Beethoven lived and composed parts of his *Third Symphony* and the *Kreuzer* sonata inside. An early—later rewritten—version of Beethoven's *Fidelio* premiered at this theater, but after an uncharitable reception by the Viennese, it was reconfigured by its composer into the form it bears today.

Continue walking northwest along Millöckergasse, then turn left onto the Lehárgasse. (The massive building on the Lehárgasse's north side at this point contains yet another annex of the Technical University.) Within about 3 blocks, Lehárgasse merges into the:

15. Gumpendorferstrasse, a street lined with the same genre of historically eclectic houses, on a smaller scale, that you'll find in larger versions on the Ringstrasse. The neighborhood you're traversing grew up from the medieval village of Gumpendorf, and was incorporated into the city of Vienna as the 6th District in 1850. Modern Viennese refer to the neighborhood as Mariahilf. At this point, it's time to:

☕ **TAKE A BREAK** at one of the most historic cafes in the district. **Café Sperl,** Gumpendorferstrasse 11 (☎ **0222/586-4158**). Until renovations in the 1960s ripped away some of its once-ornate interior, it functioned since its establishment in the mid-1800s as a pivot in the social and intellectual life of this monument-rich district. Today, hints of its original glamour and sense of nostalgia remain, albeit with many concessions to modern tastes and times. If you opt for *ein kleine brauner* here, you won't be alone: The artists who initiated the tenets that led to the Secession maintained a more or less permanent table within the confines of this cafe. The Sperl is open Monday through Saturday from 7am to 11pm, Sunday from 3 to 11pm. Coffee, depending on its size, costs from 24 to 39 AS ($2.30 to $3.70); and generous *tagestellers* of Viennese food range in price from 95 to 110 AS ($9.05 to $10.45).

After your break, walk southwest along Gumpendorferstrasse, admiring the unusual roster of historically eclectic Ringstrasse-style houses and apartment buildings that line the sidewalks. At the Köstlergasse, turn left and stroll for about a block, past more of the same ornate 19th-century architecture. At the end of Köstlergasse (at nos. 1 and 3), you'll notice apartment houses designed by Otto Wagner, and adjacent to those buildings, around the corner at Linke Weinzeile no. 40, you'll see yet another of his designs, an apartment house referred to by architecture students around the world as the Majolikahaus. Adjacent to the Majolikahaus, at 38 Linke Weinzeile, is the **Medallion House,** a building with a Secession-style floral display crafted from tiles set into its facade. It was designed by turn of the century Secessionist Koloman Moser, creator of the stained-glass windows in the Am Steinhof church.

Your tour is about over, and if you've opted to take it between Sunday and Friday, you should now consider it officially over. But if it happens to be Saturday, anytime between 7am and around 4pm, continue southwest along Linke Wienzeile (cross over the Kettenbruckengasse) toward the earthy, and evocatively seedy premises of one of Europe's most nostalgic flea markets, the:

16. Flohmarkt. Don't expect glamour, or even merchants who are particularly polite. There's lots of attitude from students eager to prove how cool they are, and lots of voyeuristic energy spent on mating games and window-shopping. But scattered amid the racks of cheap clothing, kitchenware, and hardware of this Saturday-only fair, you're likely to find painful, sometimes bittersweet vestiges of kitsch derived from the failed hopes and dreams of central Europe, and sentimental reminders of the Imperial polyglot of cultures that comprised the roots of late 19th-century Vienna.

WALKING TOUR 3
Vienna's Backstreets

Start: Maria am Gestade.
Finish: St. Stephan's Cathedral.
Time: 2¹/₂ hours (not counting visits to interiors).
Best Time: Daylight hours, when you can visit shops and cafes en route.
Worst Time: In the rain and between 4 and 6pm.

In 1192, the English king, Richard I (the Lion-Hearted), was captured trespassing on Babenburg lands in the village of Erdberg (now part of Vienna's 3rd District), after his return to England from the Third Crusade. The funds handed over from the English for his ransom were used for the enlargement of Vienna's fortifications that eventually incorporated some of the neighborhoods you'll cover on this walking tour. In horrified response, the pope excommunicated the Babenburg potentate who had held a Christian crusader, but not before some of medieval London was mortgaged to pay the ransom and, eventually, Vienna's city walls.

Much of this tour focuses on smaller individual buildings, and lesser-known landmarks on distinctive streets whose historic pavements have been trod by some of the most influential characters of Viennese history. Prepare yourself for a labyrinth of medieval streets and covered passages, and insights into the age-old Viennese congestion that sociologists claim helped catalyze the artistic output of the Habsburg Empire.

Begin your promenade slightly northwest of Stephansplatz with a visit to one of the least-frequently visited churches of central Vienna:

1. **Maria am Gestade** ("Maria-Stiegen-Kirche"/Church of St. Mary on the Strand), Salvatorgasse 1. Designated centuries ago as the Czech national church in Vienna, it replaced an older, wooden church, erected in the 800s, with the 14th century stonework you'll see today. Restricted by the narrowness of the medieval streets around it, the church's unusual floor plan is only 30 feet wide, but it's capped with an elaborate pierced Gothic steeple that soars above the district as one of the neighborhood's most distinctive features. Since the early 19th century, when the first of at least five subsequent renovations were conducted, the church has been held by art historians as one of the most distinctive but underrated in town.

From here, walk south along the alleyway that flanks its eastern edge, turning left (east) at the Wipplingerstrasse for an eventual view of the:

2. **Altes Rathaus,** Wipplingerstrasse 3. The building that was confiscated by the Habsburg ruler, Duke Frederick the Fair, in 1316, from the leader of an anti-Habsburg revolt, and subsequently donated to the city. In 1700, it was embellished with a baroque facade and a courtyard fountain (1740–41) that's famous for being one of Raphael Donner's last works. The building functioned as Vienna's Town Hall until 1885, when the city's municipal functions were moved to grander, neo-Gothic quarters on the Ring, which was completed in 1883. Today, the Altes Rathaus contains a minor museum dedicated to the Austrian resistance.

Wipplingerstrasse runs east into the:

3. Hoher Markt, the city's oldest market place. Until the early 1700s, it was the location of a public gallows, and until the early 1800s, it was the site of a pillory used to punish and humiliate dishonest bakers. Hoher Markt was originally the forum of the ancient Roman settlement of Vindobona. There are some excavations of what's believed to be a Roman barracks visible within the courtyard of the building at no. 3. It's likely, according to scholars, that Marcus Aurelius died of the plague here in A.D. 180. In the 1700s, the instruments of torture that dominated the square were replaced with several different generations of plague columns (baroque columns erected in thanksgiving for deliverance from the Turks and from the plague), the present version of which was designed by Josef Emanuele von Ehrlach in 1732 and sculpted by Italian-born Antonio Corradini. An important scene from the film *The Third Man,* was filmed at the base of the Hoher Markt's famous clock, the Ankeruhr, which—to everyone's amazement—escaped destruction during the square's aerial bombardments in 1945.

From here, walk a short block east along the Liechtensteingasse, then turn left and walk northeast along one of Vienna's most prominent shopping streets, the Rotenturmstrasse for two blocks. Then turn right (east) onto the:

4. Griechengasse. The construction of this narrow street in the 1100s was representative of the almost desperate need for expansion away from the city's earlier perimeter, which more or less followed the ancient configuration of the Roman settlement of Vindobona, centered around the previously visited Hoher Markt. Griechengasse's name derived from the influx of Greek immigrants who arrived as merchants during the 18th century, as precursors of the waves of immigrants flooding into modern Vienna from eastern Europe and the Middle East today. At Griechengasse 5, notice the unpretentious exterior of the local Greek Orthodox church, built in 1805 with the plain facade that was legally required of all non-Catholic churches up until the 19th century. At Griechengasse 7, occupying the point where the street turns sharply at an angle, stands a 14th-century watchtower, one of the few medieval vestiges left from the old city walls, that was incorporated long ago into the antique architecture that surrounds it.

The Griechengasse will narrow at this point and in some places be spanned with buttresses supporting the walls of the buildings on either side. Griechengasse soon intersects with a thoroughfare where, during the 12th century, you'd have been affronted with the stench of rancid blood from the nearby slaughterhouses.

5. Fleischmarkt. Notice the heroic frieze above the facade of the antique apartment house at no. 18 ("The Tolerance House"), which depicts in symbolic form Joseph II, son of Maria Theresa, in granting freedom of worship to what was at the time a mostly Greek Orthodox neighborhood. Number 9, begun in the 1400s and progressively improved and enlarged during the next 300 years, was used as a inn (or more likely, a flophouse) and warehouse for traders from the Balkans and the Middle East during the age of Mozart.

☕ **TAKE A BREAK**   at an inn named for the many Greeks who made it their regular dining spot for hundreds of years, **Griechenbeisl,** Fleischmarkt 11. Established in 1450, and divided into a warren of cozy and historically evocative dining rooms, it's described more fully in Chapter 5, "Vienna Dining."

Adjacent to the Greichenbeisl rise the walls of another Greek Orthodox church. It was embellished in 1858 by Theophile Hansen, the Danish-born architect of many of the grand buildings of the Ringstrasse, an ardent advocate of the Greek revival style as shown by his recent design for the Austrian Parliament.

Walking Tour: Vienna's Backstreets

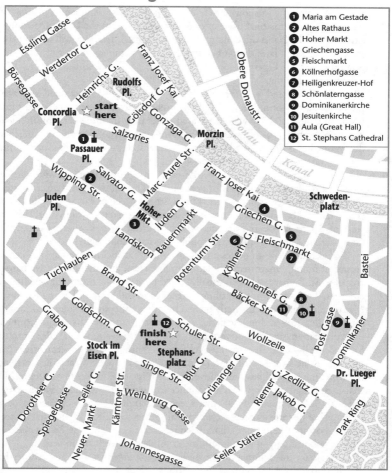

1. Maria am Gestade
2. Altes Rathaus
3. Hoher Markt
4. Griechengasse
5. Fleischmarkt
6. Köllnerhofgasse
7. Heiligenkreuzer-Hof
8. Schönlaterngasse
9. Dominikanerkirche
10. Jesuitenkirche
11. Aula (Great Hall)
12. St. Stephans Cathedral

At Fleischmarkt 15, notice the baroque facade of the birthplace of a not-very-well-known Biedermeier painter, Moritz von Schwind, whose main claim to immortality lay in his membership within the circle of friends who attended the *Schubertiades* (evenings of music and philosophy organized by Franz Schubert in Vienna during the early 19th century).

A branch of the Vienna post office lies at no. 19, within the premises of a monastery confiscated from the Dominicans by Joseph II, as part of his campaign to secularize the Austrian government. Ironically, the only ecclesiastical trappings left within an otherwise bland bureaucratic setting are the skeletons of dozens of dead brethren, unmoved and unseen since their burial in the building's crypt many generations ago.

The uninspired modern facade of the building at no. 24 Fleischmarkt was the long-ago site of a now-defunct hotel, Zur Stadt London, whose musical guests included the family of young Mozart as well as Franz Liszt, Richard Wagner (when he wasn't fleeing his creditors), and the Polish exile, Chopin. The building at no. 14 Fleischmarkt shows a rich use of *Jugendstil* detailing, and a plaque commemorating it as the birthplace of one of the directors of the Court Opera in the latter days of the Habsburg dynasty. At Fleischmarkt 1, residents will tell you about the birth here of a later director of the same opera company, after its reorganization into the State Opera.

Turn left onto the:

6. **Köllnerhofgasse** and walk for about a half block. No. 1-3 functioned long ago as the headquarters of a group of tightly interconnected merchants based on the Rhine in Cologne. They were motivated to set up a trading operation in Vienna by a complicated series of fiscal and legal perks and privileges granted to merchants during medieval times. The building you'll see today—remarkable for the number of windows that pierce its facade—dates from 1792.

At this point, turn left into a cul-de-sac that funnels through a wide gate into a courtyard that's always open to pedestrians. The cul-de-sac is Grashofgasse, at the end of which is a wall painted with a restored fresco of the Stift Heiligenkreuz (Holy Cross Abbey), a well-known 12th-century Cistercian monastery 15 miles west of town. A covered arcade, which is usually open, pierces the wall of Grashofgasse 3 and leads into the cobble-covered public courtyard of the:

7. **Heiligenkreuz-Hof,** an ecclesiastical complex that incorporates a 17th-century cluster of monk's apartments, lodging for an abbot, and the diminutive baroque chapel of St. Bernard, which is usually closed to the public except for wedding ceremonies. The courtyard's continued existence in the heart of Vienna is unusual: Many equivalent tracts formerly owned by other abbeys were converted long ago into building sites and public parks after sale or confiscation by the government.

Exit the monastery's courtyard from its opposite (southeastern) edge onto the:

8. **Schönlanterngasse.** Its name derives from the ornate wrought-iron street lamp that adorns the facade of the 16th-century building at no. 6. What hangs there now is a copy; the original has been moved to the Historical Museum of Vienna. This well-maintained street owes its appearance to a series of municipal laws enacted in the late 1960s and early 1970s that specified certain Viennese districts as neighborhoods of historic importance worthy of preservation. Renovation loans, issued at rock-bottom interest rates, have been referred to ever since as *Kultur Schillings*. The neighborhood you're in is a prime example of these loans in action.

At no. 7 on the Schönlanterngasse lies the *Basilikenhaus,* a 13th-century bakery supported by 12th-century foundations, which are the source of one of the most institutionalized neighborhood in Vienna. When foul odors began emanating from the building's well, the medieval residents of the building assumed that it was sheltering a basilisk (a mythological reptile from the Sahara Desert whose breath and gaze were fatal). The building's facade incorporates a stone replica of the beast, who was killed, according to a wall plaque, by a local baker who bravely showed the creature its own reflection in a mirror. A modern interpretation of what happened involves the possibility of methane gas or subterranean sulfurous vapors seeping out of the building's well.

The house at no. 7A on the Schonlanterngasse was the home of Robert Schumann from 1838–39, the winter he re-discovered (within another building) some of the unpublished compositions of Franz Schubert. Schumann, basking in the glory of a successful musical and social career, did more than anyone else to elevate Schubert to posthumous star status. The groundwork for the renaissance of Schubert's music was laid within this building.

The building at no. 9 on the same street has functioned as a smithy (*Die Alte Schmiede*) since the middle ages. From its outside, you can glimpse a collection of antique blacksmith tools. Continue walking eastward along the Schönlanterngasse, where you'll see the back side of a church you'll visit in a moment, the Jesuit Church. Continue walking (the street will make a sharp turn to the right) until it widens into the broad plaza of the Postgasse, where you turn right. The monument that rises in front of you, at Postgasse 4, is the:

9. Dominikanerkirche. This is the third of three Dominican churches to be built on this site. The earliest, constructed around 1237, burned down. The second, completed around 1300, was demolished by the Turks during their siege of 1529. The building you'll see today was completed in 1632, and is the most important early baroque church in Vienna. The rather murky-looking frescoes in the side chapels are artistically noteworthy, in some cases, as they are the 1726 statement of baroque artist Françoise Roettiers. However, the main allure of the building derives from the pomp of its high altar and its uncompromising allegiance to the tenets of baroque architecture. Elevated to the rank of what the Viennese clergy refers to as a "minor basilica" in 1927, it's officially referred to as the "Rosary Basilica ad S. Mariam Rotundam." Incidentally, don't confuse the Dominikanerkirche with the less architecturally significant Greek Orthodox Church of St. Barbara, a few steps to the north, whose simple facade and elaborate liturgical rituals are sited at Postgasse 10. Incidentally, Beethoven lived for about a year in a building sited adjacent to St. Barbaras, Postgasse 8.

Now, walk south along the Postgasse to its dead-end, and turn right into an narrow alley interspersed with steps. The alley will widen, within a few paces, into the Bäckerstrasse, a street noted for its imposing 18th-century architecture. Architects of such minor palaces as the ones at nos. 8 and 10, recognizing that passersby would never be able to view their creations from faraway distances, chose instead to adorn their facades with unusual details that could be appreciated from close-up views. Long ago, no. 16 contained an inn (*Schmauswaberl*—*"The Little Feast Hive"*) favored at the time by university students because of its habit of serving, at deeply discounted prices, food left over from the banquets at the Hofburg. Other buildings of architectural note include nos. 7, 12, and 14, whose statue of Mary in a niche above the door shows evidence of the powerful effect of the Virgin on the everyday hopes and dreams of Vienna during the baroque age.

Follow Bäkerstrasse for about a block until you reach the confines of the square that's referred to by locals as the Universitätsplatz, but by virtually every map in Vienna as the Dr. Ignaz Seipel-Platz, derived from a theologian/priest who bore the difficult and thankless job of functioning twice as chancellor of Austria between World Wars I and II. The building that dominates the square is the:

10. Jesuitenkirche/Universitätskirche (Jesuit Church/University Church). It was built between 1623 and 1627, and adorned with twin towers and an enhanced baroque facade in the early 1700s by the workhorses of the Austrian Counter-Reformation, the Jesuits. They were invited to Vienna by Ferdinand, the Spanish-born, fervently catholic Emperor, at a time when an estimated three-fourths of the population had converted to Protestantism. It was estimated that only four Catholic priests remained at their posts within the entire city of Vienna. From this building, the Jesuits spearheaded the 18th-century reconversion of Austria back to Catholicism, and more or less dominated the curriculum at the nearby university. For such a stern group of academics, the Jesuit's church is amazingly ornate, with allegorical frescoes and all the aesthetic tricks that make its visitors believe they've entered a transitional world midway between earth and heaven.

The western edge of Dr. Ignaz Seipel-Platz is flanked by one of the showcase buildings of Vienna's University, the:

11. Aula (Great Hall), Vienna's premier rococo attraction. A precursor of the great concert halls that dot the landmark of Austria today, musical works were presented in halls such as this one, or in private homes or palaces of wealthy patrons and art lovers. During the 1700s, the site was the venue for musical events that included the premier of Haydn's *Creation*, as well as Beethoven's *Seventh Symphony*.

Exit from the Dr. Ignaz Seipel-Platz by its northwestern corner and walk along the Sonnenfelsgasse. Flanked with 15th- and 16th-century houses, which until recently received complaints because of the number of bordellos housed within them, the street is architecturally noteworthy. The building at Sonnenfelsgasse 19, dating from 1628, once housed the proctor (administrator) of the nearby university. Other buildings of noteworthy beauty include nos. 3, 15 and 17. The street, incidentally, was named after one of the few advisors who could ever win an argument with Maria Theresa, Josef von Sonnenfels. Descended from a long line of German rabbis, and the son of a Viennese Christian convert, Sonnenfels learned a dozen languages while employed as a foot soldier in the Austrian army, and later used his influence to abolish torture in the prisons and particularly cruel methods of capital punishment. Ludwig von Beethoven dedicated his *Piano Sonata in D major* to him.

Walk to the western terminus of the Sonnenfelsgasse, then turn left and fork sharply back to the east along the Bäkerstrasse. You will, in effect, have circumnavigated an entire medieval block.

After your exploration of Bakerstrasse, turn south into a narrow alleyway, the Essigstrasse (Vinegar Street), cross over the Wollzeile, centerpiece of the wool merchants and weaver's guild during the Middle Ages and now a noted shopping district. Continue your southward trek along the Stroblgasse, which will lead into the Schulerstrasse. Turn right onto the Schulerstrasse, which will lead within a block to a sweeping view of the side of:

12. St. Stephan's Cathedral. Built over a period of 400 years, and the symbol of Vienna itself, it's one of the most evocative and history-soaked monuments of Vienna. (See "Other Top Attractions" in Chapter 6.)

Shopping 8

Visitors can spend many happy hours shopping or just browsing in Vienna's shops, where handcrafts are produced in a long-established tradition of skilled workmanship. Popular for their beauty and quality are petit-point items, hand-painted Wiener Augarten porcelain, work by goldsmiths or silversmiths, handmade dolls, ceramics, enamel jewelry, wrought-iron articles, leathergoods, and many other items of value and interest.

1 The Shopping Scene

The main shopping streets are in the city center (1st District). Here you'll find Kärntnerstrasse, between the State Opera and Stock-im-Eisen-Platz; the Graben, between Stock-im-Eisen-Platz and Kohlmarkt; Kohlmarkt, between the Graben and Michaelplatz; and Rotensturmstrasse, between Stephansplatz and Kai. There are also Mariahilferstrasse, between Babenbergerstrasse and Schönbrunn, one of the longest streets in Vienna; Favoritenstrasse, between Südtiroler Platz and Reumannplatz; and Landstrasser Hauptstrasse.

The Naschmarkt is a vegetable and fruit market, the "Covent Garden of Vienna," which has a lively scene every day. To visit it, head south of the opera district. It's at Linke and Rechte Wienzeile. (See "Open Air Markets" at the end of this chapter).

SHOPPING HOURS

Shops are normally open Monday through Friday from 9am to 6pm and on Saturday from 9am to 1pm. Small shops close between noon and 2pm for lunch. Railroad-station shops in the Westbahnhof and the Südbahnhof are open daily from 7am to 11pm, offering groceries, smoker's supplies, stationery, books, and flowers. These two stations also have hairdressers, public baths, and photo booths.

A SHOPPING CENTER

The Ringstrassen Galleries
In the Palais Corso and in the Kärntnerringhof, Kärntner Ring 5-7.

Rental fees for shop space in central Vienna are legendarily expensive. In response to the high rents, about 70 boutique-ish emporiums selling everything from hosiery to key chains to evening wear have pooled their resources and moved to labyrinthine quarters near the State Opera House, midway between the Bristol Hotel and the Anna Hotel. Its prominent location guarantees a certain glamour, although the cramped dimensions of many of the stores might be a turn-off. But the selection is broad and no one can deny the gallery's easy-to-find location. Each shop within is operated independently, but virtually all of them conduct business Monday through Friday from 10am to 7pm, and Saturday from 10:30am to 1pm. Three stores here of particular interest to fashion hounds include Yves St. Laurent, Casselli, and Agatha Paris, each of which is recommended separately within this chapter.

2 Shopping A to Z

ANTIQUES

Vienna's antiques shops constitute a limitless treasure trove. You can find valuable old books, engravings, etchings, and paintings insecondhand shops, bookshops, and picture galleries.

Since the 1980s, there's been an explosion of interest in the blonde-and-ebony woodwork abundantly produced during Austria's Biedermeier period during the first half of the 19th century. This antiques gallery stocks a worthy collection, and is ready, willing, and able to ship it virtually anywhere. There's also a stockpile of the French-inspired bombé chests and secretaries crafted in northern Europe (Germany and Sweden) in styles what was being done contemporaneously at Versailles. Nothing is cheap here, but the place might provide the kind of piece you'll treasure forever. It's open Monday through Friday from 10am to 6pm, Saturday from 10am to 1pm.

✪ Dorotheum
Dorotheergasse 17. ☎ **0222/515-60-0.**

Dating from 1707 this is the oldest auction house in Europe. Emperor Joseph I established the auction house so that impoverished aristocrats could fairly (and anonymously) get good value for their heirlooms. Today the Dorotheum is also the scene of many art auctions. If you're interested in an item, you give a small fee to a *sensal,* one of the licensed bidders, and he or she will bid in your name. The objects for sale cover a vast array of items, including exquisite furniture and carpets, delicate *objets d'art,* and valuable paintings, as well as decorative jewelry. If you're unable to attend an auction, you can still browse through the sales rooms at your own pace, selecting items you wish to purchase directly to take home with you the same day. Approximately 31 auctions are held in July alone, and, over the course of a year, these auctions are responsible for the exchange of some 250,000 pieces of art and antiques.

Flohmarkt
Linke Wienzeille.

You may find a little of everything at this flea market, which is located near the Naschmarkt and the Kettenbrückengasse U-Bahn Station. It runs every Saturday from 8am to 6pm except on public holidays. The Viennese have perfected the skill of haggling, and the Flohmarkt is one of their favorite arenas for this ritual battle of wills. It takes a trained eye to spot the antique treasures that are scattered among the junk.

ANTIQUE GLASS

Glasgalerie Kovacek
Spiegelgasse 12. ☎ **0222/512-9954.**

Its ground floor is devoted to antique glass collected from estate sales and private collections throughout Austria. The majority of these items date to the 19th and early 20th centuries, although some 17th-century pieces are displayed as well. The most appealing antique pieces boast heraldic symbols, sometimes from branches of the Habsburgs themselves. There's also a collection of cunning glass paperweights imported from Bohemia, France, Italy, and other parts of Austria.

The upper floor is devoted to classical paintings that the Secessionists revolted against. Look for canvases by Franz Makart, foremost of the 19th-century historic academics, and to a much lesser extent some works, including two by Kokoscha, a noted Secessionist. The gallery is open Monday through Friday from 9:30am to 6pm, Saturday from 9:30am to 12:30pm. It's closed Saturdays during July.

ART

✪ Ö.W. (Österreichische Werkstatten)
Kärntnerstrasse 6. ☎ **0222/512-24-18.**

This three-floor, well-run store sells hundreds of handmade art objects from Austria. Leading artists and craftspeople throughout the country organized this cooperative to showcase their wares. The location is easy to find, lying only half a minute's walk from St. Stephan's Cathedral. You'll find an especially good selection of pewter, along with modern jewelry, glassware, brass, baskets, ceramics, and serving spoons fashioned from deer horn and bone. Be sure to keep wandering through this place; you never know what treasure awaits you in a nook of this cavernous outlet. Even if you skip the other stores of Vienna, check this one out. Open Monday through Friday from 9am to 6pm and on Saturday from 9am to 1pm.

BOOKS

The British Bookshop
Weihburggasse 24-26. ☎ **0222/512-1945.**

This is the largest and most comprehensive emporium of English-language books in Austria, with a sprawling ground-floor showroom loaded with American, Australian, and English books. There are no periodicals, and no cute displays devoted to sales of such gift items as English marmalade, tea cozies, or tweed. Instead, all you'll find is enough reading material to wean you of a need for TV for the rest of your life, and educational aids for teaching English as a second language. The bookstore is open Monday through Friday from 9am to 6pm, Saturday from 10am to 1pm.

CHANDELIERS & PORCELAIN

✪ Albin Denk
Graben 13. ☎ **0222/512-44-39.**

Albin Denk is the oldest continuously operating porcelain store in Vienna, and has been doing business since its establishment in 1702. Its clients have included Empress Elizabeth, who saw the shop in almost the same format you'll see it in today. The decor of the three low-ceilinged rooms is beautiful, as are the thousands of objects from Meissen, Dresden, and other regions. With such a wealth of riches, it can be hard to make a selection, but the staff will help you. Open Monday through Friday from 9am to 6pm and on Saturday from 9am to 1pm.

Augarten Porzellan
Stock-im-Eisenplatz 3-4. ☎ **0222/512-1494.**

Established in 1718, Augarten porcelain is, after Meissen, the oldest manufacturer of porcelain in Europe. This multitiered shop is the most visible, and best-stocked outlet for the prized merchandise, in the world. Virtually anything can be shipped anywhere. Tableware, consisting of fragile dinner plates whose pattern might have been admired during the 18th century, as well as contemporary designs, are elegant and much sought-after. Also noteworthy are porcelain statues of Lippazaner horses. It's open Monday through Friday 9:30am to 6pm, Saturday 9:30am through 12:30pm.

✪ J. & L. Lobmeyr
Kärntnerstrasse 26. ☎ **0222/512-05-08.**

If during your exploration of Vienna you should happen to admire a crystal chandelier, there's a good chance that it was made by this company. It was designated in the early 19th century as a purveyor to the Imperial Court of Austria, and it has maintained an elevated position ever since. The company is credited with designing and creating the first electric chandelier, in 1883. It has also designed chandeliers for the Vienna State Opera, the Metropolitan Opera House in New York, the Assembly Hall in the Kremlin, and for many palaces and mosques in the Near and Far East, and the new concert hall in Fukuoka, Japan.

Behind its art nouveau facade on the main shopping street of town, you'll see at least 50 chandeliers of all shapes and sizes. The store also sells hand-painted Hungarian porcelain, along with complete breakfast and dinner services. They'll also engrave your family crest on a wine glass if you want it, or sell you one of the uniquely modern pieces of sculptured glass from the third-floor showroom. The second floor is a museum of some of the outstanding pieces the company has made since it was established in 1823. Open Monday through Friday from 9am to 6pm and on Saturday from 9am to 1pm.

CONFECTIONARY

Altmann & Kühne
Graben 30. ☎ **0222/533-09-27.**

Many Viennese have retained memories of marzipan, hazelnut, or nougat desserts procured for them by parents or guardians during strolls along the Graben. Established in 1928, this is the kind of cozy and nostalgic shop where virtually nothing inside is particularly good for your waistline or for your teeth, but everything is positively and undeniably scrumptious. Don't expect to consume your purchases on site, as everything is take-out. Despite that, the visuals of the inventory are almost as appealing as the way they taste. The pastries and tarts filled with fresh seasonal raspberries are, quite simply, delectable. The place is open Monday through Friday from 9am to 6:30pm, Saturday from 9am to 1pm.

DEPARTMENT STORES

Steffl Kaufhaus
Kärntnerstrasse 19. ☎ **0222/514-310.**

Rising five floors above the pedestrian traffic of one of inner Vienna's most appealing shopping streets, this is one of Vienna's most visible department stores, and the one that spends the most money on advertising. Within its well-stocked and well-accessorized premises, you'll find rambling racks of cosmetics, perfumes, a noteworthy section devoted to books and periodicals, housewares, and thousands of garments designed for men, women, and children. If there's something you forgot to pack in anticipation of your trip, chances are very good that Steffl Kaufhaus will have it for you. It's open Monday through Wednesday and Friday from 9am to 6:30pm, Thursday from 9am to 8:30pm, and Saturday from 9am to 1pm.

FASHIONS

Casselli
In the Ringstrassen Galleries, Kärntner Ring 5-7. ☎ **0222/512-53-50.**

No woman over 45 should even think about rummaging through the racks of this store devoted to the tastes and budgets of hip younger women. Many of the garments are Italian made or inspired, the remainder Austrian, and many of the younger shop assistants of downtown Vienna swear by the place for both casual street clothes and experimental evening clothes. Established in the mid-1990s, the place is open Monday through Friday from 10am to 7pm, Saturday from 10am to 1pm.

Lanz
Kärntnerstrasse 10. ☎ **0222/512-24-56.**

A well-known Austrian store, Lanz specializes in Austrian folkloric clothing. It has a rustically elegant format of wood paneling and brass chandeliers. Most of their stock is for women, although they do offer a limited selection of men's jackets, neckties, and hats. Clothes for toddlers begin at sizes appropriate for a 1-year-old child, whereas women's apparel begins at size 36 (American size 7). Open Monday through Friday from 9am to 6pm and on Saturday from 9am to 1pm.

✪ Loden Plankl
Michaelerplatz 6. ☎ **0222/533-80-32.**

Established in 1830 by the Plankl family, this store is the oldest and most reputable outlet in Vienna for traditional Austrian clothing. You'll find a collection of Austrian loden coats, shoes, trousers, dirndls, jackets, lederhosen, and suits for men, women, and children. The building, located opposite the Hofburg, dates from the 17th century. Children's clothing usually begins with items for 2-year-olds, and women's sizes range from 7 to 20 (American). Large or tall men won't be ignored either, as sizes go up to 60. Open Monday through Friday from 9am to 6pm and on Saturday from 9am to 1pm.

Mary Kindermoden
Graben 14. ☎ **0222/533-60-97.**

Here's a store specializing in children's clothing with a regional twist. If you've thought about buying a pair of lederhosen for your nephew or a dirndl for your niece, this is the place to go. In the heart of the Old Town, near St. Stephan's Cathedral, the store has two floors stocked with well-made garments, including lace swaddling clothes for a christening. Most garments are for children aged 10 months to 14 years, although lederhosen (which are adorable if you can get your child to wear them) are available for children 10 months to 8 years. The staff speaks English and seems to deal well with children. Open Monday through Friday from 9am to 6pm and on Saturday from 9am to 1pm.

Niederösterreichisches Heimatwerk
Herrengasse 6. ☎ **0222/533-34-95.**

This is one of the best-stocked clothing stores in Vienna if you're looking for traditional garments that men, women, and children still wear with undeniable style in Austria. The inventory covers three full floors, and includes garments inspired by the folkloric traditions of Styria, the Tyrol, Carinthia, and virtually every other Austrian province in between. If you're looking for a loden coat, a dirndl, a jaunty alpine hat (with or without a pheasant feather), or an incredibly durable pair of leather shorts (*lederhosen*) that look great on hikes, this is the place. You'll also find handcrafted gift items (pewter, breadboards and breadbaskets, crystal, and tableware) laden with folk-loric alpine charm. It's open Monday through Friday from 9:30am to 6pm. It's closed between late July and mid-August.

Popp & Kretschmer
Kärntnerstrasse 51. ☎ **0222/512-78-01.**

The staff here is usually as well dressed and elegant as the clientele, and if you appear to be a bona fide customer, the sales clerks will offer coffee, tea, or champagne as you scrutinize the carefully selected merchandise. The store contains three carpeted levels of dresses for women, along with shoes, handbags, belts, and a small selection of men's briefcases, and travel bags. You'll find it opposite the State Opera, near many of the grand old hotels of Vienna. Open Monday through Friday from 9am to 6pm and on Saturday from 9am to 1pm.

Sportalm Trachtenmoden
In the Haas Haus, Stephansplatz 12. ☎ **0222/535-52-89.**

If you're a woman, and looking for a coy and flattering dirndl to carry home with you, this stylish women's store stocks a staggering collection. Many are crafted as faithful replicas of designs that haven't been altered for generations; others take greater liberties and opt for brighter colors and updates that are specifically geared for modern tastes. Even if you're male and wouldn't otherwise dream of stepping into this shop, consider the possibility of procuring a lace-trimmed christening dress for a favorite niece, or a dirndl or traditional Austrian jacket or dress that would make virtually any female child look adorable. The children's department configures its stock for girls aged 1 to 14. You'll find the store, which is open Monday through Friday from 10:30am to 6:30pm and Saturday from 10:30am to 1pm, within the jarringly modern Haas Haus, across the plaza from Vienna's cathedral.

Yves St. Laurent Rive Gauche
In the Ringstrassen Galleries, Kärntner Ring 5-7. ☎ **0222/512-52-02.**

Looking for an evening gown (*abendkleide*) or cocktail dress (*cocktailkleide*) that's as divine as the Wagnerian opus you're about to hear at the State Opera? Head for the only distributor of Yves St. Laurent in Austria, a stylish street-level boutique well-stocked with a discerning sales staff and virtually every piece of *prêt-à-porter* the French master has created this season. Inventory includes a scattering of informal ensembles referred to as "sportswear" that's probably too elegant to ever actually wear out onto the tennis court. The only menswear within a shop otherwise devoted exclusively to women is a collection of neckties, many of which are purchased as peace offerings for whatever male will eventually pay the bill for the glamorous garments hauled out of here by Vienna's most stylish. The shop is open Monday through Friday from 10am to 7pm, Saturday from 10 am to 1pm.

JEWELRY

✪ A. E. Köchert
Neuer Markt 15. ☎ **0222/512-58-28.**

Here the sixth generation of the family that served as court jewelers until the end of the Habsburg empire continue their tradition of fine workmanship. The store, founded in 1814, is in a 16th-century building protected as a monument. The firm has designed many of the crown jewels of Europe, but the staff still gives attention to customers looking only for such minor purchases as charms for a bracelet. It's open Monday through Friday from 9am to 6pm and Saturdays from 9am to 1pm.

Open-Air Markets

Viennese merchants have thrived since the Middle Ages by hauling produce, dairy products, and meats, in bulk, from the fertile farms of Lower Austria and Burgenland into the city center. The tradition of buying the day's provisions directly from street stalls is so strong that there's a strong disincentive, even today, for the establishment of modern supermarkets within the city center.

Odd (and inconvenient) as this may seem, you'll quickly grasp the allure of Vienna's open-air food stalls after a brief session wandering through the Naschmarkt (a visit to which is included as part of Walking Tour 2 "South of the Ring," in Chapter 7), the Rochusmarkt, or the Brunnenmarkt. The vast majority of the hundreds of merchants operating within these markets maintain approximately the same hours: Monday through Friday from 8am to 6pm, Saturday from 8am to noon.

The largest of the city's outdoor food markets is the **Naschmarkt,** Wienzeile, in the 6th District (U-Bahn: Karlsplatz), just south of the Ring. It occupies the site of what was originally the riverbed of a branch of the Danube that was diverted and paved over during the massive public works projects of the 19th century. Insiders maintain that because of its size, it's the most evocatively seedy of the bunch, the most colorful, and the most deeply entrenched within the public consciousness of the Viennese.

Less comprehensive are the **Rochusmarkt,** at Landstrasser Hauptstrasse at the corner of the Erdbergstrasse, in the 3rd District (U-Bahn: Rochusgasse), a short distance east of the Ring, and the **Brunnenmarkt,** on the Brunnengasse, in the 16th District (U-Bahn: Josefstädterstrasse), a subway ride west of the center, a short walk north of Vienna's Westbahnhof. Even if you don't plan on stocking up on produce and foodstuffs (the staff at your hotel might not be amused if you showed up with bushels of carrots or potatoes), the experience is colorful enough, and in some cases, *kitsch* enough, to be remembered later as one of the highlights of a trip to Vienna.

Agatha Paris
In the Ringstrassen Galleries, Kärntner Ring 5-7. ☎ **0222/512-46-21.**

The concept here is small-scale and intensely decorative, with jewelry that manages to be both exotic and tasteful at the same time. Many are inset with semiprecious (i.e., affordable) gemstones, others combine gold and silver into attractive ornaments which are sometimes (but not always) based on antique models. The store is open Monday through Friday from 10am to 7pm and Saturdays from 10:30am to 1pm.

Rozet & Fischmeister
Kohlmeister 11. ☎ **0222/8061.**

Few jewelry stores in Austria attain the prestige of this 200-year-old emporium of good taste and conspicuous consumption. Owned by the same family since it was established in 1770, this store specializes in gold jewelry, gemstones set into artful settings, and both antique and modern versions of silver tableware. If you're looking for flawless copies of Biedermeir silverware or pieces inspired by 18th and 19th century aesthetics, this is where you want to go. If you opt to buy an engagement ring here or a bauble for a friend, you won't be the first. The staff here will quietly admit that Franz Joseph I made several discreet purchases here for his legendary mistress, actress Katharina Schratt. It's open Monday through Friday from 9am to 1pm, and from 3pm to 6pm; Saturdays from 9am until noon. They're closed Saturdays in July and August.

MUSIC

✪ Arcadia Opera Shop
Wiener Staatsoper, Kärntnerstrasse 40. ☎ **0222/513-95-68.**

Well respected as one of the best record stores in Austria, this establishment offers a broad range of classical music. Its staff is well educated in the lore, legend, and availability of classical recordings, and is usually eager to share its knowledge with customers. Located on the street level of the Vienna State Opera, with a separate entrance opening onto Kärntnerstrasse, the establishment also carries books on art, music, architecture, and opera, as well as an assortment of musical memorabilia. Any of these (portrait busts of Mozart, or engravings of Beethoven) would make a worthwhile souvenir of a pilgrimage to musical Austria. Guided tours of the splendid opera house end in this shop, which is open Monday through Friday from 9am to 6pm, Saturdays and Sundays from 9am to 1pm.

Da Caruso
Operngasse 4. ☎ **0222/513-1326.**

Set almost adjacent to the Vienna State Opera, this establishment is sought out by music fans and academicians around the world for its inventory of rare and unusual recordings of historic performances by the Vienna Opera and the Vienna Philharmonic. If you're looking for a recording of a magical or particularly emotional performance by Maria Callas, Herbert von Karajan, Bruno Walter, or whomever, chances are likely that this place will have a copy of it on CD. Established in the 1980s, it boasts a staff that's hip, alert, educated, and obviously in love with music. There's also a collection of taped films.

WINE

Wein & Co.
Habsburgerstrasse 3. ☎ **0222/535-09-16.**

Since the colonization of Vindobona by the ancient Romans, the Viennese have always taken their wines seriously. Wein & Co. is Vienna's largest wine outlet, a sprawling cellar-level emporium to the joys of the grape and the bounty of Bacchus. The layout resembles a supermarket as its shelves are loaded with Rheinrieslings, Blauburgunder, Blaufrankischer, Grüner Veltliners, Zweigelts, and a roster of obscure Austrian wines. You'll also find wines from around the world, including South Africa, Chile, and all the wine-producing countries of Western Europe. It's open Monday through Friday from 10am to 7pm, Saturday from 9am to 1pm.

Vienna After Dark

Come to the cabaret or the heurige, the opera or the casino—whatever nightlife scene turns you on. Vienna has a little bit of everything. You can dance into the morning hours, attend a festival, go to the theater, hear a concert, gamble, or simply indulge in Vienna's legendary spirits at a local tavern.

The best sources of information about what's happening on the cultural scene is **Wien Monatsprogramm,** which is distributed free at tourist information offices and often at many hotel reception desks. **Die Presse,** the Viennese daily, publishes a special magazine in its Thursday edition outlining the major cultural events for the coming week. It's in German but might still be helpful to you.

The Viennese are not known for discounting their cultural presentations. However, *Wien Monatsprogramm* lists outlets where you can purchase tickets in advance, thereby cutting down the surcharge imposed by travel agencies. These agencies routinely add about 22% to what may already be an expensive ticket.

If you're a student or if you'd rather not go broke attending a performance at the Staatsoper or the Burgtheater, you can purchase standing-room tickets at a cost of about 50 AS ($4.75).

Bona fide students with valid IDs are eligible for many discounts if they're under 27. For example, the Burgtheater, Akademietheater, and the Staatsoper will sell student tickets for just 70 AS ($6.65) on the night of the performance. Theaters almost routinely grant students about 20% off the regular ticket price.

Vienna is the home of four major symphony orchestras, including the world-acclaimed Vienna Symphony and the Vienna Philharmonic. Others include the ÖRF Symphony Orchestra and the Niederösterreichische Tonkünstler. There are literally dozens of others, ranging from smaller orchestras to chamber orchestras.

1 The Performing Arts

Music is at the heart of the cultural life in Vienna. This has been true for a couple of centuries or so, and the city continues to lure composers and librettists, musicians and music-lovers. You can find places to enjoy everything from chamber music to pop, from waltzes to jazz. You'll find small discos and large concert halls, as well as musical theaters. If somehow you should tire of aural entertainment, you'll find drama on Vienna's stages, from classical to modern to avant-garde. Below we'll describe just a few of the better-known spots for cultural recreation—if you're in Vienna long enough, you'll find many other delights on your own.

A NOTE ON EVENING DRESS

For concerts and theaters, dark suits and cocktail dresses are recommended. For especially festive occasions such as opera premières, receptions, and balls, tails and dinner jackets are the preferred dress for men and evening dresses for women. You can rent men's evening wear, as well as carnival costumes, from several places in Vienna, which you'll find in the telephone directory classified section (the *Yellow Pages* in the United States) under *Kleiderleihanstalten*. It's a good idea to take a light topcoat when you go out in the evening, even in summer.

AUSTRIAN STATE THEATERS & OPERA HOUSES

Reservations and information for the four state theaters—the Staatsoper (State Opera), Volksoper, Burgtheater (National Theater), and the Akademietheater—can be obtained by calling an office that unites all four theaters into a coherent system not only for reservations but for information. To reach that office—the number is likely to be busy—call **0222/51444-29-59** Monday through Friday from 8am to 5pm. The major season is from September until June, with more limited presentations in summer. Many tickets are issued, even before the box office opens, to subscribers. For all four theaters, box-office sales are made only one month before each performance at the **Bundestheaterkasse,** Goethegasse 1 (☎ **0222/51-44-40**), open Monday through Friday from 8am to 6pm, on Saturday from 9am to 2pm, and on Sunday and holidays from 9am to noon. Credit card sales can be arranged by telephone within six days of a performance by calling **0222/513-15-13,** Monday through Friday from 10am to 6pm and on Saturday and Sunday from 10am to noon. Tickets for all state theater performances, including the opera, are also available by writing to the **Österreichischer** Bundestheaterverband, Goethegasse 1, A-1010 Vienna, from points outside Vienna. Orders must be received at least three weeks in advance of the performance to be booked. No one should send money through the mails.

Note that the single most common complaint of music-lovers in Vienna is about the nonavailability of tickets to many highly desirable musical performances. If the rituals described above don't produce the tickets, you have the option of consulting a ticket broker. Their surcharge usually won't exceed 25%, except for extremely rare tickets when that surcharge might be doubled or tripled. Although at least half a dozen ticket agencies maintain offices in the city, one of the most reputable agencies is **Liener Brünn** (☎ **0222/533-09-61**). Their tickets are sometimes available months in advance, or as little as a few hours before an event.

As a final resort, remember that the concierges of virtually every upscale hotel in Vienna long ago learned sophisticated tricks for the acquisition of hard-to-come-by tickets. (A gratuity might work wonders, and will be expected anyway for the phonework. You'll pay a hefty surcharge as well.)

Akademietheater
Lisztstrasse 3. ☎ **0222/51444-26-56.** Tickets 50–500 AS ($4.75–$47.50) for seats, 30 AS ($2.85) for standing room. U-Bahn: Stadtpark.

This theater specializes in both classic and contemporary works, from Brecht to Shakespeare. The Burgtheater Company often performs here, as it's the second, smaller house of this world-famed theater (see below).

Burgtheater (National Theater)

Dr.-Karl-Lueger-Ring 2. ☎ **0222/51444-26-56.** Tickets 50–500 AS ($4.75–$47.50) for seats, 20 AS ($1.90) for standing room. Tram: 1, 2, or D to Burgtheater.

The Burgtheater produces classical and modern plays in German. Work started on the original structure in 1776, but the theater was destroyed in World War II and later reopened in 1955. It's the dream of every German-speaking actor to appear here.

✪ Staatsoper (State Opera)

Opernring 2. ☎ **0222/51444-29-60.** Tours are given almost daily year-round, often two to five times a day, depending on demand. Tour times are posted on a board outside the entrance. The cost is 40 AS ($3.80) per person. Tickets 120–2,300 AS ($11.40–$218.50). U-Bahn: Karlsplatz.

This is one of the three most important opera houses in the world, and the upkeep is apparently a necessity to the Austrians as its operation costs taxpayers some million schillings a day. With the Vienna Philharmonic Orchestra in the pit, some of the leading opera stars of the world perform here. In their day, Richard Strauss and Gustav Mahler worked as directors. Daily performances are given from the first of September until the end of June (see "Other Top Attractions" in Chapter 6).

Volksoper

Währingerstrasse 78. ☎ **0222/51444-33-18.** Tickets 80–850 AS ($7.60–$80.75). U-Bahn: Volksoper.

This folk opera house presents lavish productions of Viennese operettas and other musicals from the first of September until the end of June on a daily schedule. Tickets go on sale at the Volksoper itself only one hour before performance.

MORE THEATER & MUSIC

If your German is halfway passable, try to see a play by Arthur Schnitzler, if one is being staged during your visit. This mild-mannered playwright, who died in 1931, was the quintessential Viennese of the Austrian writers. Through his works he gave the imperial city the charm and style that often defines Paris. Whenever possible we attend a revival of one of his plays, such as *Einsame Weg* (*The Solitary Path*) or *Professor Bernhardi.* Our favorite is *Reigen,* on which the film *La Ronde* was based. Schnitzler's plays are often performed at the Theater in der Josefstadt (see below).

Konzerthaus

Lothringerstrasse 20. ☎ **0222/712-1211.** Ticket prices depend on the event. U-Bahn: Stadtpark.

This major concert hall with three auditoriums was built in 1913. It's the venue for a wide cultural program, including orchestral concerts, chamber-music recitals, choir concerts, piano recitals, and opera stage performances. Its repertoire is classical, romantic, and also contemporary. The box office is open Monday through Friday from 9am to 7:30pm and on Saturday from 9am to 1pm.

Musikverein

Dumbastrasse 3. ☎ **0222/505-8681-32** for the box office. Tickets 50 AS ($4.75) for standing room; up to 1,400 AS ($133) for seats. U-Bahn: Karlsplatz.

Consider yourself lucky if you get to hear the Vienna Philharmonic here. One of the Musikverein's two concert halls, the Golden Hall, has often served as the setting for various TV productions. Out of the 600 or so concerts that are presented here per season, (September to June), only 10 to 12 are played by the Vienna Philharmonic. These are usually subscription concerts which are always sold out long in advance. Standing room is available at almost any concert, but you must line up hours before the show. The box office, at Karlsplatz 6, is open Monday through Friday from 9am to 6pm and on Saturday from 9am to noon.

Theater an der Wien

Linke Weinzeile 6. ☎ **0222/588-85** for tickets. Tickets 90–990 F ($18–$198). U-Bahn: Karlsplatz.

This theater opened on the night of June 13, 1801, and ever since fans have been able to enjoy opera and operetta presentations here. This was the site of the première of Beethoven's *Fidelio* in 1805; in fact, the composer once lived in this building. The world première of Johann Strauss Jr.'s *Die Fledermaus* was also performed here. Invariably, an article appears every year in some newspaper proclaiming that the Theater an der Wien was the site of the première of Mozart's *The Magic Flute*—a neat trick, considering that the first performance of that great work was in 1791, 10 years before this theater existed. During the years of occupation after World War II, when the Staatsoper was being restored after heavy damage, the Vienna State Opera made the Theater an der Wien its home. The box office is open daily from 10am to 1pm and 2 to 6pm.

Theater in der Josefstadt

Josefstadterstrasse 26. ☎ **0222/402-5127.** Tickets 215–600 AS ($20.45–$57.00). U-Bahn: U-2. Tram: J. Bus: 13.

Built in 1776, this theater prides itself on presenting only comedies, dramas, and tragedies, either in their original German or in German-language translations from other languages. (Unlike most of the other theaters of Vienna, musical performances are almost never given here.) One of the most influential theaters in the Teutonic world, it reached legendary levels of excellence under the aegis of Max Reinhardt, beginning in 1924. The box office is open daily from 9am to 6pm.

Vienna's English Theater

Josefsgasse 12. ☎ **0222/402-12-60** or 0222/402-82-84. Tickets 170–460 AS ($16.15–$43.70). U-Bahn: Rathaus. Tram: J. Bus: 13A.

This is the major English-speaking theater in Vienna. It was established in 1963 and proved so popular that it has been around ever since. Many international celebrities have appeared on the stage of this neobaroque theater, in addition to many British actors. Princess Grace of Monaco played here, before her tragic death, in a performance to raise money for charity. Works by American playwrights are occasionally presented here. The box office is open Monday through Friday from 10am to 5pm and on Saturday 10am to 4pm.

Volkstheater

Neustiftgasse 1. ☎ **0222/93-27-76.** Tickets, 60–400 AS ($5.70–$38.00). Tram: 1, 2, 49, D, or J. Bus: 48A.

Built in 1889, this theater maintains a tradition of presenting plays from the classical repertoire of German-language theater, and almost never schedules a purely musical performance. Some of the pieces produced here are videotaped for distribution throughout the German-speaking world, and include original versions and translations of works by Nestroy, Raimund, and Strindberg. Modern plays and comedies are also presented. The theater's season runs from September through June. The box office is open daily from 10am to 8pm.

Wiener Kammeroper

At Schönbrunn Palace, Schönbrunner Schlossstrasse. ☎ **0222/512-01-00.** Tickets 100–800 AS ($9.50–$76). U-Bahn: Schönbrunn.

This gem of a theater opened in 1749 for the entertainment of the Maria Theresa's court. The architecture is a medley of baroque and rococo, and there's a large, plush box where the imperial family sat to enjoy the shows. The theater belongs to Hochschule für Musik und darstellende Kunst and is used for performances of the Max Reinhardt Seminar (theater productions) and opera productions throughout the year. Operettas and comic operas are performed in July and August. A wide array of different art groups, each responsible for its own ticket sales, perform here. There are various performances daily in July and August, Tuesday through Saturday nights.

2 The Club & Music Scene

AN ENTERTAINMENT COMPLEX

Volksgarten

Entrances from the Heldenplatz and from Burgring 1. ☎ **0222/533-05-180.** Cover 70 AS ($6.65) for the evergreen music (8pm–2am nightly), 70–160 AS ($6.65–$15.20) for the disco music (nightly 11pm–4am).

This is the largest and most diverse entertainment complex within Vienna's Ring. It was established in 1946 within a building very close to the Hofburg, and intersperses a series of dining and drinking emporiums within a labyrinth of rooms and outdoor spaces that interconnect into a happy-go-lucky maze. Many visitors prefer the area with the evergreen music, where everything from Tyrolean or Bavarian oom-pah-pah music alternates with rock 'n' roll from the 1950s to the 1970s. A restaurant on the premises, open continuously from 11am to midnight, serves steins of beer, wine, and main courses priced at from 60 to 160 AS ($5.70 to $15.20). A disco with up-to-date music (which, frankly, is a bit jarring when played simultaneously with the evergreen music) is open every night from 11pm, although no self-respecting Viennese hipster would even think of showing up until at least midnight.

NIGHTCLUBS/CABARET

Eden Bar

Liliengasse 2. ☎ **0222/512-74-50.** U-Bahn: Stephansplatz.

Local society figures in evening dress are often drawn to this chic rendezvous spot in Vienna. The setting is one of 19th-century grandeur. You enter a spacious room with a small mezzanine. Tables and private boxes surround the dance floor, or you can find a seat at the half-moon–shaped bar. It's open nightly from 10pm to 4am, but if you show up much before midnight you may have the place to yourself. The Eden is a popular *après-théâtre* stop, and if there's a foreign celebrity in Vienna, he or she is likely to visit here. A live band plays for dancing, and the music is of the best nightclub variety played in Vienna. Drinks begin at 210 AS ($19.95).

Moulin Rouge

Walfischgasse 11. ☎ **0222/512-21-30.** Cover 75 AS ($7.15). U-Bahn: Karlsplatz.

Established prior to World War II, this spot has been known for many years as the leading risqué nightclub of Vienna, modeled after the original Moulin Rouge in Paris. Just to the right of the opera house, its exterior has curved walls, clapboard siding, and a reconstruction of the establishment's trademark, a windmill. If you're window-shopping, you can see pictures of the "artists" who will later disrobe for you during a show. However, as the women in the pictures are stark naked, there'll be no surprise awaiting you if you decide to go into the lavishly decorated club which has two tiers of seating. The club opens nightly at 10pm, presenting two shows, at 11pm and at 12:30am. Once inside, a beer costs 180 AS ($17.10); a whisky goes for 250 AS ($23.75).

Savanna Club/Savanna Inn
Mayerhofgasse 2 at Favoritenstrasse. ☎ **0222/505-7369.** Cover (Fri–Sat only) 60 AS ($5.70).

This is the most appealing and most long-lived West African nightclub in all of Vienna, a sturdy and exotic venue that has survived where many competitors have failed. It's run by the Austrian/Nigerian husband and wife team of Eyo and Charles. Together, they run an establishment with some of the most unusual food and music in the Habsburgundian world. You might opt for a meal in the street-level dining room, the Savanna Inn, where the bar is done in a zebra theme. Collages and naïve paintings by Africa-born artists provide the decoration. Main courses range from 90 to 130 AS ($8.55 to $12.35) and include such West African dishes as *Egousi* (beef garnished with pulverized melon seeds) or stockfish (the ugliest fish in the seas) with hot sauce.

Downstairs, the music is recorded and danceable as it is produced in the electronic studios of Zaire, Nigeria, Ghana, and Senegal. These tunes are interspersed with music performed by African-American recording artists. This is a fun and cosmopolitan, albeit not particularly Viennese venue, with a crowd that hails from throughout the Arab, African, and Pacific Rim worlds. The restaurant is open Monday through Saturday from 11am to midnight. The dance club is open Tuesday through Saturday from 9pm and between 2 and 4am, depending on the night of the week.

ROCK, JAZZ & BLUES

Jazzland
Franz-Josefs-Kai 29. ☎ **0222/533-2575.** Cover 150–190 AS ($14.25–$18.05), depending on who's playing.

This is the most famous jazz pub in Austria, noted for the quality of its U.S. and Central-European–based performers. It's set within a deep, 200-year-old cellar of the type the Viennese used to store staples during the city's many sieges. Amid exposed brick walls and dim lighting, you can order either drinks or dinner, depending on your needs. Beer—which seems to be the thing to order here—costs 48 AS ($4.55) for a foaming mugful. Platters of Viennese food such as tafelspitz, Wiener schnitzel, and roulades of beef, cost from 68 to 123 AS ($6.45 to $11.70). The place is open nightly from 8am to 1:30pm. Music begins at 9pm, and every evening, three sets are performed.

Papa's Tapas
Schwarzenbergplatz 10. ☎ **0222/505-03-11.** Cover 50–150 AS ($4.75–$14.25), depending on the event.

This place attracts rock 'n' roll fans. It has the same location as the Atrium disco (see below). In a corner is the Würlitzer Bar, with its American-made jukebox. You get all vintage '50s stuff, including Elvis. It plays host to a changing roster of visiting rock stars, whose arrival is always heralded in the Vienna newspapers.

When there's no live music, Papa's operates as a bar, with a large beer costing 42 AS ($4). The club is open Monday through Thursday from 8pm to 2am and on Friday and Saturday from 8pm until 3:30am. U-Bahn: Karlsplatz.

Tenne

Annagasse 3. ☎ **0222/512-57-08.** Cover 20 AS ($1.90). U-Bahn: Karlsplatz.

Right next door to the members-only Take Five is this spot where groups play jazz music for listening or for dancing. Folk and pop music are also featured. Tenne has a log-cabin ambience, with lots of farm equipment like ox yokes comprising the decor. A one-drink minimum is required, with the first drink costing 60 AS ($5.70). The club is open Monday through Saturday from 8:30pm to 3:30am.

DANCE CLUBS/DISCOS

Atrium

Schwarzenbergplatz 10 (Schwindgasse 1). ☎ **0222/505-35-94.** Cover 30 AS ($2.85). U-Bahn: Karlsplatz.

This spot lies within a 5-minute walk of its original location, where it was Vienna's first disco. Today it caters to a young crowd who gather here Wednesday through Sunday from 8:30pm to 4am. Every Thursday and Sunday drinks are 2-for-1 for the first hour of business. Otherwise, a large beer costs 40 AS ($3.80).

Chattanooga

Graben 29A. ☎ **0222/533-50-00.** Cover for Disco, 20 AS ($1.90). U-Bahn: Stephansplatz.

Chattanooga is one of the most popular sidewalk cafés along the Graben in summer. Inside, the decor of its restaurant is like that of a railroad car in the Gay '90s. Cheeseburgers and simple meals are served upstairs, but the real reason for coming here is the disco downstairs. The half-rounded room with maroon velvet niches has stylized white tree trunks sprouting from floor to ceiling (displays are likely to change for certain musical acts). Beer starts at 58 AS ($5.50). This is the only dining establishment in the city that's open seven days a week from 8:30am to 3am, during which time all items on the menu are available.

P1 Discothek

Rotgasse 9. ☎ **0222/535-99-95.** Cover 50 AS ($4.75). U-Bahn: Stephansplatz.

The leading disco of Vienna (subject to change, of course), this lively place is filled with Viennese and visitors alike, most in their mid-20s. In what used to be a film studio, the dance club has a spacious floor that accommodates as many as 2,000 dancers. The club was launched on the road to fame when Tina Turner made an appearance here back in 1988. Two DJs alternate nightly. Once or twice per month, there's live music. The club is open Sunday through Thursday from 9pm to 4am and on Friday and Saturday from 9pm to 6am. Beer costs 45 AS ($4.30) and up.

Queen Anne

Johannesgasse 12. ☎ **0222/512-02-03.** No cover. U-Bahn: Stadtpark.

Lots of interesting people are attracted to this nightclub and disco. Patrons have included David Bowie, German playboy Gunther Sachs, the Princess of Auersperg, and the '70s heavy-metal band Deep Purple. The club has a big collection of the latest Stateside and Italian records, as well as occasional musical acts ranging from Mick Jagger lookalikes to imitations of Watusi dancers. The brown doors with brass trim are open daily from 10pm to 6am. A scotch and soda goes for 95 AS ($9.05).

Scotch Club

Parkring 10. ☎ **0222/512-94-17.** No cover. U-Bahn: Stadtpark. Tram: 1, 2.

Except for the whisky you might drink here, there's not much Scottish ambience at this disco and coffeehouse in Vienna's most fashionable area, a 5-minute walk from the Hilton, Marriott, Radisson/SAS, Parkring, and Imperial. The establishment is a popular place for society figures and others to meet. Furnished luxuriously, it has good technical equipment, including a hydraulic stage and fancy lights. The establishment has three floors, and near one of the three downstairs bars you'll find a monumental waterfall. Upstairs, the coffeehouse is cozy, and on the second floor there is a famous cocktail bar. It's open daily from 11am to 6am. Drinks begin at 90 AS ($8.55).

Titanic

Theobaldstrasse 11, (6). ☎ **0222/587-4758.** No cover.

This sprawling dance club has thrived since the early 1980s by providing two distinct dance areas (both with a different style of music), and a likable upstairs restaurant where Mexican and Italian food provides bursts of quick energy for further bouts of dancing. You'll enter a mirrored world with strobe lights and a deliberate lack of seating areas, which encourages patrons to dance, drink, and mingle, sometimes rather aggressively, throughout the evening. Many clients here come from the community of U.S. students and athletes stationed in Vienna while pursuing their studies or careers in basketball or volleyball. As far as music goes, you're likely to find everything that's playing in London or Los Angeles, with the noteworthy exception of Techno and Rave music, which this club deliberately avoids. The restaurant serves dinners every night from 8pm to 2am, with main courses priced between 50 to 90 AS ($4.75 to $8.55). The disco areas are open nightly from 10pm to around 4am, depending on business. Beer begins at around 45 AS ($4.30).

3 The Bar Scene

Viennese bars range from time-honored haunts of the Austrian aristocrats to the louder, more trendy establishments that stay open until dawn. The most popular area (among locals and visitors) for experiencing Vienna's blossoming bar scene is the **Bermuda Triangle.** It's roughly bordered by Judengasse, Seitenstättengasse Rabensteig, and Franz-Josefs-Kai. You'll find everything here from intimate watering holes to larger bars with live music. The closest U-Bahn stop is Schwedenplatz. Below is a sampling of bars that will appeal to a broad spectrum of tastes.

Barfly's Club

In the Hotel Fürst Metternich, Esterhazygasse 33. ☎ **0222/586-08-25.**

This is the most urbane and sophisticated cocktail bar in town, attended by a coterie of working journalists, actors, and politicians. It's got a laissez-faire ambience that combines aspects of Vienna's *grande bourgeoisie* with its discreetly avant garde. It's presided over by a charming and multilingual head bartender, Dutch-born René van der Graaf (whose drink-making ability puts Tom Cruise in *Cocktail* to shame). The setting, within a meticulously paneled room lined with rows of illuminated bottles is reminiscent of the bars within the transatlantic ocean liners of the 1930s. A menu will list about 250 cocktails that include every kind of mixed drink imaginable. Priced at from 85 to 100 AS ($8.05 to $9.50) each, they range from the kind of sunrise-colored libation you'd offer a tarty new acquaintance to the grand art deco classics of the Jazz Age. The only food served is toast (warm sandwiches), priced at 65 AS ($6.20) each. From May through September, it's open daily from 8pm to between

2 and 4am, depending on the night of the week. From October through April, it's open daily from 6pm to between 2 and 4pm, depending on the night of the week.

Chamäleon

Blutgasse 3. ☎ **0222/513-17-03.** U-Bahn: Stephansplatz.

A youngish crowd is drawn to this bar, which is decorated in a tongue-in-cheek style, taking its theme from the elusive chameleon. This champagne and cocktail bar—there's recorded music—has one of the widest ranges of mixed drinks in Vienna, everything from the famous Singapore Sling to "The Bronx." Of the more than 70 cocktails offered, the least expensive begin at 75 AS ($7.15). The club is open Monday through Thursday from 5pm to 2am, on Friday and Saturday from 5pm to 4am, and on Sunday 5pm to 2am. In summer, the cocktail garden is also open daily when the weather is agreeable.

Esterházykeller

Haarhof 1. ☎ **0222/533-34-82.** U-Bahn: Stephansplatz.

The ancient bricks and scarred wooden tables of this famous drinking spot are permeated with the aroma of endless pints of spilled beer. An outing here isn't recommended for everyone, although to its credit no one ever feels sloppily dressed at the Esterházykeller. If you decide to chance it, choose the left-hand entrance (while facing it from the street), grip the railing firmly, and begin your descent. A promenade through this establishment's endless recesses and labyrinthine passages could provide views of the faces you may have thought appeared only in movies. Wine, a specialty, starts at 28 AS ($2.65) a glass. Order a bottle if you plan to stay a while. The place is open Monday through Friday from 10am to 10pm and on Saturday and Sunday from 4 to 10pm.

Galerie-Bar

Singerstrasse 7. ☎ **0222/512-49-29.** U-Bahn: Stephansplatz.

Vienna is known for its fashionable bars, and one of the best is this one near St. Stephan's Cathedral. Its owner claims "it's the most beautiful bar in the world." In a warmly outfitted ambience of burled walnut, original artwork, and vaulted ceilings, the bar attracts visitors nightly from 7pm to 4am. Mixed drinks cost 70 to 120 AS ($6.65 to $11.40); beer begins at 38 AS ($3.60).

St. Urbani-Keller

Am Hof 12. ☎ **0222/533-91-02.** U-Bahn: Stephansplatz or Fahnenpasse.

Named after the patron saint of winemaking, this cellar is one of the most historic in Vienna. Carl Hipfinger renovated the cellar as a public gathering place in 1906. Many of the artifacts inside, from the paneling in the German Romantic style to the fanciful wrought-iron lighting fixtures, were designed by one of Austria's most famous architects, Walcher von Moltheim, who rebuilt Vienna's Kreuzenstein Castle at the beginning of the century. The cellar has brick vaulting dating from the 13th century and sections of solid Roman walls you can admire while listening to the folk music at night.

The most popular room is the one on the lowest level, so be sure to continue your descent down the steep stairs until you reach the room with the thick oak tables at the bottom. There you'll discover a rather large collection of art, including numerous crucifixes and a Renaissance chandelier of St. Lucretia. Many kinds of wine are served, but the featured vintage comes from the vineyards of the owner's family. That wine has been offered as gifts to everybody from the famous General Rommel (the so-called Desert Fox) to the president of Austria. The establishment is open daily from 6pm to 1am, with hot food served until midnight.

Meals begin at 50 AS ($4.75) for goulash, but if you've already eaten, no one will mind if you drop in just for a drink. Beer begins at 39 AS ($3.70). Watch your step on the way up or down.

GAY BARS

Alfi's Goldener Spiegel

Linke Wienzeile 46 (entrance on Stiegengasse). ☎ **0222/56-66-08.** U-Bahn: Schönbrunn.

This is one of the most popular gay havens in Vienna, attracting a lot of foreigners. Attached to the bar is a restaurant serving food at moderate prices and specializing in Wiener schnitzel. The bar and restaurant are open Wednesday through Monday from 7pm to 2am. Beer costs 38 AS ($3.60) and up.

Alte Lampe

Heumühlgasse 13. ☎ **0222/567-34-54.** U-Bahn: Mariahilferstrasse.

The Alte Lampe is the oldest gay bar in Vienna, established in the 1960s. Over the long decades it has attracted many visiting celebrities from the cultural world. Today's patrons listen to the same schmaltzy piano music that has been played here for years. It's open daily from 9pm to 4am. A large beer costs 35 AS ($3.35).

Eagle Bar

Blümelgasse 1. ☎ **0222/587-26-61.** U-Bahn: Neubaugasse.

This is one of the premier leather and denim bars for gay men in Vienna. There's no dancing, but virtually every gay male in town has dropped in at least once or twice for a quick look around. It's open daily from 9pm to 4am. Large beers begin at 38 AS ($3.60).

Frauencafe

Langegasse 11. ☎ **0222/43-37-54.** U-Bahn: Lerchenfelderstrasse.

Frauencafe is exactly what a translation of its name would imply: A politically conscious cafe for lesbian and (to a lesser degree) heterosexual women who appreciate the company of other women. Established in 1977 in cramped quarters in a century-old building, it has an interior filled with magazines, newspapers, modern paintings, and a clientele of Austrian and foreign women. Next door is a feminist bookstore with which the cafe is loosely affiliated. It's open Monday through Saturday; in summer from 8pm to 1am, in winter from 7pm to 1am. Glasses of wine begin at 32 AS ($3.05) each.

4 The Heurigen

These wine taverns on the outskirts of Vienna have long been celebrated in operettas, films, and song. Grinzing is the most popular district, but other heuriger-infested neighborhoods include Sievering, Neustift, Nussdorf, or Heiligenstadt.

The most-visited section, **Grinzing,** lies at the edge of the Vienna Woods, a 15-minute drive northwest of the center. Once it was a separate village until it was overtaken by the ever-increasing city boundaries of Vienna. Much of Grinzingremains unchanged, looking as it did in the days when Beethoven lived nearby. It's a district of crooked old streets and houses, their thick walls built around inner courtyards that are often grape arbors sheltering Viennese wine-drinkers on a summer night. The playing of zithers and accordions lasts long into the night.

Which brings up another point. If you're a motorist, don't drive out to the *heurigen.* Police patrols are very strict, and you're not to be driving with more than 0.8% alcohol in your bloodstream. It's much better to take public transportation. Most *heurigen* are reached in 30 to 40 minutes.

Take tram no. 38 to Grinzing; no. 41 to Neustift am Wald; and no. 38 to Sievering, which is also reached by bus no. 39A. Heiligenstadt is reached by U-Bahn line U-4.

We'll start you off with some of our favorites:

Alter Klosterkeller im Passauerhof
Cobenzigasse 9, Grinzing. ☎ **0222/320-63-45.**

One of Vienna's well-known wine taverns, this spot maintains an old-fashioned ambience little changed since the turn of the century. Some of its foundations date from the 12th century. Menu specialties include such familiar fare as tafelspitz (boiled beef), an array of roasts, and plenty of strudel. You can order a glass or bottle of wine, perhaps a meal, costing 150 AS ($14.25) and up. Drinks begin at 30 AS ($2.85). The establishment is open daily from 4pm to midnight. Music is played from 7 to 11:30pm. Closed in January and February.

Altes Presshaus
Cobenzigasse 15, Grinzing. ☎ **0222/32-23-93.**

This is the oldest *heurige* in Grinzing, with an authentic cellar you might ask to see. The interior is filled with wood paneling and antique furniture, giving the place character. The garden terrace blossoms throughout the summer. Meals cost 150 to 280 AS ($14.25 to $26.60); drinks begin at 30 AS ($2.85). It's open daily from 4pm to midnight; closed January and February.

Alt Sievering
Sieveringer Strasse 63, Sievering. ☎ **0222/32-58-88.**

This is one of several attractive *heurigen* in this Vienna suburb. The owner not only serves excellent new wine but prepares such specialties as game, lamb, fish, soufflés, dessert pancakes, strudels, and cakes. A fixed-price menu, which you can eat in summer under the shade trees, begins at 110 AS ($10.45), and à la carte meals start at 175 AS ($16.65). The restaurant is open Thursday through Monday from 9am to 11pm. If you prefer beer, the house keeps three different types on tap.

Grinzinger Hauermandl
Cobenzigasse 20, Grinzing. ☎ **0222/32-30-27.**

Many of the guests at this rustic Grinzing inn are lively Viennese escaping their city for an evening in the suburbs. You'll enter through a garden where you'll notice a Gypsy wagon perched on the roof. The farm-style cookery includes chicken noodle soup and soup with pancakes, as well as a selection of dishes so hearty they could fortify you for a day's work in the vineyards, including the schnitzel available for 95 AS ($9.05). A quarter liter of wine (about two glasses) costs 30 AS ($2.85), whereas à la carte meals run 140 to 225 AS ($13.30 to $21.40). The tavern is open Monday through Saturday from 5:30pm to midnight.

Mayer
Am Pfarrplatz 2, Heiligenstadt. ☎ **0222/37-33-61,** or 0222/37-12-87 after 4pm.

This historic house was some 130 years old when Beethoven composed sections of his *Ninth Symphony* while living here in 1817, and the same kind of fruity dry wine is still sold to guests in the shady courtyard of the rose garden. Original *heurigen* music completes the traditional atmosphere. Menu items include grilled chicken, savory pork, and a buffet of well-prepared country food.

Reservations are suggested. It's open Monday through Saturday from 4pm to midnight and on Sunday and holidays from 11am to midnight. The innkeepers, the Mayer family, sell wine for 28 AS ($2.65) a glass, with meals beginning at 200 AS ($19). Closed December 22 to January 10.

Zum Figlmüller

Grinzinger Strasse 55, Grinzing. ☎ **0222/32-42-57.**

One of the city's most popular wine restaurants is this suburban branch of a restaurant (Figlmüller's) whose main branch is recommended separately (see "Dining," in Chapter 5). Although there's a traditional set of indoor dining rooms, usually with Biedermeier furniture and accessories, most visitors prefer the flowering terrace, where garden settings while away the romance of an evening near the Vienna Woods. Known especially for the size of its enormous Wiener schnitzels 150 AS ($14.25), the restaurant prides itself on serving only wines produced under its own supervision, beginning at 32 AS ($3.05) per glass. Meals include a wide array of light salads and more substantial food designed to accompany the wine. It's open from late April to mid-November, Monday through Saturday from 4:30 pm to midnight.

5 More Entertainment

A CASINO

Casino Wien

Esterházy Palace, Kärntnerstrasse 41. ☎ **0222/512-48-36.** No cover.

For games of chance, this casino, opened in 1968, is the place to go. You can charge up to 4,000 AS ($380) on your Diners Club, MasterCard, or Visa. You'll need to show your passport to get in. There are gaming tables for French and American roulette, blackjack, and chemin de fer, as well as the ever-present slot machines. The casino is open daily from 11am to 3am with the tables opening at 3pm.

FILMS

Burg-Kino

Opernring 19. ☎ **0222/587-8406.** U-Bahn: Karlsplatz.

This theater often shows films in English, and every summer presents Carol Reed's classic *The Third Man,* starring Orson Welles and Joseph Cotten. The film was set in occupied Vienna and remains an enduring favorite. Tickets begin at around 75 AS ($7.15) but are specially priced on Monday at 60 AS ($5.70).

Filmmuseum

In the Albertina, Augustinerstrasse 1. ☎ **0222/533-70-54.** U-Bahn: Karlsplatz.

This *cinemathèque* shows films in their original languages and presents retrospectives of directors such as Fritz Lang, Erich von Stroheim, Ernst Lubitsch, and many others. The museum also presents avant-garde and experimental films, as well as classics. A monthly program is available free inside the Albertina, and a copy is posted outside. The film library inside the government-funded museum includes more than 11,000 book titles, and the still collection numbers more than 100,000. A recent retrospective featured movies from the 30s. The theater is closed from June through September. The nominal fee of 45 AS ($4.30) is requested upon entrance, but you must take out a 24-hour membership for 45 AS ($4.30), which entitles you to all of the day's screenings.

6 Only in Vienna

We've recommended a variety of night spots, but none seem to capture the true Viennese spirit quite like the establishments below. Each is unique in its own atmosphere and decor and each continues to remain unique to Vienna.

Alt Wien
Bäckerstrasse 9 (1). ☎ **0222/512-5222.**

Set on one of the oldest, narrowest, and most evocative streets of medieval Vienna, a short walk north of the cathedral, this is the kind of smoky, mysterious, and shadowy cafe where—with a bit of imagination—you might imagine subversive plots, doomed romances, and revolutionary art movements being hatched and plotted. During the day, it's a busy, workaday restaurant patronized by virtually everybody. As the night progresses, you're likely to rub elbows with denizens of late-night Wien whose dialogue and demeanor gets sudsier and, often, more sentimental and schmaltzy. Beer is the preferred drink, and is quaffed in quantities that might rival those of such beer-loving cities as Bamburg and Munich. Foaming mugfuls sell for 24 AS ($2.30) each, and are often accompanied with heaping platters of traditional food, especially goulasch and schnitzels, whose nuances and composition have been sampled by many generations, and many thousands, of diners before you. Main courses range from 85 to 160 AS ($8.05 to $15.20). U-Bahn: Stephansplatz.

Kaffeehäuser Drechsler
Linke Weinzeile 22. ☎ **0222/587-8580.**

It's the best antidote for insomnia in Vienna, presenting a worthy early-morning diversion for anyone whose sleeping habits have been interrupted by jet lag after a long transatlantic flight. Established around 1900, this is the largest and busiest cafe in the neighborhood of the Naschmarkt, the vast open-air food market that sits on what used to be a branch of the Danube before urban renewal and flood control projects in the 19th century diverted the river to another location outside town. Part of the fun of a visit to the market involves wandering through a labyrinth of outdoor food stands early in the morning as restaurants and hotels around Vienna stock up on provisions for the day. Entire books have been written about the subcultures and linguistic dialects that flourish among the Naschmarkt's many generations of entrepreneurs, but for a worthwhile insight into what some travelers compare to the old (and now defunct) Les Halles of Paris, head for the Café Drechsler.

Its bizarre hours reflect those of the wholesale food industry itself: Monday through Friday from 3:30am to 8pm, Saturday from 3:30am to 6pm. Platters of hearty food (concocted from very fresh ingredients procured at the stalls outside) sell for between 55 AS ($5.25) and 100 AS ($9.50) each. No one will mind if you begin quaffing beer, priced at 34 AS ($3.25) each, as the sun rises (you won't be alone if you do). And if you need a dose of caffeine, coffee pours out of urns in ways that might remind you of the flooding of the Danube in pre-flood-control days of yore. U-Bahn: Karlsplatz.

Karl Kolarik's Schweizerhaus in Prater
In the Prater, Strasse des Ersten Mai, 116. ☎ **0222/728-01520.**

The references to this old-fashioned eating house are about as old as the Prater itself. Awash with suds and nostalgia, and laden with *kitsch* of a type possible only within central Europe, it sprawls across a *biergarten* landscape that might remind you of the Habsburg Empire at its most cosmopolitan and most indulgent.

Indulgence is indeed the word, as you'll note when you order any of the vastly proportioned main courses that might have been conceived as provisions for a 19th-century army. If you're looking for *neuen kuchen,* this isn't the place for you, as the menu stresses old-fashioned schnitzels and its house specialty, roasted pork hocks (*Hintere Schweinsstelze*) served with dollops of mustard and horseradish. Anything here is especially appealing when washed down with foaming mugs of Czech *Budweiser* that elderly—and usually solidly built—waitresses pull from taps. During clement weather, the spot moves outside to a verdant corner close to the entrance of Europe's most famous amusement park, the Prater. Main courses range from 75 to 120 AS ($7.15 to $11.40). Service is perfunctory and unfanciful, but food is flavorful, simple, and served in huge portions. Consequently the place is usually packed. Bring your appetite. It's open daily from 10am to midnight.

Pavillion

Burgring 1. ☎ **0222/532-0907.** No cover. U-Bahn: Volkstheater.

Even the Viennese stumble when trying to define a civic monument that has survived in the same format since the 1950s. By general consensus, it's usually labeled as a music cafe, with a clientele that grows much, much more animated after music (funk, soul, blues, and jazz) is broadcast throughout the place every evening beginning around 8pm. During the day, it's well known as a particularly accommodating, Sputnik-era cafe, with a multigenerational clientele and a sweeping garden that boasts a panorama of the Heldenplatz (forecourt to the Hofburg). Come here to peruse the newspapers, chitchat with the Wieners, drink coffee, wine, beer, or schnapps, and consume platters of Viennese food priced at from 65 to 170 AS ($6.20 to $16.15) each. There's no dancing on site, but the disco dancing venues of the Volksgarten, separately recommended, lies a few steps away. The place is open daily from 11am to 2am, with warm food being served from 11am to midnight.

Schnitzelwirt Schmidt

Neubaugasse 52 (7). ☎ **0222/523-3771.**

Its waitresses wear dirndls, its portions are huge, and in a form that celebrates the culinary folklore of central Europe, the only meats on the menu are pork and— to a much lesser extent—chicken. The setting is rustic, a kind of tongue-in-cheek and bucolic homage to the Old Vienna Woods, and schnitzels are almost guaranteed to hang over the sides of whatever platter they're served on. Regardless of what youorder, it will almost invariably be accompanied with French fries (*pommes frites*) and salad, and often copious quantities of beer and/or wine. Don't expect music, as there isn't any, or surges of historicity, as the place was established as recently as the early 70s. Despite that, the dive packs in its clients, who appreciate the good value, the availability of an ambience that's unmistakably Viennese, and easy access to lots of cronies, characters, and gourmands. Main courses cost from 60 to 115 AS ($5.70 to $10.95), and opening hours are continuously, Monday through Saturday, from 11am to 10pm. Drinks are served till 11pm. Closed Sunday. Tram 29 or U-3 to Mariahilferstrasse.

Side Trips from Vienna

10

Vienna lies at the doorstep of some of the most exciting one-day trips. Many visitors head for destinations in the Vienna Woods or else the small towns and villages along the Danube, particularly the vineyards of the Wachau. Another major attraction is the small province of Burgenland, which evokes Hungary, lying as it does between Vienna and the Hungarian border.

Lower Austria (*Niederösterreich*), known as the "cradle of Austria's history," is the biggest of the nine federal states that make up the country today. While this province may seem to you more like *Upper* Austria because of its geographic location, it is in fact named *Lower* Austria because the Danube flows into it from the east. The 7,402 square miles of the state are bordered on the north by the Czech Republic, on the east by Slovakia, on the south by the province of Styria, and on the west by Upper Austria.

This historic area was once heavily fortified, as some 550 fortresses and castles—many still standing, but often in ruins—testify. The medieval Kuenringer and Babenberger dynasties had their hereditary estates here. Many monasteries and churches, ranging from Romanesque and Gothic to the much later baroque abbeys, are also found in Lower Austria. The province is covered with vineyards, and in summer it booms with music festivals and classical and contemporary theater.

It's relatively inexpensive to travel in Lower Austria, where prices are about 30% lower than those in Vienna. This price differential explains why many people stay in one of the neighboring towns in Lower Austria when they come to explore Vienna. However, you may not always have a private bath if you check into one of the many old inns that service this region. (Unless otherwise noted, however, all recommended accommodations have private bath.) Parking is also more accessible in the outlying towns, which makes them even more appealing.

Lower Austria is divided into five distinct districts, the best known being the **Wienerwald (Vienna Woods)** completely surrounding Vienna. Another district, **Alpine Lower Austria,** lies about an hour's drive south of Vienna, containing mountains up to 7,000 feet high.

The **foothills of the Alps,** beginning about 30 miles west of Vienna, comprise a district extending to the borders of Styria and Upper Austria. This area has some 50 open-air swimming pools that are busy in summer and nine chair lifts that go up to the higher peaks, such as Ötscher and Hochkar, each around 6,000 feet.

One of the most celebrated districts of Lower Austria is the **Waldviertel-Weinviertel** (a *viertel* is a traditional division of Lower Austria). In this case, the viertels are the *wald* (woods) and *wein* (wine) areas. They contain thousands of miles of marked hiking paths and, of course, many mellow old wine cellars.

Another district, **Wachau-Nibelungengau,** boasts both historical and cultural significance. One of the most historic valleys in central Europe, it's a land of castles and palaces, abbeys and monasteries, and wine making. Lying on both banks of the Danube, this area begins about 40 miles west of Vienna.

Some 60% of Austria's grape harvest is produced in Lower Austria, from the rolling hillsides of the Wienerwald to the terraces of the Wachau. Many visitors like to take a "wine route" through the province, stopping off at cozy taverns to sample the vintages from Krems, Klosterneuburg, Dürnstein, Langenlois, Retz, Gumpoldskirchen, Poysdorf, and other towns.

Lower Austria is also home to more than a dozen spa resorts like Baden, which is the most frequented. Innkeepers welcome families with children at these resorts, which can prove to be an inviting retreat from the city. Most hotels accommodate children up to 6 years old free; between ages 7 and 12 they stay for half price. Many towns and villages have attractions designed just for kids. Some hotels have only a postal code for an address, as they do not lie on a street plan. (If you're writing to them, this is their complete address.) When you reach one of these small towns, finding a hotel isn't a problem because they're signposted at the various approaches to the resort or village. Parking is rarely a problem in these places, and, unless otherwise noted, you park for free.

Burgenland, the newest and easternmost province of Austria, is a stark contrast to Lower Austria. It's a little border region, formed in 1921 from German-speaking border areas of what was once Hungary. The province marks the beginning of a flat steppe (*puszta*) that reaches almost to Budapest, but it also lies on Vienna doorstep. It shares a western border with Styria and Lower Austria, and the long eastern boundary separates Burgenland from Hungary.

Burgenland joined Austria after an election by its citizens in the aftermath of World War I, although when the vote was taken in 1919, its capital, Ödenburg, now called Sopron, chose to remain with Hungary. The Hungarian city of Sopron actually lies to the west of Lake Neusiedl (*Neusiedler See*), a popular haven for the Viennese. During the Cold War era, Sopron represented the "Iron Curtain" between Austria and Hungary.

Called "the vegetable garden of Vienna," Burgenland is mostly an agricultural province, also growing wheat and fruit. It's noted for its wines, producing more than one-third of all the wine made in Austria. Its Pannonian climate translates into hot summers with little rainfall, and moderate winters. For the most part you can enjoy sunny days from early spring until late autumn.

The capital of Burgenland, **Eisenstadt,** a small provincial city, was for many years the home of Joseph Haydn, and the composer is buried here. Each summer there's a festival at Mörbisch, using Lake Neusiedl as a theatrical backdrop. Neusiedl is the only steppe lake in central Europe. If you're visiting in summer, you'll most certainly want to explore it by motorboat. Lots of Viennese flee to Burgenland on weekends for sailing, birdwatching, and other outdoor activities.

Accommodations in this province are extremely limited, but they're among the least expensive in the country. The area is relatively unknown to North Americans, which is a pity. Like Lower Austria, Burgenland contains many fortresses and castles, often in ruins, but you'll find a few castle hotels in the Romantic style. Or perhaps you'll prefer to settle into a *gasthof*-type place. The touring season in Burgenland lasts from April through October.

1   The Wienerwald (Vienna Woods)

The Vienna Woods—romanticized in operetta, literature, and the famous Strauss waltz—have already been introduced in Chapter 6, "What to See and Do in Vienna."

The woods stretch from Vienna's city limits to the foothills of the Alps to the south. You can hike through the woods along marked paths or drive through at a leisurely pace, stopping off at country towns to sample the wine and the local cuisine, which is usually hearty, filling, and reasonably priced. The Viennese and a horde of foreign tourists, principally German, usually descend on the wine taverns and cellars here on weekends—we advise you to make any summer visit on a weekday. The best time of year to go is in September and October, when the grapes are harvested from the terraced hills.

TIPS ON EXPLORING THE VIENNA WOODS

You can visit the expansive and pastoral Vienna Woods by car or by public transportation. We recommend renting a car so that you can stop and explore some of the villages and vineyards along the way. Public transportation will get you around, but it will take much more time. Either way, you can easily reach all of the destinations listed below within a day's trip. If you have more time, spend the night in one or more of the quintessential Austrian towns along the way, where you can feast on traditional Austrian fare and sample the exquisite local wines.

Before you go, visit the tourist office for **Lower Austria**, Heidenschuss 2, A-1010 (☎ **0222/533-3114-0;** fax 0222/535-0319) in Vienna. They are the best source of information and maps for the Vienna Woods. Tourist offices for some the smaller towns in the area appear in their individual listings.

If you don't want to go on your own, **Vienna Sightseeing Tours,** Stelzamergasse 4 Suite 11(☎ **0222/712-468-30;** fax 0222/714-11-41) operates a 4-hour tour called, **"Vienna-Mayerling"**. It goes through the Vienna Woods past the Castle of Liechtenstein and the old Roman city of Baden. There's also an excursion to Mayerling, where Crown Prince Rudolf and his mistress died violent deaths. Other highlights include a trip to the Cistercian abbey of Heiligenkreuz-Höldrichsmühle-Seegrotte and a boat ride on Seegrotte, the largest subterranean lake in Europe. It runs April through October, daily at 9:30am and 2:30pm; and November through March, daily at 9:30am only. The cost is 480 AS ($45.60) for adults and 160 AS ($15.20) for children, including admission fees and a guide.

KLOSTERNEUBURG

On the northwestern outskirts of Vienna, Klosterneuburg is an old market town in the major wine-producing center of Austria. The Babenbergs established the town on the eastern foothills of the Vienna Woods, making it an ideal spot to enjoy the countryside and also to participate in the cultural and entertainment activities of Vienna, seven miles southeast.

ESSENTIALS

GETTING THERE   Motorists from Vienna can take Route 14 northwest, following the south bank of the Danube to Klosterneuburg. If you opt for public transportation, take the U-Bahn (U4, U6) to Heiligenstadt, and catch bus no. 239

Lower Austria & the Danube Valley

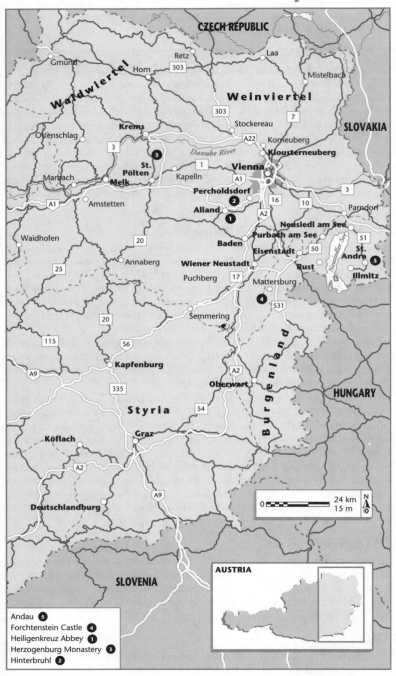

CZECH REPUBLIC

Gmünd
Retz
303
Laa
Horn
Mistelbach

Waldwiertel

Weinviertel

SLOVAKIA

Ostenschlag
303
Stockereau
7

Krems
Korneuberg
A22
Danube River
Kloustenneuberg

Marbach
3
St. Pölten
Kapelln
1
Vienna
A1

Melk
Percholdsdorf
2

Amstetten
Alland
1
A2
16
10
Parndorf
3

A1

Waidhofen
20
Baden
Neusiedl am See
Purbach am See
51

Annaberg
Wiener Neustadt
Eisenstadt
50
St. Andrä
5

Puchberg
17
Rust
Illmitz

25
Mattersburg

Semmering
4
S31

20

115
S6

A9
Kapfenburg
Burgenland

335
Oberwart
A2
HUNGARY

Styria
54

Köflach
Graz

A2

Deutschlandburg
A9

SLOVENIA

0   24 km
    15 m
N

AUSTRIA

Andau 5
Forchtenstein Castle 4
Heiligenkreuz Abbey 1
Herzogenburg Monastery 3
Hinterbruhl 2

or 341 to Klosterneuburg, or take the Schnellbahn (S-Train) from Franz-Josef Bahnhof to Klosterneuburg-Kierling.

VISITOR INFORMATION Contact the Klosterneuberg **tourist information office** at Niedermarkt 4, A-3400, (☎ **02243/320-38;** fax 02243/867-33).

VISITING THE ABBEY

Austrians and tourists gather in Klosterneuburg annually to celebrate St. Leopold's Day on November 15, with music, banquets, and a parade.

East of the Upper Town, ✪ **Klosterneuburg Abbey** (Stift Klosterneuburg), Stiftsplatz 1 (☎ **02243/411-212**), is the most significant abbey in Austria. The monastery of Klosterneuburg was once the residence of the famous Habsburg emperor, Charles VI. It was originally founded however, in 1114 by the Babenberg margrave, Leopold III. It's visited not only for its history but for its art treasures. The most valuable treasure is the world-famous enamel altar of Nikolaus of Verdun, a work created in 1181. The monastery also boasts the largest private library in Austria, with more than 1,250 handwritten books and many antique paintings. Guided tours of the monastery are possible daily throughout the year. On the tour you visit the Cathedral of the Monastery (unless masses are under way), the cloister, St. Leopold's Chapel (with the Verdun altar), the former wellhouse, and the residential apartments of the emperors.

The Museum of the Monastery can be visited May 1 through November 15 on Friday from 2 to 5pm and on Saturday and Sunday from 10am to 5pm. Guided tours of the monastery itself are possible on Sunday and holidays throughout the year at 11am and on the half hour between 1:30 and 4:30pm. From April through October, tours are possible Monday through Saturday every hour from 9 to 11am and 1:30 to 4:30pm. In the off-season, November through March, tours leave Monday through Saturday at 10 and 11am, and then every hour from 1:30 to 4:30pm.

For the tour and the museum, adults pay 50 AS ($4.75); students, children, and senior citizens are charged 40 AS ($3.80).

The abbey has an old restaurant, the **Stiftskeller,** Albrechtsbergergasse 1 (☎ **02243/32070**), where you can dine well for 180 AS ($17.10), enjoying classic Austrian specialties. The kitchen is especially known for its fish dishes, and the menu, which is translated into English, also features dishes low in calories and sodium. The restaurant, which is child-friendly with a playground, also has one of the largest and most beautiful outdoor terraces in the vicinity of Vienna, with old chestnut trees and views over Klosterneuburg. It's open throughout the year, Monday through Saturday from 11am to midnight and on Sunday from 11am to 10pm. Warm food is served throughout all the open hours. In summer, the restaurant opens at 10am.

Nearby, guests can relax in the cozy Stiftskaffe (coffee shop), which is open Tuesday through Sunday throughout the year from 10am to 7pm. It serves coffee and pastries among other items. If you don't choose to eat here, you can patronize one of several *heurigen* in the district, enjoying good wine and country food.

WHERE TO STAY & DINE

Hotel-Restaurant Josef Buschenretter

Wienerstrasse 188, A-3400 Klosterneuburg. ☎ **02243/32385.** Fax 02243/3238-5160. 40 rms. TEL. 860–1,000 AS ($81.70–$95) double. Rates include breakfast. No credit cards. Closed Dec 15–Jan 15. Free parking.

Built in 1970 a mile south of the town center, this hotel is white walled with a mansard roof rising above the balcony on the fourth floor. A terrace on the roof and an indoor swimming pool provide diversion for hotel guests, who will also find a bar decorated with earth-colored patterns. The bedrooms are comfortably furnished and well kept, and some of the more expensive doubles contain a minibar and TV, although all accommodations have a phone.

Hotel Schrannenhof
Niedermarkt 17-19, A-3400 Klosterneuburg. ☎ **02243/32072.** Fax 02243/320-72-13. 13 rms. TV TEL. 950–1,200 AS ($90.25–$114) double. Rates include breakfast. MC, V. Free parking.

Originally dating from the Middle Ages, this hotel was completely renovated and equipped for modern comfort in 1986. The owners rent units with large living and sleeping rooms and small kitchens, as well as quiet and comfortable double rooms with showers. International and typical Austrian specialties are served in the hotel's cafe-restaurant next door, Veit. The hotel also runs the Pension Alte-Mühle (see below).

ⓢ Pension Alte Mühle
Mühlengasse 36, A-3400 Klosterneuburg. ☎ **02243/37788.** Fax 02243/377-88-22. 13 rms. TV TEL. 840 AS ($79.80) double. Rates include breakfast. MC, V. Free parking.

Housed in an uncomplicated two-story building, this hotel is gracious in hospitality. The breakfast room offers a bountiful morning buffet; a comfortable restaurant-cafe, Veit, 2,300 feet away, has upholstered banquettes and a sunny modern decor of bright colors. The Veit family owns the place, and in summer their pleasant garden lures guests.

PERCHTOLDSDORF

This old market town with colorful buildings, referred to locally as Petersdorf, is one of the most visited spots in Lower Austria when the Viennese go on a wine tour. You'll find many heurigen, where you can sample local wines and enjoy good, hearty cuisine. Perchtoldsdorf is not as well known as Grinzing, which is actually within the city limits of Vienna, but many discriminating visitors find it less touristy. It has a Gothic church, and part of its defense tower dates from the early 16th century. A vintners' festival is held annually in early November. Local growers make a "goat" from grapes for this festive occasion, which attracts many Viennese.

ESSENTIALS

GETTING THERE   Head for Liesing (23rd district) via Wiener Stasse to Perchtoldsdorf, 11 miles southwest of the city center. From the Westbahnhof, you can take a *Schnellbahn* heading for Liesing. From here, Perchtoldsdorf is just a short ride away by taxi (cabs are found at the train station). Bus 256 runs from Vienna, but it runs infrequently.

VISITOR INFORMATION   Contact the **tourist information office** in Perchtoldsdorf (☎ **0222/869-7634-34**).

WHERE TO DINE

Restaurant Jahreszeiten
Hochstrasse 17. ☎ **0222/86-53-129.** Reservations recommended. Main courses 290–320 AS ($27.55–$30.40). Fixed-price lunch 330–500 AS ($31.35–$47.50); fixed-price dinner 500–800 AS ($47.50–$76). AE, DC, MC, V. Tues–Fri and Sun 11:30am–2pm; Tues–Sat 6–10pm. Closed July 25–Aug 15. AUSTRIAN/FRENCH/INTERNATIONAL.

Set within what was once a private villa in the 1800s, this restaurant—the best in town—provides a welcome and romantic haven for escapist Viennese looking for hints of the country life. In a pair of elegantly rustic dining rooms illuminated at night with flickering candles, you can enjoy such dishes as deliberately underdone poached salmon served with herbs and truffled noodles; Chinese-style prawns in an "Asiatic" sauce as prepared by a duet of Japanese cooks working in the kitchens; filet of turbot with morels and asparagus-studded risotto; and braised filet of roebuck served with autumn vegetables. Try one of the soufflés for dessert. Service is polite, hard-working, and discreet.

HINTERBRÜHL

In his hamlet, you'll find good accommodations and good food. This is no more than a cluster of bucolic homes, much favored by the Viennese who like to escape the city for a long weekend. Hinterbrühl holds memories of composer Franz Schubert, who wrote *Der Lindenbaum* here. This tiny area is also home to the largest subterranean lake in Europe, which you can explore on a guided motorboat tour.

ESSENTIALS

GETTING THERE   This village is 16 miles south of Vienna, just west of Mölding, the nearest large town. To reach Hinterbrühl from Vienna, drive southwest along the A21, exiting for the signs to Gisshubel. From there, follow the signs posted to Hinterbrühl (which you'll reach first) and Mödling (a few miles after Hinterbrühl). To reach Hinterbrühl by public transport, take the S-Bahn train from the Südbahnhof to Mölding (trip time: 15 minutes), then catch a connecting 12-minute bus to Hinterbrühl, the last stop.

VISITOR INFORMATION   Contact the **tourist information office** in Mölding (☎ **02236/267-27**).

WHERE TO STAY

Hotel Beethoven

Bahnplatz 1, A-2317 Hinterbrühl. ☎ **02236/26252.** Fax 02236/27-70-17. 20 rms. MINI-BAR TV TEL. 900–1,180 AS ($85.50–$112.10) double. Rates include breakfast. AE, MC, V. Free parking.

This hotel lies in the heart of the hamlet, and boasts as its core one of the village's oldest buildings, a private house originally constructed around 1785. In 1992 the hotel was expanded with a new wing and most of the interior was renovated. There's no formal restaurant on the premises, although management maintains an all-day cafe where coffee, drinks, pastries, ice cream, salads, and platters of regional food are served daily from 9am to 11pm.

WHERE TO DINE

Hexensitz

Johannesstrasse 35. ☎ **02236/22937.** Reservations recommended. Main courses 200–285 AS ($19–$27.10). MC. Tues–Sun noon–2pm; Tues–Sat 6–10pm. AUSTRIAN/INTERNATIONAL.

Permeated with impeccable service rituals, this restaurant celebrates the subtleties of Austrian country cooking in an upscale setting. It's in a century-old building whose trio of dining rooms are outfitted "in the Lower Austrian style" with wood paneling and well-scrubbed country antiques. In summer, the restaurant expands outward into a well-kept garden studded with flowering shrubs and ornamental trees. Established in 1985 by Alfred and Ulriche Maschitz, it offers daily changing dishes such as asparagus-cream soup; Styrian venison with kohlrabi, wine sauce, and homemade noodles; medaillons of pork with spinach and herbs; and sea-bass with forest mush-rooms. Desserts are luscious, highly caloric, and traditional. The restaurant's name

Twilight of the Habsburgs

Mayerling was the setting on January 30, 1889, for a grim tragedy that altered the line of succession of the Austro-Hungarian Empire and shocked the world. On a snowy night, Archduke Rudolf, the only son of Emperor Franz Joseph and Empress Elizabeth, and his 18-year-old mistress, Maria Vetsera, were found dead in the hunting lodge at Mayerling and called suicide victims. Supposedly, they were shot, although no weapon, if found, ever surfaced for examination. All doors and windows to the room of the victims were also locked when the bodies were discovered. All evidence that might have shed some light on the deaths—double suicide or assassination—was subsequently destroyed.

Rudolf, a sensitive eccentric, was locked in an unhappy marriage, and neither his father nor Pope Leo XIII would allow an annulment. He had fallen in love with Maria immediately after they met at a German embassy ball when she was only 17. Maria's public snubbing of Archduchess Stephanie of Belgium, Rudolph's wife, at a reception given by the German ambassador to Vienna led to a heated discourse between Rudolph and his father Franz Joseph. Because of the young archduke's liberal leanings and sympathy for certain Hungarian partisans, he was not popular with his country's aristocracy, which of course gave rise to lurid speculation as to whether the couple actually killed themselves or were the victims of a cleverly designed assassination. Among those who supported this theory was Empress Zita von Hapsburg who in 1982 told the *Kronen Zeitung,* the Vienna daily, she believed their deaths were the culmination of a conspiracy against the family.

Maria Vetsera was buried in Heilgenkreuz at a village cemetery, where today the inscription over her tomb reads *Wie eine Blume sprosst der mensch auf und wird gebrochen* ("Human beings, like flowers, bloom and are crushed.") In 1988, her coffin was exhumed and stolen by a Linz executive distraught by the death of his wife, and obsessed with the Mayerling affair. It took police four years before the coffin was reclaimed and passed along to the Medical Institute of Vienna. As it turned out, if Rudolf, who died at age 30, had lived he would have succeeded to the already-tottering Habsburg throne in 1916 in the middle of World War I, shortly before the collapse of the empire. Franz Joseph, grief-stricken at the loss of his only son, ordered the hunting lodge torn down and a Carmelite nunnery built in its place.

incidentally, translates as "the Witch's Chair," and was chosen as a humorous reference to a regional fairy tale.

MAYERLING

This beautiful spot, 18 miles west of Vienna in the heart of the Wienerwald, is best known for the tragedy of the unresolved double suicide/homicide of Archduke Rudolph, son of Emperor Franz Joseph, and his mistress in 1889. This event, which took place in a hunting lodge (now a Carmelite convent), altered the line of Austro-Hungarian succession, giving rise to Archduke Ferdinand whose murder in Sarajevo was the principal impetus for World War I.

ESSENTIALS

GETTING THERE   Head southwest on A-21 to Alland and take 210 to Mayerling. If you opt for public transportation from Vienna, take buses 1123, 1124, or 1127 from Südtirolerplatz, marked *Alland,* (trip time: 90 minutes); from Baden hop on buses 1140 or 1141.

VISITOR INFORMATION   Contact the local authorities, **Gemeindeamt,** in nearby Heiligenkruz, Haus Nr.15, A-2532 (☎ **02258/2266**).

WHAT TO SEE & DO

The **Jagdschloss at Mayerling** (☎ **02258/2275**) is a Carmelite abbey that is the site of the infamous hunting lodge where Rudolf and his mistress committed suicide (see "Twilight of the Habsburgs" above). The hunting lodge, if it hadn't been torn down, would have been a much more fascinating—if macabre—attraction. It is the history that happened here that compels visitors to come and take a look—not the actual attractions remaining today. It's open for tours Monday through Saturday from 9am to 12:30pm and 1:30 to 5pm (until 6pm in summer). Admission is 20 AS (95¢).

We recommend a short trip (3 miles via Heiliqenkreuzstrasse) to nearby **Heiligenkreuz** for a glimpse of one of the oldest Cistercian abbeys in Austria, dating from 1133. Known as the ۞ **Abbey Heiligenkreuz** (Abbey of the Holy Cross) (☎ **02258/2286**). The church, founded by Leopold III, was built in the 12th century, but there has been an overlay of Gothic and baroque additions in subsequent centuries, with some 13th- and 14th-century stained glass still in place. The Romanesque and Gothic cloisters date from 1240, with some 300 pillars of red marble. Some of the dukes of Babenberg were buried in the chapter house, including Duke Friedrich II, the last of his line. Heiligenkreuz has more relics of the Holy Cross than any other site in Europe except Rome.

Today a vital community of 50 Cistercian monks lives in Heiligenkreuz. In summer at noon and 6pm daily, visitors can attend the solemn choir prayers of the monks. Tours are conducted Easter through September, daily at 10am, 11am, 2pm, 3pm, and 4pm. Admission is 35 AS ($3.35) for adults and 20 AS ($1.90) for children.

WHERE TO STAY

Mayerling's best-managed enclave of hotel and restaurant facilities is in one interconnected complex of buildings in a verdant forest about half a mile from the town center. Managed by members of the Hanner family, it was originally built in the *blockhaus* (log-cabin) style in the 1930s, and enlarged in 1962 and again in 1985. Within its well-scrubbed confines, you'll find a hotel and two restaurants, the combination of which are the most popular and best-recommended in town.

Hotel Mayerling (also known as Hotel Marienhof)
Mayerling 1, A-2534 Mayerling. ☎ **02258/237846.** Fax 02258/237841. 28 rms. MINIBAR TV TEL. 900–1,600 AS ($85.50–$152) double. Rates include breakfast. AE, DC, MC, V. Free parking.

Clean, comfortable, unpretentious, and well maintained, this hostelry offers simple but cozy bedrooms, focusing on country living and plentiful portions of good food. Guests appreciate the proximity of the hotel's two restaurants (see below) and the abundance of natural beauty outside.

WHERE TO DINE

۞ Restaurant Kronprinz
Mayerling 1. ☎ **02258/237846.** Reservations required. Main courses 260–420 AS ($24.70–$39.90); fixed-price menu 495–720 AS ($47.05–$68.40). AE. Wed–Sun noon–2pm; Wed–Sat 6–9:30pm. MODERN AUSTRIAN.

This small-scale hideaway is the most elegant dining venue in the region, with a cuisine created by the self-taught owner/chef, Heinz Hanner. Despite its allegiance to its namesake (Crown Prince Rudolf), it contains few, if any, portraits or remembrances of him. (Too many reminders of his grisly death, we were told, would not be appetizing.) Instead, the place is outfitted in a coolly conservative decor of beige marble and sweeping views through large windows to the verdant forest.

Menu items have been praised by gastronomes throughout Austria, and include a series of delectable dishes which change with the seasons and the inspiration of the chef. These might include truffled pâté of goose liver with artichokes; cream of zucchini soup with black truffles and parmesan; medaillons of venison with wild mushrooms and fried onions and braised breast of Bresse chicken with paprika noodles.

Restaurant Landhaus

Mayerling 1. ☎ **02258/237846.** Reservations not required. Main courses 80–215 AS ($7.60–$20.45). AE, DC, MC, V. Daily noon–2:30pm and 6pm–midnight. AUSTRIAN.

Unlike its more glamorous nearby cousin (see above), this restaurant makes no pretense to modern cuisine or new-fangled combinations of ingredients. Instead, specialties are conservative, Austrian, and filling, and the staff and at least some of the guests are likely to appear in traditional Austrian costumes (*dirndls* and *trachten*). In a rustic and woodsy set of dining rooms, the restaurant features tafelspitz, Wiener schnitzel, fresh salads, schnitzels of pork, roast lamb, and—throughout the day—steaming bowls of soup and strong cups of coffee.

2 Baden bei Wien

Tsar Peter the Great of Russia ushered in Baden's golden age by establishing a spa at the beginning of the 18th century. The Soviet army used the resort city as its headquarters from the end of World War II to the end of the Allied occupation of Austria in 1955. But there's not much that's Russian about Baden, which was once known as "the dowager empress of health spas in Europe."

The Romans, who didn't miss many natural attractions, began in A.D. 100 to visit what they called Aquae, which had 15 thermal springs whose temperatures reached 95° Fahrenheit. You can still see the Römerquelle (Roman spring) in the Kurpark, which is the center of Baden today.

This lively casino town and spa in the eastern sector of the Vienna Woods was at its most fashionable in the early 18th century, but it lured royalty, sycophants, musicians, and intellectuals for much of the 19th century. For years the resort was the summer retreat of the Habsburg court. In 1803, when he was still Francis II of the Holy Roman Empire, the monarch (who became Francis I of Austria when the vast empire originated by Charlemagne ended in 1806) began annual summer visits to Baden.

During the Biedermeier era (mid to late 19th century), Baden became known for its Schönbrunn yellow (Maria Theresa ochre) Biedermeier buildings, which still contribute to the spa city's charm. The Kurpark, Baden's center, is handsomely laid out and beautifully maintained. Public concerts performed here keep the magic of the great Austrian composers alive.

The bathing complex was constructed over more than a dozen sulfur springs. In the complex are some half a dozen bath establishments, plus four outdoor thermal springs, to which visitors flock from Vienna and elsewhere. These thermal springs reach temperatures ranging from 75° to 95° Fahrenheit. The thermal complex also has a "sandy beach" and a restaurant. It lies west of the center in the Doblhoffpark, a natural park with a lake where you can rent boats for sailing. There's also a garden restaurant in the park which is known for its roses.

Emperor Karl made this town the Austrian army headquarters in World War I, but a certain lightheartedness persisted. The presence of the Russians during the post-World War II years brought the lowest ebb to the resort's fortunes.

The resort is officially named Baden *bei Wien* to differentiate it from other Badens *not* near Vienna.

THE ROAD TO BADEN

From Vienna, Baden is 15 miles southwest. Head south on Autobahn A-2, cutting west at the junction of Route 210 which leads to Baden. If you go by train, Baden is a local (rather than an express) stop. Trains depart from 4:40am until 11:15pm at intervals of between 8 and 20 minutes from Vienna's Südbahnhof (trip time: 20 minutes, with two intermediary stops). For schedules, call **02252/17-17.** Also, the *Badner Bahn* leaves every 15 minutes from the State Opera (trip time is 1 hour). Buses to Baden leave out of Vienna's Westbahnhof.

Visitors should head to the Baden **tourist information office** at Brusattiplatz 3 (☎ **02252/445-31**).

WHAT TO SEE & DO

In the **Hauptplatz** (main square) is the **Trinity Column,** built in 1714, which commemorates the lifting of the plague that swept over Vienna and the Wienerwald in the Middle Ages. Also here are the **Rathaus** (town hall) and at No. 17, the **Kaiserhaus,** which was Franz II's summer residence from 1813–1834.

At **Beethovenhaus,** Rathausgasse 10 (☎ **02252/86800-231**), a little museum has been set up. The composer lived here in the summers of 1821–23. It's open year-round Saturday, Sunday, and holidays from 9 to 11am and 4 to 6pm, and Tuesday through Friday from 4 to 6pm. Admission is 15 AS ($1.45) for adults and 5 AS (50¢) for children.

Among the other sights in Baden, there's the celebrated death mask collection at the **Städtisches Rolletmuseum,** Weikersdorfer-Platz 1 (☎ **02252/48255**). The museum possesses many items of interest to history and art lovers. Furniture and art of the Biedermeier period are especially represented. The museum is open Wednesday through Monday from 3 to 6pm and on Sunday from 9am to noon. Admission is 15 AS ($1.45). To reach the museum from Hauptplatz in the center, cut south onto Josefs Platz, then continue south along Vöslauer Strasse, cutting right when you come to Elisabeth Strasse which leads directly to the square on which the museum sits.

Northeast of Hauptplatz on the Franz-Kaiser Ring is the **Stadttheater** (Municipal Theater), built in 1909, and on Pfarrgasse, the nearby parish church, **St. Stephan's,** which dates from the 15th century. Inside there's a commemorative plaque to Mozart, who allegedly composed his "Ave Verum" here for the parish choirmaster.

The real reason, however, to come to Baden is the sprawling and beautiful ✪ **Kurpark,** which lies to the north of town. Here, you can attend concerts, plays, and operas at an open-air theater, or try your luck at the casino (see "Baden After Dark," below). The **Römerquelle** (Roman Springs) can be seen gurgling from an intricate rock basin, which is surrounded by monuments of Beethoven, Mozart, and the great playwright Grillparzer. There are also numerous paths where visitors can stroll and also enjoy a view of Baden and the surrounding hills from various points, some over 1,000 feet in elevation.

WHERE TO STAY
EXPENSIVE
✪ Grand Hotel Sauerhof zu Rauhenstein

Weilburgstrasse 11-13, A-2500 Baden bei Wien. ☎ **02252/41251.** Fax 02252/48047. 88 rms, 7 suites. MINIBAR TV TEL. 2,200–2,950 AS ($209.00–$280.25) double; 3,900–5,400 AS ($370.50–$513.00) suite. Rates include buffet breakfast. Half board 300 AS ($28.50) per person extra. AE, DC, MC, V. Free parking.

Although the history of this estate goes back to 1583, it became famous in 1757 when a sulfur-enriched spring bubbled up after a cataclysmic earthquake in Portugal. The present building was constructed in 1810 on the site of that spring, which continues to supply water for its spa facilities today. During the 19th century it welcomed visits from Beethoven (who wrote his *Wellington Sieg* here, and enjoyed a dinner with Karl Maria von Weber) and Mozart's archrival Salieri. Since then, the property has served as an army rehabilitation center, a sanatorium during the two world wars, and as headquarters for the Russian army. In 1978, after extravagant renovations, the Sauerhof reopened as one of the region's most upscale spa hotels.

Today, it rambles across a wide lawn in a three-story neoclassical style with steeply sloping slate roofs. Few of the original furnishings remain, although the management has collected a handful of vintage Biedermeier sofas and chairs to fill the elegant but somewhat underfurnished public rooms. A covered courtyard, designed in the style of ancient Rome, has a vaulted ceiling supported by chiseled stone columns. The bedrooms are outfitted with a comfortable and contemporary decor. There's a collection of Russian icons and a series of medieval halberds in the richly decorated, farmer-style restaurant, which serves some of the best food at the resort. The resort boasts two tennis courts, a jogging course, an indoor swimming pool, a terrace, a spa (offering treatments such as sulfur baths, mud wraps, and electro-acupuncture), and a nearby golf course. Room service and laundry service are available.

MODERATE
Hotel Gutenbrunn

Pelzgasse 22, A-2500 Baden bei Wien. ☎ **02252/48171.** Fax 02252/45758. 78 rms. 2 suites. MINIBAR TV TEL. 1,310–1,820 AS ($124.45–$172.90) double; 1,760–2,270 AS ($167.20–$215.65) suite. Rates include breakfast. AE, DC. Free parking.

This hotel in the town center, a minute's walk from the main square, was originally named after the healthful waters (*Gutenbrunn*) which bubbled up from the earth nearby. In 1480, Holy Roman Emperor Friedrich III paid a visit to its predecessor, and by around 1890 the neobaroque building received visitors from throughout the Austrian Empire. Today the old-world pink-and-white facade sports a hexagonal tower and a slate roof with a baroque steeple; a wing was added in 1972. The interior has a skylit reception area with a double tier of neoclassical loggia. Bedrooms are well furnished, frequently housing clients of the town's spa, to which the hotel is directly connected by a passageway. In back of the hotel, guests can promenade in the privately owned park dotted with old trees. The hotel has a restaurant, a sauna, and indoor and outdoor swimming pools. Baby-sitters and laundry service are available, as well as room service every day from 7am to 10pm.

Krainerhütte

Helenental, A-2500 Baden bei Wien. ☎ **02252/44511.** Fax 02252/44514. 110 rms. 3 suites. MINIBAR TV TEL. 1,680 AS ($159.60) double; 2,500 AS ($237.50) suite. Rates include breakfast. AE, MC, V. Parking 150 AS ($14.25).

Run by Josef Dietmann and his family, this hotel stands on tree-filled grounds five miles west of Baden at Helenental. It's a large A-frame chalet with rows of wooden balconies. The interior has more detailing than you might expect in such a modern hotel. There are separate children's rooms and play areas. In the cozy restaurant or on the terrace, you can dine on international and Austrian cuisine, with fish and deer from the hotel grounds offered. On the premises is an indoor swimming pool, plus a tennis court, a sauna, and an exercise room. Hiking in the owner's forests, and hunting and fishing are possible. "Postbus" service to Baden is available all day.

Schloss Weikersdorf
Schlossgasse 9-11, A-2500 Baden bei Wien. ☎ **02252/48301.** Fax 02252/48301-150. 102 rms. TV TEL MINIBAR. 1,570–1,900 AS ($149.15–$180.50) double. Rates include breakfast. AE, DC, MC, V. Free parking.

This hotel has massive beams, along with arched and vaulted ceilings. The oldest part of the hotel has an Italianate loggia stretching toward the manicured gardens, and an inner courtyard with stone arcades. The rooms in the newer section repeat the older section's arches and high ceilings, and sport ornate chandeliers and antique or reproduction furniture. The nearby sports center has an indoor swimming pool, bowling alleys, tennis courts, and a sauna. On the premises are a charming baroque bar and two restaurants. Accommodations are handsomely furnished and most comfortable. There are 76 bedrooms in the main house, plus 26 in the annex.

INEXPENSIVE

Parkhotel
Kaiser-Franz-Ring 5, A-2500 Baden bei Wien. ☎ **02252/44386.** Fax 02252/80578. 77 rms, 15 suites. MINIBAR TV TEL. 1,820 AS ($172.90) double; 2,120 AS ($201.40) suite. Rates include breakfast. AE, DC, MC, V. Free parking.

This contemporary hotel is in the middle of an inner-city park dotted with trees and statuary. The high-ceilinged lobby has a marble floor padded with thick Oriental carpets and ringed with richly grained paneling. Most of the sunny bedrooms have their own loggia overlooking century-old trees; each contains a radio. The hotel has a heated indoor swimming pool, two Finnish saunas, a restaurant, a coffee shop, and a terrace overlooking the park.

WHERE TO DINE

Badner Stüberl
Gutenbrunnstrasse 19. ☎ **02252/41232.** Reservations recommended. Main courses 88–215 AS ($8.35–$20.45); fixed-price menu 88–138 AS ($8.35–$13.10). No credit cards. Wed–Mon 11am–2pm and 6–9:30pm. AUSTRIAN.

In the center of the older section of Baden, this old-fashioned coffeehouse and restaurant is filled with black and red upholstery and unusually designed lighting fixtures. Specialties of the house include a generous beef dish served with roasted garlic and onions that draws visitors from Vienna, along with a green salad garnished with chicken, and pork and beef steaks grilled to savory tenderness.

BADEN AFTER DARK

Casino Baden
In the KurPark. ☎ **02252/444960.** Free admission, 300 AS ($28.50) worth of chips can be obtained for 260 AS ($24.70).

The major attraction in town is the casino, where you can play roulette, blackjack, baccarat, poker (seven-card stud), money-wheel, and slot machines. Many visitors from Vienna come down to Baden for a night of gambling, eating, and drinking; on the premises are two bars and a restaurant. Guests are often most fashionably dressed, and you'll feel more comfortable if you are, too (men should wear jackets and ties).

Open daily from 3pm to 3am. A less formal casino, the Casino Leger, is open daily from 1pm to 1am on the premises.

3   Wiener Neustadt

When you head south from Vienna on the Südautobahn (A-2), Wiener Neustadt, a former imperial city might be your first stopover. It was once the official residence of Emperor Friedrich III of the Habsburgs. Called *Allzeit Getreue* because of its loyalty to the throne, this thriving city between the foothills of the Alps and the edge of the Pannonian lowland has a strong historical background.

Unfortunately, Wiener Neustadt was a target for Allied bombs during World War II, because it lay at the point where the routes from Vienna diverge, one going to the Semmering Pass and the other to Hungary via the Sopron Gate. The 200-year-old military academy that turned out officers for the Austrian army may have been an added attraction to bombers. German Gen. Erwin Rommel, "the Desert Fox," was the academy's first commandant during the Nazi era. At any rate, the Allies did bomb the city—more than any other town in the country. It's estimated that some 60% of its buildings were leveled.

The town was founded in 1192, when its castle was built by Duke Leopold V of the ruling house of Babenberg. He had it constructed as a citadel to ward off attacks of the Magyars from the east. From 1440 to 1493 Austrian emperors lived at this fortress in the southeastern corner of what is now the old town. Maximilian I, called "the last of the knights," was born here in 1459 and lies buried in the Church of St. George in the castle. It was Maria Theresa who in 1752 ordered that the structures comprising the castle be turned into a military academy.

ESSENTIALS
GETTING THERE

From Vienna, Wiener Neustadt is 28 miles south of Vienna. Head south along Autobahn A-2, until you reach the junction with Route 21, at which point you head east to Wiener Neustadt. Trains leave for Wiener Neustadt daily from Vienna's Südbahnhof, from 4:30am until midnight (trip time: between 27 and 44 minutes, depending on the number of stops). For schedules, call **0222/17.** Buses depart daily from the Wiener Mitte bus station at intervals of 15 to 30 minutes (trip time: 65 minutes) In Weiner Neustadt, buses drop off passengers in the town center, at Ungargasse 2. Most visitors opt for the train.

VISITOR INFORMATION

The Wiener Neustadt **tourist information office** (☎ **02622/29551**) is at Hauptpaltz in Rathaus.

WHAT TO SEE & DO

You can visit the **Church of St. George,** Burgplatz 1 (☎ **02622/38-10**), daily from 8am to 6pm. The gable of the church is adorned with more than 100 heraldic shields of the Habsburgs. It's noted for its handsome interior, decorated in the late Gothic style.

   Neukloster, Neuklostergasse 1 (☎ **02622/23102**), a Cistercian abbey, was founded in 1250 and reconstructed in the 18th century. The New Abbey Church (Neuklosterkirche), near the Hauptplatz, is Gothic with a beautiful choir. It contains the tomb of the Empress Eleanor of Portugal, wife of Friedrich III and mother of

Maximilian I. Mozart's *Requiem* was first presented here in 1793. Admission is free, and it's open Monday through Friday from 6am to 7pm.

Liebfrauenkirche, on the Domplatz (☎ **02622/23202**), was once the head-quarters of an Episcopal see. It's graced by a 13th-century Romanesque nave, but the choir is Gothic. The west towers have been rebuilt. Admission is free, and the church is open daily from 6am to 9pm (until 8pm in winter).

In the town is a **Recturm,** Babenberger Ring (☎ **02622/235-310**), a tower in the gothic style said to have been built with the ransom money paid for Richard the Lion-Hearted. It's open March through October, on Tuesday through Thursday from 10am to noon and 2 to 4pm, and on Saturday and Sunday from 10am to noon only. Admission is free.

WHERE TO STAY

Hotel Corvinus
Bahngasse 29-33, A-2700 Wiener Neustadt. ☎ **02622/24134.** Fax 02622/24139. 68 rms. MINIBAR TV TEL. 1,390 AS ($132.05) double. Rates include breakfast. Children under 12 stay free in parents' room. AE, DC, MC, V.

The best hotel in town, built in the 1970s, this place has a color scheme of white and weathered bronze. It sits in a quiet neighborhood near the city park, a two-minute walk south of the main rail station. The bedrooms have modern comforts and a decor of solid colors. Hotel guests can use the sauna, Turkish bath, and whirlpool. Also on the premises are a modern bar area, a parasol-covered sun terrace, and a light-heartedly elegant restaurant serving Austrian and international dishes.

WHERE TO DINE

Gelbes Haus
Kaiserbrunnen 11. ☎ **02622/26400.** Reservation recommended. Main courses 145–275 AS ($13.80–$26.15); fixed-price lunch 295 AS ($28.05); fixed-price dinners 550–580 AS ($52.25–$55.10). DC, MC, V. Mon–Sat noon–2pm and 6:30–10pm. Closed Christmas, New Year's Day, and Easter. AUSTRIAN/INTERNATIONAL.

Set in the historic heart of town, this long-enduring and well-respected restaurant (whose name translates as "the yellow house") takes its name from the vivid ochre color of its circa 1911–13 exterior. Inside, you'll find an art-nouveau dining room where colors include touches of green and an emphasis on style and comfort. The Austrian and international cuisine is prepared with fresh ingredients, imagination, and flair. Examples include a succulent version of tafelspitz (boiled beef); an assortment of carpaccios arranged with herbs, truffle oil, goose liver, and exotic mushrooms on a platter; duck breast in orange sauce, fresh Canadian lobster, rumpsteak stuffed with goose liver, tomatoes, and onions; and filets of pork in red wine sauce with cabbage and herbs. Dishes based on the repertoires of France and Italy are change depending on the whim of the chef.

4 The Wachau-Danube Valley

The Danube is one of the most legendary rivers in Europe, rich in scenic splendor, historic wealth, and all forms of architecture. The Wachau, a section of the Danube Valley northwest of Vienna, with rolling hills and fertile soil, is one of the most beautiful and historic parts of Austria. Throughout this part of the Danube Valley, you'll pass ruins of castles reminiscent of the Rhine Valley, some of the most celebrated vineyards in Austria, some of the most famous medieval monasteries in central Europe, and ruins from the stone age, the Celts, the Romans, and the Habsburgs.

Unrelentingly prosperous, the district has won many awards for the authenticity of its historic renovations.

If you like the looks of this district, take a paddleboat steamer, most of which operate only between April 1 and October 31. You can travel by armchair, lounging on the deck along the longest river in central Europe.

If you're really "doing the Danube," you can begin your trip at Passau, Germany, and go all the way to the Black Sea and across to the Crimean Peninsula, stopping over at Yalta, scene of the controversial meeting of Roosevelt, Churchill, and Stalin. However, the Vienna–Yalta portion of the trip alone takes nearly a week and few travelers can devote that much time. Most visitors limit themselves to a more restricted look at the Danube, taking one of the many popular trips offered from Vienna.

TIPS ON EXPLORING THE DANUBE VALLEY

If you only have a day to see the Danube Valley, we highly recommend one of the tours listed below. If you have more time, however, rent a car and explore this district yourself, driving inland from the river, now and then, to visit the towns and sights listed below. You can also take public transportation to the towns we've highlighted below (see individual listings).

The Danube and Wachau Valley contain some of the most impressive monuments in Austria, but because of their far-flung locations, many readers prefer to participate in an organized tour. The best of these are conducted by **Vienna Sightseeing Tours,** Stelzhamergasse 4, Suite 11 (☎ **0222/712-46-830;** fax 0222/714-11-41), which offers guided tours by motorcoach in winter and both motorcoach and boat in summer. Stops on this 8-hour trip include Krems, Durnstein, and Melk Abbey. Prices are 770 AS ($73.15) for adults, 330 AS ($31.35) for children under 12, and does not include lunch. Advance reservations are required.

Before you venture into the Danube Valley, pick up maps and other helpful information at the **tourist office for Lower Austria,** Heidenschluss 2, A-1010, Vienna (☎ **0222/533-3114-0;** fax 0222/535-0319).

TULLN

This is one of the most ancient towns in Austria. Originally a naval base, Comagena, and later a center for the Babenberg dynasty, Tulln, on the right bank of the Danube, is called "the flower town" because of the masses of blossoms you'll see in spring and summer. It's the place, according to the saga of the Nibelungen, where Kriemhild, the Burgundian princess of Worms, met Etzel, king of the Huns. A famous "son of Tulln" was Kurt Waldheim, former secretary-general of the United Nations and one of Austria's most controversial former presidents (because of his previous Nazi affiliations).

ESSENTIALS

GETTING THERE   From Vienna, head 26 miles north and west along Route 14 to reach Tulln. S-Bahn trains depart from both the Wien Nord Station (at Praterstern) and, more frequently, from the Franz-Josefs Bahnhof, daily from 4:30am to 8:30pm at intervals ranging from 50 to 120 minutes. Although Tulln lies on the busy main rail lines linking Vienna with Prague, most local timetables will list Gmund, an Austrian city on the border of the Czech Republic, as the final destination (trip time: from 27 to 45 minutes). For more information, call 0222/17-17 in Vienna. A bus ride to Tulln from Vienna is not recommended as it would require multiple transfers in at least two (and sometimes three or more) suburbs. Between mid-May and late September, river cruisers owned by the DDSG-Donaureisen Shipping Company (☎0222/727-500; fax 0222/72-892-38) leave

Vienna on Saturday and Sunday at 9am en route to Passau, Germany and arrive in Tulln around 11:45am.

VISITOR INFORMATION   The **tourist information office** in Tulln (☎ 02272/ 58-36) is at Albrechtsgasse 32.

WHAT TO SEE & DO

The twin-towered **Church of St. Stephan** on Wiener Strasse grew out of a 12th-century Romanesque basilica. Its west portal is from the 13th century. A Gothic overlay added in its early centuries gave way in the 18th century to the baroque craze that swept the country. A 1786 altarpiece commemorates the martyrdom of St. Stephan. Ogival vaulting was used in the chancel and the nave.

Adjoining the church is the **karner** (charnel or bone house). This funereal chapel is the major sight of Tulln, the finest of its kind in the entire country. Built in the mid-13th century in the shape of a polygon, it's richly decorated with capitals and arches. The Romanesque dome is adorned with frescoes.

In a restored former prison, Tulln has opened the **Egon Schiele Museum,** Donaulände 28 (☎ 02272/4570), devoted to its other most famous son, born here in 1890. Schiele is one of the greatest Austrian artists of the early 1900s. The prison setting might be appropriate, as the Secessionistic painter spent 24 days in jail in 1912 in the town of Neulengbach. He was sentenced to three days' imprisonment for possession of what back then was regarded as "pornography." While awaiting trial, he produced 13 watercolors, most of which are now in the Albertina Collection in Vienna. The works of this great artist, who died in Vienna in 1918, now sell for millions of dollars. The Tulln museum has more than 90 of his oil paintings, watercolors, and designs, along with much memorabilia. It's open Tuesday through Sunday from 9am to noon and 2pm to 6pm. Admission is 30 AS ($2.85) for adults and 15 AS ($1.45) for children.

WHERE TO STAY & DINE

Hotel/Restaurant Römerhof Stoiber

Langenlebarnerstrasse 66, A-3430 Tulln an der Donau. ☎ 02272-62954. 49 rms. TV TEL MINIBAR. 770 AS ($73.15) double. Rates include breakfast. MC, V. Closed Mon. Free parking.

Built in 1972, this establishment is near the train station. It has a simple modern facade of white walls and unadorned windows. The interior is warmly outfitted with earth tones, a macramé wall hanging, and pendant lighting fixtures. The bedrooms are comfortable. A restaurant serves well-prepared meals in an attractive, rustic setting; traditional and good-tasting specialties include Wiener schnitzel and roast beef in sour-cream sauce. Meals in the restaurant begin at 135 AS ($12.85) each. Only dinner is served, May through October, from 5 to 8pm. There's a little beer garden as well as a parking lot.

Hotel zur Rossmühle

Hauptplatz 12, A-3430 Tulln an der Donau. ☎ 02272/24110. Fax 02272/24-11-33. 106 rms. TV TEL. Main building, 1,120 AS ($106.40) double. Annex, 910 AS ($86.45) double. Rates include breakfast. AE, MC, V. Free parking. Coming from Germany, exit the autobahn at St. Christopher; from Vienna it's a 30-minute drive west on Route 14.

Despite its relative newness as an edifice (constructed in 1977), this hotel combines many old-fashioned architectural features. A yellow building on the town's main square, the hotel has an arched entryway protected with a wrought-iron gate, a collection of antique furniture, and crystal chandeliers. About half of the bedrooms are in an older annex, set nearby, and are less expensive than the 56 in the newer main building. Regardless of their position, the bedrooms are outfitted in a modernized country baroque style.

The hotel contains one of the region's most glamorous restaurants, an all-Austrian enclave of good food and *Gemütlichkeit*, where fixed-price menus begin at 150 AS ($14.25) each. Meals are served daily from noon to 2pm and 7 to 10pm.

HERZOGENBURG MONASTERY

Founded in the early 12th century by a German bishop from Passau, the ✪ **Augustinian Herzogenburg Monastery,** A-3130 Herzogenburg (☎ **02782/3315** or **3112**), 7 miles south of Traismauer, has a long history. Take Wiener Strasse (Route 1) out of St. Pölten. Head east for 8 miles toward Kapelln, but turn left at the sign along a minor road to Herzogenburg. The present complex of buildings comprising the church and the abbey was reconstructed in the baroque style. That master of baroque, Fischer von Erlach, designed some of the complex. The art painted on the high altar of the church is by Daniel Gran, and the most outstanding art owned by the abbey is a series of 16th-century paintings on wood, displayed in a room devoted to gothic art. The monastery is known for its library containing more than 80,000 works.

Hourlong guided tours take visitors through the monastery daily from the first of April until the end of October, from 11am and 1 to 5pm for an admission of 40 AS ($3.80); closed November through March. There's a wine tavern in the complex where you can eat platters of Austrian specialties and drink the product of local grapes.

KREMS

In the eastern part of the Wachau on the left bank of the Danube lies Krems, a city some 1,000 years old. The city today encompasses Stein and Mautern, once separate towns.

Krems is a mellow town of courtyards, old churches, and ancient houses in the heart of vineyard country, with some partially preserved town walls. Just as the Viennese flock to Grinzing and other suburbs to sample new wine in heurigen, so the people of the Wachau come here to taste the vintners' products, which appear in Krems earlier in the year.

ESSENTIALS

GETTING THERE   Krems is 50 miles west of Vienna and 18 miles north of St. Pölten. To reach Krems from Vienna, drive north along the A22 superhighway until it splits into three near the town of Stockerau. There, drive due west along Route 3, following the signs to Krems. Trains depart from both the Wien Nord and the Wien Franz-Josefs Bahnhof for Krems, daily from 5am to 8:30pm. Many are direct, although some will require a transfer in at Absdorf-Hippersdorf or St. Pölten (trip time: from 60 to 95 minutes. Call **0222/17-17** for schedules. Traveling by bus to Krems is not recommended; however, Krems is well-connected by local buses to surrounding villages. Between mid-May and late September, the **DDSG-Donaureisen Shipping Company** (☎ **0222/727-500;** fax 0222/72-892-38) runs river cruisers departing Vienna Saturday and Sunday at 9am en route to Passau, Germany. They arrive in Krems around 2:10pm.

VISITOR INFORMATION   The Krems **tourist information office** (☎ **02732/ 82676**) is at Undstrasse 6.

WHAT TO SEE & DO

The most interesting part of Krems today is what was once the little village of **Stein.** Narrow streets are terraced above the river, and the single main street, **Steinlanderstrasse,** is flanked with houses, many from the 16th century. The Grosser

Passauerhof, Steinlanderstrasse 76, is a Gothic structure decorated with an oriel. Another house, at Steinlanderstrasse 84, which combines Byzantine and Venetian elements among other architectural influences, was once the imperial toll house. In days of yore, the aristocrats of Krems barricaded the Danube and extracted heavy fines from the river traffic. Sometimes the fines were more than the hapless victims could pay, so the townspeople just confiscated the cargo.

The **Pfarrkirche St. Viet** (parish church) of Krems stands in the center of town at the Rathaus, reached by going along either Untere Landstrasse or Obere Landstrasse. It's somewhat overadorned, rich with gilt and statuary. Construction on this, one of the oldest baroque churches in the province, began in 1616. In the 18th century Martin Johann Schmidt painted many of the frescoes you'll see inside the church. In the Altstadt, or Old Town, the **Steiner Tor**, a 1480 gate, is a landmark.

You'll find the **Historisches Museum der Stadt Krems** (Historical Museum of Krems), Körnermarkt 14 (☎ **02732/801-567**), in a restored Dominican monastery. The abbey is in the Gothic style from the 13th and 14th centuries. It has a gallery displaying the paintings of Martin Johann Schmidt, a noted 18th-century artist better known as Kremser Schmidt (mentioned earlier). The complex also has an interesting **Weinbaumuseum** (Wine Museum), exhibiting artifacts, many quite old, gathered from the vineyards along the Danube. The cost of admission 40 AS ($3.80) for access to both areas of the museum. The museum is open only between March and November, Wednesday through Sunday from 1 to 6pm.

The Historical and Wine Museums are open from around Easter until the middle of November, Tuesday through Saturday from 9am to noon and 2 to 5pm, and on Sunday from 9am to noon. Admission is 35 AS ($3.35) for both museums.

WHERE TO STAY

Donauhotel Krems
Edmund-Hofbauer-Strasse 19, A-3500 Krems. ☎ **02732/87565.** Fax 02732/87565-52. 60 rms. TV TEL. 1,080 AS ($102.60) double. Rates include breakfast. Half board 180 AS ($17.10) per person extra. AE, MC, V.

This large glass-walled hotel built in the 1970s has a wooden canopy stretched over the front entrance. Meals are available in the airy cafe, on the terrace, or in the more formal restaurant serving typically Austrian food. The waitresses, all of whom wear regional garb, will bring you wine from the Wachau district. The hotel's fitness center includes a sauna and solarium. The bedrooms are comfortably furnished and well maintained.

Hotel-Restaurant am Förthof
Donaulände 8, A-3500 Krems. ☎ **02732/83345.** Fax 02732/833-4540. 20 rms. TV TEL. 1,200–1,400 AS ($114–$133) double. Rates include breakfast. Half board 250 AS ($23.75) per person extra. DC, MC, V. Free parking.

In the Stein sector of the city, this big-windowed hotel has white stucco walls and flower-covered balconies which date from the 1970s. A rose garden surrounds the base of an al fresco cafe, whereas the inside is decorated with Oriental rugs and a scattering of antiques amid newer furniture. On the grounds is an outdoor swimming pool bordered in stone. The high-ceilinged bedrooms each have a foyer and a shared balcony. At dinner, hotel guests have a choice of contemporary cuisine or traditional Austrian cooking.

WHERE TO DINE

✪ Restaurant Bacher
Südtiroler Platz 208, A-3512 Mautern. ☎ **02732/82937.** Fax 02732/74337. Reservations required. Main courses 195–355 AS ($18.50–$33.75); fixed-price meals 385–555 AS

($36.60–$52.75) at lunch, 625–885 AS ($59.40–$84.10) at dinner. DC, V. Wed–Sat 11:30am–2pm and 6:30–9pm; Sun 11:30–9pm. Closed mid-Jan–mid-Feb. AUSTRIAN/INTERNATIONAL.

Lisl and Klaus Wagner-Bacher operate this excellent restaurant-hotel, with an elegant dining room and a well-kept garden. Lisl cooks à la Paul Bocuse, serving an imaginative array of fresh ingredients. Specialties include crabmeat salad with nut oil, zucchini stuffed with fish, and two kinds of sauces. Dessert might be *beignets* with apricot sauce and vanilla ice cream. She has won awards for her cuisine, as her enthusiastic clientele will tell you. The wine list includes more than 600 selections.

Eight double and three single rooms are offered. Rooms contain TVs, minibars, phones, and radios, and each is attractively furnished. The rates are 700 to 970 AS ($66.50 to $92.15) per person in a double. The establishment is 2¹/₂ miles from Krems.

DÜRNSTEIN

Less than 5 miles west of Krems is, in our opinion, the loveliest town along the Danube, Dürnstein, which draws throngs of tour groups in summer. Terraced vineyards mark this as a Danube wine town, and the town's fortified walls are partially preserved.

ESSENTIALS

GETTING THERE Dürnstein is 50 miles west of Vienna. To reach it by car, take Route 3 west from the city. From Krems, continue driving west along Route 3 for five miles. Train travel to Dürnstein requires a transfer in Krems (see above). In Krems, trains leave every two hours on river-running routes. Call **0222/17-17** in Vienna for schedules. There's also bus service (trip time: 20 minutes) between Krems and Dürnstein.

VISITOR INFORMATION Dürnstein has a little **tourist office** (☎ **02711/200**), housed in a shed in the east parking lot, called Parkplatz Ost. It's open only from April to October.

WHAT TO SEE & DO

The ruins of a **castle fortress,** 520 feet above the town, are a link with the Crusades. Here Leopold V, the Babenberg duke ruling the country at that time, held **Richard the Lion-Hearted** of England prisoner in 1193. It seems that Richard had insulted the powerful Austrian duke in Palestine during one of the frequent religious forays of the Middle Ages to get the Holy Sepulcher and its appurtenances into Christian hands. The story goes that when Richard was trying to get back home, his boat went on the rocks in the Adriatic and he tried to sneak through Austria disguised as a peasant. Somebody probably turned stool pigeon, and the English monarch was arrested and imprisoned by Leopold.

For quite some time nobody knew exactly where Richard was incarcerated in Austria, but his loyal minstrel companion, Blondel, had a clever idea. He went from castle to castle, playing his lute and singing Richard's favorite songs. The tactic paid off, the legend says, for at Dürnstein Richard heard Blondel's singing and sang the lyrics in reply. This discovery forced Leopold to transfer the English king to a castle in the Rhineland Palatinate, but by then everybody knew where he was, so Leopold set a high ransom on the Plantagenet head, which was eventually met and Richard was set free.

The castle was virtually demolished by the Swedes in 1645, but you can visit the ruins if you don't mind a vigorous climb (allow an hour). The castle isn't much, but the view of Dürnstein and the Wachau is more than worth the effort.

Back in the town, stroll along the principal artery, **Hauptstrasse,** which is flanked by richly embellished old residences. Many of these date from the 1500s and have been well maintained through the centuries. In summer the balconies are filled with flowers.

The 15th-century pfarrkirche (parish church) also merits a visit. The building was originally an Augustinian monastery and was reconstructed when the baroque style swept Austria. The church tower, identified by its reddish color, is the finest baroque example in the whole country and is a prominent landmark in the Danube Valley. There is also a splendid church portal. Kremser Schmidt, the noted baroque painter, did some of the altar paintings here.

WHERE TO STAY & DINE

⑤ Gartenhotel Pfeffel

A-3601 Dürnstein. ☎ **02711/206.** Fax 02711/20688. 40 rms, 4 suites. TEL. 920–1,120 AS ($87.40–$106.40) double; from 1,300 AS ($123.50) suite. Rates include breakfast. MC, V. Closed Dec–Feb. Free parking.

This black-roofed, white-walled hotel is partially concealed by well-landscaped shrubbery. The public rooms are furnished with traditional pieces. The hotel rates as one of the best bargains in this much-frequented tourist town. The hotel takes its name from its garden courtyard with flowering trees where tasty but not fancy meals are served. The bedrooms are handsomely furnished in a traditional Austrian motif, with comfortable armchairs, beds, and tables. Leopold Pfeffel, your host, serves wine from his own terraced vineyard. He's also added a swimming pool.

Gasthof-Pension Sänger Blondel

A-3601 Dürnstein. ☎ **02711/253.** Fax 02711/2537. 16 rms. TEL. 970–1,250 AS ($92.15–$118.75) double. Rates include breakfast. No credit cards. Closed Dec–Feb and the first week in July. Parking 80 AS ($7.60).

Lemon-colored and charmingly old-fashioned, with green shutters and clusters of flowers at the windows, this hotel is named after the faithful minstrel who searched the countryside for Richard the Lion-Hearted. There's a good and reasonably priced restaurant, serving a regional cuisine. Bedrooms are furnished in an old-fashioned, rustic and traditional style and are quite comfortable, containing such amenities as hair dryers. Each Thursday an evening of zither music is presented. If the weather is good, the music is played outside in the flowery chestnut garden near the baroque blue church tower of Dürnstein.

✪ Romantik-Hotel Richard Löwenherz

A-3601 Dürnstein. ☎ **02711/222.** Fax 02711/22218. 40 rms. TV TEL. 1,680 AS ($159.60) double. Rates include breakfast. AE, DC, MC, V. Closed Nov–Mar. Free parking.

This establishment was founded as a hotel in the 1950s on the site of a 700-year-old nunnery which was originally dedicated to the sisters of Santa Clara in 1289. Its richly historical interior is filled with antiques, Renaissance sculpture, elegant chandeliers, stone vaulting, and paneling which has been polished over the years to a mellow patina. An arbor-covered sun terrace with restaurant tables extends toward the Danube. Best of all, the hotel offers a swimming pool; you'll see the apse of a medieval church reflected in the water. The spacious bedrooms, especially those in the balconied modern section, are filled with cheerful furniture.

The restaurant offers excellent local wines as well as fish from the Danube among its many regional specialties. The dining room is open daily from 11:30am to 11:30pm. A fixed-price menu costs 380 AS ($36.10).

✪ Hotel Schloss Dürnstein

A-3601 Dürnstein. ☎ **02711/212.** Fax 02711/351. 37 rms, 2 suites. MINIBAR TV TEL. 2,500–4,200 AS ($237.50–$399.00) double; 2,100 AS ($180.60) per person suite. Rates include half board. AE, DC, MC, V. Closed Nov 10–Mar 25. Parking garage 100 AS ($9.50). A pickup can be arranged at the Dürnstein rail station.

The baroque tower of this Renaissance castle rises above the scenic Danube. It's one of the best-furnished hotels in Austria, with white ceramic stoves, vaulted ceilings, parquet floors, Oriental rugs, gilt mirrors, and oil portraits of elaborately dressed courtiers. Below the ochre facade of one of the wings, an ivy-covered wall borders the swimming pool. The real beauty of the grounds, however, is found on the shady terrace a stone's throw from the river. The most expensive double is the hotel's most elegant room (rare antiques, beautiful upholstery, and beds worthy of Napoléon).

The restaurant is outfitted with velvet armchairs. Here you'll be served well-prepared dishes from the kitchen of an experienced chef. Fixed-price menus begin at 380 AS ($36.10) including appetizer.

MELK

Finally, you arrive at one of the chief sightseeing goals of every pilgrim to Austria, or in the words of Empress Maria Theresa, "If I had never come here, I would have regretted it." The main attraction here is the Melk Abbey, a sprawling baroque abbey that overlooks the Danube basin. Melk marks the western terminus of the Wachau and lies upstream from Krems.

ESSENTIALS

GETTING THERE   Melk is 55 miles west of Vienna. Motorists can take Autobahn A1, exiting at the signs for Melk. If you prefer a more romantic and scenic road than the autobahn, then try Route 3, which parallels the Danube, but takes between 30 to 45 minutes longer. Trains leave frequently from Vienna's Westbahnhof to Melk, with two brief stops en route (trip time: about 1 hour).

VISITOR INFORMATION   The **Melk tourist office** (☎ **02752/23-07-32** or **33**), is at Babenberger strasse 1 in the center of town.

WHAT TO SEE & DO

One of the finest baroque buildings in the world, ✪ **Melk Abbey,** Dietmayerstrasse 1, A-3390 Melk (☎ **02752/2312**), and the **Stiftskirche** (the abbey church) are the major attractions here today. However, Melk has been an important place in the Danube Basin since the establishment of a Roman fortress on a promontory looking out onto a tiny "arm" of the Danube. Melk also figures in *The Nibelungenlied* (the German epic poem), in which it is called *Medelike*.

The rock-strewn bluff where the abbey now stands overlooking the river was the seat of the Babenbergs, who ruled Austria from 976 until the Habsburgs took over. In the 11th century Leopold II of the House of Babenberg presented Melk to the Benedictine monks, who turned it into a fortified abbey. It became known as a center of learning and culture, and its influence spread all over Austria, a fact that is familiar to readers of the *The Name of the Rose* by Umberto Eco. However, it did not fare well during the Reformation, and it felt the fallout from the 1683 Turkish invasion, although it was spared from direct attack when the armies of the Ottoman Empire were repelled at the outskirts of Vienna. The construction of the new building began in 1702, just in time to be given the full baroque treatment.

Most of the design of the present abbey was by the baroque architect Jakob Prandtauer. Its marble hall, the Marmorsaal, contains pilasters coated in red marble. A richly painted allegorical picture on the ceiling is the work of Paul Troger. The library, rising two floors, again with a Troger ceiling, contains some 80,000 volumes. The Kaisergang, or emperors' gallery, 650 feet long, is decorated with portraits of Austrian rulers.

Despite all this adornment in the abbey, it still takes second place in lavish glory to the Stiftskirche, the golden abbey church, damaged by fire in 1947 but now restored, even to the regilding with gold bullion of statues and altars. Richly embellished with marble and frescoes, the church has an astonishing number of windows. Many of the paintings are by Johann Michael Rottmayr, but Troger also had a hand in decorating the church. The Marble Hall banquet room next to the church was also damaged by the fire but has been restored to its former ornate elegance.

Melk is still a working abbey, and you may see black-robed Benedictine monks going about their business or schoolboys rushing out the gates. Visitors head for the terrace for a view of the river. Napoleon probably used it for a lookout when he made Melk his headquarters during the campaign against Austria.

Throughout the year, the abbey is open every day, with tours that depart at intervals of between 15 and 20 minutes, depending on business. The first tour departs at 9am, the last at 5pm, and guides make efforts to translate into English a running commentary that is otherwise German. Adults pay 70 AS ($6.65) for guided tours and 55 AS ($5.25) for unguided tours: children 45 AS ($4.30) and 30 AS ($2.85), respectively.

WHERE TO STAY

Hotel Stadt Melk

Hauptplatz 1, A-3390 Melk. ☎ **02752/2475.** Fax 02752/247519. 15 rms. MINIBAR TV TEL. 1,050 AS ($99.75) double. Rates include breakfast. MC, V.

Positioned just below the town's palace, a five-minute walk from the train station, this four-story hotel has a gabled roof and stucco walls. Originally built a century ago as a private home, it was eventually converted into this cozy family-run hotel. The pleasant restaurant has leaded-glass windows in round bull's-eye patterns of greenish glass. Meals are served on a balcony, decorated with flowers, at the front of the hotel. The food is quite good, including, for example, a pâté of wild mushrooms, followed by venison, and ending with a white mousse with a "web" of crystallized caramel. Meals begin at 400 AS ($38). The simply furnished bedrooms are clean and comfortable. Rooms in the rear open onto views of the abbey, and a sauna is on the premises.

WHERE TO DINE

Stiftrestaurant Melk

Abt-Berthold-Dietmayrstrasse 3. ☎ **02752/2555.** Fixed-price menus 125–215 AS ($11.90–$20.45). AE, MC. Daily 8am to 6pm. BURGENLANDER.

For a tourist visiting Melk, this is required eating. Don't allow the cafeterialike dimensions of this eatery sway you from its very fine cuisine. This modernly decorated place is well-equipped to handle large groups: 3,000 visitors a day frequent the establishment during peak season. The dining rooms are typically Austrian clean, and the price is reasonable. From their fixed-menu you might opt for the asparagus and ham soup with crispy dumplings; hunter's roast with mushrooms, potato croquettes, and cranberry sauce, and a choice of desserts—one of which being the famed, highly caloric Sachertorte.

5 Eisenstadt

When Burgenland joined Austria in the 1920s, it was a province without a capital. In 1924 its citizens agreed on Eisenstadt for the honor. This small town lies at the foot of the Leitha mountains, at the beginning of the Great Hungarian Plain. Surrounded by vineyards, forests and fruit trees. It's a convenient stopover for exploring Lake Neusiedl, six miles east.

Even before assuming its new role as the capital, Eisenstadt was renowned as the place where the great composer Joseph Haydn lived and worked while under the patronage of the Esterházys. For a good part of his life (1732–1809), Haydn divided his time between Eisenstadt and the Esterházy Castle in Hungary. Prince Esterházy eventually gave him his own orchestra and a concert hall in which to perform.

EN ROUTE TO EISENSTADT

From Vienna, Eisenstadt is 31 miles southeast. Motorists can take Route 10 east to Parndorf Ort, then head southwest along Route 304 to Eisenstadt. Trains for Eisenstadt leave from the Südbahnhof daily, heading toward Budapest. Change at the railway junction of Neusiedl am See, where connections are carefully timed to link up with the trains to Eisenstadt (trip time: around 90 minutes). Call **0222/17-17** for schedules. You can take a bus from the City Air Terminal at the Vienna Hilton. Buses marked EISENSTADT-DOMPLATZ, depart daily every 20 minutes.

When you arrive, go directly to the **Eisenstadt tourist office,** Franz-Schubert-Platz 1 (☎ **02682/67390**) distributes information about Eisenstadt and Burgenland and will also book rooms.

WHAT TO SEE AND DO

Bergkirche (Church of the Calvary)

Josef-Haydn-Platz 1. ☎ **02682/626-38.** Admission to church, free; Haydn's tomb, 20 AS ($1.90) adults, 10 AS (95¢) students and senior citizens, 5 AS (50¢) children 17 and under. Daily 9am–noon and 1–5pm. Closed Nov–Mar. From Esterházy Platz at the castle, head directly west along Esterházystrasse, a slightly uphill walk.

If you want to pay your final respects to Haydn, follow Hauptstrasse to Esterházystrasse, which leads to this church containing Haydn's tomb, built of white marble. Until 1954 only the composer's headless body was here. His skull was in the Music Museum in Vienna, where curious spectators were actually allowed to feel it. Haydn's head was stolen a few days after his death and did not get back together with his body for 145 years!

Haydn Museum

Haydn-Gasse 21. ☎ **02682/626-52.** Admission 20 AS ($1.90) adults, 10 AS (90¢) children, senior citizens, and students. Daily 9am–noon and 1–5pm. Closed Nov–Easter. Pass Schloss Esterházy and turn left onto Haydn-Gasse.

The little home of the composer from 1766 to 1778 is now a museum honoring its former tenant. Although he appeared in court nearly every night, Haydn actually lived very modestly when he was at home. However, the home wasn't exactly bleak, as he had a little flower-filled courtyard. The museum has collected mementos of Haydn's life and work.

○ Schloss Esterházy

Esterházy Platz. ☎ **02682/633-84**. Admission 50 AS ($4.75) adults, 30 AS ($2.85) children, senior citizens, and students. Daily 9am–5pm. From the bus station at Domplatz, follow the sign to the castle (a 10-minute walk).

Haydn worked in this château built on the site of a medieval castle and owned by the Esterházy princes. The Esterházy clan was a great Hungarian family with vast estates who ruled Eisenstadt and its surrounding area. They claimed descent from Attila the Hun. The Esterházys helped the Habsburgs gain control in Hungary. So great was their loyalty to Austria, in fact, that when Napoléon offered the crown of Hungary to Nic Esterházy in 1809, he refused it.

The *schloss* (castle), built around an inner courtyard, was designed by the Italian architect Carlone and fortified because of its strategic position. Carlone started work on the castle in 1663, but subsequently it was remodeled by many other architects, resulting in sweeping alterations to its appearance. In the late 17th and early 18th centuries it was given a baroque pastel facade. On the first floor, the great baronial hall was made into the Haydnsaal, where the composer conducted the orchestra Prince Esterházy had provided for him and often performed his own works before the Esterházy court. The walls and ceilings of this concert hall are elaborately decorated, but the floor is of bare wood, which, it is claimed, is the reason for the room's acoustic perfection.

A complete tour of Esterházy Palace takes 45 minutes, whereas a tour of Haydnsaal lasts about 20 minutes. Both tours are conducted for a minimum of 10 people.

Franz-Liszt-Geburtshaus (Franz Liszt's Birthplace)

Raiding. ☎ **02619/72-20**. Admission 20 AS ($1.90) adults; 10 AS (95¢) children, students, and senior citizens; 40 AS ($3.80) family ticket. Daily 9am–noon and 1–5pm. Closed Nov–Easter. Take Route S31 south of Eisenstadt, then cut east onto a minor, unmarked road at Lackenbach (follow the signs to Raiding from there).

In the small nearby village of Raiding (south of Eisenstadt), this museum contains many mementos of the composer's life, including an old church organ he used to play. Liszt's father worked as a bailiff for the princes of Esterházy, and this was his home when little Franz was born in 1811.

WHERE TO STAY & DINE

Hotel Burgenland

Schubertplatz 1, A-7000 Eisenstadt. ☎ **02682/696**. Fax 02682/65-5-31. 88 rms, 8 suites. MINIBAR TV TEL. 1,590 AS ($151.05) double; from 2,080 AS ($197.60) suite. Rates include breakfast. AE, DC, MC, V. Parking 100 AS ($9.50).

The Hotel Burgenland opened in 1982 and quickly established itself as the class act of Eisenstadt. A mansard roof, white stucco walls, and big windows form the exterior of this contemporary hotel in the center directly northeast of the bus station at Domplatz. The comfortable bedrooms have lots of light, wood-grained headboards, functional furniture, and radios. A swimming pool, a sauna, two restaurants, and a cafe are on the premises.

One of the best restaurants in Burgenland is the hotel's G'würzstockl, the more formal of its two restaurants, open Sunday and holidays from noon to 2:30pm and Monday through Friday from 6 to 10pm. Of bright, airy design, it serves such traditional and old-fashioned dishes as cabbage soup, veal steak with fresh vegetables, and a host of other platters, some Hungarian. Fixed-price meals cost 200 to 700 AS ($19.00 to $66.50), with à la carte meals running 135 to 320 AS ($12.85 to $30.40).

Reservations are suggested. A less formal option is the Bianankorb, a cafe-restaurant open daily from 7am with last orders taken at 9pm.

ⓢ Wirtshaus zum Eder

Hauptstrasse 25, A-7000 Eisenstadt. ☎ **02682/626-45.** 13 rms. 590 AS ($56.05) double. Rates include breakfast. AE, DC, MC, V. Free parking on side streets.

Filled with modern furniture, deer antlers, and iron chandeliers, this family-style guesthouse also has a garden terrace surrounded with a thick wall of greenery. It's in the town center, north of the bus station at Domplatz. The simple bedrooms are clean and comfortable. The hotel's restaurant serves hot and cold Austrian and Hungarian specialties at reasonable prices. Meals cost 160 AS ($15.20) and are served daily from 11am to 10pm.

6 Lake Neusiedl

The Neusiedl Lake region is famous getaway for the Viennese, and North Americans will also find it a desirable vacation spot. The lake offers countless recreational opportunities, making it an ideal destination for families and active travelers. The steppe landscape will intrigue you and so will the geological anomaly the Neusiedler Lake (see box below).

NEUSIEDL AM SEE

On the northern bank of Lake Neusiedl lies this stopover, which is likely to be crowded on summer weekends. Water sports prevail here, and sailboats can be rented. The parish church, in the Gothic style, is noted for its "ship pulpit." A watchtower from the Middle Ages still stands guard over the town, although it's no longer occupied. Many vineyards cover the nearby acreage. If you plan to be here on a weekend in summer, make advance reservations.

ESSENTIALS

GETTING THERE   Neusiedl am See lies 28 miles southeast of Vienna and 21 miles northeast of Eisenstadt. Neusiedl am See should be viewed as your gateway to the lake, as it's less than an hour by express train from Vienna. Motorists can reach it by taking the A-4 or Route 10 east from Vienna. If you're in Eisenstadt, head northeast along Route 50, cutting east along Route 51 for a short distance. It's better to have a car if you're exploring Lake Neusiedl, although there are bus connections, departing several times daily from the Domplatz bus station at Eisenstadt.

VISITOR INFORMATION   The **Neusiedler See tourist office** is in the Rathaus (town hall) at Hauptplatz 1 (☎ **02167/2229**). It distributes information about accommodations in the area and will also explain how to rent sailboats for cruising the lake.

WHERE TO STAY

Gasthof zur Traube

Hauptplatz 9, A-7100 Neusiedl am See. ☎ **02167/2423.** Fax 02167/24236. 7 rms. TV TEL. 630–660 AS ($59.85–$62.70) double. Rates include breakfast. No credit cards. Free parking.

This small hotel stands on the bustling main street of town. The pleasant restaurant on the ground floor is filled with country trim and wrought-iron table dividers. You can stop in for a meal from 11am to 10pm or book one of the cozy upstairs bedrooms for an overnight stay (you have to register at the bar in back of the restaurant). In summer guests can relax in the garden. Franz Rittsteuer and his family are the owners.

The Capricious Lake

Called **Neusiedler See** in German, Lake Neusiedl is a steppe lake lying in the northern part of Burgenland. Strange and mysterious, the lake will come and go in parts—in fact, from 1868 to 1872 it desiccated completely as it has done periodically throughout its known history. This creates intriguing real-estate disputes among bordering landowners. The lake was part of a body of water that once blanketed all of the Pannonian Plain. Today it's only about six feet deep at its lowest point, and the wind can shift the water dramatically, causing parts of the lake to become dry. A broad belt of reeds encircles the huge expanse of lake, about 115 square miles. This thicket is an ideal habitat for many varieties of water fowl. In all some 250 different species of birds inhabit the lake including the usual collection of storks, geese, duck and herons. It's between $4^1/_4$ and $9^1/_4$ miles wide, and about 22 miles long. If you're tall enough you could walk across it, but we're not recommending that!

Because of the curvature of the earth, the middle of the lake is about 80 feet higher than the longitudinal axis. The Neusiedler See possesses no natural outlets; it is fed by underground lakes. Its water is slightly salty, and the plants and animal life here are unique in Europe. This is the meeting place of alpine, Baltic, and Pannonian flora and fauna.

The Viennese flock to the lake throughout the year, in summer to fish and windsurf, and in winter to skate. If you're a sunbather, nearly every village nearby has a beach (although on any given day it might be swallowed up by the sea or miles from the shore depending on which way the wind blows). The fertile soil and temperate climate surrounding the west bank is ideal for vineyards. Washed in sun, the orchards in Rust produce famous, award-winning vintages.

Hotel Wende

Seestrasse 40-50, A-7100 Neusiedl am See. ☎ **02167/8111.** Fax 02167/8111-649. 105 rms, 1 suite. MINIBAR TV TEL. 1,365–1,765 AS ($129.70–$167.70) double; 3,660 AS ($347.70) suite for two. Rates include half board. AE, DC, V. Closed last week in Jan and first two weeks in Feb. Parking garage 100 AS ($9.50). Free pickup at the train station.

The walls of this hotel are dotted with maps of Burgenland, and its dining room serves many recipes from the region. The place is actually a complex of three sprawling buildings, interconnected by rambling corridors. Set at the edge of town, on the road leading to the water, the hotel is almost a village unto itself. The aura here is one of clean but slightly sterile propriety, although the indoor pool and sauna, along with the glass-enclosed clubhouse, offer diversion. The bedrooms are well furnished, and the in-house restaurant is recommended separately (see below). The luxury suite of the hotel is named after Joseph Haydn.

WHERE TO DINE

Hotel Wende Restaurant

In the Hotel Wende, Seestrasse 40-50. ☎ **02167/8111.** Fixed-price menus 155–570 AS ($14.75–$54.15). AE, DC, V. Daily noon–2:30pm and 6:30–9:30pm. Closed last week in Jan and first two weeks in Feb. AUSTRIAN/HUNGARIAN.

The best food and best service, as well as the most formal setting, are found at the previously recommended Hotel Wende. Under a wood-beamed ceiling, the rich and bountiful table of Burgenland, both in food and wine, is set to perfection here.

In summer, tables are placed outside overlooking the grounds. Since Burgenland is a border state, the menu reflects the two different cultures of both Hungary and Austria.

A choice of 21 fixed-price menus appeals to those wishing to dine inexpensively as well as those who want to order more lavishly. Menu items include a savory soup made with fresh carp from nearby lakes; cream of zucchini soup; medaillons of pork with Roquefort-flavored cream sauce and herb-flavored rice; pork cutlets with home-made noodles, bacon-flavored rösti, baby carrots, and fresh herbs; breast of chicken with polenta and fresh herbs; roast beef in the style of the Esterházy family, with salty strudel and green salad; smoked filet of eel with black bread toast; filet of zander in a potato crust with a sherry-cream sauce and wild rice; crêpes stuffed with minced veal in the Hungarian style and served with paprika-cream sauce; and a dessert specialty of an iced honey parfait with seasonal fresh fruits, or perhaps a strudel studded with fresh dates, served with marzipan-flavored whipped cream.

PURBACH AM SEE

If you take Route 50 south from the northern tip of Lake Neusiedl, your first stop-over might be in this little resort village, which has some recommendable accommo-dations. Purbach boasts a well-preserved circuit of town walls, which were built to stop Turkish invasions during the 16th and 17th centuries. It's also a market town, where you can buy some of Burgenland's renowned wines from local vendors.

ESSENTIALS

GETTING THERE   Purbach is 31 miles southeast of Vienna and 11 miles north-east of Eisenstadt. From Eisenstadt, you can take a daily bus leaving from the station at Domplatz. Motorists in Eisenstadt can head northeast along Route 50, whereas motorists from Vienna can cut southeast along Route 10 or Autobahn A4.

VISITOR INFORMATION   Contact the **Neusiedler See tourist office** in Neusiedl am See, Hauptplatz 1 (☎ **02167/2229**).

WHERE TO STAY

Am Spitz

A-7083 Purbach am See. ☎ **02683/5519.** Fax 02683/551-920. 12 rms, 4 apts, TV TEL. 720–760 AS ($68.40–$72.20) double; 1,200 AS ($114) apt. Rates include breakfast. No credit cards. Closed Christmas to Easter. The hotel will pick up guests at the bus station. Free parking.

The main building of this hotel features a gable trimmed with baroque embellish-ments. The Holzl-Schwarz family are your hosts here, where a hotel has stood on the premises for more than 600 years. The current incarnation include accommodations with panoramic views of the lake. The hotel is well directed, conservative, and deserving of its three-star rating. The adjoining restaurant, rustically decorated to provide an air of coziness, is one of the best places in the region for Burgenland cookery. Specialties include chicken soup, bacon salad, lamb cutlets with potatoes and spinach, and a array of local wines. It closes on Monday and Tuesday, and reservations are suggested.

WHERE TO DINE

Romantik-Restaurant Nikolauszeche

Bodenzeile 3. ☎ **02683/5514.** Reservations recommended. Main courses 185–245 AS ($17.60–$23.30); fixed-price menu (including wine) 200–1,000 AS ($19–$95). AE, DC, MC, V. Thurs–Mon 12:30–3pm; Wed–Mon 6–11pm. Closed Dec 12–Mar 15. AUSTRIAN.

This upscale restaurant is housed in what was constructed five centuries ago as a cloister for monks. In a niche high above the rest of the baroque decor here, someone has placed a statue that looks more like the Madonna than the namesake of this establishment, Saint Nicholas. The food, however, is authentically regional, attracting a wide cross section of Austrians. The menu changes every two weeks. Diners can order the rich bouillon or cabbage soup, the *fogosch* (a white fish), and the chef's special ham crêpes, as well as select from a well-chosen wine list. Accordion or organ music is played. If you seek privacy and calm, you can find a quiet corner in the interior courtyard.

RUST

Leaving Purbach, head south towards Rust, a small resort village with limited accommodations. It's famous for its stork nests, which are perched on chimneys throughout the town. The antiquated, charming town center is well-preserved and clean. Its walls were built in 1614 for protection against the Turks.

Rust is the capital of the Burgenland lake district, lying in a rich setting of vineyards that produce the Burgenlander grape. If it's available, try the *Blaufränkisch,* a red wine that seems to be entirely consumed by the locals or the Viennese, who flock to the area and return home with bottles of the region's vintage. Sometimes you can go right up to the door of a vintner's farmhouse, especially if a green bough is displayed, and sample wine and buy it on the spot, as at a *heurige.*

The taverns in the town have lively Gypsy music. Some local residents, when the wine is in their blood, like to dance in regional costume wearing high boots. You're left with the distinct impression that you're in Hungary.

Rust has a *Gemütlich* atmosphere, especially on weekends. Summers are often hot, and the lake water can get warm. You can rent sailboats and windsurfers on the banks of the shallow Neusiedler See.

ESSENTIALS

GETTING THERE   Rust lies 11 miles northeast of Eisenstadt and 44 miles southeast of Vienna. From Eisenstadt head east on Route 52. From Purbach, motorists can take Route 50 south toward Eisenstadt. At Seehof take a left fork to Oggau and Rust.

VISITOR INFORMATION   The **Rust tourist office (☎ 02685/502)** is in the Rathaus (town hall) in the center of the village. It can arrange inexpensive stays with English-speaking families if asked.

WHERE TO STAY & DINE

Hotel-Restaurant Sifkovitz

Am Seekanal 8, A-7071 Rust. ☎ **02685/276.** Fax 02685/36012. 34 rms. 860–1,180 AS ($81.70–$112.10) double with bath. Rates include breakfast. No credit cards. Closed Dec–Mar. Free parking.

Attracting summer visitors, many from Vienna but also from Hungary, this hotel consists of both an older building and a new wing. Both were fully renovated in the mid-1980s. The facade is concrete and stucco, and the older building has a format of red-tile roofs and big windows. The bedrooms get a lot of sun and are comfortably furnished with rather functional pieces. Singles are very hard to get during the busy summer season. Facilities include a sauna, an exercise room, a cafe, and a sun terrace. There is access to tennis courts, but they're on the grounds of another hotel nearby (the staff will make arrangements). Food, both an Austrian and a Hungarian-inspired cuisine, is served daily from 11am to 10pm.

Seehotel Rust

A-7071 Rust. ☎ **02685/382.** Fax 02685/381419. 110 rms. MINIBAR TV TEL. 1,900 AS ($180.50) double. Rates include half board. MC, V. Free parking.

The Seehotel Rust is one of the most attractive hostelries in the lake district. Well designed and dating from 1982, it's set on a grassy lawn at the edge of the lake and remains open year-round. It has an appealing series of connected balconies, rounded towers that look vaguely medieval, and a series of recessed loggias. The hotel rents pleasantly furnished bedrooms. On the premises are an indoor swimming pool, a sauna, two tennis courts, and a bar area.

Offerings in the restaurant include tafelspitz (boiled beef) with chive sauce, calves' brains with a honey vinegar, watercress soup, and sole meunière. Meals begin at 190 AS ($18.05), whereas brunch costs 300 AS ($28.50). A Gypsy band provides the evening's entertainment.

ILLMITZ

This old *puszta* (steppe) village on the east side of the lake has grown into a town with a moderate tourist business in summer. From Eisenstadt, motorists should take Route 50 northeast, through Purbach, cutting southeast on Route 51, via Pordersdorf, to Illmitz. The distance from Eisenstadt to Illmitz is 38 miles, which seems long because traffic must swing around the northern perimeter of the lake before heading south to Illmitz.

NEARBY ATTRACTIONS

Leaving Illmitz, head east on the main route, then cut north at the junction with Route 51. From Route 51, both the little villages of St. Andrä bei Frauenkirchen and Andau are signposted. Near the Hungarian border, the hamlet of **St. Andrä bei Frauenkirchen** is filled with thatch houses. The town is known for its basket weaving, so you might want to drive here for a shopping expedition.

A short drive farther will take you to **Andau,** which became the focus of world attention in 1956 during the Hungarian uprising. It was through this point, almost on the border, that hundreds of Hungarians dashed to freedom in the West, fleeing the grim massacres of Budapest.

Starting in the late 1940s, the border with Hungary was closely guarded and people who tried to escape into Austria were shot from the Communist-controlled watchtowers. But now all that has changed. In 1989 the fortifications were rendered obsolete as hundreds of East Germans fled across the border to freedom in the West. Before the year was out, their own Berlin Wall came tumbling down and they didn't need this means of escape anymore.

The surrounding marshy area of this remote sector of Austria, called **Seewinkel,** is a haven for birds and contains many rare flora, plus many small *puszta* animals. This is a large natural wildlife sanctuary. You'll see a few windmills and expanses of reeds, which are used to make roofs and shelters.

This area, very different from the celebrated Austria of alpine lore, is little known to North Americans or even to most Europeans. The landscape is perfect for an off-beat adventure.

WHERE TO STAY & DINE

Ⓢ Weingut-Heurigenrestaurant/Pension Rosenhof

Florianigasse 1, A-7142 Illmitz. ☎ **02175/2232.** Fax 02175/22324. 15 rms. 270–350 AS ($25.65–$33.25) per person. Rates include breakfast. No credit cards. Closed Nov–Easter. Free parking.

A block from the main highway running through the center of town, this charming baroque hotel is in an agricultural area. The arched gateway at its gold-and-white facade takes visitors into a rose-laden courtyard filled with arbors. A tile-roofed affiliated building, capped with platforms for storks' nests, contains cozy bedrooms.

In an older section you'll find a wine restaurant whose star attraction is the recent vintage produced by the Haider family's wine presses. Many of your fellow diners live in the neighborhood, coming for the Hungarian and Burgenland specialties. These might include dishes as exotic, for example, as wild boar cooked in a marinade and thickened with regional walnuts. Local fish, such as carp, are available, including the meaty zander from the Danube. In the autumn the inn serves Traubensaft from freshly harvested grapes—delectable grape juice consumed before it becomes alcoholic. In the evening, musicians fill the air with Gypsy music. Meals are served daily from 11am to 3pm and 5 to 10pm, costing 70 to 170 AS ($6.65 to $16.15).

PODERSDORF

Podersdorf am See is one of the finest places for swimming in the mysterious lake, as its shoreline is relatively free of reeds. As a result, the little town has become a modest summer resort. The parish church in the village is from the late 18th century. You'll see many storks nesting atop chimneys, and some of the cottages have thatch roofs. The Viennese like to drive out here on a summer Sunday to go for a swim and also to purchase wine from the local vintners.

ESSENTIALS

GETTING THERE   Podersdorf lies nine miles south of the major center along the lake, Neusiedl am See (see above). It's most often visited by car, although buses run throughout the day from Eisenstadt, going via Neusiedl am See. Motorists leaving Eisenstadt can head northeast along Route 50, via Purbach, cutting southeast at the junction with Route 51, driving through Neusiedl am See before cutting south along the lake to Podersdorf.

VISITOR INFORMATION   A small **tourist office** operates during summers only in Pordersdorf at Hauptstrasse 2 (☎ **02177/2227**).

WHERE TO STAY

Gasthof Seewirt
Strandplatz 1, A-7141 Podersdorf. ☎ **02177/2415.** Fax 02177/246530. 16 rms. TV TEL. 570–685 AS ($54.15–$65.10) per person. Rates include half board. No credit cards. Closed Dec 1–Feb 15. Free parking.

Solidly built in 1924, then gutted and renovated in 1979, this hotel sits at the edge of the lake, within a short walk from the expanses of marshland. It charges the same prices, and shares the same owners, as the roughly equivalent but newer Haus Attila, with which it frequently compared. Bedrooms are well scrubbed, comfortable, and utilitarian, and public rooms include one of the best recommended restaurants at the resort (see below.) There's a sauna on the premises, and touches of personalized, English-speaking charm from the hardworking owners.

⑤ Haus Attila
Strandplatz 8, A-7141 Podersdorf. ☎ **02177/2415.** Fax 02177/246530. 36 rms. 570–685 AS ($54.15–$65.10) per person, double. Rates include half board. No credit cards. Closed Nov 1–Mar 30. Free parking.

Newer and more recently renovated than its sibling, the Seewirt, with whom it shares the same owners, this hotel was built in 1975, and renovated and enlarged in 1992.

The light-grained balconies are partially shielded from public scrutiny by a row of trees, and many overlook the lake. Each of the bedrooms is clean, comfortable, and filled with durable, utilitarian furniture. Many clients check in for lakeside holidays for several days at a time, consuming their meals in the dining room of this hotel's sibling; the Seewirt, which rises less than a hundred yards away.

Seehotel Herlinde
Strandplatz 7, A-7141 Podersdorf. ☎ **02177/2273.** Fax 02177/2273-12. 40 rms. TV TEL MINIBAR. 540–590 AS ($51.30–$56.05) per person. Rates include breakfast and lunch. No credit cards. Free parking.

An excellent two-star choice, this holiday hotel is on the beach of Lake Neusiedl away from the main highway. All the functionally furnished bedrooms have their own balconies; the best ones open onto views of the lake. The food and wine are plentiful, the latter often enjoyed on a 200-seat terrace.

WHERE TO DINE

Gasthof Seewirt Café Restaurant
Strandplatz 1. ☎ **02177/2415.** Main courses 80–195 AS ($7.60–$18.50). No credit cards. Daily noon–2:30pm and 6–9:30pm. Closed Dec 1–Feb 15. Closed Mon–Tues Feb 16–Apr 30 and from Sept 15–Nov 30. BURGENLANDER/INTERNATIONAL.

The preferred place for dining at the resort is this likable and unpretentious restaurant, which prepares a bountiful cuisine served by formally dressed waiters who are well trained in describing the nuances of the local cuisine. The Karner family, well-known vintners whose excellent rieslings, red and white *pinots,* and *weisserburgundens* are available for consumption, are proud of their long-established traditions and a local cuisine that in some ways resembles that of neighboring Hungary. A specialty of the house is *palatschinken marmaladen,* consisting of tender roast beef glazed with apricot jam, and a dessert called *Somloer Nockerl,* vanilla pudding, whipped cream, raisins, and nuts encased in a biscuit shell. The goulasch soup of the restaurant is very similar to that served across the eastern border. Other items include baked zander from the Danube, veal Cordon bleu, a succulent version of Wiener schnitzel, and such exotica as eel.

7 Forchtenstein

ESSENTIALS
GETTING THERE
Forchtenstein lies 44 miles south of Vienna. From Eisenstadt, take Route S31 southwest to Mattersburg, and from here follow the signs along a very minor road southwest to Forchtenstein. Three buses per day run from Vienna's bus station to Forchtenstein.

VISITOR INFORMATION
In lieu of a tourist office, information about the area is provided by the **town council** in the mayor's office at Hauptstrasse 54 (☎ **02626/63125**).

WHAT TO SEE & DO
Visitors come here chiefly to look at **Burg Forchtenstein** (Forchtenstein Castle), Burgplatz 1 (☎ **02626/81212**), 9 miles southeast of Wiener Neustadt in Lower Austria. From a belvedere here you can see as far as the Great Plain of Hungary. The castle was constructed on a rocky base by order of the counts of Mattersdorf in the 13th century. The Esterházy family had it greatly expanded around 1636.

The castle saw action in the Turkish sieges of Austria, both in 1529 and in 1683. A museum since 1815, the castle holds the Prince Esterházy collections, which consist of family memorabilia, a portrait gallery, large battle paintings, historical banners, and Turkish war booty and hunting arms. It's the largest private collection of historical arms in Austria. Legend has it that Turkish prisoners carved out of the rock the castle cistern more than 450 feet deep.

Admission is 55 AS ($5.25) for adults and 30 AS ($2.85) for children, and the castle is open April through October, daily from 8am to noon and 1 to 4pm. From November through March, they offer tours only when requested in advance. A guide shows you through.

WHERE TO STAY

Gasthof Sauerzapf

Rosalienstrasse 39, A-7212 Forchtenstein. ☎ **02626/81217.** 11 rms. 400–500 AS ($38.00–$47.50) double. Rates include breakfast. No credit cards. Closed Wed. Free parking.

A long, grangelike building, this hotel has two stories of weathered stucco, renovated windows, and a roofline that's red on one side and black on the other. The updated interior is cozy and appealing, albeit simple, and is kept immaculate. Anna Daskalakis-Sauerzapf, the owner, rents modestly furnished rooms that are reasonably comfortable for the price. The restaurant serves good regional food and an array of local wines.

⑤ Gasthof Wutzlhofer

Rosalia 12, A-7212 Forchtenstein. ☎ **02626/81253.** 6 rms. 400 AS ($34.40) double. Rates include breakfast. No credit cards. Closed Nov–Mar. Free parking.

The core of this hotel was built in the 1640s as a private house. Greatly enlarged and improved over the years, it became a hotel in 1955. The view from the rooms of this family-run guesthouse encompasses the whole valley and many square miles of forested hills. Herbert Wutzlhofer, the owner, offers one of the bargains of the area—good food and comfort.

Although the hotel closes in winter, the restaurant remains open year-round, as it attracts a lot of local trade, who know of its reputation for hearty regional cookery. Main courses in the restaurant cost 105 to 150 AS ($9 to $12.90).

WHERE TO DINE

⑤ Reisner

Haupstrasse 141. ☎ **02626/63139.** Reservations recommended. Main courses 90–240 AS ($8.55–$22.80); five-course fixed-price menu 495 AS ($47.05). No credit cards. Fri–Tues 11:30am–2:30pm and 6–10pm. Closed three weeks in Feb. AUSTRIAN.

This restaurant, the best in the area, has expanded over the years from its original century-old core. Well managed, it offers good food, featuring the regional specialties and wines of Burgenland. The main dining room is perfectly acceptable, but our favorite area is the cozy, rustic Stüberl, which the locals prefer as well. Besides the especially good steaks, you might enjoy trout filet served with a savory ragoût of tomatoes, zucchini, potatoes, and basil. The five-course fixed-price menu is a gargantuan repast.

Index

210 Index

WHEREVER YOU TRAVEL, *H*ELP IS NEVER FAR AWAY.

From planning your trip to providing travel assistance along the way, American Express® Travel Service Offices are always there to help.

> *Vienna*

American Express Travel Service
Kaerntnerstrasse 21-23
Vienna
1/515-40770

Travel

http://www.americanexpress.com/travel

American Express Travel Service Offices are found in central locations throughout Austria.